Exclusionary Empire

English Liberty Overseas, 1600–1900

Consisting of an introduction and ten chapters, *Exclusionary Empire* examines the transfer of English traditions of liberty and the rule of law overseas from 1600 to 1900. With each chapter written by a noted specialist and focusing on a particular area of the settler empire – Colonial North America, the West Indies, Ireland, the early United States, Canada, Australia, New Zealand, and South Africa – and one nonsettler colony, India, it examines the ways in which the polities in each of these areas incorporated these traditions, paying particular attention to the extent to which these traditions were confined to the independent white male segments of society and denied to most others. This collection will be invaluable to all those interested in the history of colonialism, European expansion, the development of empire, the role of cultural inheritance in those histories, and the confinement of access to that inheritance to people of European descent.

Jack P. Greene is Andrew W. Mellon Professor in the Humanities, Emeritus, in the Department of History at Johns Hopkins University. He has also taught at Michigan State University, Western Reserve University, the University of Michigan, and the University of California at Irvine. A specialist in Colonial British and Revolutionary American history, he has published and edited many books, chapters in books, articles, and reviews. Perhaps his best-known books are *The Quest for Power: The Lower Houses of Assembly in the Southern Royal Colonies, 1689–1776* (1963); *Peripheries and Center: Constitutional Development in the Extended Polities of the British Empire and the United States, 1607–1789* (1986); *Pursuits of Happiness: The Social Development of the Early Modern British Colonies and the Formation of American Culture* (1988); and *The Intellectual Construction of America: Exceptionalism and Identity from 1492 to 1800* (1993).

D1211670

For all of those subordinated people who lost their lands, cultures, freedoms, and lives in the construction of Britain's empire of liberty, which denied them civic space.

Exclusionary Empire

English Liberty Overseas, 1600–1900

Edited by
JACK P. GREENE
Johns Hopkins University

CAMBRIDGE
UNIVERSITY PRESS

CAMBRIDGE UNIVERSITY PRESS
Cambridge, New York, Melbourne, Madrid, Cape Town, Singapore,
São Paulo, Delhi, Dubai, Tokyo

Cambridge University Press
32 Avenue of the Americas, New York, NY 10013-2473, USA

www.cambridge.org
Information on this title: www.cambridge.org/9780521132701

First published 2010

Printed in the United States of America

A catalog record for this publication is available from the British Library.

Library of Congress Cataloging in Publication Data

Exclusionary empire : English liberty overseas, 1600–1900 / edited by Jack P. Greene.
　p. cm.
　Includes bibliographical references and index.
　ISBN 978-0-521-11498-1 (hardback) – ISBN 978-0-521-13270-1 (pbk.)
1. Political rights – Great Britain – Colonies – History. 2. Rule of law – Great Britain –
Colonies – History. 3. Civil rights – Great Britain – Colonies – History. 4. Great Britain – Colonies –
Administration – History. I. Greene, Jack P. II. Title.

JV1096.E97 2009
323.09171′2410903–dc22　　　　2009009884

ISBN 978-0-521-11498-1 Hardback
ISBN 978-0-521-13270-1 Paperback

Cambridge University Press has no responsibility for the persistence or accuracy of URLS
for external or third-party Internet Web sites referred to in this publication and does not
guarantee that any content on such Web sites is, or will remain, accurate or appropriate.

Contents

Notes on Contributors   *page* vii

Preface   ix

Introduction: Empire and Liberty   1
    Jack P. Greene

1 The Languages of Liberty in British North America,
    1607–1776   25
    Elizabeth Mancke

2 Liberty and Slavery: The Transfer of British Liberty
    to the West Indies, 1627–1865   50
    Jack P. Greene

3 "Era of Liberty": The Politics of Civil and Political Rights
    in Eighteenth-Century Ireland   77
    James Kelly

4 Liberty and Modernity: The American Revolution and the
    Making of Parliament's Imperial History   112
    Eliga H. Gould

5 Federalism, Democracy, and Liberty in the New
    American Nation   132
    Peter S. Onuf

6 Liberty, Order, and Pluralism: The Canadian Experience   160
    Philip Girard

7 Contested Despotism: Problems of Liberty in British India   191
    Robert Travers

8 ". . . a bastard offspring of tyranny under the guise
    of liberty": Liberty and Representative Government
    in Australia, 1788–1901   220
    Richard Waterhouse

9 How Much Did Institutions Matter? Cloning Britain
   in New Zealand   248
   James Belich

10 The Expansion of British Liberties: The South
   African Case   269
   Christopher Saunders

Index   289

Notes on Contributors

James Belich is Research Professor of History at the Stout Research Centre, Victoria University of Wellington. He has published extensively on New Zealand history and is now working on the history of settler societies in general. His most recent book, *Replenishing the Earth: The Settler Revolution and the Rise of the Anglo-World*, is being published by Oxford University Press in 2009.

Philip Girard is Professor of Law, History, and Canadian Studies and University Research Professor at Dalhousie University, Halifax, Nova Scotia. Among his many publications on Canadian legal and socio-legal history is *Bora Laskin: Bringing Law to Life* (2005), a biography of Canada's best-known chief justice.

Eliga H. Gould is Associate Professor of History at the University of New Hampshire, where he teaches early American and British Atlantic history. His books include *The Persistence of Empire: British Political Culture in the Age of the American Revolution* (2000) and *Empire and Nation: The American Revolution in the Atlantic World* (2005), co-edited with Peter Onuf. Gould is currently finishing a book, *Zones of Law, Zones of Violence*, on the American Revolution and the pacification of the Atlantic world.

Jack P. Greene, Andrew W. Mellon Professor in the Humanities, Emeritus, at Johns Hopkins University, has written extensively on the early modern British empire in America. He is currently completing a volume entitled *Speaking of Empire: Confronting Colonialism in Eighteenth-Century Britain, 1739–1785.*

James Kelly, MRIA, is head of the History Department, St Patrick's College, Dublin City University. He is the author of, among other works, *That Damn'd Thing Called Honour: Duelling in Ireland, 1570–1860* (Cork, 1995); *Henry Flood: Patriots and Politics in Eighteenth-Century Ireland* (Cork, 1998); *Poynings' Law and the Making of Law in Ireland, 1660–1800* (Dublin, 2006); and *Proceedings of the Irish House of Lords, 1771–1800* (3 vols, Dublin, 2008).

Elizabeth Mancke, Professor of History at the University of Akron, is the author of *The Fault Lines of Empire: Political Differentiation in Massachusetts and Nova Scotia, ca. 1760–1820,* and the co-editor with Carole Shammas of *The Creation of the British Atlantic World,* as well as the author of numerous essays on the relation between the British empire and state.

Peter S. Onuf, Thomas Jefferson Professor of History at the University of Virginia, has written extensively on the history of the early American republic, including most recently *The Mind of Thomas Jefferson* (2007).

Christopher Saunders is a Professor in the Department of Historical Studies at the University of Cape Town (UCT), South Africa. Educated at UCT and Balliol and St. Antony's Colleges, Oxford University, he returned to lecture at UCT and there pioneered the teaching of African history in the 1970s. He has written widely on topics in the history of southern Africa and is perhaps best known as the co-author of *South Africa: A Modern History* (5th ed., 2000). He is currently working on a chapter on South African historiography for the *Oxford History of Historical Writing.*

Robert Travers is Associate Professor of History at Cornell University and the author of *Ideology and Empire in Eighteenth-Century India: The British in Bengal* (Cambridge, 2007).

Richard Waterhouse, Bicentennial Professor of Australian history at the University of Sydney, is the author of five books on aspects of United States and Australian social and cultural history, the most recent of which is *The Vision Splendid: A Social and Cultural History of Rural Australia* (2005).

Preface

The idea for this volume came to me in March 2003 during a colloquium I organized for Liberty Fund, Inc., in Santa Fe, New Mexico. Entitled "William Molyneux and Irish Liberty in the Eighteenth Century" and examining Molyneux's *The Case of Ireland's Being Bound by Acts of Parliament in England Stated* and the contemporary responses to it, the colloquium generated a lively discussion of the parallels and contrasts between Irish efforts to incorporate English ideas of liberty into the Irish polity during the Protestant Ascendancy and the attempts of free settlers to do the same in the new polities they constructed in North America and the Atlantic and West Indian islands during the seventeenth and eighteenth centuries. This discussion immediately suggested to me the desirability of a colloquium with a wider spatial and temporal focus that would explore the experience of the transmission, application, adaptation, and operation of English ideas of liberty – especially as they involved consensual governance, trial by jury, and the rule of law – to the wide variety of settlement societies associated with the British empire.

Although the spread of English liberty overseas through colonization has long been a central trope in popular works, in school books, and, before the advent of decolonization after World War II, in the historiography of the British empire, I was astonished to discover that no single work had ever taken up this subject in detail and began to think about organizing a book consisting of case studies, written by specialists, of each of the major settlement polities established by British people overseas between the advent of successful colonization around the turn of the seventeenth century and the turn of the nineteenth century, a book that would consider not just the spread of English liberty to those polities but also the extent and form that it took and the particular exclusions it involved. The book I envisioned was never intended to be comprehensive even of all those portions of the empire that experienced extensive British settlement. In particular, it did not include treatments of twentieth-century settler polities in Kenya and Rhodesia as they developed and applied their own practices of exclusionary liberty. Nor in the original formulation did the volume give any space to the vast nonsettler empire in India, southeast Asia, the Mediterranean, the Middle East, and Africa. Partially to remedy this neglect, I ultimately decided that a chapter on India, Britain's principal non-settlement colony, would provide a useful contrast to the experiences of the settler empire, which indeed turned out to be the case. The Indian example underlines the degree to which the spread of self-government to and the estab-lishment of wider franchises in the settler colonies forced imperial thinkers and managers to articulate their rationale for denying self-government to the non-settlement portions of the British imperial world, while in the process delineat-ing more fully the underlying cultural and racialist assumptions for the exclusion of various categories of people from civic participation within the settler empire.

Once Liberty Fund had generously agreed to support this project by com-missioning ten original papers and sponsoring a conference of myself and the authors, I recruited the best authors I could find to write them. These included Elizabeth Mancke, on colonial British North America; Christopher Leslie Brown, on the West Indian and Atlantic island colonies; James Kelly, on Ire-land under the Protestant Ascendancy; Eliga Gould, on the relationship between the British Parliament and provincial parliaments during the eight-eenth century; Peter S. Onuf, on the republican United States that emerged out of the American Revolution; Philip Girard, on British North America/Canada; Robert Travers, on the early debate over extending British liberty to India; Richard Waterhouse, on the Australian colonies; James Belich, on New Zealand; and Christopher Saunders, on South Africa. Each of these people produced a discussion paper and, with the exception of Christopher Brown, who was unable to attend because of a medical emergency, came together in Cincinnati for four days in November 2007 at the Hilton Cincinnati Nether-lands Plaza Hotel, a magnificent art deco edifice, to discuss them. Over the next few months the authors proceeded to revise their contributions along lines articulated in these discussions, and, together with my introduction, they constitute this book. When Christopher Brown had to withdraw from the project, I took on the assignment of writing the chapter on the West Indies and Atlantic islands, a subject in which I had had a strong interest for more than forty years.

Too broad to fit comfortably within an *Atlantic* framework and too narrow to represent a *global* perspective, albeit James Belich's imaginative chapter on New Zealand reaches in many interesting ways in that direction, this volume eschews both of those modern scholarly constructs in favor of an *imperial* approach, the empire being the largest unit with which most contemporaries among the settler populations that dominated these overseas polities custom-arily identified. Each chapter looks carefully at a specific subject – the transition of liberal traditions – within a broad British imperial context. In addition, these studies fit within the framework of state formation studies with its emphasis, in the case of colonial polities, on the construction of legal, political, and constitu-tional regimes in newly conquered or newly occupied areas, and they are sensitive to the post-colonial emphasis on the high cost paid by subaltern populations caught up in the colonial process.

The authors of these broad interpretive essays had considerable freedom in developing them, and many of the specific questions they examine are peculiar to the subjects they treat. Indeed, one of this volume's primary objectives is to show the variety in outcomes and experiences arising out of the process of adapting English political, legal, and constitutional traditions to differing environments at different times. If the specification of spatial variations is a central concern of each chapter, together they call attention to important temporal variations. Just as the experience of the Seven Years' War focused metropolitan attention on the looseness of British imperial governance and saw the beginnings of efforts to tighten it, the revolt of the American colonies stimulated Irish and West Indian political establishments to secure firmer control over their internal governance. Within a decade, the American republican experiment and the French Revolution served as a countervailing model for those who sought or opposed more liberty and self-government in Canada, Australia, and India, while Canada's invention of responsible government in the 1830s and 1840s strongly affected the movement for self-government in New Zealand, Australia, and South Africa.

Yet, because they all focus on the self-governing process as it took shape in the entities they cover, they all engage, to one degree or another, with a common set of topics. These include: (1) the intellectual and cultural traditions that underlay and informed that process and the social and economic conditions that nurtured and sustained it; (2) the crucial relationship of property to this process; (3) the nature of the conflicts with the metropolis that arose over settler self-governing claims and how those conflicts were resolved; (4) the character of the conflicts arising between national and provincial levels of government over issues involving the distribution of authority in federal polities (the new United States and most subsequent settler colonies); (5) the process of negotiation and implementation involved in the superimposition of English ideas of governance and law in polities encompassing territories with established European-style institutions (Ireland, Canada, and South Africa); (6) the scope of self-government within the polities, especially as it involved indigenous, enslaved, transported, and propertyless people, and the ways in which that scope changed over time; (7) how British traditions were modified and sustained during the first century or two of polity formation; and (8) the political and legal legacy of the early experience in self-government.

Despite their presentation and consideration at the same conference, these essays rarely speak to one another or move beyond the boundaries of their respective subjects. Yet, attentive readers will not fail to grasp the volume's comparative dimensions. They will appreciate the centrality of the liberal tradition in British overseas expansion. From the seventeenth through the nineteenth centuries, those traditions informed and shaped the British colonizing process at every stage and in every settler colony, at once energizing that process by providing *independent* settlers with a personal stake in the empire and stimulating the emergence of competing concepts of liberty that elicited resistance to metropolitan direction, fueled provincial movements for self-governance, and led to one major rupture, with the withdrawal of thirteen colonies from the empire. Readers will also recognize the crucial relationship between personal independence and liberty and the logic of exclusion that, inherited from the metropolis itself, throughout the empire limited the civic space accorded to *dependent* populations. Indeed, the title, *Exclusionary Empire*, is intended to direct attention to the exclusionary character of these avowedly liberal regimes. Readers will also see the parallels among those societies – principally Ireland under the Protestant Ascendancy, the West Indies, those North American colonies with large enslaved populations, India, and South Africa – where dependent peoples often constituted a majority of the population. In two cases, notably Ireland and the West Indies, those dependent majorities became so restive as to persuade politically dominant populations to abandon self-government altogether: in Ireland, through incorporation into Great Britain, and in almost all of the West Indian colonies, by abandoning representative institutions, some of which were two centuries old.

This volume intentionally breaks out of the boundaries of several conventional historical categories. By including a chapter on Ireland, it intends to focus on the similarities and variations between the colonial status of Ireland in relation to the metropolis, and the status of more distant contemporary colonies in the Americas. By including chapters on the West Indies and India, it endeavors to blur the sharp distinctions drawn by many scholars between colonies of settlement and colonies of exploitation and to suggest that *settler* and *nonsettler* colonies might profitably be studied together as mutually enlightening. By including a chapter on the United States, it intends at once to highlight the continuing importance of the British inheritance in American political and legal culture; to bring the history of the United States within a broader global context of emerging nations; to provide a comparative perspective with contemporary developments in the West Indies, Canada, India, Australia, New Zealand, and South Africa; and to transcend the conventional confines of both American national history and a British imperial history that takes no further interest in the thirteen North American colonies after 1783, as if political boundaries put an end to cultural and other influences. By including chapters on the early modern or first empire in the same volume with chapters on the modern or second empire, it asks the reader to reconsider the question of periodization in British imperial history. By juxtaposing chapters on the older Atlantic empire and the newer African, Asian, and Pacific empires, it seeks to call attention to the global dimensions of national cultural transmissions in the imperial process.

I thank the nine other authors who contributed to this volume and Christopher Brown for his early participation. I and authors alike are especially grateful to officers of Liberty Fund, Inc., whose sponsorship of the conference that led to this book was essential. We owe a particular debt to Dr. Hans Eicholz, a Senior Fellow at Liberty Fund, who recommended a conference on this subject to Liberty Fund and was the Liberty Fund representative in charge of it. His contributions to the discussions helped to reshape several of the chapters. Dr. Amy Turner Bushnell assisted in many ways in making that conference run smoothly and in the preparation of this book. We are also grateful to our copy editor, Elise Oranges, and to our indexer, Russell Stoermer.

Jack P. Greene
East Greenwich, Rhode Island

Introduction

Empire and Liberty

Jack P. Greene

The "birthrights and privileges of Britons," the agricultural writer Arthur Young declared in 1772, "form a system of liberty, so happily tempered between slavery and licentiousness, that the like is not to be met with in any other country of the globe."[1] Widely shared by Young's contemporaries, this claim had a long genealogy – and enormous staying power. Rooted in a jurisprudential tradition that emphasized the role of law as a restraint on the power of the Crown, it dated back to such older writings as Sir John Fortescue's *De Laudibus Legum Angliae*, written during the fifteenth century and always familiar to the English law community but not published until 1616, and to the early seventeenth-century writings of Sir Edward Coke, Sir John Davies, Nathaniel Bacon, and others who elaborated on Fortescue in a series of learned works. Writing in an age when, except for the Netherlands, every other major European state was slipping into absolutism and when England's first two Stuart kings seemed to be trying to extend the prerogatives of the Crown and perhaps even to do away with Parliaments in England altogether, these early seventeenth-century legal writers all were eager to erect legal and constitutional restraints that would ensure security of life, liberty, and property against such extensions of royal power.[2]

This early modern jurisprudential tradition rested on a distinction, already fully elaborated by Fortescue, between two fundamentally different kinds of monarchies that Fortescue called *regal* monarchy and *political* monarchy. Whereas, in the former, the prince's will was absolute, in the latter, it was "restrained by political law" that, in the case of England, expressed "the will of the people" and ensured that they would be able to use the law to maintain their liberty and avoid arbitrary and unjust encroachments on their persons and

[1] Arthur Young, *Political Essays Concerning the Present State of the British Empire* (London, 1772), p. 50.
[2] J. G. A. Pocock, *The Ancient Constitution and the Feudal Law: English Historical Thought in the Seventeenth Century* (Cambridge: Cambridge University Press, 1957).

properties. Thus founded in consent and favoring "liberty in every case," English law, Fortescue predicted, would "always be exceptional among all the other laws of the earth, among which I see it shine like a Venus among the stars." It is no wonder that, as he noted, "among the English the law" and reverence for it were so "deeply rooted."[3]

By the term *law*, English jurisprudential writers meant, of course, both statute law and common law, or custom. The common law, or *lex non scripta*, was the product of time, continuous usage, and the quiet and common consent of the people. Exhibited in the decisions of judges and juries, it performed two vital functions. First, it provided guidelines for the courts in both civil and criminal matters affecting the protection and transfers of properties of all sorts and the penalties for temporal offenses. Second, and even more important, the common law provided the foundations for all of the most cherished liberties of English people. Most significantly, these included the rights of every person not to be taxed or subjected to laws without his consent and not to be deprived of life, liberty, or property without due process of law, including an accused's right to a jury trial in which judgment would be rendered by the accused's peers drawn from the neighborhood where the alleged offense had been committed.

If, according to English jurisprudential writers, statute law, which represented the formal "assent of the whole realm" through the medium of Parliament, carried more authority than the common law, statutes were, as Sir William Blackstone affirmed in the 1760s in his *Commentaries on the Laws of England*, very often "either *declaratory* of the common law or *remedial* of some defects therein." Indeed, said Coke, even the Magna Charta and other important statutes in the constitutional tradition were "but a confirmation or restitution of the common law" that, as the Whig publicist Henry Care wrote in the late seventeenth century in paraphrasing Fortescue and Coke, were "coeval" with the formation of English political society. The liberties referred to in the Magna Charta, Care explained, should never be understood as "meer Emanations of Royal Favour granted, which the People ... had not a Right unto before."[4]

Thus were the "absolute rights of every Englishman, (which, taken in a political and extensive sense, are usually called their liberties)," "deeply implanted" in the laws and constitution of England. Defined generally by Blackstone as the capacity of every subject to be the "entire master of his own conduct, except in those points wherein the public good requires some direction or restraint," and by the popular Whig theorists John Trenchard and

---

[3] Sir John Fortescue, *De Laudibus Legum Angliae* (Cambridge: Cambridge University Press, 1942), pp. 25, 27, 31, 33, 79, 81, 87, 89, 105, 115, 139.

[4] Ibid., 41; Sir William Blackstone, *Commentaries on the Laws of England*, 4 vols. (Philadelphia, 1771), vol. 1, pp. 67–68, 86; Sir Edward Coke, *Institutes*, Part One, 2 vols. (London, 1832), vol. 2, pp. 4, 10, 108, 171; Coke, *Institutes*, Part Two (London, 1797), ch. 30, p. 60; Henry Care, *English Liberties*, 5th ed. (Boston, 1721), pp. 3, 6–7, 23–24, 27.

Thomas Gordon as "the Power which every Man has over his own Actions, and his Right to enjoy the Fruit of his Labour, Art, and Industry, as far as by it he hurts not the Society, or any Member of it, by taking from any Member or by hindering him from enjoying what he himself enjoys," liberty in English thought consisted of four principal legal rights. As Blackstone systematically specified them, they were (1) the right to personal security in terms of life, limbs, well-being, and reputation; (2) the right to personal liberty, including "the power of loco-motion, of changing situation, or removing one's person to whatsoever place one's own inclination may direct"; (3) freedom from "imprisonment without cause"; and (4) the right to "the free use, enjoyment, and disposal of all" property "without any control or diminution, save only by the laws of the land."[5] Not just common-law lawyers and political writers but also the leading liberal natural rights philosopher John Locke drew a similar connection between law and liberty during the closing decades of the seventeenth century.[6]

The happy capacity of English people to preserve this liberty rested on two institutions for determining and making law: juries and Parliament. By guaranteeing that "no Causes" would be "tried, nor any Man adjudged to lose Life, Members, or Estate, but upon the Verdict of his Peers, (or Equals) his Neighbours, and of his own Condition," the first gave every person "a Share in the executive Part of the Law." By giving each independent person through "his chosen Representatives" a share "in the Legislative (or Law-making) Power," the second ensured that no law should be passed without the consent of the nation's property holders. Over the centuries, Parliament had taken a conspicuous role in maintaining the "vigour of our free constitution: from the assaults of would-be tyrants, through not just Magna Charta but the Petition of Right under Charles I, the Habeas Corpus Act under Charles II, the Bill of Rights during the Glorious Revolution, and the Act of Settlement," Blackstone proudly noted, and had repeatedly acted to restore "the ballance of our rights and liberties" to their "proper level." Occasionally in these efforts, Englishmen had had to resort to arms, and they were careful to preserve their right to bear arms in order to be able to do so when necessary. But most of the time Parliaments and juries, those "two grand Pillars of English Liberty" through which "the Birth-right of Englishmen" had always shone "most conspicuously," had functioned effectively to ensure that in England the law would continue, as Coke said, to be "the surest sanctuary that a man can take" and "the best Birthright of the Subject."[7]

For Englishmen, liberty was thus, according to the English jurisprudential and libertarian traditions, not just a condition enforced by law, but the very

---

[5] Blackstone, *Commentaries*, vol. 1, pp. 126–40; John Trenchard and Thomas Gordon, *Cato's Letters*, in David L. Jacobson, ed., *The English Libertarian Heritage* (Indianapolis: Bobbs Merrill, 1965), #62, pp. 127–28.

[6] John Locke, *Two Treatises on Government*, ed. Peter Laslett (Cambridge: Cambridge University Press, 1960), p. 348.

[7] Care, *English Liberties*, pp. 3–4, 27; Blackstone, *Commentaries*, vol. 1, pp. 126–28, 144; Coke, *Institutes*, Part Two, ch. 29, p. 55.

essence of their national identity. In most early modern countries, noted Trenchard and Gordon quoting the republican Algernon Sydney, rulers *"use[d] their Subjects like Asses and Mastiff Dogs, to work and to fight, to be oppressed and killed for them,"* considering "their People as Cattle, and" using "them worse, as they fear[ed] them more. Thus," had "most of Mankind" become "wretched Slaves" who maintained "their haughty Masters like Gods," while "their haughty Masters often use[d] them like Dogs." Elsewhere – English writers invariably singled out Turkey, France, and sometimes Spain – "the meer Will of the Prince is Law; his Word takes off any Man's Head, imposes Taxes, seizes any Man's Estate, when, how, and as often as he lists; and if one be accused, or but so much as suspected of any Crime, he may either presently execute him, or banish, or imprison him at pleasure." Only in England were "the Lives and Fortunes" of the people not subject to the "Wills (or rather Lusts)" of "Arbitrary" tyrants. Only in England did the monarchs, in Fortescue's words, have *"two Superiours, God and the Law."* Only in England was "the Commonality . . . so guarded in their Persons and Properties by the Sense of Law, as" to be rendered "Free-men, not Slaves." Only in England did law require the consent of those who lived under it. Only in England was "the Law . . . both the Measure and the Bond of every Subject's Duty and Allegiance, each Man having a fixed fundamental Right born with him, as to Freedom of his Person, and Property in his Estate, which he cannot be deprived of, but either by his Consent, or some Crimes for which the Law has impos'd such Penalty or Forfeiture." Few early modern English people had any doubt, as Care put it, that "the Construction of our English Government" was "the best in the World."[8]

Despite this national mystique, not all English people enjoyed liberty to its fullest extent. English society, like early modern society all over Europe, was divided between independent people, who were few and possessed sufficient property to ensure that they would not be subject to the will of others, and dependent people, who constituted the overwhelming majority and, by contemporary understandings, had, in Blackstone's words, no wills of their own. At least theoretically, everyone, regardless of gender or dependency, had access to those liberties associated with the rule of law, albeit all dependent people and even many lesser property holders were, as Robert Zaller has recently put it, "held fast within a hierarchy of authority, status, and property" that was dominated by and no doubt partial to the independent classes that presided over it.[9] Moreover, except in a few borough constituencies, custom and statute law excluded everyone who was not an adult male property holder from voting. In this exclusionary polity, only those few who met the property requirements for the franchise thus fully enjoyed that most celebrated right of Englishmen,

---

[8] Trenchard and Gordon, *Cato's Letters*, #25, pp. 68, 70; Care, *English Liberties*, pp. 1–3.
[9] Robert Zaller, "Representative Government: How Sure a Thing," in Maija Jansson, ed., *Realities of Representation: State Building in Early Modern Europe and America* (New York: Palgrave, 2007), p. 216.

not to be taxed or governed without their consent. Only they had an active voice in making and enforcing laws and levying taxes. The rest of the population consented to laws only passively, through their obedience to them and the implicit acceptance such obedience implied.[10]

As English people increasingly after 1600 established settlements overseas in Ireland and the Americas, sometimes with authorization from the Crown under the initial aegis of chartered companies or landed proprietors, sometimes on their own, and always with their active participation, they took these ideas about their libertarian inheritance with them and used them to shape the new polities they created. In their earliest forms, these polities, at least in America, assumed a variety of forms, some remarkably experimental, but they all shared two fundamental objectives. The first was to recreate and adapt to their new homes the English common-law culture they had left behind; the second was to found, in the English manner, their polities on a consensual base through the creation of a representative institution through which they could ensure that they would have a say in making the laws under which they lived and in levying the taxes necessary to support their polities.

Nothing less seemed appropriate for English people who, using their own resources, industry, and initiative, had created social spaces for themselves in Ireland or America and thereby created for themselves status, capital, and power. Especially on the North American continent, where indigenous people were less densely settled and land abundant, but also, if to a lesser extent, in Ireland, where the indigenous people were both far more similar in their cultures to English and Scottish invaders and offered more effective resistance, and in the West Indies and Atlantic islands, where, except for Jamaica, the amount of land was finite and quickly taken up, independent individual settlers engaged in a deep and widespread process of individual and corporate self-empowerment. In contrast to England, where only a small fraction of the population ever managed to achieve the civic competence, the full right to a voice in political decisions that was the preserve of independent property holders, in the colonies a very large proportion of the adult male white settlers acquired land or other resources, built estates, and achieved individual independence.

This development produced strong demands on the part of the large empowered settler populations for the extension to the colonies of the same rights to security of property and civic participation that appertained to the empowered, high-status, and independent property holders in England. These demands included the right "to enjoy the advantages of the colonists' former betters in the society they had left behind," including their many "exemptions and privileges," and the right to exclude dependent peoples from those same rights and exemptions.[11] In the settler view, colonial governance, no less than

---

[10] Jack P. Greene, *All Men Are Created Equal: Some Reflections on the Character of the American Revolution* (Oxford: Oxford University Press, 1976), explores the logic of franchise exclusion in both early modern England and colonial America.

[11] Zaller, "Representative Government," p. 216.

metropolitan governance, should guarantee that men of their standing would not be governed without consultation or in ways that were patently against their interests. Along with the vast distance of the colonies from Europe, these circumstances encouraged those who were nominally in charge of the colonies toward the establishment and toleration of political structures that involved the active consent of local independent settlers. Consultation meant that local populations would more willingly both acknowledge the authority of private agencies of colonization and contribute to local costs. The earliest stages of English colonization thus resulted in the emergence, in new colonial peripheries, of many new and relatively autonomous centers of authority effectively under local control. How this process worked is the subject of the first three chapters of this volume: Chapter 1, by Elizabeth Mancke, on the North American colonies; Chapter 2, by Jack P. Greene, on the island colonies in the Atlantic and the West Indies; and Chapter 3, by James Kelly, on Ireland during the Protestant Ascendancy.

In addition to occupying large segments of Ulster, Munster, and Leinster in Ireland, English migrants had, by 1660, created through settlement seven separate plantations in mainland North America and six in the Atlantic and Caribbean islands, and had occupied Jamaica following its conquest from the Spanish in 1655. Over the next half-century, they re-peopled seven new colonies on the mainland and one in the Atlantic, while continuing to occupy more and more of Ireland and to add to the population streams that extended the settlements in the older American colonies into ever widening areas, two of those colonies amalgamating with other colonies during the closing decades of the seventeenth century. Although the next half-century was primarily a period of consolidation and growth in already established colonies, just two continental colonies and one island colony being settled between roughly 1710 and 1760, British conquests in the Seven Years' War led to the incorporation of the old French colony of Quebec into the British Empire and the formation of seven new colonies, three on the continent and four in the West Indies. With the partial exception of Quebec, which had a substantial French population that retained its French-derived private law, each of these post-1763 colonies became yet another American setting into which British immigrants could, in conscious imitation of settlers in early colonies, transplant English legal and political forms and ideas. Not counting Newfoundland, which remained a fishing settlement without regular participatory government, the British empire, on the eve of the American War for Independence, had twenty-nine colonies in America, eleven in the islands, and eighteen on the continent, only one of which, Quebec, was not a regular British-style polity with representative institutions. This proliferation of polities represented an astonishing spread of English common-law culture and modes of representative government across the Irish Sea and the Atlantic and provided abundant evidence of their adaptability to radically different physical, social, and economic contexts.

With regard to representative government, both the Irish House of Commons and the American assemblies consciously endeavored to model themselves as closely as possible on the English House of Commons. In this effort, they had many sources to draw on, including the several parliamentary commentaries and procedural books published in the seventeenth century. Working out the logic of the analogy between the assemblies and the House of Commons, colonial legislative leaders not only copied the forms and procedures of the metropolitan body but also insisted that they were constitutionally vested with the same powers and privileges in the colonies as the House of Commons in Britain.[12]

Notwithstanding this powerful mimetic impulse, however, legislative development in the colonies diverged considerably from that in the parent state. Having exercised wide authority over revenues from their earliest days, colonial legislatures gradually refined and extended that authority over every phase of raising and distributing public revenue. They acquired a large measure of legislative independence by winning control over their procedures and obtaining guarantees of basic English parliamentary privileges, and they extended their power well beyond that of the House of Commons by gaining extensive authority in handling executive affairs, including the rights to participate in formulating executive policy and to appoint most officials concerned with the collection of provincial revenues and many other executive officers.

In still other ways, legislative development in the colonies differed from that of the House of Commons. Elections were more frequent; residential requirements for legislative seats were the norm; most colonies paid their representatives for their services as legislators and endeavored, in many colonies successfully, to exclude placemen from holding legislative seats; and representatives were far more closely monitored by their constituents in electoral environments in which a vastly higher proportion of the adult male inhabitants met franchise requirements.[13]

Of course, the Irish experience was in many ways strikingly different from the American. On a general level, the parallels were strong. The *over*settlement of Ireland and the resettlement of the colonies occurred at the same time. Both involved similar *colonial* processes and were products of the same extensive settler migration. Both required the dispossession of native peoples from their lands. Both created polities that existed in a dependent relationship with England or, after 1707, Britain. Both sets of polities enjoyed a considerable measure

---

[12] See Jack P. Greene, "Political Mimesis: A Consideration of the Historical and Cultural Roots of Legislative Behavior in the Eighteenth Century," *American Historical Review* 75 (1969): 337–67.

[13] On these points, see Robert J. Dinkin, *Voting in Provincial America: A Study of Elections in the Thirteen Colonies, 1689–1776* (Westport, CT: Greenwood Press, 1977); Edmund S. Morgan, *Inventing the People: The Rise of Popular Sovereignty in England and America* (New York: Norton, 1988); J. R. Pole, *Political Representation in England and the Origins of the American Republic* (New York: St. Martin's Press, 1966), and *The Gift of Government: Political Responsibility from the English Restoration to American Independence* (Athens: University of Georgia Press, 1983); Jack P. Greene, *The Quest for Power: The Lower Houses of Assembly in the Southern Royal Colonies, 1689–1776* (Chapel Hill: University of North Carolina Press, 1963); and Mary Patterson Clarke, *Parliamentary Privilege in the American Colonies* (New Haven, CT: Yale University Press, 1943).

of consensual self-government and developed localized versions of the English legal inheritance. Both functioned within the same Anglophone cultural system and constituted peripheral or provincial variants of that system. Both operated within economic restrictions imposed by London. And, after 1760, both demonstrated a common front, as they articulated a view of the imperial constitution that left them with full autonomy over their internal affairs.

But there were also profound differences. No American colony enjoyed Ireland's special status as a separate, if dependent, kingdom, and none formally called its legislative institutions a Parliament. Although most of the American colonies had significant native populations, at least initially, population density in America was low relative to Ireland, much of the land was uncultivated and lacked domestic herding and was, therefore, according to contemporary European theory, a "waste" land available for colonization. Furthermore, the native population was both pagan and deemed culturally backward by European standards. By contrast, the new plantations in Ireland were established on territories conquered from a people who were numerous, Christian, and, by European standards, civilized. Although a few of the earliest American colonies had, like Ireland, also been conquered from rival European powers – Jamaica having been wrested from Spain in 1655, New York from the Dutch in 1664, and Nova Scotia and half of St. Christopher from the French in 1713 – the American colonies were mostly the products of a dual process of extensive settlement and, as a concomitant, the expulsion or marginalization of most of the land's existing inhabitants, so that the settlers and their descendants quickly came to constitute a majority of the free population. Even with the conquered colonies in which the old European populations chose to remain under British governance, like New York and Nova Scotia, incoming immigrants from the British Isles eventually became a majority and established their cultural, as well as political, predominance over the earlier inhabitants. Unlike the situation in the colonies, in Ireland, English and Scottish immigrants and their progeny became a majority only in a few localities and thus had to live in the midst of a numerically superior and often hostile native population.

And there were still other differences. Although most of the American colonies placed civil restrictions on Catholics and Jews, the number of such people constituted such a small percentage of the population in every colony except Maryland, where Catholics may have accounted for about a quarter of the free inhabitants, that the colonies have to be considered as *inclusionary* polities, inclusionary, that is, of the independent male population and their dependents, who constituted the majority of the settlers, whereas Ireland after the Glorious Revolution, with its intricate system of penal laws that disabled its Catholic majority from civic participation and many avenues of economic opportunity, was an explicitly *exclusionary* polity.

Unlike Ireland, none of the colonies supported a permanent military establishment of any size, except Jamaica, where the threat of domestic upheaval among the majority slave population and of foreign invasion from neighboring islands controlled by the French and Spanish lay behind settler willingness to pay for such an establishment beginning in the 1720s. Nor did the metropolis have any regular forces in any of the other colonies before the Seven Years' War. This situation stands in profound contrast to the situation in Ireland, where the Protestant minority felt the need of such forces in the face of the possibility of revolt by the Catholic majority and paid for an annual military establishment of 12,000 men from the 1690s.

The relationship between church and state and the structure of landholding also diverged. Even where colonies established a particular church, the laity controlled it, even in the surveillance societies of seventeenth-century Massachusetts and Connecticut, and nowhere did there appear the sort of confessional state that characterized Ireland during the Protestant Ascendancy, with its extensive religious hierarchy, large concentration of wealth in church hands, and close association with the civil arm. Nor did landlordism of the variety that was so pronounced in eighteenth-century Ireland develop to any significant degree in the American colonies, where, at least on the continent, the wide availability of cheap land meant that tenancy was often a temporary condition and that tenants were not without leverage in negotiating contracts with landlords. St. John's Island (Prince Edward Island) was a notable exception to this observation.

In many ways the most important difference was geographical. The American colonies were 3,000 miles away from London, and distance meant that they were subject to much less supervision and had far more political autonomy, that they were far less thoroughly drawn into the metropolitan patronage network, that they contributed much less to metropolitan pension lists, and that they had far fewer absentees among their landholding populations. To take one example, while every piece of Irish legislation was vetted and re-vetted by the Crown-appointed Irish Privy Council and the British Privy Council, the vast majority of colonial laws were wholly ignored by the British Privy Council, usually being read by the Board of Trade and often sent to legal authorities for opinions but rarely, at least before 1748, being referred to the Privy Council for either allowance or disallowance. The attempt to apply Poyning's Law to Virginia and Jamaica in the 1670s failed abysmally, and colonial legislatures strongly and successfully resisted metropolitan efforts to require the inclusion of suspending clauses in unusual laws after 1750. Political discourse in Ireland and the American colonies frequently addressed the same issues, such as the initiation of money bills and the tenure of judges, and thus bore some degree of similarity. But the contexts in which those issues were discussed were radically different.

These many differences strongly suggest that, by the middle of the eighteenth century, Ireland, notwithstanding its superior development; its greater social, economic, and cultural complexity; and certainly its far more extensive urbanization, was, by modern understandings of the term *colonial*, considerably more colonial than Britain's more distant colonies.[14] Modern understandings, however, differ profoundly from those of contemporaries.

[14] A point confirmed in James Kelly, *Poyning's Law and the Making of Law in Ireland, 1660–1800* (Dublin: Four Courts Press, 2007).

If, at the beginning of English expansion in the early seventeenth century, the Irish plantations were not wholly dissimilar to those being undertaken at the same time across the Atlantic, by the mid-eighteenth century, contemporaries such as the Scottish economic writer John Campbell, whose extended two-volume *Political Survey of Britain* was published in 1774,[15] thought of Ireland, not as a British colony, but as a subordinate polity within the British Isles.

Not only members of the settler establishments in Ireland and the American colonies, but also many metropolitan Britons celebrated the development of representative government and the transfer and creolization of the common law overseas as appropriate expressions of the longstanding commitment of the English nation to liberty and precisely the characteristics that distinguished the British empire from others. In America, declared the agricultural writer Arthur Young in 1772, "Spain, Portugal and France have planted despotisms; only Britain liberty."[16] "From the earliest and first instance of the establishment of a BRITISH SENATE," declared the political writer Thomas Pownall in the mid-1760s, *"the principle of establishing the Imperium of government, on the basis of a representative legislature"* had been the defining feature of British governance.[17] "By extending this beautiful part of our constitution" to the colonies, George Dempster told the House of Commons in October 1775, "our wise ancestors have bound together the different and distant parts of this mighty empire" and "diffused in a most unexampled manner the blessings of liberty and good government through our remotest provinces."[18] "Without freedom," Edmund Burke remarked in 1766, the empire "would not be the British Empire."[19] Some European analysts agreed. By thus permitting the colonies to adopt "the form of its own government," observed Montesquieu, Britain had effectively ensured that the colonies would prosper, that "great peoples" would "emerge" from the forests and islands to which their ancestors had migrated, and that the colonists would be able to think of themselves and be thought of by others as "intrinsically British."[20]

[15] John Campbell, *A Political Survey of Britain: being a Series of Reflections on the Situation, Lands. Inhabitants, Revenues, Colonies, and Commerce of this Island*, 2 vols. (London, 1774), vol. 1, pp. 263–448.

[16] Arthur Young, *Political Essays Concerning the Present State of the British Empire* (London, 1772), p. 20.

[17] Thomas Pownall, *The Administration of the Colonies*, 4th ed. (London: J. Walter, 1768), p. 175.

[18] George Dempster, speech, Oct. 27, 1775, in Richard Simmons and P. D. G. Thomas, eds., *Proceedings and Debates of the British Parliament Respecting North America, 1754–1783*, 6 vols. (Millwood, NY: Krauss International, 1982–87), vol. 6, p. 640.

[19] Edmund Burke, Speech on the Declaratory Act, Feb. 3, 1766, in Paul Langford, ed., *The Writings of Edmund Burke, Vol. 2: Party, Parliament, and the American Crisis, 1766–1774* (Oxford: Oxford University Press, 1981), p. 47.

[20] Quoted in Richard Koebner, *Empire* (Cambridge: Cambridge University Press, 1961), pp. 92, 297.

In his extensive dilation in the *Wealth of Nations* in 1776 on the causes of the rapid development in new colonial societies in the English-speaking world, Adam Smith agreed that Britain had "dealt more liberally with her colonies than [had] any other nation." He linked the colonies' rapid development directly to their extensive self-governing authority. "Plenty of good land, and liberty to manage their own affairs their own way," he argued, were "the two great causes of the prosperity" of the British colonies. "In every thing except their foreign trade," he observed, "the liberty of the English colonists is complete. It is in every respect equal to that of their fellow-citizens at home, and is secured in the same manner, by an assembly of the representatives of the people." "The government of the English colonies," he observed, "is perhaps the only one which, since the world began, could give perfect security to the inhabitants of so very distant a province."[21] "The Case of a Free country branching itself out in the manner Britain has done and sending to a distant world colonies which have there, from small beginnings and under free legislatures of their own, increased and formed a body of powerful states," echoed the philosopher Richard Price, was unprecedented "in the history of mankind."[22]

By no means were all metropolitan Britons comfortable with this conception, however. It implied an association of polities, each exercising authority over its internal sphere through the instruments of consensual governance while maintaining a common attachment to a parent culture through well-defined political ties to a central state, whatever the institution, Crown or Parliament, that held the preponderance of power within that state. For the later Stuarts, and especially for James II, this sort of arrangement contributed to a larger empire that was too loose and too free from central direction, especially during wartime. Although James II had an additional agenda, such concerns also lay behind his attempts to consolidate the colonies into manageable regional blocs and to curtail their extensive self-governing powers. While the Glorious Revolution brought an end to this particular effort and essentially left the English empire organized along the same lines on which it had originally developed, it did not put an end to concerns that authority within the empire was far too dispersed for its own good, and throughout the early decades of the eighteenth century, metropolitan administrators made occasional, desultory, and largely ineffective efforts to strengthen London's authority. Notwithstanding substantial colonial contributions to the inter-colonial wars between 1739 and 1763, London officials became ever more convinced, especially during the Seven Years' War, that the colonies were too free of central direction to be counted on to contribute effectively or systematically to the extension to a wider empire

[21] Adam Smith, *An Inquiry into the Nature and Causes of the Wealth of Nations* [1776], in *The Glasgow Edition of the Works and Correspondence of Adam Smith*, ed. R. H. Campbell and A. S. Skinner, 6 vols. (Oxford: Oxford University Press, 1976–83), vol. 2, pp. 572, 583–85.

[22] Bernard Peach, ed., *Richard Price and the Ethical Foundations of the American Revolution* (Durham, NC: Duke University Press, 1979), p. 82.

of the fiscal military state that had come into being in Britain in the decades since the Glorious Revolution.[23]

As Eliga Gould shows in Chapter 4, such concerns lay behind Parliament's efforts in the mid-1760s to add its authority to that of the Crown in an attempt to curtail the centrifugal tendencies that had traditionally characterized the British imperial polity, asserting its jurisdiction over the colonies in unprecedented ways by taxing them for revenue; otherwise interfering in the internal affairs; and, for the first time during peace time, saddling them with a substantial military force. In the vigorous debate that erupted during the Stamp Act crisis of 1764–1766 and escalated over the following decade, it rapidly became clear to antagonists on both sides of the Atlantic and throughout the settler empire that Parliament's emergence during the decades following the Glorious Revolution as the unchallenged site of sovereign authority within Britain was at odds with the unwritten constitution that had taken shape over the previous century and a half for governing the empire as a whole, a constitution that had been founded and had always operated on the assumption that colonial Britons might not be taxed or subjected to laws relating to their internal affairs without the consent of the representatives in their own parliamentary bodies.

Colonial resistance to Parliament's efforts to enforce its authority through legislation and, after 1774, through force was strongest and most persistent in the North American mainland colonies. Although many political spokesmen for the island colonies in the Atlantic and the West Indies and in Ireland endorsed the constitutional stance of the North Americans, recognizing their greater vulnerability to British force and their dependence on metropolitan protection against the majority disenfranchised populations among whom they lived, they stopped short of offering armed resistance and subsequently provided material support for British arms in the long war that followed the failure to find a peaceful resolution. When the metropolitan government, under the mistaken notion that colonial resistance could be easily put down by force, refused to accept any limitation on its sovereign authority in the empire, thirteen of the eighteen North American colonies raised armies, offered military resistance, formed themselves into a loose political coalition, reluctantly declared themselves independent in the summer of 1776, and, after nearly eight years of a costly war, forced the British government to recognize that independence.

This event changed the face of the British settler empire. On the surface, the change was most pronounced among the former colonies that proceeded to organize themselves into the independent, republican, and, by the late 1780s, explicitly federal United States. But the transition to republicanism and federalism represented less of a change than modern historians have often suggested.

[23] On this point, see Jack P. Greene, *Peripheries and Center: Constitutional Development in the Extended Polities of the British Empire and the United States, 1607–1788* (Athens: University of Georgia Press, 1988), and Peter J. Marshall, *Making and Unmaking of Empire* (Oxford: Oxford University Press, 2005).

As Adam Smith remarked in *The Wealth of Nations* in 1776, Britain's American colonies – and he did not here exclude the island colonies – were "republican" in "their manners ... and their governments" long before thirteen of them became formally republican in 1776.[24] The extensive authority of the legislative branch, he thereby suggested, had made Britain's American colonies functionally republican long before they became anti-monarchical. Similarly, the operative division of authority within the empire, with the metropolitan government's being responsible for the regulation of trade, diplomacy, and other external concerns, and the provincial governments of the various parts of the empire's having authority over matters of their internal governance, represented a de facto form of federalism well before the Constitution of 1787 made the United States a federal nation.

To a considerable degree, these conditions explain why, during the North American settler revolt that began in 1774–76, the transition from monarchy to republican government was so easy in those polities that had the wherewithal to participate in that revolt; why the revolution it produced required no disavowal of a British-style representative government or of British common-law legal traditions; why, when those polities moved to strengthen the national government in 1787–88, they never considered any form except a federal system that left control of their internal affairs to the individual states; and why, as settlements spread to new areas after 1790, every new state, with the partial exception of Louisiana, founded itself on an English common-law legal culture. To be sure, as Peter Onuf shows in Chapter 5, the creation of a new national arena disattached from the old empire provided a forum for the development of a distinctive national political culture that in many ways departed significantly from that of contemporary Britain or from those areas of the overseas empire that remained within the empire, and each of those departures took a distinctive shape fitted to the particular context in which it developed. But the limited scope of the national government guaranteed that individual states would continue to exert the predominant influence over their local affairs, including especially the perpetuating of a slave labor regime and the exclusionary political system that it involved. In this way and many others, the construction of the United States provided a political framework for the achievement and expansion of the provincial autonomy British overseas settlers had long sought through their quest for metropolitan recognition of their right to British liberty, as defined by consensual government through representative institutions and a legal system rooted in English traditions of the rule of law.

Elsewhere in the old settler empire – in Ireland, the West Indies and Atlantic island colonies, and those North American colonies that either did not revolt or were retroceded to Spain as a result of the Treaty of Paris of 1783, as was the case with East and West Florida – the American situation also resulted in the extension of provincial autonomy, at least in the short run. In the case of Ireland, Britain's difficulties in America emboldened the Protestant political

[24] Smith, *Wealth of Nations*, vol. 2, p. 585.

nation to mount a vigorous and successful campaign to eliminate British restrictions on Irish trade and legislative independence. While Britain's suspension of the Navigation Acts in the case of Ireland in 1780 put Ireland on an equal commercial footing with the metropolis, the repeal of the Declaratory Act of 1720 and the repeal of Poynings' Law in 1782 freed the Irish Parliament from all limitations on its legislative jurisdiction and thus not only paved the way for the adoption of habeas corpus, judicial tenure during good behavior, and local control over military forces, but also, at least with respect to Ireland's internal affairs, put the Irish Parliament on a level with the British Parliament. All of these achievements represented the culmination of a campaign of almost a century, spearheaded by the Irish House of Commons and generations of its protagonists for the removal of any restrictions on their British liberty.

If, as James Kelly explains in Chapter 3, "the liberties available to the Protestant subjects of Ireland were greater than they had been at any point in Irish history," Irish legislative independence did not survive the end of the century. The Protestant Ascendancy in Ireland after the Glorious Revolution was built on a series of penal laws that placed drastic social, legal, and political disabilities on all the vast majority of Irish Catholics who refused to become Protestant. Although the newly liberated Irish Parliament considered ameliorating these laws in the early 1780s, it consciously avoided easing the most significant political exclusions. When the French Revolution inspired the majority Catholic population to demand the elimination of these laws in the 1790s and to rise in rebellion in 1798, Irish Protestant leaders, more intent on maintaining Protestant control in Ireland than on preserving Irish self-government in the face of the prospect of sharing it with Catholics, voted in 1800 to abolish their Parliament altogether and enter into a formal legislative union with Britain.

A similar course of development occurred in the old West Indies colonies. During the Stamp Act crisis, the British Parliament passed the Declaratory Act of 1766, which, modeled after the 1720 statute applying only to Ireland, asserted its legislative jurisdiction over Britain's overseas possessions in all cases whatsoever. However, as it became evident that the revolting colonies could not be easily and inexpensively subdued, the government in 1778 sought to entice them back into the imperial fold by repealing that measure and replacing it with a new Declaratory Act that acknowledged the exclusive legislative jurisdiction of colonial assemblies over taxation in their respective colonies, a measure that applied to all American colonies, including those that were not in revolt. In the West Indies, this concession had the effect of giving provincial legislatures a free hand over their internal affairs. Except for their continued subjection to the Navigation Acts, West Indian legislatures thereafter were almost as autonomous in their internal polities as were the Irish after Britain's 1782 concessions to Ireland, although their legislation was still subject to royal veto. This enhanced autonomy would be useful to West Indian legislatures during the half-century after 1789.

For the first six decades of the eighteenth century, Britons had, to the extent that they thought about empire at all, embraced it as a source of national prosperity and, especially after the great victory in the Seven Years' War, an emblem of national greatness. But exposés after 1770, such as the revelation of the mistreatment and exploitation of India by East India Company employees in the early 1770s, the iniquities of the slave trade and slavery brought to light during the press wars over American resistance in the mid-1770s, the injustices of Irish Protestant discrimination against Catholics compared with the more favorable treatment of Catholics in Quebec in the mid-1770s, and the shocking use of slaves and Indians against the American rebels during the American war, all tended to produce a re-evaluation of empire, especially among those who, responding to the wave of humanitarian sentiment generated by Enlightenment thinkers, liked to think of Britain as a humane nation. Deeply embarrassed by such behavior, these critics pursued a variety of strategies. Some sought to distance themselves and their country from empire by suggesting that greedy Guinea merchants on the African coast, plundering nabobs in India, despotic slaveowners in the American colonies, persecuting Protestants in Ireland, and debauched British generals in North America were not true Britons but some debased variety of the sorts that had always been the principal recruits for Britain's overseas adventures. A few wanted Britain to sever its ties to empire altogether. Arguing for "the real inutility of external territories to Britain," James Thomson Callender called attention to "the unfathomable waste of money requisite to retain them, the injustice and guilt that constantly attend such acquisitions, and the intolerable ravages that we suffer from internal taxes, in consequence of national wars about them."[25] Most critics, however, merely demanded that the empire's greatest excesses be reformed.[26]

In regard to the West Indies, this re-evaluation of empire produced increasingly strident demands within metropolitan Britain for metropolitan intervention, first to stop the slave trade, then to ameliorate slavery, and eventually to end slavery altogether. With the help of the powerful West Indian and slave trade lobby, West Indian legislatures managed to stave off the abolition of the slave trade for nearly two decades and then to localize or even subvert metropolitan initiatives to register slaves and ameliorate their conditions of life. Even after Parliamentary legislation emancipated – with compensation to their owners – all slaves throughout the empire, West Indian legislatures exerted enormous influence on the process of emancipation, especially during the five years of apprenticeship before slaves acquired their full freedom, and they made no effort to ease the slaves' transition to freedom, carefully restricting political

[25] James Thomson Callender, *The Political Progress of Britain: Or, an Impartial History of the Abuses of the Government of the British Empire in Europe, Asia, and America* (Philadelphia, 1795), p. 19.
[26] These observations derive from the editor's largely completed book manuscript, which is tentatively entitled *Speaking of Empire: The Metropolitan Reevaluation of Britons Overseas, 1730–1790*.

access to independent property holders. They had no intention of sharing their liberty with former slaves or of making island liberty less exclusive. Gradually losing confidence in their capacity to control an increasingly restive population of former slaves, West Indian legislatures, after two centuries of existence, led by the Jamaican Assembly, which abolished itself after the uprising at Morant Bay in 1865, exchanged consensual for Crown colony governance that had no representative element but seemed to promise metropolitan support for the continuation of white control. Of all the British West Indian colonies only Barbados, which had the highest proportion of whites, retained its old constitution. The Barbadian Assembly ranked just behind those of Virginia, Bermuda, Massachusetts, Maryland, and Connecticut in being the oldest continuously functioning parliamentary bodies in the English-speaking world outside of Britain itself. Elsewhere in the West Indies, the early generations of settlers had created societies that were so exclusive that the small remaining settler populations found their security, such as it was, not in the robust assertion of their rights as Britons, in the manner of their ancestors, but in the forfeiture of those rights. In the end, they had to acknowledge that the colonies they inhabited were no longer settler colonies but economic entities populated largely by people who, having, as they thought, no capacity for self-government, required the authoritarian hand of the metropolis.

In contrast to Ireland and the West Indies, the three remaining and highly disparate British settlement colonies on the North American continent after 1783 – Nova Scotia, St. John's Island (renamed Prince Edward Island in 1799), and Quebec – had no substantial populations to exclude from the civic sphere, although none of them extended full civic status to whatever indigenous peoples yet lived among them, and Quebec, with its predominantly Catholic and French population, lacked formal representative government of the British kind. But the Quebec situation was rather a concession to majority sensibilities than a deprivation of liberty, whatever the small local British population thought. The legislatures in Nova Scotia (1758) and St. John's Island (1773) both enjoyed considerable authority over internal affairs, especially after the Declaratory Act of 1778 guaranteed colonial assemblies the exclusive power of internal taxation. Moreover, the influx of loyalists, who might have abhorred resistance to legitimate government but were no less committed to British principles of consensual governance and the rule of law than the Whig leaders they had left behind, proved sturdy advocates for the creation or expansion of the authority of representative assemblies wherever they settled – whether in Nova Scotia or in the new colonies of New Brunswick (1784) and Upper Canada (eventually renamed Ontario). Indeed, in the 1791 act that separated Upper Canada from Quebec (renamed Lower Canada), the metropolitan government provided for representative governments for both colonies, thereby extending consensual government to the French Canadians. Thereafter all new British settler colonies established north of the United States partook of the same privilege. In contrast to the older colonies of Nova Scotia and St. John,

Catholics in Lower and Upper Canada enjoyed the franchise from the beginnings of representative government.

Philip Girard treats this subject at length in Chapter 6 as well as the demand for responsible government that emerged in the older colonies in the 1840s and the union of Ontario, Quebec, New Brunswick, and Nova Scotia in the new federal Dominion of Canada by the British North America Act of 1867, a union soon joined by Manitoba, British Columbia, and Prince Edward Island. Although it did not become fully independent until 1931, Canada was the first new settler nation to grow out of the British empire after the creation of the United States in the late 1770s.

The demand for responsible government emerged out of settler dissatisfaction with the existing structure of governance. Despite the wide authority exerted by the legislatures of every colony over internal affairs, the executive arm of these relatively new polities was far more independent and powerful than had been the case in the older colonies, founded to the south and in the West Indies more than a century earlier. As the population grew during the early decades of the nineteenth century and provincial identity became more coherent, widespread discontent developed in all the colonies over restrictions on their self-governing powers, especially the power of appointed governors and upper houses (who together came to be seen as irresponsible oligarchies beyond the control of citizens) to veto measures passed by the assemblies. In 1837 the movement for responsible government, which envisioned a parliamentary regime in which the royal governor would become a mere figurehead and executive authority would be exercised by the prime minister and a cabinet selected out of the legislature and thus indirectly accountable to the broader public, culminated in rebellions in both Upper and Lower Canada. In response, the metropolitan government sent to Canada Lord Durham, who produced a report recommending the institution of responsible government in all the British North American colonies as well as the union of Upper and Lower Canada, a device intended further to acculturate French Canadians to English forms of parliamentary governance.

This change, with the formal approval of the metropolitan government, represented a devolution of authority to provincial political establishments. Thereafter, British North American colonies had, in a strikingly new form, the self-government that settler colonies in the British empire had always claimed as their inheritance. Nor did the British North American Act of 1867 that created the Dominion of Canada diminish this achievement. Although the act assigned broad powers to the national government, in practice that government proved less intrusive than London had been, and provincial governments continued to exercise broad authority over provincial affairs.

In the era of the American Revolution, the extension of British liberty overseas through the devices of representative institutions and the rule of law did not necessarily apply to all parts of the empire. India, treated by Robert Travers in Chapter 7, is the principal case in point. The East India Company presided over British commercial interests there for a century and a half before its territorial acquisitions in 1757 during the Seven Years' War brought portions of India under its direct political jurisdiction. These acquisitions quickly raised the question of how far the British government should be responsible for India's governance, a question that became more pressing with the revelations of extensive corruption on the part of company officials in Bengal during the late 1760s and early 1770s. After 1774 the company had to operate with considerably more oversight from Westminster.

But the question of how India ought to be governed remained a thorny problem. The considerations that prompted Ireland and most of the West Indian colonies to abandon consensual government existed in abundance in India. Like Ireland, it had a large settled population with deeply embedded cultural mores and traditions of religion, jurisprudence, and governance. In contrast to Ireland, however, cultural differences, most British observers of India argued, were so extreme as to preclude the eventual assimilation of the indigenous population to British traditions of free governance. As in the West Indies, a small cadre of white inhabitants existed in a vast sea of alien peoples; however, in contrast to the West Indies, the subaltern peoples were not imported and culturally vulnerable, but indigenous and thoroughly rooted in an ancient civilization. Moreover, in further contrast to the West Indies in their earliest days, British people had never been sufficiently numerous to create their own polity with the consensual apparatus that existed throughout the old settler empire. For these reasons, neither the company nor the metropolis ever seriously entertained the possibility of extending British parliamentary government to India.

But representative institutions were only part of the British libertarian inheritance, and the debate over Indian governance quickly began to turn around the question of how far British law should extend in India. Company representatives soon managed to crush an early effort to use British-manned courts to protect indigenous people from British rapacity, arguing that British liberty could not be transferred to non-British people without undermining the system of economic and political subordination on which the profits of the company were based. Instead, they advocated the creation of a two-tier legal system in which indigenous laws and institutions would be left to adjudicate problems among Indians, while the protections of British law would be reserved exclusively for Britons. Although the questions of whether parts of India might become settler enclaves that could be trusted with representative institutions and whether privileged and assimilated Indians might eventually be permitted to enjoy British legal rights remained open well into the nineteenth century and occasionally generated heated debates, the sort of two-tier system advocated by the company supporters in the 1770s soon became the norm, with British courts in the presidency towns ensuring that British residents would be governed by British legal traditions, and company tribunals presiding over the indigenous population using forms of jurisprudence supposedly modeled on traditional Indian laws combined with codes of administrative regulations issued by British colonial governors.

New settler colonies in Australia, New Zealand, and South Africa, respectively treated herein by Richard Waterhouse in Chapter 8, James Belich in Chapter 9, and Christopher Saunders in Chapter 10, did not suffer the fate of India and other nonsettler colonies that Britain acquired during the nineteenth century. All three represented variants of the Canadian experience. For reasons peculiar to their origins as convict colonies, the Australian colonies were the slowest to follow the Canadian path. Initially, the original colonies of New South Wales and Van Diemen's Land (Tasmania) functioned under a joint military government, for which the closest model was the government of Newfoundland. Presided over by a naval or military officer, these governments did not even have an appointed advisory council until the early 1820s. Governors made, executed, and enforced, with little check except from the distant metropolitan government, a system that left no room for consensual institutions, juries, the rule of law, or any of the other traditions of British liberty and stood in stark contrast to conceptions of the British empire as a free empire.

Unlike the enslaved people in the American colonies, the convicts who formed the bulk of the European population in Australia during the early decades of settlement had fixed terms and defined rights, including by the first decade of the nineteenth century the right to acquire property. As the number of emancipated convicts steadily increased, joined by a few free immigrants, they became a significant settler population, and, like free settlers throughout the empire over the previous two centuries, began by 1819 to press for the extension to Australia of jury-based common law and representative government. Opposed by colonial officials in both the colony and London, these early efforts were largely unsuccessful, although in 1823 London did provide for the appointment of an advisory council to assist the governor in making and enforcing rules of governance.

But dissatisfaction continued, especially after Lord Durham's report in the early 1840s led to the granting of responsible government to the Canadian colonies, all of which had already long enjoyed representative government. By this time, convicts had long been a dwindling minority of the white population, and, with the metropolitan government having stopped transportation to New South Wales in the 1840s and to Van Dieman's Land (Tasmania) in 1853 and the vast majority of emancipated convicts having become law-abiding and property-owning settlers, the convict origins of the colony no longer seemed like a viable pretext for depriving Australians of their inherited British rights. Nevertheless, social conservatives in Australia and the colonial office continued to resist settler agitation for consensual governance, which had now escalated to a demand for responsible government of the kind that had recently been granted to the Canadian colonies. Although London authorities took the first tentative step in this direction in 1842 by expanding the size of the advisory council and making two-thirds of its members elective, another decade elapsed before they directed the legislative councils of New South Wales, Victoria, and South Australia, three of the six colonies then existing in Australia, to draft constitutions providing for bicameral legislatures and responsible government, and Tasmania, Queensland, and Western Australia soon followed suit. Debate over what form these constitutions should take and London's slowness in yielding control over customs, Crown lands, and the civil lists to the new colonial governments delayed this process for a few years, but, by the end of the 1850s, all of the Australian colonies had responsible governance that was remarkable both for the breadth of the franchise and the low qualifications for office-holding. The aboriginal population did not participate in this debate and had no access to civil space either before or after the achievement of responsible government. With this significant exception, however, Australian liberty, as enshrined in both the provincial constitutions and the federal constitution adopted later in the century, seemed to be the least exclusive variant of British liberty established anywhere in the British empire before the twentieth century, including Britain itself.

The journey to the same destination of New Zealand, which did not become a British colony until 1840, was much more rapid. Notwithstanding the fact that its indigenous Maori occupants were more densely settled, sedentary, and militarily formidable than Australia's aborigines, British settlers poured into the new colony in droves during its earliest years. To provide some order over the society they were creating, metropolitan authorities sent a governor from London to establish an interim government composed of himself and an appointed advisory council with temporary law-making powers, and this body presided over the colony until 1853. Already in 1841–42, it issued ordinances to establish courts and ensure that British common law complete with juries would form the foundations of the legal system for the settler populations, leaving the Maoris free to use their customary law to determine legal matters in the portions of the colony they still controlled. Despite sporadic pressure from the settler population to bring the Maoris under settler law, this two-tiered legal system lasted until the 1880s, by which time further immigration, wars of conquest, and the spread of British settlement had largely overwhelmed the last vestiges of Maori independence. In contrast to Australia, where the Crown, ignoring aboriginal rights, had simply declared all land to be Crown land, the colonial office insisted that New Zealand authorities seek Maori consent and purchase land before British settlement.

Settler agitation for self-government was coincident with the first settlement, and metropolitan authorities, with Lord Durham's report in hand, always expected that New Zealand would proceed rapidly to the creation of consensual governance in the British manner. In 1846, just six years after the initial British settlements, Parliament passed an act providing for the creation of an elected legislature. Colonial authorities managed to delay the implementation of this measure for eight years, during which time New Zealand's governor and council divided New Zealand into six provinces, each with its own government. Thus, when the measure was finally implemented in 1854, New Zealand had both a general legislature and six provincial legislatures, each of which enjoyed authority over Crown lands in its province and a share of customs revenues. This step, which, like contemporary arrangements adopted for the Australian colonies, included an extremely wide franchise for property-owning males and amply provided New Zealand settlers with representative government of the kind traditionally found throughout the settler empire before 1840, but not with responsible government, which, at metropolitan insistence, came in 1856. In a reversal of the process that made the United States, Canada, and, by 1900, Australia federal governments, the New Zealand general government in 1876 abolished the provinces in the name of social and economic progress.

Already a century and a half old at the time of its conquest from the Dutch in 1795, the Cape colony provides yet another variant on settler acquisition of British liberty. Although the Cape had a substantial number of Dutch settlers with a well-established settler culture, the vast majority of its population consisted of the indigenous Khoi people, who were free but subordinated to Dutch rule, and slaves imported from Asia or brought in from other parts of Africa, and slavery and racial hierarchy were firmly in place under a system of Roman-Dutch law. As had been the case with Quebec after the Seven Years' War, the British conquerors permitted the Dutch to retain their old legal system but slowly introduced features of the common law and, eventually in 1826, trial by jury in civil and criminal cases. The new administration soon moved to ameliorate the worst conditions of Dutch slavery by eliminating torture and endeavored with some success to extend British law over the Khoi, providing them with access to the courts and equal justice. Meanwhile, an 1808 ordinance subjecting Africans whom the royal navy liberated from captured slave vessels to fourteen years of labor before they could exercise their freedom introduced a new form of forced labor that was de facto slavery. As elsewhere in the empire, the Emancipation Act of 1832 brought an end to slavery, with compensation to owners. Although immigration from Britain was substantial, it was never high enough to produce a settler majority, and, as territorial expansion brought additional indigenous people under British authority, settlers constituted a declining proportion of the total population.

This situation made many members of the settler community skeptical about any move toward consensual government, even while many others, resentful of the arbitrary practices of some governors, agitated for representative institutions that would extend to them the traditional British right not to be taxed or governed by laws or ordinances to which they had not consented. The creation in 1834 of a locally nominated council to provide some check on governors was in part a response to this agitation, but it would take another twenty years before the Cape would get its own legislature. London authorities agreed in 1846 that the Cape should have representative government on the condition, which would not be applied to the Australian colonies or New Zealand, that any laws it might pass would be nonracial and apply to all equally, and a massive settler protest against admitting transported British criminals into the colony in 1849 hastened Parliament's grant of representative government in 1853.

But the new regime provided liberty only to the propertied white minority, which, like its counterparts in the continental and island slave colonies in the

Americas, never seriously considered extending that liberty to the indigenous majority. The white property holders quickly turned the Cape Parliament into a bastion of settler privilege, a development that the grant of responsible government in 1872 only consolidated, by freeing the Cape government from any possible check from London. A bit later than the Cape, the neighboring colony of Natal exhibited a similar development, as did the Boer republics following their defeat by the British in the Boer War in 1899–1902. When representatives from all over South Africa joined together to form the Union of South Africa in 1910, which, unlike Canada and Australia, rejected federalism as a form of organization, they created a national parliamentary government that continued to enable the settler minority to exclude the indigenous majority from any effective role.

During its first three centuries, the English or, after 1707, British empire produced an extraordinarily wide diffusion of the English libertarian inheritance overseas through the creation of polities in a wide variety of physical and social settings: Ireland, continental North America, the Atlantic and West Indian islands, India, Australia, New Zealand, and South Africa. For the first two centuries, most of these new polities were created on territories acquired by conquest. Significantly, however, with the exception of Jamaica, New York, India, Quebec, the Cape colony, and, to a partial extent, Ireland, these conquests were not the work of metropolitan navies or armies but of British settlers and other agents of colonization. Showing little concern for the rights or persons of the existing inhabitants, they proceeded, with slight help from the parent state, to subjugate or drive them out; take possession of the vacated property; repopulate it; and create, insofar as possible, new anglicized societies and polities. Even in territories acquired by military conquest, settlers supplied most of the initiative and man and woman power necessary to make the spaces they inhabited productive and congenial to their inherited norms. After 1750, the metropolitan government took a more active role in this process as colonies were established in India, Canada, Florida, and the West Indies, areas acquired as a result of the Seven Years' War. Throughout the settler empire, however, settlers continued to exert a disproportionate amount of the agency involved in the creation of every new colony.

From first to last, settler claims to their inherited rights of Englishmen, by which they principally meant the rights to consensual governance and the rule of law, were a critical element in the dispersal of authority throughout the settler empire. Already by the mid-seventeenth century, they had worked out a theory justifying their assertions that those rights were theirs by inheritance, were neither the grant nor the gift of any superior government, and necessarily required full access to the corpus of English law and the parliamentary institutions that could alone guarantee that, like English people at home, they should be governed only by laws and pay only taxes to which they had, through their representatives, given their consent. The implementation of these ideas, first through representative and then, after 1840, through responsible government, resulted in the high degree of self-government over local affairs that underlay British pride, especially evident from the middle decades of the eighteenth century, in having created a free empire. If India, with its varied indigenous polities and small cadre of British agents, represented a significant exception to this pattern, it was the exception that proved the rule, and its British inhabitants all had access to British legal protections and procedures.

Of course, British conceptions of liberty and who might enjoy it did not remain static during the long era covered by this volume. In the generations immediately following the American War for Independence, demands for free trade and the abolition of chattel slavery in the empire, agitation for electoral reform in Britain, the adoption of universal white male suffrage in most of the American states, and the extension of self-government to new Canadian provinces all seemed to herald an expansion of traditional British notions about liberty within the English-speaking world, an expansion that appeared to be confirmed after the middle of the nineteenth century by the achievement of self-government in all those British colonies that had been heavily settled by Britons and other Europeans. If, at the same time, however, the abolition of the Irish Parliament at the beginning of the nineteenth century and of most of the West Indian assemblies after 1865 represented significant exceptions to this general trend, a far more general exception involved India and the many new colonies that Britain acquired during the last half of the nineteenth century with indigenous inhabitants too numerous to displace and (it was often argued) culturally backward, unschooled in the merits and practice of British liberty, or not the right color for it. The anomaly of such polities within a "free" empire demanded explanation, and increasingly around and after mid-century imperial thinkers developed a rationale for the accommodation with authoritarian imperialism in reference to nonsettlement colonies. Amplifying the stadial theories of their early modern predecessors, they emphasized the incapacity of people at "lower stages" of civilizational development to enjoy self-government and the correlative necessity for British tutelage and stewardship until those people had advanced to a "higher stage" of cultural development.[27] Such theories in reference to Indians and other culturally different people only operated to reinforce the idea that English people "were peculiarly adapted . . . to self-government" and "fitted by the nature" and traditions "to guide the government[s]" of the many societies over which they presided, thus employing "their imperial power for the good of all mankind."[28]

These theories also served to highlight the underlying assumptions that had long functioned to exclude various categories of people from self-government within the self-governing portions of the empire and thereby to make it

---

[27] See Uday Singh Mehta, *Liberalism and Empire: A Study in Nineteenth-Century British Liberal Thought* (Chicago: University of Chicago Press, 1999), and Jennifer Pitts, *A Turn to Empire: The Rise of Imperial Liberalism in Britain and France* (Princeton, NJ: Princeton University Press, 2005).

[28] The quotations are from Catherine Hall, *Civilising Subjects: Metropole and Colonies in the English Imagination, 1830–1867* (Chicago: University of Chicago Press, 2002), pp. 426–27.

increasingly clear, though it had always been the case in fact, that the British empire might be a free empire for settlers but not for anyone else. As in England itself, the capacity to enjoy fully liberty, in the way it was traditionally defined, was limited to independent property owners with wills of their own and people who could claim a British cultural inheritance either by birth or naturalization. Not only did colonial self-government empower the enfranchised to disempower all those whom they found politically or socially threatening, but the very concept of liberty as they had inherited and understood it required them to do so. Within the settler empire, as Christopher Saunders has aptly expressed the situation in reference to South Africa in Chapter 10, the liberal British idea "that people should have the right to rule themselves" actually "helped promote illiberalism" in respect to subaltern peoples.

Not even the expansion in Britain in 1867 of the franchise to include most male property holders and rate payers, regardless of their religious affiliations, fundamentally challenged the ancient connection between personal independence and a civic voice. On the contrary, the broader franchise reached only, as Catherine Hall has put it, to "independent Englishmen: those with homes and families" and pointedly excluded "the residuum" of "the poor, the rough and those lacking in respectability on account of their religious or ethnic considerations" who "were not yet ready to enjoy the vote."[29] For the time being, in Britain and in the "free" segments of the empire, political liberty would continue to be an exclusionary liberty.

If the amount and scope of self-government achieved by the British colonies were extraordinary in comparison with those of any other European empire, the denial of citizenship to indigenous peoples in Ireland, the Americas, Canada, Australia, New Zealand, and South Africa; the denial of self-ownership to imported peoples and their descendants in North America, the Atlantic islands, and the West Indies; and the systematic discrimination on religious or racial and cultural grounds against the majority populations in Ireland and South Africa all made Britain's settler empire, like its nonsettler empire in India and other parts of Asia, Africa, and the Americas, exclusionary.

[29] Ibid., 425, 426, 430.

The Languages of Liberty in British North America, 1607–1776

Elizabeth Mancke

In the seventeenth century, beginning with the settlement of Jamestown, Virginia, in 1607, English subjects of middling and poor circumstances settled in the temperate zones of North America, often under the auspices of companies or proprietors. All participants in planting these colonies soon realized that their greatest assets were labor, land, and their identity as natural-born English subjects, and that returns on investments would be slow to achieve. For settlers, these three assets reinforced one another in dialectical complementarity: Labor invested in land created wealth and legitimated a claim; ownership of land gave them the right to participate in government and the exercise of traditional English liberties, such as trial by jury, deliberative assemblies, and local government; and self-government could protect their land and labor. While charters acknowledged that overseas English subjects were entitled to traditional English legal and political protections, they did not spell out what institutional forms the protections of English rights and liberties should take. Thus, in addition to establishing farms and families, colonists from New England to the Carolinas established the institutions of self-government, with a particular emphasis on their rights to assemblies and rule by law.[1] This chapter seeks to position British American expressions of traditional English liberties within a broader transatlantic context in which claims to liberty were frequently deployed in the struggle to define the nature and character of overseas expansion.

The ideologies informing English overseas expansion borrowed from, elaborated on, reconstructed, and made anew four expressions of liberty. One drew on the ancient Afro-Eurasian practices concerning the liberty of travel or passage for certain groups, most particularly merchants, but also students

---

[1] Jack P. Greene, "Traditions of Consensual Governance in the Construction of State Authority in the Early Modern Empires in America," in Maija Jansson, ed., *Realities of Representation: State Building in Early Modern Europe and European America* (New York: Palgrave Macmillan, 2007), pp. 171–186; John Phillip Reid, *Rule of Law: The Jurisprudence of Liberty in the Seventeenth and Eighteenth Centuries* (DeKalb: University of Northern Illinois Press, 2004).

and later missionaries, and which European commentators argued originated in natural law or in the law of nations. A second expression of liberty was the English liberties that inhered in the person of a subject and which, in the words of the seventeenth-century jurist, Sir Matthew Hale, "the English planters carried with them" overseas. These liberties, including protection of person and property from unwarranted seizure, due process in law, and trial by jury, were specifically English, ostensibly dating back to William the Conqueror and listed in the Magna Charta (1215).[2] Liberty of self-government, a third distinct expression, drew its rationale from the two previous expressions of liberty. Merchant communities in foreign cities, students in foreign universities, and members of religious orders were generally accorded the liberty of self-government for members of their "nation" or order.[3] In England, self-government was associated with local government of various forms – village, borough, and city – and by the late middle ages had also become associated with the right to consent to statutes by which the English were governed and taxed, a right metropolitan authorities acknowledged when authorizing many colonies and that colonists quickly came to claim as an inherited English right. The fourth, and for most people newest, was liberty of conscience. Ancient iterations of liberty of conscience in England were manifest in practices such as the right of members of Parliament to speak freely without fear of arrest.[4] With the religious ferment of the sixteenth and seventeenth centuries, liberty of conscience in matters of religion was demanded by people throughout Europe and by the mid-seventeenth century was widely accorded to dissenting Protestants in the English world.

Many English overseas enterprises justified their agendas using one or more of these expressions of liberty, so that the language of liberty became entwined in the ideology of the British empire, and at the same time became central to the identities of Britons, in both Britain and its overseas dependencies.[5] For some members of the larger British world, the concept of liberty became naturalized, expressed most famously in the Declaration of Independence: "We hold these truths to be self-evident that all men are created equal, that they are endowed by their Creator with certain inalienable rights, that among these are life,

---

2 Sir Matthew Hale, *Prerogatives of the King* (1650), as quoted in Ken MacMillan, *Sovereignty and Possession in the English New World: The Legal Foundations of Empire, 1576–1640* (Cambridge and New York: Cambridge University Press, 2006), p. 37.

3 Andrew C. McLaughlin, *The Foundations of American Constitutionalism* (rpt. Gloucester, MA: Peter Smith, 1972 [1932]), pp. 38–65.

4 The right of members of Parliament to speak without fear of arrest was a source of great contention with James I. For documentation on the points on each side see, Michael Kammen, *Deputyes & Libertyes: The Origins of Representative Government in Colonial America* (New York: Alfred A. Knopf, 1969), pp. 73–85.

5 David Armitage, *The Ideological Origins of the British Empire* (New York and Cambridge: Cambridge University Press, 2000); Jack P. Greene, "Empire and Identity from the Glorious Revolution to the American Revolution," in P. J. Marshall, ed., *The Eighteenth Century*, Vol. 2, *The Oxford History of the British Empire* (Oxford: Oxford University Press, 1998), pp. 208–230.

liberty, and the pursuit of happiness." In this iteration, liberty was ostensibly no longer tied to social condition, to privileges that arose out of specific political, religious, or commercial contexts, but was a natural condition arising out of life itself; as the next sentence of the Declaration of Independence notes, governments exist "to secure these rights," and therefore not to grant them.[6]

All four expressions of liberty were current in the seventeenth- and eighteenth-century British world, and were instrumentally important first in attracting, cajoling, and luring English people into transatlantic expansion, and then in negotiations between colonists and the metropolitan government over the nature of the privileges and rights of British subjects in overseas settler colonies. As well, the multiple meanings of liberty made it possible to elide the contradictions and tensions in one expression of liberty by shifting to another, or to forestall recognizing one expression of liberty by extending another. It was not the specificity of the meaning of liberty but its plural and plastic meanings that allowed ideas and applications of liberty to become abstracted from their commercial, political, and religious contexts, so that Britons throughout the world could espouse loyalty to the empire based on a shared sense that the expansion of liberty was central to the empire's meaning and distinguished it from other empires, both European and Asian. Indeed, the abstracting, and for some the ostensible naturalizing, of liberty contributed to the emergence of another iteration in the mid-eighteenth century, one deployed against the institution of slavery so that every person's natural right to a free body became a fifth powerful meaning attached to liberty. This new definition of liberty was one that Britons used against British American colonists in the revolutionary era to suggest that colonists had very instrumental and self-serving definitions of liberty.[7] Thus the abstraction, naturalization, and eliding of meanings of liberty and the concomitant loyalty to it exposed contradictions and tensions of such a contested nature that disagreements over what liberty specifically entailed contributed to a permanent renting of the British empire.

The ability of the British to convince themselves and other Europeans that their culture and their empire embodied and exemplified liberty more fully than did those of other empires rested on a set of ideas that Europeans were widely engaged in debating and which provided the conceptual foundations for some of the central texts of early modern political thought. While colonial self-government and liberty of conscience were, indeed, more widely applied in overseas British dependencies than in those of the Spanish, Portuguese, and French, ideas about liberty were not exclusively British. Indeed, three of the

---

[6] See Michal Jan Rozbicki, "Between Private and Public Spheres: Liberty as Cultural Property in Eighteenth-Century British America," in Robert Olwell and Alan Tully, eds., *Cultures and Identities in Colonial British America* (Baltimore: Johns Hopkins University Press, 2006), pp. 293–318, for a discussion of the way the expression of liberty became naturalized and universalized, in part, as a strategy of elites "to anchor [themselves] ... in universals and inalienables that appeared to transcend the current power struggles" (quote on 304).

[7] Christopher Leslie Brown, *Moral Capital: Foundations of British Abolitionism* (Chapel Hill: University of North Carolina Press, 2006), pp. 105–153.

four expressions of liberty drew on a common European legacy of custom and law, although they did assume distinctively British configurations and expressions – and with time new meanings – when applied in an Atlantic context.[8]

Liberties traditionally associated with the English – protection of person and property from unwarranted seizure, due process in law, trial by jury, and the right to consent to statutes by which they were governed and taxed – all dealt with aspects of governance in which recognition of contingent and local details was relevant to decision-making. Trial by jury and assembly representation, in particular, provided English subjects access to the processes of governing in which it was especially critical that the contingencies of situations be factored into the final outcome of decisions. In the transatlantic British contestations over the nature of liberties that colonists enjoyed, authorities in the metropole frequently argued that these traditional liberties were themselves contingent in the colonies because of the complexities involved in governing an empire. The emphatic responses from colonists that these liberties could not be qualified were often phrased in ways that shifted their contextual meanings so that liberty became something both natural and not intrinsically connected to the processes of governing, but indeed outside of and separate from government. During the American Revolution, colonists deftly deployed the language of liberty in their cause against Britain, especially through documents such as the Declaration of Independence, so that liberty achieved an iconic association with the values of the United States that only furthered the abstraction and essentializing of it, lifting it above the messy particulars of the historical contexts in which it had been used. To a great extent, the American Revolution was a British war *over* the meanings of liberty as much as *for* liberty, with much of it reflecting significant differences in how liberties were understood.[9]

The British recognition of American independence and the end of the Anglo-American military confrontation did not resolve questions about the definitions of liberty, their interconnections, and who could claim liberty. Colonists who left the British empire to form the United States were not alone in birthing these new contextualizations of liberty, which were reinforced by and drew on various strains of Enlightenment thought. Nevertheless, the abstraction of liberty and its separation from specific concrete meanings made many Britons who remained within the empire, especially those in British North America (later Canada), wary of deploying the languages of liberty. Indeed, the latter tended to frame their political negotiations with imperial authorities, for example, those that led to reforms such as responsible government in the 1840s, in terms of the processes of government to which they were entitled as British subjects.

---

[8] David Armitage in *The Ideological Origins of the British Empire*, 125–145, frames his discussion of "liberty and empire," and the problems with combining the two, in terms of the intellectual legacy of Machiavelli and Italian humanism. This chapter, in contrast, argues that British uses of liberty and understandings of its limitations in imperial contexts drew from a much broader set of English and European traditions.

[9] Kathleen Wilson, *The Sense of the People: Politics, Culture and Imperialism in England, 1715–1785* (New York and Cambridge: Cambridge University Press, 1995), pp. 237–284.

Meanwhile, the American sense that there were indeed liberties to which citizens had claims that were outside of government, and indeed society, took new expression in the nineteenth century.

This chapter seeks to recapture the plural and plastic meanings of liberty in British America and the British Atlantic contexts in the early modern era when the language of liberty was both a tool of expansion and a weapon against imperialism, used to exclude many people, especially non-Europeans, as well as a discourse of nationalist inclusion. The cultural divergences and tensions over the meanings and contexts of liberty remain alive and continue to take part of their resonance from echoes of the early modern transatlantic debates and struggles.

The principle of liberty of passage and commerce is of such antiquity that it is impossible to locate its origins in either time or place, and over the centuries commentators have attributed it to natural law, the law of nations, or both.[10] Restrictions on it are easier to establish, and arguments and agitation against restrictions provide much of the evidence for this principle of liberty. European expansion is associated with wholesale restrictions on navigation by the Spanish and Portuguese beginning with the Treaty of Alcaçovas in 1479, followed by the 1494 Treaty of Tordesillas and the 1529 Treaty of Zaragoza. Through these treaties and the attendant papal bulls, Spain and Portugal attempted to regulate and limit oceanic navigation, thereby resolving conflicting claims between those two powers, while at the same time proscribing their rivals' access to overseas commerce, colonization, and empire. As we know, other European powers, particularly France and England but later also the Dutch, protested these expansive Iberian claims and challenged their validity by emphasizing how they violated liberty of passage and commerce. The challenges, coming as they did from state and quasi-state actors, shifted the principle of liberty of passage and commerce from being a temporally and spatially bounded liberty that discrete groups – primarily merchants and traders – negotiated on a case-by-case basis with local princes and rulers to being a liberty claimed by states and which they negotiated in the interest of their own subjects, and at times to the exclusion of others. As James I argued in the 1604 negotiations for the Anglo-Spanish Treaty of London, he could not agree to Spain's navigational restrictions because he would "deny his subjects the liberty to employ themselves in service abroad."[11] This shift also made liberty of passage and commerce one of the first expressions of liberty that was widely negotiated and legitimized at the multilateral international level; the liberty of a person's physical body leading to the abolition of the slave trade and slavery would be a second.[12]

---

[10] Hugo Grotius, *The Free Sea*, ed. David Armitage (Indianapolis: Liberty Fund, 2004), pp. 49–51.

[11] Quote in MacMillan, *Sovereignty and Possession*, 182.

[12] The Universal Declaration of Human Rights, passed by the UN General Assembly on December 10, 1948, is the most fully expressed multilateral statement; http://www.un.org/Overview/rights.html, accessed April 7, 2008.

During the sixteenth century, the articulation of the principle of liberty of passage and commerce occurred most frequently in diplomatic exchanges. By the 1520s, French corsairs, traders, and royally sponsored explorers were active enough in Spanish-claimed waters that the Castilian Cortés complained formally to the French Crown in 1523 and 1525; Francis I responded with claims to liberty of navigation and trade. Iberian protests intensified with the accession of Elizabeth I to the throne of England in 1558. The Portuguese immediately demanded that she prohibit her subjects from trading in Africa and seized English property in Lisbon; she refused to accede to their demands and instead insisted that her subjects had liberty of navigation and commerce. During negotiations for the 1559 Treaty of Cateau-Cambrésis, France asserted that French subjects had the right as a matter of natural law to sail anywhere they wanted and that French diplomats could not abridge that liberty in the face of Spanish demands.[13] The sophistication of the English diplomatic arguments for liberty of trade and navigation during the negotiations for the 1604 Treaty of London reflected their heightened importance in international political discourse.[14] A nearly simultaneous set of negotiations between the Spanish and the Dutch over the Dutch seizure of a Portuguese ship in Southeast Asian waters in 1603 catapulted the issue to the level of a general European debate. Hugo Grotius, a Dutch lawyer, published a defense of liberty of navigation and trade (*commeandi commercandique libertas*), called *Mare Liberum* or *The Free Sea*, in 1609, a treatise that transformed a century of diplomatic debate over the issues into a broader philosophical and political debate over international law, international relations, and the nature of sovereign property rights in maritime space.[15]

The trend toward treating navigation and trade as conjoined liberties that states negotiated for their subjects and citizens enhanced the ability of states to impose internal restraints on liberty of passage and commerce. In France, Cardinal Richelieu, who came to power first as the secretary of state and then in 1624 as Louis XIII's chief minister, undertook to break the influence of Huguenots by prohibiting their participation in some branches of overseas trade in which they had been prominent in the sixteenth century. French overseas expansion, in turn, became closely associated with Catholicism, including numerous missions to the natives of the Americas, as part of a strategy both to consolidate royal power within France and to prove their faith to the pope in the power struggle within Europe between Spain and France. Such a firmly Catholic policy in France precluded an association of liberty of conscience with

---

[13] Frances Gardiner Davenport, ed., *European Treaties Bearing on the History of the United States and its Dependencies*, 4 vols. (Washington, DC: Carnegie Institution of Washington, 1917–37), vol. 1, pp. 219–22; Elizabeth Mancke, "Oceanic Space and the Creation of a Global International System, 1450–1800," in Daniel Finamore, ed., *Maritime History as World History* (Gainesville: University Press of Florida, 2001), pp. 155–56.

[14] MacMillan, *Sovereignty and Possession*, 180–194.

[15] Grotius, *The Free Sea*, xv and passim; Armitage, *The Ideological Origins of the British Empire*, 100–124.

liberty of trade and navigation in contrast to the way that the two would become ideologically linked in the English world.[16] The subsequent revocation of the Edict of Nantes in 1685 ending French toleration of Protestants forced many Huguenots out of France and into Protestant countries, particularly England and the Netherlands. Indeed, English acceptance of French Protestant refugees, both within England and in its American colonies, became a way to reinforce that their culture was one of liberty, in contrast to absolutist and Catholic French culture.[17] After the passage of navigation acts beginning in 1651, the English metropolitan government would also find itself negotiating liberty of trade with its own colonists in the Caribbean and North America, but those negotiations were framed against the other liberties that colonists claimed for themselves by virtue of English identity and their needs in overseas contexts.

In addition to challenging the Iberians' hegemonic restrictions on trade and navigation, the French and English also challenged their territorial claims to the extra-European world, arguing that discovery and papal donation were insufficient to establish a perpetual claim. They dismissed any pretense of the Portuguese discovering Asia, as distinct from a sea route to Asia, because Europeans had long known of Asia and knew it was occupied.[18] The American continents were another matter. With the extent of indigenous settlement unknown, Europeans could conceptualize these continents as partially unoccupied land that had arguably been "discovered" by the Spanish. Invoking Roman law concerning licit appropriation of unoccupied territory, the French and English argued that claims had to include occupation by one's subjects. In the absence of natural-born subjects on the ground, rivals could establish a claim by settling their own subjects.[19] By acting on this principle to settle colonies, the English created ambiguous linkages among Roman law, transplanted English legal regimes, and English customs, which asserted that the bodies of English subjects carried English liberties with them overseas. The English use of merchant companies as agents and vehicles for overseas expansion drew on common international understandings and practices concerning merchant privileges, including the self-government of merchant communities overseas, and contributed to controversies among the English over the definition of many enterprises, whether they should be governed as companies or civil societies, and whether governments in the colonies were effectively English municipalities or freestanding dominions of the Crown. These legal and constitutional ambiguities arising over what liberties English subjects carried

---

[16] Philip P. Boucher, *France and the American Tropics to 1700: Tropics of Discontent?* (Baltimore: Johns Hopkins University Press, 2008), pp. 63–69; W.J. Eccles, *France in America*, rev. ed. (Markham, Ont.: Fitzhenry & Whiteside, 1990), pp. 27–28; Linda Colley, *Britons: Forging the Nation, 1707–1837* (New Haven, CT: Yale University Press, 1992), pp. 11–54.

[17] Julian Hoppit, *A Land of Liberty?: England 1689–1727* (Oxford: Clarendon Press, 2000), pp. 69, 214–15.

[18] See Grotius's dismissal of Portuguese claims in Asia in *The Free Sea*, 13–20.

[19] MacMillan, *Sovereignty and Possession*, 17–48.

overseas in their bodies were still contested at the time of the American Revolution.[20]

The Virginia Company, chartered in 1606, is one of the best known of a number of joint-stock companies that pioneered English overseas expansion, both commercial and colonial. In 1607, it planted the first persisting English settlement in the Americas at Jamestown and established the first English overseas assembly in 1619. It failed, though, as a profit-making enterprise. After a decade of martial-style government, Edward Sandys assumed control of the struggling company and articulated a new governing policy, referred to by Virginians as the "Great Charter."[21] Land was granted to English subjects willing to grow vendable crops, particularly tobacco; settlers were organized into four boroughs; and new regulations, modeled on English local governments, were implemented. Company officials also recognized that settlers needed a voice in governing the colony, so the commission of Virginia's new governor, Sir George Yeardley, included authorization to call an assembly. On July 30, 1619, the first English colonial assembly, composed of the governor, six councillors, and twenty-two burgesses, convened in the church at Jamestown. For five days they dealt with myriad details of government – legislative, executive, and judicial – until heat, the death of one burgess, and "the alteration of the healthes of diverse of the general Assembly" prompted Yeardley to prorogue the first assembly until the following March.[22]

The Virginia Company lasted for another five years until its dissolution by the King's Bench in 1624. Charles I emphasized that the colony would remain under royal control rather than return to company control, "to whom it may be proper to trust matters of Trade and Commerce, but cannot bee fit or safe to communicate the ordering of state-affaires, be they of ever so meane consequence,"[23] and appointed commissioners to be the colony's governing council in England. They seemed disinclined to continue an assembly, but the new governor, Sir Francis Wyatt, called one on his arrival in the colony, notwithstanding the absence of any authorization to do so. This new assembly sent a request to the king when George Yeardley returned to England asking that the "liberty of General Assemblies" that they had enjoyed under the company be continued. The Privy Council equivocated, the executive council in Virginia requested permission for assemblies in special cases, and, in 1627, Wyatt's

[20] Kammen, *Deputyes & Libertyes*, 11, 13; James Muldoon, "Discovery, Grant, Charter, Conquest, or Purchase: John Adams on the Legal Basis for English Possession of North America," in Christopher L. Tomlins and Bruce H. Mann, eds., *The Many Legalities of Early America* (Chapel Hill: University of North Carolina Press, 2001), pp. 27–46.

[21] See, e.g., "John Pory's Report of the Proceedings of the First Assembly in Virginia, July 30 to August 4, 1619," in Kammen, *Deputyes & Libertyes*, 95.

[22] Warren M. Billings, *A Little Parliament: The Virginia General Assembly in the Seventeenth Century* (Richmond: The Library of Virginia, 2004), pp. 5–10; quote from "John Pory's Report" in Kammen, *Deputyes & Libertyes*, 99.

[23] Charles Andrews, *The Colonial Period of American History*, 4 vols (New Haven, CT: Yale University Press, 1934), vol. 1, p. 194.

replacement, Captain Francis West, carried authorization for an assembly to discuss tobacco marketing, which convened on November 27, 1627. Another assembly met the following March, and in the minds of Virginians it established a precedent for annual meetings, although the practice did not receive royal sanction until 1639. For settlers in Virginia, the calling of an assembly was both functionally important in the running of the colony and culturally and symbolically important in affirming their English identity and liberties. In their minds, their assembly was the Virginian equivalent of the House of Commons; in 1641, they built a state house with an assembly chamber modeled on St. Stephen's Chapel, the home of the House of Commons.[24]

In 1620, the Somers Island Company, formerly affiliated with the Virginia Company, convened an assembly for settlers on Bermuda. The nearly simultaneous inclusion of settlers in the governments of Virginia and Bermuda bears brief contextualization. Commercial governance of overseas enterprises remained widely practiced in the British empire from its earliest manifestations in the sixteenth century through to decolonization in the twentieth century. At overseas factories, company governance tended to be hierarchical, if not garrison-style. Shipboard governance, both in the merchant marine and the navy, was similarly, if not more, hierarchical. During the early modern era, thousands of overseas British subjects worked in such environments, and for much of the seventeenth century they conceivably numbered more than the white settlers if one counts all the people employed in merchant shipping, in the East India Company (EIC), the Levant Company, the Royal African Company (RAC), the Hudson's Bay Company (HBC), and the North Atlantic fishery. Company governance in these environments persisted for centuries, and was not seriously challenged from inside, notwithstanding important concessions to some employees, such as the independent trading privileges extended to officers of the EIC, RAC, and HBC.[25]

The transition from company to civilian governance in Virginia and Bermuda was, therefore, situationally specific to enterprises with settlers and not a consistent trend in the nature of English expansion. The survival of these two enterprises depended on large labor inputs from settlers that neither of the two companies had funds to compensate. The Virginia Company and the Somers Island Company became colonial agents, institutions that facilitated the settlement of American lands. Land grants, not wages, became the material lure for associates; settlers dispersed and could not be kept centrally located as could employees for solely mercantile establishments. Planters, especially those who were landholders, wanted a say in determining the nature and amount of their contributions to the larger enterprise and its common elements. Stated in

---

[24] Billings, *A Little Parliament*, 11–23; Andrews, *The Colonial Period*, vol. 1, pp. 194–204; Kammen, *Deputyes & Libertyes*, 16.

[25] Jerry Bannister, "The Oriental Atlantic: Governance and Regulatory Frameworks in the British Atlantic World," in Huw V. Bowen, Elizabeth Mancke, and John G. Reid, eds., *British Asia and the British Atlantic, 1500–1820: Two Worlds or One?* (forthcoming).

economic terms, the Virginia Company and the Somers Island Company shifted much of the burden of capital investment and risk-taking onto the settler associates, and those settlers wanted a say in the disposition of their investments and the management of risk. One of the laws the Virginia assembly sent to England at the time of the dissolution of the company stated that "The governor shall not lay any taxes or ympositions upon the colony, their lands or commodities other way than by the authority of the General Assembly, to be levied and ymployed as the said Assembly shall appoint,"[26] a law that also evoked the legislative powers of the House of Burgesses that mirrored those of Parliament.

The calling of an assembly in Virginia had variable meanings. For company officials, it was a modification of company governance rather than the establishment of a civilian government, which was not in their power to effect. But for planters in Virginia, it established a practice that could easily shift from being an extension of company governance within the colony to being a "liberty" or privilege associated with the civil governance of a polity, from being a "corporate appendage to miniature parliament." Indeed, later petitions from planters to the king and Privy Council for continuance of the "liberty of General Assemblies" indicate that the transition to English civilian government, with the attendant association of the "rights of freeborn Englishmen," had occurred ideologically, if not constitutionally and legally, for Virginians with the convening of the 1619 assembly.[27]

As the Virginia Company was reorganizing its governance structure in the 1610s, it was also searching for more settlers and invited English Separatists in Leiden to relocate to Virginia, and offered them a land patent for a settlement of their own that would be autonomous from the Jamestown settlement. For the Separatists, a central issue in the negotiations was the kinds of liberties they could expect to have in Virginia. At play was a shifting combination of liberty of conscience, the liberties of free-born English subjects, liberty of self-government, and liberty of movement. Virginia was ostensibly an Anglican colony, so Edwin Sandys, the treasurer, approached the archbishop of Canterbury for permission for the Leiden Separatists and a group of Brownists to settle back in the king's domains. He refused on the grounds that the Brownists "claimed liberty of worship and a disregard of monarchy." The Separatists addressed the latter concern by drafting seven articles outlining the tenets of their faith, including assurances of their loyalty to James I. But they also intended to govern themselves under a Geneva-style congregational system, which the archbishop would not countenance. James I, when he heard of the Separatists' plans and their desire for "liberty of conscience," declined to sanction their settlement in Virginia, but indicated that he would not block it.

[26] Quoted in Andrews, *The Colonial Period*, vol. 1, p. 191.
[27] Billings, *A Little Parliament*, 12–23, quote on 12. In Massachusetts, the shift from company to commonwealth was more summary and happened shortly after Puritans settled in the 1630s; see Andrews, *The Colonial Period*, vol. 1, pp. 437–442.

The settler-hungry Virginia Company, untroubled by the Separatists' needs, issued them a land patent in 1619. Thus, when they set out across the Atlantic in 1620, they anticipated liberty of conscience, including liberty to worship publicly in their own fashion, and liberty of self-government.[28]

These Separatists, or Pilgrims, as history better knows them, landed in territory of the Council of New England, not the Virginia Company, and named their landing site and colony Plymouth. In 1629, they finally received a patent for land from the Council of New England, which included "liberty of fishinge uppon any parte of the sea coaste and sea shoares of any the seas or islands adjacente and not beinge inhabited or otherwise disposed of by order of the said presidents and councell," liberties that the Council of New England had fought in Parliament to maintain as their own. As well, the council assured them of the right "Freely and lawfully [to] goe and returne trade and traffique."[29] However, it did not have the right to authorize the establishment of civil governance by the Plymouth Colony. Indeed, neither the joint-stock company organized to support the colony nor the colony itself ever received a royal charter. From 1620 to 1685, when the Plymouth Colony was folded into the Dominion of New England, the Pilgrims governed themselves "according to the free liberties of a free people," as the Code of 1685 described their actions. In 1636 they codified their affairs in a document called the "Great Fundamentals," which was eventually printed in 1671. It laid out the "Orders and Constitutions that are so fundamentally Essential to the just Rights, Liberties, Common Good, and Special End of this Colony." The initial government established by the Plymouth Plantation consisted of a governor and council, who occasionally consulted the larger body of freemen in the colony. Not until 1639 was an assembly, or General Court, established, probably modeled on that of Massachusetts.[30]

The 1685 self-description of the Plymouth Colony government as deriving from "the free liberties of a free people" suggests both the ambiguity that existed about the establishment of English governments in North America and the kinds of liberties English subjects overseas could expect. Were liberties extended by the Crown or a royally created corporation such as the Council of New England? Or were there "free liberties," ones that existed from the condition of being English or simply from being human? The evidence from the first half of the seventeenth century suggests that English colonists were transplanting and cultivating liberties in quite discretionary and diverse fashions; as the relationship of the Virginia Company and the Leiden Separatists indicates, those liberties did not have to be compatible. The liberties desired by Virginians, for whom an assembly was important, were not the same liberties desired

---

[28] Andrews, *The Colonial Period*, vol. 1, pp. 256–58, 264; quote on p. 256.
[29] "Charter of the Colony of New Plymouth Granted to William Bradford and His Associates: 1629," The Avalon Project at Yale Law School, http://www.yale.edu/lawweb/avalon/states/mass02.htm, accessed August 31, 2007.
[30] Andrews, *The Colonial Period*, vol. 1, p. 297; Kammen, *Deputyes & Libertyes*, 24–25, 54.

by the Separatists who landed in Plymouth and for whom an assembly seemed less necessary, at least in the early years. The negotiations by the Virginia Company to get the Separatists to settle in Virginia, not New England, and its willingness to countenance practices distinctly different from those being developed for Jamestown, indicate that in the early seventeenth century there was no understood package of liberties that would be transplanted into colonies. Indeed, it was as though the opportunity to move to North America offered the liberty of choosing liberties. Disaffected members of the *Mayflower* associates announced after they landed at Plymouth that "they would use their own libertie, for none had power to command them, the patent they [the Separatists] had being for Virginia and not for New England."[31] Yet their sentiment is not substantively different from that of some Puritans, such as Roger Williams, who, on settling in Massachusetts Bay, discovered that the liberty of conscience he espoused was not that of the colony's leadership, and he resettled on Narragansett Bay.

The various configurations and prioritizations of liberties in English America posed few immediate concerns for metropolitan officials, though disparate negative reactions pepper the record. As noted previously, the archbishop of Canterbury would not sanction the settlement of Separatists in Virginia, while James I chose to ignore it. The legal advisor to Charles I's Privy Council opined that the Maryland charter granted such extensive powers to Lord Baltimore that they threatened to infringe on traditional English rights. Jesuit affiliates of Baltimore, meanwhile, were disaffected with his attitudes toward religion toleration.[32] But before the 1650s, metropolitan authorities took few measures to check the liberties that colonists pursued, except in the case of the Massachusetts Bay Company. The Puritans' removal of the charter from the realm, the blatant creation of a civil government from company government, and other challenges to royal authority, such as the prohibition on colonists appealing legal cases to the Crown, contributed to the attempt by the King's Bench in the 1630s to revoke the charter, which it could not do because John Winthrop, governor of the Bay Colony, refused to return the charter, and without the physical document the court could not finalize its case against the company.

During the early seventeenth century, the struggles over liberties took place within colonies (and within the Three Kingdoms) more than in a transatlantic context. Settlements established by people seeking a place where they would have liberty of conscience and freely express and exercise their religious beliefs could become a place of new religious orthodoxy, as like-minded co-religionists expelled dissenters. The Massachusetts Bay Colony became the most notable case of such practices as it expelled people who did not conform to its orthodoxy. Some of those exiles, such as Roger Williams, established settlements to

[31] Andrews, *The Colonial Period*, vol. 1, p. 292.
[32] Andrews, *The Colonial Period*, vol. 2, p. 284; John D. Krugler, *English and Catholic: The Lords Baltimore in the Seventeenth Century* (Baltimore: John Hopkins University Press, 2004), pp. 166–170.

the south around Narragansett Bay, in what would become Rhode Island. Other Massachusetts residents decided that economic opportunities along the Connecticut River and Long Island Sound were more conducive to their interests and settled the Connecticut and New Haven colonies. Leaders of colonies attempting to maintain a specific religious integrity were not always responsive to representative assemblies. Settlers who remained in Massachusetts chaffed under the executive-style government of John Winthrop, the colony's first governor, and demanded an elected representative assembly, but the franchise was tied to religious conformity, and thus liberty of self-government was restricted by liberty of conscience, but of a single dissenting kind. In New England, the exception was Rhode Island, where religious toleration was an ideological tenet and the electoral franchise was tied only to property ownership, not church membership.[33]

One of the distinctive qualities of these early decades of English settlement in the Americas is the liberty of movement that splintered the Puritans from their original settlement in the Massachusetts Bay Colony and resettled the disaffected elsewhere in the northeast. Most charters included a clause allowing the grantees to take subjects out of the realm to settle in a colony, and subjects leaving the realm had to register with authorities.[34] The Massachusetts Bay charter stated that the company could take "out of any our Realmes or Domynions ... soe many of our loving Subjects, or any other strangers that will become our loving Subjects, and live under our Allegiance, as shall willinglie accompany them in the same Voyages and Plantacon."[35] Once outside of Europe and the international agreements regulating the movement of people, English subjects in the Atlantic world accepted a great liberty of movement as a right, which metropolitan officials tended to support. The power some proprietors tried to wield over colonists, including restrictions on the movement of settlers, prompted Charles I to issue a proclamation declaring that colonists without legal constraints, such as debts or indentures, "were free to remove themselves out of the several Islands and places of their residence."[36]

People in settlements arising after splintering tended to establish rather quickly assemblies or ally with existing assemblies. The first assembly in Connecticut was in 1637, called to raise men and money for the Pequot War; the Fundamental Orders adopted two years later provided for an assembly to meet two sessions per year. Puritans who settled on Long Island sent delegates to the Connecticut assembly until those settlements became part of New York in 1664, after which there was a two-decade-long struggle between colonists and the Duke of York before an assembly was called for that colony in 1683.

---

[33] Andrews, *The Colonial Period*, vol. 1, pp. 433–446, 470–495; vol. 2, pp. 1–36, 67–99.

[34] Alison Games, *Migration and the Origins of the English Atlantic World* (Cambridge, MA: Harvard University Press, 1999).

[35] The Charter of Massachusetts Bay, 1629, http://www.yale.edu/lawweb/avalon/states/mass03.htm, accessed April 7, 2008.

[36] Quoted in MacMillan, *Sovereignty and Possession*, 102.

The New Haven Colony first convened an assembly in 1639 that met regularly until it merged with Connecticut in 1664. Rhode Islanders, who were notorious for their independence, began holding assemblies in the 1640s, but their assembly took longer to regularize than others. Indeed, only with Rhode Island does one sense that the liberty of movement (and resettlement) that English colonists exercised in the seventeenth century was an attempt to move beyond the pale of government, and that was largely a central government as opposed to local ones. But in most instances resettlement appears to have been for reasons of conscience, to find better land, or for commercial opportunities, and most people formed governments or allied with existing governments shortly after resettlement.[37]

Liberty of movement was often necessary for survival. Edward Johnson, in his 1654 *History of New England*, noted that the New England colonies "fed their Elder Sisters, Virginia, Barbados, and many of the Summer Islands"; liberty of trade, in his assessment, had quickly turned "this Wilderness . . . [into] a mart for Merchants."[38] The Massachusetts Bay Colony could banish people, and others could leave before banishment, and set up new settlements because they had great liberty of movement. These cases illustrate how claims to one "liberty" could be both infringed on and protected by asserting a person's access to another form of "liberty." Puritans searching for a place where they would be at "liberty" from the writ of the archbishop of Canterbury and his interpretation of the Church of England in turn restricted the "liberty of conscience" of others, who had recourse to a "liberty" to leave the Bay Colony and settle elsewhere. If liberties in the seventeenth-century English world were a kind of privilege, then they were also a kind of social property that one could protect, if necessary at the expense of someone else's property. These seventeenth-century English Puritans understood "liberty of conscience" as a privilege more than a right, and therefore banishment of others and recourse to liberty of movement were solutions to conflicting property rights in liberty of conscience.

During the 1640s, Europeans were distracted by war. On the continent they were slogging through the third decade of the Thirty Years' War; civil war, meanwhile, engulfed England, Scotland, and Ireland. People operating in the Atlantic Basin were left without significant oversight from their home governments, and many engaged in free trade to compensate for disruptions in shipping from their home societies. The Dutch were the great winners, though many English colonists found that the loosening of restrictions on international trade suited their needs. With the end of civil war in England, the execution of Charles I in 1649, and a modicum of stabilization under the Commonwealth government, English officials turned their gaze outward, with a particular concern to curb Dutch commercial ascendancy, within both Europe and the

[37] Andrews, *The Colonial Period*, vol. 2, pp. 7–17, 26–28, 89–92; vol. 3, pp. 106–110.
[38] Carla Gardina Pestana, *The English Atlantic in an Age of Revolution, 1640–1661* (Cambridge, MA: Harvrd University Press, 2004), pp. 158–160; quote on p. 160.

Atlantic, and to bring the English colonies within their purview, including an English controlled system of overseas trade. In the fall of 1650 Parliament passed legislation authorizing the reduction of the royalist colonies of Barbados, Antigua, Virginia, and Bermuda, followed in 1651 by the Navigation Act. The 1650 act included a trade embargo on the royalist colonies by other English polities, including the colonies that recognized the Commonwealth government. Massachusetts claimed that its merchants were honoring the embargo, but also protested Parliament's intention of greater oversight and regulation of overseas trade and colonization. Ironically, free trade became associated with the royalist cause, a perspective that would only apply while the monarchy was in exile. Once restored to the throne, Charles II pursued a mercantilist policy more stridently restrictive than that of the interregnum governments.[39]

In 1651, acting on the 1650 legislation, the Commonwealth government sent the navy to force the royalist colonies, beginning with Barbados, to submit to its authority. One of the conditions of submission that Barbadians negotiated was the continuance of free trade with countries in amity with England. With Barbados acknowledging the Commonwealth, Sir George Ayscue, the naval officer in charge of reducing the Caribbean colonies, turned his attention to Antigua, which asked for the same terms that Barbados had received. Settlers on St. Christopher added the proviso of the right to an assembly, to which Ayscue acceded. The ships sent to Virginia under the command of Edward Courtis finally reached terms with those colonists in March 1652, including free trade. One characteristic of these negotiations was the nature of the liberties that Parliament, or at least its agents, would honor. Free trade was a concession to the colonists and in opposition to the Navigation Act, but the men negotiating for Parliament operated under the motto "Keepers of the Liberties of England," and in the immediate instance were more interested in the loyalty of English Americans to the Commonwealth than their trading practices.[40] These negotiations also highlight the ambiguity that made it increasingly difficult to define the nature of liberties in the Atlantic world. Were they privileges granted, conditions sought outside the realm, practices developed in new settlements, rights embedded in being a free-born English subject, rights by nature, or concessions negotiated? The seventeenth-century hiatus and then reassertion of metropolitan control of English America helped engender and embed these ambiguities, which would become points of strong contention in the eighteenth century.

After the restoration of the monarchy in 1660, Charles II and his ministers pursued an aggressive policy of expansion, both commercial and colonial, and awarded shares in proprietary colonies and joint-stock companies to men who had been loyal to the monarchy during its exile.[41] The king and Privy Council

---

[39] Pestana, *The English Atlantic in an Age of Revolution*, 99–103, 220–221.

[40] Pestana, *The English Atlantic in an Age of Revolution*, 99–120.

[41] David S. Lovejoy, *The Glorious Revolution in America* (New York: Harper & Row, 1972), pp. 1–20.

also attempted to craft a new balance of liberties in the Atlantic world, recognizing that protection of liberties was important for attracting settlers; those liberties, however, would not include free trade, at least not in the guise taken by the colonies during the interregnum. Most prominently and liberally bestowed was liberty of conscience, which early seventeenth-century Europeans associated with Venice and the Netherlands, Catholic and Protestant, respectively, and their commercial power.[42] One of the most aggressive agendas of the Restoration Stuarts was the commercial ascendancy of England, particularly vis-à-vis the Dutch, and liberty of conscience in English overseas territories was part of that agenda. All the colonial charters granted after 1662 provided for liberty of conscience, and Charles II required Massachusetts to allow Anglicans to worship in that colony, though not until the rechartering of Massachusetts in 1691 would a broader liberty of conscience be mandated, one that included protections for Quakers, Baptists, and other Protestant dissenters.

The recipients of the new proprietary charters for the Carolinas (1663), East and West Jersey (1664), and Pennsylvania (1681) all recognized the importance of both liberty of conscience and assemblies for attracting settlers, though all proprietors attempted to protect their large governmental powers by delaying the calling of assemblies or granting them limited powers. In 1679, New Hampshire became a royal colony separate from Massachusetts after sufficient agitation from John Mason, a great landowner without governmental powers who had long chaffed under the control of the Bay Colony. Of all the Restoration colonies, the New Hampshire assembly was the easiest to establish; most of the first delegates had been former delegates to the Massachusetts General Court.[43] James, Duke of York and proprietor of New York after its cession by the Dutch in 1664, was the most powerful of the restoration-era proprietors and the most resistant to calling an assembly. Despite vehement protests from colonists and pleas from governors, he did not authorize the calling of any assembly until 1683. His secretary, Sir John Werden, wrote Lt. Anthony Brockholls, the governor of New York, in 1682, that "Though I cannot yet positively assure you that it will be so, yet I may hint to you that we believe his R[II] H[s] will condescend to the desires of that Colony in granting them equall priviledges in chooseing an Assembly &[c] as the other English plantations in America have."[44] When an assembly finally met in October 1683, it promptly drafted a "Charter of Liberties and Priviledges" designed to protect "the colonists' individual liberties, the rights of property, and the right to consent to their laws and taxes." Some sections of the charter drew directly from the Magna Charta while others evoked Paliament's 1628 Petition of Right made to Charles I, thus underlining that English subjects in New York believed they still had traditional English rights even though they lived outside the realm. Other sections, such as those

---

[42] Christopher Hill, *Intellectual Origins of the English Revolution Revisited* (Oxford: Clarendon Press, 1997), pp. 245–252.

[43] Kammen, *Deputyes & Libertyes*, 46.

[44] Quoted in Andrews, vol. 3, p. 113.

dealing with liberty of conscience, were adapted to the heterogeneous religious environment of the colony. James as the Duke of York initially approved the charter, but never returned it to New York. After the death of his brother, Charles II, in 1685 and his accession to the throne, he and the Privy Council revoked the earlier approval and rejected the charter.[45]

In the early 1680s, Charles II's Privy Council had begun a review of all the charters and succeeded in having those of Massachusetts and Bermuda revoked and the colonies made royal domains.[46] James II and his advisors temporarily combined Massachusetts, New Hampshire (a royal colony), and Maine (James II's portion) into a single polity and appointed a president to govern it. By the following year, they had decided that the chartered colonies, Rhode Island and Connecticut, and the never-chartered Plymouth Colony would cease to be autonomous entities and included them in the omnibus colony named the Dominion of New England, governed by a royally appointed governor general and appointed council, but without an assembly. When some Massachusetts residents protested the lack of an assembly by refusing to pay taxes levied through executive order, they were arrested. In the trial of men from Essex County, they defended themselves in terms of traditional English liberties, to which magistrates responded "that they need not expect the laws of England to follow them to the ends of the earth." In 1688, New York and New Jersey were added to the Dominion, with New York having a lieutenant governor.[47] Some erstwhile colonies sent agents to England to lobby for their interests; Increase Mather, negotiating on behalf of Massachusetts, couched his requests in terms of the restoration of "privileges [because] no colonist spoke to James about rights."[48]

If colonists found political life under James II limiting, circumstances in England were little better. Parliament had not met since his coronation in 1685. Anglican bishops found themselves being investigated by Catholic appointees of the king. And in June 1688, James II and his Catholic wife, Mary Modena, had a baby boy, James, Prince of Wales, and first in line to the throne. The birth of an heir who would be raised Catholic, coming in tandem with other grievances, prompted seven prominent Englishmen to invite James II's son-in-law, Prince William of Orange, to come to England in the Protestant interest. He and an entourage of troops landed at Tor Bay in the West Country in November 1688 and marched to London, arriving in December. James and his family took flight to France, Parliament deemed him to have abdicated, and asked William and Mary to be joint monarchs.[49]

Colonists received fragmented, embellished, and unreliable reports of events in England, while instructions and orders to royal officials were delayed or

[45] Lovejoy, *The Glorious Revolution in America*, 114–121, 170–173; quote on 115.

[46] Philip S. Haffenden, "The Crown and the Colonial Charters, 1675–1688," *William and Mary Quarterly*, 3rd ser., 14 (1958), 297–311, 452–466.

[47] Lovejoy, *The Glorious Revolution in America*, 179–208; quote on 185.

[48] Lovejoy, *The Glorious Revolution in America*, 223.

[49] Lovejoy, *The Glorious Revolution in America*, 220–34.

waylaid, leaving everyone anxious and uncertain. Significant numbers, however, realized the occasion as one for rising up against unwanted government and reclaiming usurped liberties. Appealing to the ancient rights of free-born English subjects that had been eroded by prerogative acts – such as governing without an assembly, royal seizure of land in New England because the legal status of ownership did not conform to common law, and the suspension of the Connecticut and Rhode Island charters when those colonies were included in the Dominion of New England – colonists marched on assembly houses, arrested and jailed Dominion of New England officials, organized provisional governments, and, where possible, restored suspended but not judicially revoked charters.

In these circumstances, ambiguities over the legitimacy of colonial governments created volatile, exploitable, and potentially explosive conditions, and indeed intemperate remarks by Lieutenant Governor Francis Nicholson in New York helped precipitate the uprising of rebel militiamen under Captain Jacob Leisler. The outbreak of the Nine Years' War (1689–1697) compounded tensions as the French and their Indian allies unleashed attacks on outlying settlements in New England and New York, which elicited fresh fears of Catholic absolutism and popish plots. These circumstances also produced a remarkable concern about the nature of liberty among colonists. Plymouth colonists petitioned William for a restoration of their liberties, particularly liberty of conscience, their primary reason for settling in New England. In New York, Leisler's government brought back the Charter of Libertyes and Priviledges passed by the 1683 New York assembly, but rejected by James II in 1686. With the overthrow of Leisler in 1691, the New York council made the Charter of Libertyes statute law, but in 1696 the Board of Trade recommended it for a royal veto and William obliged. Thus, in New York, the meeting of an assembly to vote taxes and pass necessary laws was a privilege granted through gubernatorial commission and not a right or liberty protected by statute law. In Maryland, colonists attempted to protect the rights of free-born English subjects by repeatedly embedding language to that effect in bills to establish the Anglican Church, only to face repeated vetoes for their presumption that the Magna Charta applied in America. This stratagem of Marylanders to protect their liberties through statute law ultimately failed after a royal veto in 1696. Massachusetts did receive a new charter, thanks to vigorous lobbying by Increase Mather, that protected the right of an assembly, but it also required concessions: The colony had to extend toleration to all Protestants; colonists would have the right to appeal legal cases originating in the colony to the Privy Council; the colony would have to use the common law more consistently; and the king would appoint the governor.[50]

[50] Lovejoy, The Glorious Revolution in America, 251–270; Richard R. Johnson, Adjustment to Empire: The New England Colonies, 1675–1715 (New Brunswick, NJ: Rutgers University Press, 1981), pp. 136–182.

The Glorious Revolution left a murky and contested legacy of liberty in the English world. In the colonies, liberty of conscience for Protestants was more uniformly observed, though Massachusetts and Connecticut would only recognize dissenters from the established Congregational Church who were recognized members of another religious society. Individual right of dissent and relief from taxes for support of religion was not countenanced at the provincial level, though the odd town may have allowed it. In Maryland, Catholics were granted liberty of conscience, though they could no longer vote or hold public office, underscoring that liberty of conscience was a granted privilege and not a guaranteed right. Within England, the 1689 passage of the Bill of Rights (or An Act Declaring the Rights and Liberties of the Subject and Settling the Succession of the Crown) protected Parliament's rights, and by extension the liberties of English subjects within the realm were better protected from the arbitrary and unchecked exercise of prerogative power. But those achievements within the realm did not necessarily extend overseas. William III and Parliament struggled over whether oversight of colonies and foreign trade would be by parliamentary or Privy Council committee; William prevailed, and in 1696 he established the Lords Commissioners for Trade and Plantations (or Board of Trade) as a standing committee that reported to the Secretary of State for the Southern Department and which on paper reinforced prerogative powers in the colonies.[51]

Liberty of colonial self-government in the wake of the Glorious Revolution was more ambiguous than ever. In the cases of Maryland and New York, the calling of assemblies had been defined as a privilege granted by the Crown after William vetoed legislation defining it as a right in 1696. In Massachusetts, the calling of an assembly was defined in the new 1691 charter and colonists tended to interpret it as a right, but as the 1774 Massachusetts Government Act suspending the charter unequivocally underscored, metropolitan powers perceived it as a revocable privilege. Over the eighteenth century, however, colonists proceeded as though assemblies were a right established through customary practice and thus embedded in the colonial constitutions and had ceased to be a royally granted privilege, if indeed colonists had ever really conceded it might be, notwithstanding their cognizance of prerogative claims.[52] From the first decades of settlement, colonists had insisted on the right to an assembly to vote taxes, pass necessary laws, and establish other institutions of government at the local level, though frequently they received and achieved less than that to which they aspired. In British North America, royal officials relied on assemblies to vote taxes for operating expenses including, in most instances, their salaries,

---

[51] Charles M. Andrews, *British Committees, Commissions, and Councils of Trade and Plantations, 1622–1675* (Baltimore: Johns Hopkins Press, 1908); Ian K. Steele, *The Politics of Colonial Policy: The Board of Trade in Colonial Administration, 1696–1720* (Oxford: Clarendon Press, 1968), pp. 3–18.

[52] Jack P. Greene, *Peripheries and Center: Constitutional Development in the Extended Polities of the British Empire and the United States, 1607–1788* (Athens: University of Georgia Press, 1986), pp. 47–54.

and the control of the provincial purse strings gave assemblies considerable power.[53] By the mid-eighteenth century, the Board of Trade had come to accept assemblies as a traditional part of colonial governments. When Charles Lawrence, the governor of Nova Scotia, resisted pressure from colonists to call an assembly, the Board of Trade told him he had to call one, and in October 1758 the colony's first assembly convened.[54] Over the next two decades, however, the ministry and Parliament reversed the seeming universality of that position that colonies would have assemblies as they used executive and legislative suspensions of colonial assemblies to punish colonists. Shortly after passing the Massachusetts Government Act in 1774, Parliament passed the Quebec Act that established a government without an assembly for that colony. These nearly back-to-back pieces of legislation seemed to confirm colonists' fears that, not only did Parliament and the ministry not consider assemblies to be inviolable parts of the colonial constitutions, they considered them privileges to be manipulated capriciously to intimidate colonists.[55]

Parliament's attempts to legislate for the colonies in the 1760s and 1770s and the attacks on assemblies to punish colonists seemed to belie the claim that the British empire was built on liberty. But from a metropolitan perspective, the liberty most salient to empire was not liberty of self-government in the colonies but liberty of commerce and navigation. In the sixteenth century, English appeals to it had been the primary diplomatic response to Iberian protests over English incursions in Africa, Asia, and the Americas. A century later it had become woven into the emerging ideology of the British empire so that "trade depended upon liberty, and that liberty could therefore be the foundation of empire."[56] The language of commerce permeated international relations. In the War of the Spanish Succession, the allied English and Dutch were known as the Maritime Powers, both for their maritime-based trade and, in the case of the English, the growing navy to protect that trade.[57] The rapid expansion of British trade in the eighteenth century seemed to confirm the superiority of commerce as the engine of expansion over the more authoritarian imperial regimes of the Spanish, French, and Portuguese.

During the negotiations to end the War of the Spanish Succession (1702–1713), the Spanish transferred the *asiento*, the contract to supply African slaves

[53] Leonard Woods Labaree, *Royal Government in America: A Study of the British Colonial System before 1783* (New Haven, CT: Yale University Press, 1930), pp. 312–72; Jack P. Greene, *The Quest for Power: The Lower Houses of Assembly in the Southern Royal Colonies, 1689–1776* (Chapel Hill: University of North Carolina Press, 1963), pp. 129–47.

[54] "Establishment of the House of Assembly of Nova Scotia, 1758," *Report*, Public Archives of Nova Scotia, 1956 (Halifax: Public Archives of Nova Scotia, 1957), 15–71; Elizabeth Mancke, "Colonial and Imperial Contexts," in Philip Girard, Jim Phillips, and Barry Cahill, eds., *The Supreme Court of Nova Scotia, 1754–2004: From Imperial Bastion to Provincial Oracle* (Toronto: University of Toronto Press, 2004), pp. 30–50.

[55] David Ammerman, *In the Common Cause: American Response to the Coercive Acts of 1774* (Charlottesville: University Press of Virginia, 1974).

[56] Armitage, *The Ideological Origins of the British Empire*, 143.

[57] Colley, *Britons*, 55–100.

to Spanish America, from the French to the British. Spain contracted for African slaves because it still observed the terms of the Treaty of Tordesillas, which put Africa outside Spain's zone of trade. Its insistence that Tordesillas was still operable gave it international leverage that it could wield against competitors, particularly the British, by attempting to regulate (including prohibit) navigation in major parts of the world. In the Western Atlantic, Spain attempted to restrict British navigation in the Caribbean and Gulf of Mexico to specifically negotiated routes and times. British merchants, however, exploited Spanish American demand for both slaves and manufactures and supplied more than the *asiento* allowed; in turn, Spain seized British ships it claimed were in restricted waters. Incensed British merchants demanded that the British government not be supine in the face of Spanish threats to liberty of navigation. Diplomatic solutions, which the government of Robert Walpole conceded could include Spanish rights to stop and search British ships, failed to appease British merchant groups and their supporters, who characterized the differences "in the stark and dramatic terms of a struggle between liberty and slavery."[58] Rising militant sentiment in Britain against both Spain and the Walpole government, which to detractors seemed more intent on making concessions in continental European politics than in protecting British commercial interests in the Atlantic trades, finally led to a British declaration of war against Spain in October 1739, the War of Jenkins' Ear, which then blended into the War of the Austrian Succession (1741–48).

Overall these wars were British military debacles, except for a few spectacular victories that only highlighted the otherwise desultory military performance. Vice-Admiral Edward Vernon captured the Spanish American cities of Porto Bello in November 1739 and Chagres the following March. The British press heralded Vernon as a "Son of Liberty" and a "Heroic asserter of English Liberties" in his valiant efforts to "maintain and defend our ancient Trade, Commerce and Navigation."[59] In 1745, New Englanders took the French fortress of Louisbourg on Cape Breton, only to have British negotiators return it. Perhaps the most useful outcome of these wars for British commercial interests was the formal Luso-Spanish revocation in 1750 of the Treaty of Tordesillas, a diplomatic gesture that ended any exclusionary Iberian claims to the Atlantic, though not to the Pacific; it would be another four decades before Spain abandoned its exclusionary claims to that ocean in the 1790 Nootka Sound Agreement.

These international struggles over liberty of trade and navigation were also contested domestically in Britain in the halls of Parliament and Whitehall. Since the late seventeenth century, provincial merchant groups in England had sought an end to the monopoly control of overseas trade, particularly by the RAC, the EIC, the Levant Company, and the HBC. As well, Scottish subjects of the Stuart

---

[58] Kathleen Wilson, *The Sense of the People: Politics, Culture and Imperialism in England, 1715–1785* (New York and Cambridge: Cambridge University Press, 1995), p. 141.

[59] Quoted in Wilson, *The Sense of the People*, 143, 146, 149.

kings sought unsuccessfully to compete with the large English overseas companies by chartering their own monopolistic companies, endeavors that contributed to the Union of the Kingdoms in 1707. The ease of interloping in the slave trade effectively ended monopoly control at the end of the seventeenth century and which Parliament acknowledged in various ways until the final revocation of the RAC charter in 1750, the same year the Levant Company charter was vacated. Challenges against the EIC and HBC were less successful, and their monopoly privileges were more slowly eroded and challenged.[60] Nevertheless, arguments for free trade became a prominent part of Enlightenment thought, especially coming out of Scotland and associated most closely with Adam Smith and *The Wealth of Nations*.

These arguments emanating from Britain in support of an empire of liberty played well in the colonies because their survival depended on vibrant trade. What British subjects on the east and west sides of the Atlantic did not seem to appreciate fully, however, was that they did not necessarily agree on what specific liberties were inviolable parts of the empire.

The Union of the Kingdoms in 1707 made it possible for Scots to move to the English colonies and engage in British transatlantic trade without restrictions. But by the early eighteenth century, the English overseas dominions had thousands of European settlers who were not natural-born English subjects. Many charters for companies and colonies had provisions for including friendly aliens as associates. The 1611 Virginia charter provided for the company to include as associates "Strangers and Aliens born in any Part beyond the Seas wheresoever ... as our natural Liege Subjects born in any our Realms and Dominions."[61] Irish Catholic political prisoners had been dispatched to the Caribbean at various times in the seventeenth century. Many Dutch in New Netherland chose to remain in the colony under English governance rather than relocate. Huguenot refugees from France had settled in England and England's colonies throughout the seventeenth century, a process that accelerated in 1685 when Louis XIV revoked the Edict of Nantes. Colonial assemblies exercised as one of their powers the right to naturalize foreigners as English subjects within a polity; similarly, royally appointed governors had the power to endenize foreigners.[62] In all of the above instances, except the Dutch and Irish, these non-English Europeans in English colonies settled voluntarily. The attractions of these colonies for many European Protestants were the liberties accorded, including liberty of trade and navigation within the British world, liberty of conscience, and the liberty to participate politically in colonial governments.

[60] Elizabeth Mancke, "Chartered Enterprises and the Evolution of the British Atlantic World," in Elizabeth Mancke and Carole Shammas, eds., *The Creation of the British Atlantic World* (Baltimore: Johns Hopkins University Press, 2005), pp. 237–262.

[61] The Third Charter of Virginia; March 12, 1611, on http://www.yale.edu/lawweb/avalon/states/va03.htm, accessed May 25, 2008.

[62] James H. Kettner, *The Development of American Citizenship, 1608–1870* (Chapel Hill: University of North Carolina Press, 1978), pp. 65–105.

These liberties continued to attract immigrants to Anglophone North American societies down to the present. Many immigrants lacked these liberties in their home societies, and thus it was not a case of exchanging one set of liberties for another but a true addition of liberties, as was the case with French Huguenots at the end of the seventeenth century. But for some groups – particularly indigenous Americans, Catholic Europeans in the Americas, and peoples of African descent – inclusion into the British colonial world entailed significant exchanges of liberties or losses of liberties. Governor Richard Philipps of Nova Scotia promised Acadians "le libre Exercise de leur Religion," and "de Droits et privileges Civils comme S'ils estoint Anglois," if they would swear an oath of allegiance, though what exactly those rights and privileges would be was not spelled out. As their deportation beginning in 1755 made clear, they did not include due process under the law in the seizure of their persons and property.[63] Many native peoples found that the law as practiced in British American colonies was less supportive of their interests than direct diplomacy with the metropolitan government. Inclusion in Anglo-American communities often entailed a loss of liberties for native peoples, including liberty of self-government, rather than an expansion of liberties. And, as is well known, Africans were enslaved by the millions, and in the British American colonies, the loss of control over the liberty of one's own body prefigured the loss of all manner of liberties from self-government, to due process of law, to rights to off-spring, to rights to read and write, to rights to property.

No country and no government in Europe was more associated with liberty than Great Britain. The constitutional system to which people pointed as providing for so much liberty arose out of a careful balancing of monarchy, aristocracy, and commoners. Liberty and social inequality, therefore, were two sides of the same coin, and at the beginning of the eighteenth century there was no serious alternative coinage of liberty circulating in Europe. By the end of the century there was new coinage, one that paired liberty with equality, minted from an amalgam of Enlightenment thought and anti-slavery agitation and fired in the caldron of the French Revolution.

As noted at the beginning of this chapter, in the sixteenth century, the French and English used arguments about the liberty of trade and navigation against the Spanish and Portuguese, and in the process states appropriated that language of liberty. Once the French government was confident that Iberian hegemony had been seriously weakened, Huguenot merchants who had helped France gain footholds overseas were first excluded from the liberty of trade and navigation and then in 1685 had liberty of conscience removed with the revocation of the Edict of Nantes. Thus, when issues of liberty reemerged in the French world in the late eighteenth century, they were not encased in decades of

---

[63] Elizabeth Mancke, 'Imperial Transitions,' in John G. Reid et al., eds., *The 'Conquest' of Acadia, 1710: Imperial, Colonial, and Aboriginal Constructions* (Toronto: University of Toronto Press, 2004), pp. 178–202; quotes on p. 185. Translations of quotes by the author: "the free exercise of their religion" and "civil rights and privileges as if they were English."

practice as were British concerns with liberty. The French could pair liberty and equality in ways that were problematic in the British world in which liberty and inequality were closely associated, whether in class-bound Britain or in British America, where widespread slavery offered a glaring example of lack of liberty and highly visible inequality.

Within the British world, the medieval freedom of merchants to peaceful passage and trade became in the context of overseas expansion a liberty of subjects that the British state was to protect militarily and to the exclusion of others. This state obligation, coupled with the importance of trade to the British economy and to a British identity, contributed to the decision to fight the Seven Years' War (1756–63) at all costs. That decision, in turn, created the conditions that prompted British ministers and Parliament to seek revenues in the colonies to pay the war debt. The protection of one kind of liberty, trade, would contribute to the violation of another kind of liberty, colonial self-government. As well, the costly successes of the war included the acquisition of territories with thousands, if not millions, of non-British peoples, whether in Canada, the trans-Appalachian West, or Bengal, leading many in the ministry and Parliament to ask whether the preservation of local systems of law and some aspects of government was not the most humane course of action, as manifested in the 1763 Royal Proclamation and the 1774 Quebec Act.[64] Those decisions, however, effectively limited the extension of traditional English liberties, primarily associated with law, into major sections of the British world. The acquisition of new territories challenged the expansion and transmission of English liberties and contributed to imperial tensions and intra-British debates over the nature of liberties in the British world.

Much of the burgeoning trade of the British world depended on the labor of African slaves, and over the course of the eighteenth century, the size of the slave populations in the Caribbean and North America had grown, and many Britons sensed, whether rightly or wrongly, a rise in the numbers of African slaves in Britain, many of them the personal servants of West Indian planters, ships' captains, naval officers, and merchants active in the Atlantic trades. The consequences of overseas expansion, in the minds of some Britons, would soon contaminate Britain itself as a bastion of liberty, and slavery might well be legalized in Britain as it was in the American colonies. Others on both sides of the Atlantic began to question the morality and ethics of the slave trade and slavery and to argue that Africans had certain claims to liberty of their bodies simply as a condition of being human. Similarly controversial was the idea that liberty of the body could imply equality of any sort.[65]

---

[64] [George Johnstone], *Thoughts on our Acquisitions in the East Indies, Particularly Respecting Bengal* (London, 1771), pp. iv, xiii; "Proceedings in the Commons on the Bill for the Government of Quebec," *Parliamentary History*, vol. 17, col. 1362; Sir William Meredith, *A Letter to the Earl Chatham on the Quebec Bill* (London, 1774).

[65] Brown, *Moral Capital*, passim.

The plural and plastic meanings of liberty in the seventeenth- and eighteenth-century British world suggest that liberties in the colonies of British North America that became the United States were their own form of social property. Indeed, as Michal Rozbicki notes, liberties in the medieval world were privileges, tied to one's social condition and frequently inheritable. He argues that Americans during the revolutionary era spoke of liberties as natural and universal but operated in a world in which they were privileges, a kind of social property, that people would militantly defend. Thus we might ask to what extent seventeenth- and eighteenth-century British expansion involved not just the transmission and transplanting of liberties, but also the active creation of liberties. The "frontier thesis," that distinctly American idea of expansion, is not so much about the transmission of liberty as going to a place where liberty is fashioned anew. Liberty, then, is not natural but a social construction and hence a social property, whether it is the liberty of Virginians to meet in an assembly, of Puritans to observe a particular and exclusive liberty of conscience, of Pilgrims to worship in their own fashion, of Barbadians to trade with the Dutch, of Puritans on Long Island to send delegates to the Connecticut assembly, or of the British government to redefine liberty of trade to be a state obligation. These are by no means universal or natural expressions but social constructs, social property. They were highly dependent on liberty of movement, with the expectation that the state would provide protection, as the British navy increasingly did in the Atlantic basin. Similarly, Americans rewrote the constitution in part to provide the resources to protect the liberty of movement of merchants outside the country and the liberty of settlers to move into the trans-Appalachian West. This idea of liberty operated well within a world of inequality and exclusion while still holding up liberty of movement as a kind of equality of opportunity, whether Thomas Hooker and his Puritan associates moving to the Connecticut River to set up a new colony, Scots moving into western Pennsylvania, or Virginians settling in Kentucky and the Ohio Country. In the British world, this subject-driven transmission of liberty and culture ended in the eighteenth century, partly in response to the American Revolution and partly in response to the French Revolution and its espousal of liberty and equality. But it continued in the United States, with citizen-initiated expansion across the continent, often beyond the national boundaries, engaging in what Thomas Jefferson called an "Empire of Liberty," one in which the liberties sought and the liberties constructed in new places of settlement were often ones in which the object was not simply to transmit and transplant existing liberties, but to make laboratories of liberty.[66] It is in the tension between the invocation of an abstract ideal of liberty and the plural, plastic, particularistic, and often exclusionary expressions of liberty that the early modern legacy of English liberties continues to have resonance.

---

[66] David Thomas Konig, ed., *Devising Liberty: Preserving and Creating Freedom in the New American Republic* (Stanford, CA: Stanford University Press, 1995).

2

Liberty and Slavery

The Transfer of British Liberty to the West Indies, 1627–1865

Jack P. Greene

English promoters and settlers were active participants in the settlement of the numerous islands adjacent to the continental Americas. During the two centuries after 1600, English men and women, operating under the auspices of chartered companies, proprietary groups, or the Crown, established thirteen separate island colonies: Bermuda, Barbados, the four Leeward Island colonies of Antigua, Montserrat, Nevis, and St. Kitts, and Jamaica during the first six decades of the seventeenth century; the Bahamas in the early eighteenth century; the Virgin Islands in the 1750s; and the four ceded islands of Dominica, Grenada, St. Vincent, and Tobago just after the Seven Years' War. Two of these island colonies, Bermuda and the Bahamas, were in the Atlantic, the rest in the West Indies. Later, as a result of the Napoleonic Wars, the British acquired St. Lucia from the French and Trinidad from the Spanish. Every polity answered directly to the metropole. If the Leeward Islands had a common governor, each of the four islands also had its own lieutenant governor and a local system of governance with exclusive jurisdiction over the island's internal affairs.

Unlike the Atlantic islands of Bermuda and the Bahamas, which were of marginal economic or strategic importance within Britain's larger American empire, the early West Indian settlements had, by the late seventeenth century, become the nation's most valuable American colonies. First Barbados, then Jamaica and the Leeward Islands, quickly developed into sites for the production of sugar and its by-products and other tropical crops that the islands sent in increasing quantities to Britain and to the British colonies in North America. Using vast numbers of unfree laborers, at first European indentured servants in Barbados and the Leeward Islands, and then slaves imported mainly from Africa throughout the West Indies, the islands' economic success could be measured by their expanding trade with the British Isles and by their ravenous demand for imported labor. The wealth they generated enriched many free settlers and traders in the colonies; large numbers of merchants, refiners, processors, shopkeepers, and other middlemen in the metropolis and Ireland; and the purveyors of slaves on the African coast.

From the beginning, however, the free settlers in these island colonies thought of their new island homes as more than economic factories. Like the English settlers on the North American mainland whose status within the empire they shared, they came to America fully intending to reproduce the old world in the new. Subscribing to the idea, articulated by many prominent English writers and foreign observers and supported by a sturdy corpus of English jurisprudential opinion, that the English system of law and governance, with its emphasis on the rule of law and consensual governance through juries and parliaments, had provided English people with a degree of liberty unique on the face of the globe,[1] they insisted on taking their laws and institutions with them and making them the primary foundations for the new political societies they hoped to create.

If, for Englishmen in the home island, liberty was the very essence of their emerging national identity, for English people migrating overseas, liberty was equally crucial to their ability to think of themselves and be thought of as English. For that reason, as well as because they regarded English legal and constitutional arrangements as the best way to preserve the properties they hoped to acquire, it is unsurprising that English settlers establishing new enclaves of authority in the islands, as on the continent, should make every effort to construct them on English legal foundations. As the legal historian George Dargo has observed, "the attempt to establish English law and the 'rights and liberties of Englishmen' was constant from the first settlement."[2] How settlers translated the English liberal and legal inheritance to the slave regimes they were creating in the West Indian and Atlantic island colonies, and how slavery affected this process, are the principal subjects of this chapter, which will focus on the experiences of Barbados and Jamaica, Britain's most successful sugar colonies.

Their extensive use of unfree labor and their creation of societies in which the overwhelming majority of the population was enslaved did not lessen the determination of West Indian settlers to achieve for the free segments of the population all the rights and privileges associated with their liberal English inheritance. Of course, none of the earliest island political societies began as a slave regime; all of them were, rather, communities of settlers seeking economic opportunities in the Americas, even Jamaica, conquered from the Spanish in 1655 and initially populated by disbanded soldiers. If these early settlers employed unfree labor, they mostly used servants from the British Isles

---

[1] See Liah Greenfeld, *Nationalism: Five Roads to Modernity* (Cambridge, MA: Harvard University Press, 1992), pp. 27–87, and, especially, the rich and penetrating study by Richard Helgerson, *Forms of Nationhood: The Elizabethan Writing of England* (Chicago: University of Chicago Press, 1992), of the process of national self-fashioning undertaken during the half-century from 1575 to 1625 by English intellectuals, who in a variety of discursive communities – poetry, law, chorography, travel writing, drama, and religious discourse – self-consciously sought to identify what was distinctive about the emerging English national state and the people who lived in it.

[2] George Dargo, *Roots of the Republic: A New Perspective on Early American Constitutionalism* (New York: Praeger, 1974), p. 58.

who labored under term contracts and, although worked unmercifully, could look forward to regaining their freedom. Notwithstanding its vaunted liberty, early modern England was a profoundly exclusionary society with a deep fault line between independent and dependent peoples. Theoretically, both categories enjoyed the legal rights to trial by jury, habeas corpus, and due process of law, but dependents, those without wills of their own, could claim no right to consent through elected representatives to the laws under which they lived. The right to vote was the exclusive preserve of independent people; dependents could only gain the franchise by acquiring sufficient property to make them independent.

As long as European servants constituted the bulk of the labor force in the islands, island political societies thus mirrored that of England itself. Servants and former servants had ostensible access to the traditional legal rights of English people but not, unless they managed to change their status to independent property owners, to the franchise. By contrast, enslaved Africans, who everywhere in the English West Indies soon constituted a growing majority, enjoyed no formal legal rights whatever and had no way to obtain them except through the relatively rare route of manumission in some islands at some times. In effect, the creation of a special group of people without civil rights converted English West Indian societies into rigid caste societies. This development was not limited to the island colonies, of course. To one degree or another, it characterized all early modern British American slave regimes from Barbados north to Nova Scotia. But it was most evident in the islands, where, except for Bermuda, enslaved people of African descent soon constituted a substantial and, in most islands, the overwhelming majority of the population.

As many contemporaries observed, the presence of a numerous slave caste in the fundamentally exclusionary political societies settlers created in English America functioned to make the empowered and possessing classes intensely concerned with asserting, constitutionalizing, and defending the attributes of English liberty that legally set them apart from the enslaved. Long before the introduction of slavery, however, the island colonies, like their continental counterparts, had begun to develop some form of representative government as a response to the settlers' demands for consensual governance and the sponsors' need for money to meet public expenses. Within twenty years of its founding, and often much earlier, every English colony with a substantial body of settlers adopted some form of elected assembly to pass laws for the polity it was creating, including those in the islands: Bermuda in 1620s, Barbados in 1639, St. Kitts and Antigua in the 1640s, Montserrat and Nevis in the 1650s, and Jamaica in the mid-1660s. By 1670, all thirteen settled colonies in the Americas had functioning representative assemblies. From New England to Barbados, colonial English America proved to be an extraordinarily fertile ground for parliamentary governance.[3]

[3] See Michael Kammen, *Deputyes & Libertyes: The Origins of Representative Government in Colonial America* (New York: Knopf, 1969), pp. 11–12.

Even in situations in which company officials or proprietors took the initiative in establishing these early law-making bodies, as was the case with Bermuda, the representative bodies never acted as the "passive servants and petitioners of the prerogative" as had been the case with the medieval House of Commons. On the contrary, modern historians have been impressed by their "effectiveness and spirit of assertiveness." "Usually from their very first meetings," Michael Kammen has noted, they acted as the aggressive spokesmen for the proliferating settlements within the colonies. Claiming their constituents' right to the English tradition of consensual governance, they early insisted that no laws or taxes could take effect without their assent, demanded the initiative in legislation, turned themselves into high courts of appeal and original jurisdiction in the manner of the medieval House of Commons, and they rarely shrank from controversy with "local executives, proprietors, or the Crown."[4]

To be sure, it took up to twenty years for these bodies "to materialize, stabilize, and take permanent form in each colony." During the early years, they usually did not sit as a separate body but met together with the governor's council or even with the governor himself to hear cases and pass laws.[5] But they early set course toward achieving their independence from the executive, and by the 1640s the larger colonies, each of them on its own initiative, had all moved toward a bicameral legislature, with the lower house sitting separately from the governor and council: Virginia in 1643, Massachusetts Bay in 1644, Maryland in 1650, and Barbados in 1652. Local exigencies, not emulation, drove this development. In every case, the specific shape of a provincial polity was the product of what Yunlong Man, in his careful study of the first half-century of provincial political institutions in England's five most successful colonies, calls an "indigenous development." Some popular provincial governors, such as Philip Bell in Barbados, fostered these changes, but in doing so they were invariably consolidating the political frameworks already worked out by emerging local leaders and acknowledging that the capacity to govern, in Man's formulation, "compelled [Crown, company, or proprietary] recognition of the indigenous structures of colonial government that had emerged out of colonial conditions," whatever the Crown's reservations about representative government in the colonies.[6]

If these indigenous developments "firmly rooted" the tradition of consensual governance in colonial English America,[7] the form such governance took increasingly came to resemble the English model. Once their governments had acquired a bicameral form, provincial magnates in the colonies had no difficulty in noting "the remarkable resemblance" between colonial polities

---

[4] Ibid., 7, 9, 62, 67.

[5] Ibid., 11.

[6] Yunlong Man, "English Colonization and the Formation of Anglo-American Polities, 1606–1664," unpublished Ph.D. dissertation, Johns Hopkins University (1994), 232–414, traces these developments in detail. The quotations are from pp. 416 and 455.

[7] Kammen, *Deputyes & Liberties*, 61.

and the traditional form of metropolitan English governance, and they began, as did the Barbadian government in 1651, to defend the polities they had created on the grounds that they represented "the nearest model of conformity to that under which our predecessors of the English nation have lived and flourished for above a thousand years." English officials were also impressed by the structural similarities between the colonial polities and the metropolitan government. At the same time, the enunciation and proliferation in England of the classical theory of mixed government during and after the English Civil War, and its rapid installation as the official interpretation of the English constitution, provided additional justification for the application of that theory to the "indigenous colonial tri-partite government of governor, council, and assembly." The Stuart monarchy provided "official sanction" for this "conceptual transformation" in 1661 when it "introduced just such a government in Jamaica," recently captured from the Spanish and only the second English colony to come under royal control, instructing its new governor "to proceed 'according to such good, just and reasonable customs and institutions as are exercised and settled in our colonies and plantations.'"[8]

Yet, this action with regard to Jamaica did not completely settle the issue of the structure of English colonial governance. During the Restoration, English officials made a serious attempt to impose metropolitan authority on the local centers of power that had emerged in America. Throughout the decades from 1660 to 1690, the metropolitan government undertook a variety of measures intended to reduce the colonies to what it called "an absolute obedience to the King's authority."[9] These included the subordination of the economies of the colonies to that of the metropolis through the navigation acts, passed between 1651 and 1696; bringing as many as possible of the still mostly private colonies under the direct control of the Crown; and curtailing the powers of colonial political institutions. As a theoretical support for these efforts, metropolitan officials in the late 1670s enunciated the new doctrine that the extension of representative government to the colonies was an act of royal grace.

Everywhere in the colonies, these metropolitan intrusions into colonial affairs encountered stiff resistance. In response, provincial assemblies expressed the determination of the property holders they represented to secure both their estates and their claims to an English identity by obtaining metropolitan recognition that, as English people or their descendants, they were entitled to enjoy the same rights and legal protections as English people in the home island. Thus, in protesting metropolitan efforts to take away the legislative initiative of the Jamaica legislature during the late 1670s and early 1680s, did Samuel Barnard, speaker of the Assembly, express the determination of Jamaica settlers "to continue under our old form of Government, which his Majesty had been

---

[8] Man, "English Colonization and the Formation of Anglo-American Polities," 15–16, 391–92.

[9] Report of the Commissioners sent to New England, [April 30,] 1661, in W. Noel Sainsbury et al., eds., *Calendar of State Papers, Colonial*, 44 vols. (London: His Majesty's Stationery Office, 1860–), *1661–68*, p. 25.

pleased to constitute at [the] first [political organization of the colony], as near that of his Realm of England, as so great a Volume could be comprised in so small an Epitome, and to preserve the quiet fruition of those Estates which our industry (blest be divine Providence) had acquired, under the same method of making Laws, as is observed in our Native Country."[10]

This determination stimulated an extensive constitutional discussion intended to identify explicit legal defenses that would put colonial claims to English rights and legal protections on a solid foundation and thereby protect the colonies from a repetition of such wholesale intrusions of metropolitan power.[11] In these discussions, colonial spokesmen articulated an elaborate argument designed to strengthen existing colonial claims to inherited rights. According to this argument, the original settlers and their descendants were all equally free-born English subjects who had left their native country to establish English hegemony over portions of the New World. Denying that they could lose any of their inherited rights simply by migrating to America, they pointed out that they had created their own civil governments with the specific purpose of securing those rights for themselves. At the same time, they argued that, so far from being a grant from the Crown, their assemblies derived from their basic English right to representative government and many decades of customary practice. They contended that no charter or other instrument could grant English people a right that they already enjoyed by inheritance. Instruments like the Magna Charta merely constituted an acknowledgment on the part of the Crown that such rights inhered in the people themselves. In the colonies, no less than in the metropolis, they thus insisted, parliaments were the bulwark of the people's liberties and properties.

In the West Indies, the most intense and sustained battles over these issues occurred in Barbados and Jamaica. Parliament's efforts early in the interregnum to force Barbados to comply with the earliest English Navigation Act of 1651 and confine its trade to England met with stubborn resistance, with the Barbadians boldly publishing a Declaration on February 19, 1651, denying Parliament's right to legislate for them on the grounds that they were unrepresented in it and that such legislation violated their traditional English right to be governed only by laws to which they had formally consented. Declaring that they would never "alienate ourselves from those old heroick virtues of true Englishmen" or "prostitute our freedom and privileges, to which we are borne, to the will and opinion of any one," the Declaration expressed the Barbadians' determination to "chuse a noble death" rather "than forsake their ould liberties and privileges," and, dominated by adherents to the monarchy, they organized a military force to resist the expeditionary force Parliament sent to ensure that

---

[10] Speech of Samuel Barnard, September 21, 1683, in *A Narrative of Affairs Lately Received from his Majesties Island of Jamaica* (London, 1683), 3.

[11] This subject is discussed more fully in Jack P. Greene, *Peripheries and Center: Constitutional Development in the Extended Polities of the British Empire and the United States 1607–1788* (Athens: University of Georgia Press, 1986), pp. 12–18.

Barbados would acknowledge its authority.[12] If the parliamentary expedition ultimately forced the islanders into a nominal submission, that submission did not change their minds. For a decade or more, they continued to deny Parliament's authority to interfere with their freedom of trade and to demand exclusive control over their internal affairs and taxation, including their selection of their own governors and other public officials. Although they did not achieve all their objectives, they did succeed in creating a tradition of "local independence" that subsequently "proved strong enough to withstand the centralizing policies" of the metropolitan government during the Restoration and beyond.[13]

When the Crown took over Barbados in the early 1660s, it seemed to gain a significant advantage in this struggle. In return for quieting proprietary claims that made land titles in the island uncertain, the Barbadian Assembly in 1663 agreed to grant the Crown a permanent revenue to defray the colony's civil expenses, thereby appearing to give up the financial leverage that had enabled it to keep a large measure of control over Barbados' internal governance. But the Crown forfeited whatever advantage it might have gained by this grant by refusing for at least a century to apply the monies raised to the grant's intended purpose. While this diversion of funds was a source of great resentment in Barbados, the Crown's continuing need for money to defray civil and military costs served as the device by which the Barbadian Assembly became one of the most powerful representative bodies in the American colonies. Although it had to give up its pretensions to secure free trade, the assembly managed not just to fend off the centralizing tendencies of the Crown but to expand and consolidate its authority over most aspects of Barbadian life, including the courts, the militia, public works, all aspects of financial administration, and the appointment and auditing of revenues officers.[14]

Jamaica's peculiar status as a conquered colony raised the possibility that the Crown might choose to govern it without representative institutions, and the struggle of the Jamaican Assembly to secure metropolitan acknowledgment that independent Jamaicans possessed the traditional English right to consensual governance was a salient issue in Jamaica's political life for the next seven decades. In the end, the assembly was victorious, first beating back a metropolitan effort in 1679–80 to limit its legislative independence by requiring, as was the case with the Irish Parliament in Poynings' Law, metropolitan approval before passing any legislation and then adamantly refusing to vote a permanent revenue until the Crown had formally acknowledged Jamaica's entitlement to the protection of English laws. This last issue was not settled until 1728–29, when the Crown finally agreed to accept a clause in a permanent revenue act

---

[12] This declaration is reprinted in Jack P. Greene, ed., *Great Britain and the American Colonies, 1606–1763* (New York: Harper & Row, 1970), pp. 47–50.

[13] See Vincent T. Harlow, *A History of Barbados 1625–1685* (Oxford: Clarendon Press, 1926), pp. 98–99, 124, 127, 140.

[14] Ibid., 145–47, 158–59, 172–73, 196, 234, 259; F. G. Spurdle, *Early West Indian Government: Showing the Progress of Government in Barbados, Jamaica, and the Leeward Islands, 1660–1783* (Palmerston, NZ: The author, 1963), pp. 50–110.

declaring that "all such laws, and statutes of England as have been at any time esteemed, introduced, used, accepted, or received, of this Island shall, and are hereby declared to be and continue to be laws of this His Majesty's Island of Jamaica for ever." Jamaicans regarded this declaration as the "Magna C[h]arta of Jamaica."[15] In contrast to the situation in both Barbados and the Leeward Islands, the Crown never diverted the permanent revenue of Jamaica from its intended purpose – the payment of the civil establishment – but Jamaica's growing public expenses throughout the eighteenth century ensured that the assembly would continue to have extraordinary financial leverage and to exert wide authority over the colony's internal polity.

Stimulated by efforts of a few royal governors such as Daniel Parke of Antigua, Robert Lowther and Henry Worsley of Barbados, and Lord Archibald Hamilton of Jamaica "to govern, in a more absolute and unlimited manner" in the colonies "than ever the Queen her self can, according to Law, or ever did attempt to exercise in *Great Britain*,"[16] West Indian legislatures continued through the eighteenth century to hold tightly to the extensive powers they had acquired during their first half-century of existence and to resist metropolitan efforts to curtail the autonomy of the several provincial governments. As a concomitant of this impulse, West Indian settlers also continued, usually with vehemence, to proclaim their Englishness. Insisting that they were not "*Aliens*" but "English Men," albeit Englishmen "Beyond Sea," "Free-born Subjects" of the British Isles, who, "by removing to the Colonies," had by no means "forfeited their Pretensions to" those English rights to which they were "entitled ... by Birth," settler spokesmen interpreted most efforts at enhanced metropolitan authority in terms similar to those applied to the first navigation act by the Barbados Assembly, as "Slavish imposition[s] beyond what [any] Englishmen ever yet suffered." They protested against recurring efforts to treat them as "Strangers," as "Tenants at Will," or "as a conquered People" without legitimate claims to an English heritage, identity, or rights and expressed their determination to remain "*freemen* (whithout [sic] which) our lives will be but lothsome to us."[17]

To these ends, West Indian settler protagonists took special pains to refute metropolitan suggestions that they were conquered polities whose rights and liberties depended, not on the national inheritance of their English settlers, but on royal favor. Barbados, explained the Barbadian lawyer Jonathan Blenman in 1742, had certainly "not [been] ... acquired ... by Conquest." Rather, at the time it "was settled by Englishmen," it had been "a Country not inhabited, but

[15] Agnes Whitson, *The Constitutional Development of Jamaica* (Manchester: Manchester University Press, 1929), pp. 70–158.

[16] *The Groans of Jamaica: Express'd in a Letter from a Gentleman Residing There to his Friend in London* (London, 1714), vi.

[17] Edward Littleton, *The Groans of the Plantations* (London, 1689), 20; *A Declaration Set Forth by the Lord Lieutenant Generall, the Gentlemen of the Councell & Assembly* (Hague, 1651), 2; *Groans of Jamaica*, vi; [James Knight], *The State of the Island of Jamaica* (London, 1726), 36; William Duke, *Some Memoirs of the first Settlement of the Island of Barbados and Other Carribee Islands* (Barbados, 1741), 32.

overgrown with Wood." "To the great Emolument of the Kingdom, as well as their own private Profit," Barbadian settlers, said Blenman, at "their own Trouble and Expence," had "brought" this "waste and desolate Place ... to Perfection."[18] Jamaican partisans could not deny that Jamaica had come "to England by Conquest," but they argued that the English men who took and subsequently began to people and develop the island had been, not the *conquered*, but the *conquerors*, and they protested the absurdity of looking on the "Conquerors themselves ... as a conquered People," who, by bringing "Countries under the Dominion of England, and maintain[ing] the possession [of them], should by doing so lose their own English Liberties" and the identities implicit in those liberties.[19]

In these contentions, West Indian settler protagonists, like those of similar status in the continental colonies, expressed great pride in the fact that, whatever their social origins in Britain, they, "by their own, or their Forefather[']s Industry" had "acquired the Property and possession of very considerable Plantations and Estates" that placed them firmly within the category of empowered independent people and thereby entitled them to all the privileges enjoyed by such people in Britain, including, not just the right to consensual governance, but also the right to enjoy the exclusive civil space reserved by the contemporary British world to such people, especially the rights to deny the franchise to dependent peoples in their midst and to secure their property, in whatever form that property existed.[20] But West Indian writers were under no illusions that the settlers for whom they spoke had achieved these ends merely by dint of their own industry. In a 1682 petition appealing to the English monarch to restore their old constitution, the Jamaican Assembly also thanked him for his "favour in ordering us supplies of Negroes at reasonable rates." West Indian settlers knew that their plantations had been cleared and were subsequently "work'd and cultivated mostly by the hands of Negroes," work that they and their predecessors had quickly persuaded themselves "would be hard to do ... by any" other hands.[21] That people of African descent constituted by far the greater proportion of the population of every colony in the British West Indies and that as an enslaved people they had no access to the rights and privileges that formed the foundation of English liberty and identity, they did not trouble to deny. How societies composed so largely of slaves could claim to be free was not a question that, before the final third of the eighteenth century, many West Indian political writers would explore in any detail.[22]

---

[18] Jonathan Blenman, *Remarks on Several Acts of Parliament Relating More Especially to the Colonies Abroad* (London, 1742), 91.

[19] Littleton, *Groans of the Plantations*, 16.

[20] *Groans of Jamaica*, iv–v.

[21] *Narrative of Affairs*, 3; *A Letter from a Merchant at Jamaica to a Member of Parliament in London. Touching the African Trade to Which Is Added. A Speech ade by a BLACK of Guadeloupe at the Funeral of a Fellow-Negro* (London, 1709), 14.

[22] For a fuller discussion of the subjects treated over the next few pages, see Jack P. Greene, "Liberty, Slavery, and the Transformation of British Identity in the Eighteenth-Century West Indies," *Slavery and Abolition*, 21 (2000): 1–31, from which they have been adapted.

A 1710 pamphlet published anonymously by a Jamaica merchant represents an impressive exception to this generalization. In *A Letter from a Merchant at Jamaica to a Member of Parliament in London, Touching the African Trade; To which Is Added, A Speech made by a BLACK of Guadeloupe at the Funeral of a Fellow-Negro*, published in London in 1710, the writer offered a scathing indictment of Jamaican slave society that both anticipated most of the objections anti-slavery writers would make later in the century and called into question the humanity, if not the Englishness, of free West Indian settlers.

Much of this pamphlet consisted of a withering attack on West Indian slaveowners and the labor system they had devised. That system, the writer charged, had reduced the enslaved to "a base servile tedious Life, a Life beneath the State of Brutes," a life of "perpetual Bondage" characterized by "hard Labour, and harder Fare," and "cruel Punishments." To support his suggestion that the institution of slavery made a mockery of the settlers' much vaunted commitment to liberty, he turned, not to the English inheritance, but to natural rights theory. As men, Africans and their Creole descendants, he argued, citing the Dutch theorist Hugo Grotius, "had a plain and natural Right to Life and Liberty" and ought never to have been deprived of "the *just Rights and Libertys of Mankind*" on the sorts of weak legal grounds that supported slavery in the early modern Atlantic world. Contending that "Life and Liberty" were "hardly things" that could be purchased or sold at such "a low rate, that they're to pass as lightly from the [legitimate] Owner, to whom God gave the sole certain Property, as Beasts, or Birds, or [other] Things Inantimate," he questioned whether sellers, in either Africa or the colonies, had anything more than "a weak, presumptive, or a may-be Title." Without either "know[ing] or regard[ing]" the legitimacy of the sellers' titles, slave purchasers, he charged, had bought slaves "at randome, without Regard to Right or Wrong." Even if such purchases were sanctioned by the "Laws of [the] particular Societys" to which the purchasers belonged, he contended that "by Reason's Law" these purchasers could "at best" have a title only "[un]till they're reimburs'd the Cost and Charge they've been at" in the original purchase. "That for so small a Sum, so soon repaid," slaveowners would reduce adult people and all their "guiltless Children" to "perpetual Slavery" and thereby "exact what makes" their "Fellow-Creature[s], from whom," they had "nought to fear, so miserable for life," seemed to the author of the *Letter* to be a blatant sacrifice of humanity and justice to interest and avarice.[23]

Such a discriminatory system, the author suggested, was hardly commensurate with English traditions of the rule of law. By those traditions, even those parts of the population that had no direct voice in making laws – women, servants, and the unpropertied free – could, at least in theory, be deprived of neither life, liberty, nor property without due process of law. In England, even the lowliest could count on the protection of the law, or so jurisprudential

[23] *Letter from a Merchant at Jamaica*, 4, 19–21, 23–25, 30.

writers said. But that was obviously not the case in the slave colonies of English America. There, slaveowners, the author charged, were in their governance of the enslaved "bounded by no Fences of *human* Law." Devised entirely by free settlers to promote their own individual and collective interests, "the Law" in the colonies gave the enslaved absolutely "no Protection or Redress." Rather, in direct violation of English jurisprudential traditions, it "indulg'd or conniv'd at" the slaveowners' "being Judges in" their "own Cause." For the enslaved, the owners' "Will's" were thus the enslaved's only "Law."[24]

If the anonymous author of *A Letter from a Merchant at Jamaica* used the slave systems of the West Indian colonies to raise profound questions about the credibility of the settlers' oft-claimed identities as English people, no spokesperson for settler interests bothered to answer him, and for the next half-century few people explored the relationship between Englishness and slaveholding, between freedom and slavery. Calling himself Sempronius, an anonymous Barbadian author, observing that "a great Part of our Interests here consists of the property we have in human Creatures," published in the *Barbados Gazette* in 1735 a learned discourse on the "Nature of Servitude" among the ancient Romans and expressed his interest in discussing "several other Matters concerning Slavery in general" and taking "into particular Consideration the present trade to *Africa*." "Apprehensive that" his "Notions on that Head" were "too unpopular for this Part of the World," however, Sempronius instead chose to suppress them.[25] The relationship between slavery and the identity of settlers as free-born English people had clearly become a taboo subject, the implications of which were too dangerous and disturbing for systematic public discussion.

When before the mid-eighteenth century the enslaved did appear in political literature they usually, as had been the case since the introduction of chattel slavery in the colonies, did so as a security issue. Thus did Edward Littleton in 1689 worry that Barbados's loss of a white population would render settlers incapable of defending themselves "either against a Forrain Enemy, or against our own *Negroes*."[26] Thus in 1716 did William Wood, noting that Jamaica contained more than 80,000 blacks and only a few thousand whites, deplore the "weak Condition" of Jamaica's settler population and its vulnerability "to Insurrections of *Negroes*," who might "at any time rise and destroy the White People."[27] Thus in 1755 did an anonymous writer calling himself Veridicus anxiously predict that foreign invaders would "easily find 10,000 *Corromantees*, and 30,000 other able-bodied Negroes and fighting Men, who ... would

---

[24] Ibid., 10–11, 13–14, 28.
[25] Sempronius, Dec. 17, 1735, in Samuel Keimer, ed., *Caribbeana*, 2 vols. (London, 1741), vol. 2, pp. 105–06, 115.
[26] Littleton, *Groans of the Plantations*, 14.
[27] William Wood, *A View of the Proceedings of the Assemblies of Jamaica, for Some Years Past, with some Considerations on the Present State of That Island* (London, 1716), 15, 33.

embrace the Opportunity with all their Hearts, and perhaps not fail to fight with their Hands, in order to change Condition with their Masters."[28]

But such security concerns were never powerful enough to inhibit settler leaders from contending among themselves or with metropolitan authorities. In contest after contest, in Barbados before the late 1740s and in Jamaica between 1710 and 1730 and again for a decade and a half beginning in the late 1740s, they showed that they were prepared to go to extraordinary lengths to defend their identities as English or British people by standing up to London authorities, royal governors, and any local supporters who threatened, as a Barbadian author declared in 1720, "to infringe upon those Privileges which ... the Laws of my Country have given every Britton an undoubted Title to," privileges and rights that, perhaps more than anything else, defined their Britishness. Celebrating, throughout these contests, the fact that "*British* Blood runs in our Veins, and the Spirit of *Englishmen*, in our Hearts," they invariably insisted that their actions were "consistent with the Principles of our happy [English] Constitution, and the Liberties and Privileges of *Englishmen*," and they contrasted their good fortune in this regard with the neighboring French or "*Spaniards*, who [had] never tasted the Sweets of *English* Liberty." The author of the *Barbadoes Packett*, published in London in 1720, was one of the few analysts to suggest that "God and Nature seem[ed] to have design'd" the rights enjoyed by British people "for all Men," a dangerous defense for people who had made human beings property. Rather, West Indian settler writers usually eschewed natural rights theory in favor of English jurisprudential traditions, which provided clearer support for making categorical legal distinctions among various classes of people in the same society.[29]

The most systematic exposition of settler West Indian political thought was a pamphlet published in Kingston in 1765 and in London in 1766 and entitled *The Privileges of the Island of Jamaica Vindicated*. Apparently written by Nicholas Bourke, an Anglo-Irishman who, in about 1740, had emigrated to Jamaica, acquired a very large estate, and since the late 1750s had been a prominent member of the Jamaica Assembly, this pamphlet presented the assembly's view of the controversy with Governor William Henry Lyttelton over the nature, extent, and origins of the parliamentary privileges of the

---

[28] Veridicus, *The Merchants, Factors, and Agents, Residing at Kingston in the Said Island, Complainants, against the Inhabitants of Spanish-Town, and of the Four Adjacent Pasrishes, and against the Members of the Honourable Assembly, Annually and Constitutionally Held at Saint Jago de la Vega, and against the Planters, Freeholders, Settlers, and Chief Body of the People of the Island of Jamaica, Respondents: The Respondents Case* (London, 1755), 30.

[29] *The Barbadoes Packett* (London, 1720), [i–ii]; *A Letter from a Citizen at Port-Royal in Jamaica, to a Citizen of New-York* (Dublin, 1756), 19; *An Historical Account of the Sessions of Assembly, for the Island of Jamaica* (London, 1757), [Knight], *State of the Island of Jamaica*. 36; Jamaicanus, *The Jamaica Association Develop'd* (London, 1757), 17. See also Jack P. Greene, "'Of Liberty and the Colonies': A Case Study of Constitutional Conflict in the Mid-Eighteenth-Century British American Empire," in David Womersley, ed., *Liberty and American Experience in the Eighteenth Century* (Indianapolis, IN: Liberty Fund, 2006), pp. 21–102.

assembly. The most profound constitutional crisis in Jamaica since at least the 1720s, this controversy raged for more than eighteen months from December 1765 through the summer of 1766, brought legislative governance in the island to a complete halt, and led to Lyttelton's attempted impeachment and eventual recall.[30]

In a dazzling display of learning in English, Irish, and Jamaican constitutional, legal, and parliamentary history, Bourke laid out the traditional colonial case about the political status of colonial settlers within the larger British imperial polity. Arguing that, "by settling in a British colony," no "British subject became a slave, or forfeited any of the Rights and Privileges of an Englishman," he asserted, taking the classic settler political position, that Jamaica's "Inhabitants" (a term that did not for him include the island's enslaved majority) were "all British subjects, entitled to the laws of England, and to its Constitution, as their inheritance; possessing those Rights and Privileges, by as free and certain a tenure, as that [tenure], by which they hold their lands, as that [tenure], by which the King holds his crown." Not "concessions from the crown," as Lyttelton had contended, "but the right and inheritance of the people" (another term that did not include the enslaved) were the sources of the assembly's privileges, which, in Bourke's view, were absolutely essential to provide the British "people of this Colony [with] that protection against arbitrary power, which nothing but a free and independent Assembly can give."

Bourke left no doubt that the stakes in this controversy were high: They reached to the very British identities of the settlers themselves. "If our lives, liberties, and properties are not our inheritance, secured to us by the same laws, determined by the same jurisdictions, and fenced in and defended by the same constitution, as the wisdom of our ancestors found it necessary to establish, for the preservation of these blessings in our mother country; then," Bourke wrote, the condition of British colonists resembled that of "our neighbours, the American Spaniards" in terms of the "oppression, injustice or hardship" they "do at this time endure." Indeed, they were, "to all intents and purposes, ... as much slaves ... as the aforesaid unhappy Spaniards, or any other slaves." If "the [British] subjects of the Colonies" did not enjoy the traditional rights of English people, Bourke declared, then were they "*not* freemen but slaves; not the free subjects, but the outcasts of Britain; possessing these invaluable blessings, only as tenants at will, the most uncertain and wretched of all tenures; and liable to be dispossessed, by the hand of power." Elaborating on "the distinction between freedom and slavery," Bourke made the implicit parallel between political slavery and chattel slavery explicit. Whereas "a freeman" had "his life, his liberty, and his property, secured to him by known laws, to which he has

---

[30] I have treated this controversy at length in "The Jamaica Privilege Controversy, 1764–66: An Episode in the Process of Constitutional Definition in the Early Modern British Empire," *Journal of Imperial and Commonwealth History,* 22 (1994): 16–53, which is reprinted in Jack P. Greene, *Negotiated Authorities: Essays in Colonial Political and Constitutional History* (Charlottesville: University of Virginia Press, 1994), pp. 350–393.

given his consent; and" could not "be divested of any right, but by a judgment of a lawful court, and for breach of some law of the land," "a slave" held "every thing at the pleasure of his master, and has no law, but the will of his tyrant." The *"power which any man has of taking my life, my liberty, or property without my consent,"* wrote Bourke, *"constitutes and defines slavery."*[31]

To impose any "form of Government, repugnant to the English constitution" and incompatible with an English identity on Jamaica without the consent of Jamaican settlers, Bourke contended, would be to degrade Jamaica's settler population "from the rank of Englishmen, and" reduce them "to a condition of Slavery." Jamaica, he suggested, was at a pivotal crossroads. If Jamaican settlers "retain[ed] any degree of love for the laws of England and for civil liberty," he thought, they had to demonstrate their entitlement to an English identity by standing up, in the classic manner of English men, for their liberties. For the free inhabitants of a slave society, the alternative was unthinkable. They knew, as Bourke observed, that it was "the part of slaves, to submit to Oppression," and, if Jamaican settlers had become "base enough to ... give up" the liberties long associated with their English inheritance, they must themselves have become slaves.[32]

The possible sources of such baseness had been discussed in some detail by an anonymous author almost two decades earlier. The title of this 1746 work, *An Essay Concerning Slavery, and the Danger Jamaica Is Expos'd to from the Too Great Number of Slaves, and the Too Little CARE that Is Taken to Manage THEM, And a Proposal to Prevent the Further Importation of Negroes into That Island*, announced the author's purpose: to persuade Parliament to cut off the slave trade to the British colonies and to persuade Jamaican planters to manage their slaves more carefully, perhaps even to take measures that would lead to the gradual emancipation of some privileged slaves.[33]

As the title made clear, the author's principal concern was the security of white settlers who without foresight were "indulging themselves both in their Indolence and fond Desire of more and more Negroes." As a consequence, he lamented, Jamaica had far "too great [a] Number of Negroes in Proportion to white Persons, being at least ten to one." To compound this problem, settlers, driven by indolence, stupidity, and "a narrow Selfishness, and total Unconcern for every Thing that doth not regard their immediate [economic] Interest," took far "too little Care to manage those Negroes." "If some Stop [were] not ... put to" the "Rage that Planters have for buying Negroes" and more "Care or Conduct ... used in the Management of them," the author observed, "the Island must [sooner or later] be over-run, and ruined by its own Slaves." No wonder,

[31] Greene, "Jamaica Privilege Controversy," 44–45, 57.

[32] Ibid., 44, 48, 57, 66.

[33] *An Essay Concerning Slavery, and the Danger Jamaica Is Expos'd to from the Too Great Number of Slaves, and the Too Little CARE That Is Taken to Manage THEM, and a Proposal to Prevent the Further Importation of Negroes into That Island* (London, 1746). I am grateful to James Robertson for nailing down the publication date of this pamphlet, a subject of considerable scholarly confusion in the past.

then, that Jamaican white settlers were "not only alarm'd by every trifling Armament of the Enemy [in the West Indies], but under the greatest Apprehensions frequently from their own Slaves."[34]

But the author of the *Essay Concerning Slavery* moved, if somewhat cautiously, beyond such security concerns to what he called "the moral one." Denouncing the slave trade as a trade "in human flesh, in the Lives and Liberties of our own Species," he suggested in invoking natural rights theory that, by actively encouraging and sanctioning both the slave trade and such a brutal violation of human rights, the British nation – including Parliament, "All the merchants, all the trading towns, and all the makers and dealers in goods sent to Africa or the West Indies" – had effectively indulged colonial white settlers with a liberty based on the slavery of others, a "Liberty [that was] contrary to the Laws of God and Nature."[35]

That such a system of trade and labor should be employed by free English people seemed to the author of the *Essay Concerning Slavery* to be totally out of character. To explain the contradiction between British self-conceptions and British willingness to enslave other peoples, he turned to the peculiar nature of the slave societies that developed in early modern plantation America. In a society composed mostly of enslaved people, he suggested, the need to draw a sharp distinction between free men and slaves provided an especially powerful impulse for settler claims, of the most extreme variety, to an identity as free-born Britons. But such claims, the author appreciated, required settlers to justify their enslavement of others on other than legal grounds. They could only be founded on the assumption that the enslaved were incapable of achieving such an identity. "One would imagine," he observed in articulating the implicit cultural assumptions that underlay the slave trade and slavery, "that Planters really think that Negroes are not of the same Species with us, but that being of a different Mold and Nature, as well as Colour, they were made intirely for our Use, with Instincts proper for the Purpose, having as great a Propensity to Subjection, as we have to command, and loving Slavery as naturally as we do Liberty."[36]

Like the 1710 *Letter from a Merchant at Jamaica*, the *Essay Concerning Slavery* received no immediate answer from any protagonist of West Indian settler societies, but this deafening silence on the relationship between settler identities as free-born Britons and the massive employment of slave labor in the colonies was broken in 1772 in the wake of the Somerset Case. To question the decision by the Court of King's Bench at Westminster to free the enslaved Somerset, West Indians produced three substantial pamphlets, two

[34] Ibid., i–ii, v, 18, 22, 37.

[35] Ibid., v, 24–26, 31, 38.

[36] Ibid., 19, 53. Twenty years later, in 1768, the Reverend James Ramsay of St. Christopher prepared a memorial in a similar vein, but Ramsay did not publish this manuscript until 1784. See Christopher Brown, "Empire without Slaves: British Concepts of Emancipation in the Age of the American Revolution," *William and Mary Quarterly*, 3d ser., 56 (1999), 286–87.

of which – the first by Edward Long, a Jamaican who just two years later would publish his three-volume *History of Jamaica*,[37] and the second by Samuel Estwick, a Barbadian[38] – marshalled learned and sophisticated arguments that explored the legal, historical, and cultural foundations of slavery, not just in the *colonial* but also in the *metropolitan* British world, in an attempt to reconcile colonial settler claims to an identity as free-born Britons with their enslavement of the vast majority of their colony's inhabitants.

Mounting a broad attack on, not just the views of Lord Mansfield, the principal judge in the Somerset Case, but also the arguments offered by a growing anti-slavery literature that, since the late 1750s, had been demanding the extinction of the slave trade and slavery within the British world, these West Indian pro-slavery writers did not deny either that English law tended, as Long put it, to favor "liberty" or, as Estwick suggested, that slavery, at least to some measure, appeared to be "inconsistent with the principles of the constitution" of England. They also admitted that, as Estwick wrote, because "Negroes" were "human creatures," it seemed logical "that they should be allowed the privileges of their nature; which" for Britons meant "in part the enjoyment of person and property."[39] But they argued that, not only colony slave codes, but the principles and customs of British commerce, the English common law of property, and many parliamentary statutes provided sturdy legal foundations for slavery throughout the British world.

Both Long and Estwick acknowledged that there was no counterpart to colonial slavery in the contemporary British Isles, but they insisted that "slavery" had been "part of the constitution" in "the antient law of England," when, as Estwick wrote, "slavery was the law, and slaves the object of that law." In medieval England, they noted, when even "*freemen* owed service to their lords" and therefore enjoyed only a limited "liberty which was not many removes from slavery," the "class of people called Villeins" labored under a "severe bondage" in which almost "the only right ... they had by the *Lex Terre*, or common law, [was] that of not being detained in prison *without some cause shewn*." Noting "that neither *Magna Charta*, nor" the "several statutes reiterating or confirming it" applied to villeins, they pointed out that "*freemen* were alone the chief objects of these statutes," none of which "impeached the power which a master" exercised over "his Villein; but, on the contrary, that other statutes were passed contemporary with the latter, to aid and enforce this

---

[37] A Planter [Edward Long], *Candid Reflections Upon the Judgement Lately Awarded by the Court of King's Bench in Westminster-Hall, on What Is Commonly Called The Negroe-Cause* (London, 1772). Edward Long, *History of Jamaica*, 3 vols. (London, 1774).

[38] A West Indian [Samuel Estwick], *Considerations on the Negroe Cause Commonly So Called, Addressed to the Right Honourable Lord Mansfield, Lord Chief Justice of the Court of King's Bench* (London, 1772), and Samuel Estwick, *Considerations on the Negroe Cause Commonly So Called, Addressed to the Right Honourable Lord Mansfield, Lord Chief Justice of the Court of King's Bench*, 2d ed. (London, 1773).

[39] Long, *Candid Reflections*, 42; Estwick, *Considerations on the Negroe Cause*, 34–35; Estwick, *Considerations on the Negroe Cause*, 2d ed., 86.

power." Quoting Lord Chancellor Hardwicke "that the state or situation of Negroes towards their masters or owners arose out of, and was founded upon, the remains of the antient laws of villenage in this country," they argued that in conditions in which Africans "were instruments necessary for the colonizing of America" settlers had had no choice but to render them the legal equivalents of the villeins of medieval England.[40]

Like medieval England, then, colonial British America, according to Long and Estwick, consisted of two principal and quite distinct categories of people, one legally free and the other subjected to harsh legal disabilities. If, they contended, the colonial and metropolitan British worlds were indeed part of the same general legal system and were governed on the same legal principles and if enslaved people of African descent were, as they claimed, legally similar to medieval English villeins, then, they reasoned, it seemed, as Long phrased it, "preposterous to say," as did Mansfield in the Somerset Case, that "Negro slaves emigrating from our plantations to this kingdom" were not commodities, "the absolute property of the purchasor[s]," but *free subjects of the realm,*" who were "entitled to all the rights, liberties, and privileges of natural, or free-born subjects." At most, Long suggested, "this class of men," that is, the colonial enslaved, could be placed "in no higher degree of franchise than was allowed ... to *villeins*" under the "*Magna Charta,* and the subsequent statutes passed in confirmation of this Great Charter."[41]

Because the colonial enslaved were property, because the sanctity of property was one of the principal rights of free-born Britons, and because colonial slaveowners were free-born Britons, Long said, "the pretended magical touch of the *English air*" could not, "like the *presto* of a juggler, turn" slaveowners' "gold into counters" without divesting them of a property that had been "solemnly guaranteed by the consent of the nation in Parliament." Such a development, he believed, would deprive slaveowners of their British rights; deny them their inherited identities as Britons who were absolute masters of their properties and their liberties, including their liberty to own slaves; and render them as far from a free condition as their own slaves. In caste societies such as those that had taken shape in early modern plantation America, the need to distinguish the free from the enslaved provided an especially powerful impetus for settler claims to an identity as free-born Britons.[42]

Even before Long and Estwick used the Somerset Case to reaffirm the Britishness of West Indian settlers, other events and developments were forcing still other West Indian settler protagonists to consider the disturbing question of whether the wide extent and deep entrenchment of chattel slavery in West Indian societies had already effectively transformed the identity of the settler populations by reducing them to a degree of dependence on the parent state

---

[40] Estwick, *Considerations on the Negroe Cause,* 27; Estwick, *Considerations on the Negroe Cause,* 2d ed., xiv, 85, 94–95; Long, *Candid Reflections,* 3, 5, 7, 10.

[41] Long, *Candid Reflections,* 4–5, 33.

[42] Ibid., 41.

that was incompatible with their claims to an identity as free-born Britons. This development can be explored through an analysis of the West Indian response to the great debate on the constitutional status of the colonies that divided the British world in the 1760s and 1770s.

The reaction of the settler leaders of Barbados to the Stamp Act crisis is a case in point. While almost all of the other American colonies, including Jamaica, were protesting that measure, the Barbadian Assembly, alone among the legislatures of the older colonies, contented itself with entering a "dutiful representation" against the act in a letter from its committee of correspondence to the island's agent in London. Although the committee protested the act as a "deprivation of our *old and valuable rights*," it emphasized that the colony had "submitted, with all obedience, to the act of Parliament" out of "a *principle of loyalty* to our King and Mother Country." Condemning the "violent spirit raised in the North American colonies against this act," it characterized North American behavior as "REBELLIOUS *opposition to ... authority*." Although the committee subsequently decided to omit the word "rebellious" from the version actually sent to London, the initial draft found its way to North America, where reaction was swift and negative.[43]

In *An Address to the Committee of Correspondence in Barbados*, the Pennsylvania lawyer John Dickinson denounced Barbadians for having at once "cast a most high and unprovoked censure on a gallant, generous, loyal people" and raised questions about the legitimacy of Barbadian settler claims to an identity as Englishmen. By submitting to the detestable Stamp Act, Dickinson charged, Barbadian settlers had reduced themselves "to the miserable dilemma of making a choice between two of the meanest characters – of those who *would be slaves* from *inclination*, tho they pretend to love liberty – and of those who *are dutiful* from fear, tho they pretend to love submission." Refusing to believe that any British people would actually choose to be slaves, Dickinson concluded that Barbadian settlers were "*loyal* and *obedient*, as you call yourselves, *because you apprehend you can't safely be otherwise*." Suggesting that this preference for safety over liberty could only be the product of frightened "dreams of submission," Dickinson dismissed the Barbados committee's letter as "the timid murmurs of slaves" and declared that such "unmanly timidity" belonged "not to *Britons* or [to] their true sons."[44]

For Barbadian settlers, "Gentlemen, and the Descendants of Britons," to be thus accused of being no different from their own slaves and "painted as *Slaves prostrate* in the Dirt" was unbearable, and Barbadian settler leaders rushed to defend themselves in three separate pamphlets, including one written by the

---

[43] Charles Price et al., To Stephen Fuller, Dec, 1764, Lyttelton Papers, BA 5806/12 (iii), 926, Worcester Record Office, Worcester, England; "A Letter from the Committee of Correspondence of Barbados, to Their Agent in London" [April 1766], in Paul Leicester Ford, ed., *The Writings of John Dickinson* (Philadelphia: Lippincott, 1895), pp. 254–56.

[44] John Dickinson, "An Address to the Committee of Correspondence in Barbados" (Philadelphia, 1766), in ibid., 259, 265–68, 275–76.

speaker of the assembly, John Gay Alleyne.[45] Alleyne freely admitted that the character of the Barbadian response had been determined by the island's weakness. Whereas "North America, boundless in its Extent of Territory, and formidable in its Numbers," had sufficient "resources of Empire within itself" to be "*fearless* of the Consequences of Resistance," Barbados was only "a small island, containing only a Handful of [free] Men." In "struggling for the Liberties she demanded," the former "might possibly have arrived at a State of Independence." But Barbados, "a well-cleared ... little Spot" with "no Woods, no Back-Settlements to retreat to," Alleyne declared, "could only have suffered by a Revolt." Highly vulnerable to naval attack and to some extent dependent on the outside world for supplies of food, clothing, and the slave labor necessary to produce its principal export, Barbados "could not so much as exist without the constant Protection and Support of some superior State." Thus condemned "ever [to] be dependant," Barbadians could expect nothing from a more spirited resistance than the loss of the liberties they already enjoyed and "the Horror of an *unavoidable Subjection.*"[46]

But all three writers insisted that Barbadians had not abandoned ancient settler claims to traditional British liberty. When the anonymous author of *Candid Observations on Two Pamphlets Lately Published*, one of the three Barbadian pamphlets issuing out of the paper war with Dickinson, included an extended rumination on the meaning of political liberty for the empowered classes within the British world, his discussion represented a reaffirmation and an extension, in the new context created by the Stamp Act, of traditional settler concerns. Spelling out the implications of a century and a half of settler discourse, the author boldly argued that, for colonial settlers to enjoy British liberty, they had to have their own "separate" and largely "independent Governments," and the British empire had to be a polity in which "the Form of Government in the People abroad," though "founded on similar Principles," was "as little connected with that of the English, as the Counties or Soils themselves which both People inhabit."[47]

The liberty that concerned the author of *Candid Observations* was thus the liberty of colonial settlers in relation to the parent state, specifically the settlers' entitlement to the traditional English liberty to consent to the laws that bound them. In the process of articulating this concern, however, he approvingly quoted Joseph Addison to the effect that "*Liberty should reach every Individual of a People, as they all share one common Nature*; If it spreads only among particular Branches [those who have their Representatives for Instance] there had better be none at all, since such a Liberty only aggravates the Misfortunes

---

[45] [John Gay Alleyne], *A Letter to the North American, on Occasion of his Address to the Committee of Correspondence in Barbados* (Barbados, 1766), 9–10, 23, 46; A Native of Barbados, *Candid Observations on Two Pamphlets Lately Published* (Barbados, 1766), 6, 11; [Kenneth Morrison], *An Essay Towards the Vindication of the Committee of Correspondence in Barbados* (Barbados, 1766), 4.

[46] [Alleyne], *Letter to the North American,* 10–12, 27.

[47] *Candid Observations,* 17–20.

of those [the Colonists] who are deprived of it by setting before them a disagreeable Subject of Comparison." Betraying no awareness of the implications
of this quotation for a society like that of Barbados, both free and enslaved, the
author of *Candid Observations* obviously did not mean to include the slaves
when he referred to the Barbadian "*People*." "Provided it be consistent with
public Peace and Tranquility," a system of equal liberty, Addison thought, was
desirable because it was "most conformable to the Equality that we find in
human Nature," but the author of *Candid Observations* certainly did not
believe that free Barbadians "*share[d] one common Nature*" with their slaves.
Nor, apparently, despite its obvious applicability, was he thinking of the
enslaved when he endorsed Addison's observation that a liberty confined to a
"particular" section of the population operated as "a disagreeable Subject of
Comparison" for those segments that were deprived of that liberty. For free
settlers in the slave societies of the West Indies and elsewhere in British
America, a system of equal liberty would not have been compatible with their
own "public Peace and Tranquility" or with their exclusive identity as free-born
Britons, an identity sustained by its denial to the enslaved. Nonetheless, the
author's use of this quotation from Addison inadvertently called attention to
the settlers' dilemma in claiming freedom for themselves while living in societies in which the vast majority of inhabitants were enslaved. In so doing, he
implicitly anticipated the problem posed for free West Indians by the Somerset
Case a few years later.[48]

Although Alleyne hinted darkly at "other Considerations ... arising out of
Circumstances of Distress and Hazard from within" that tempered Barbadian
opposition to the Stamp Act, none of these writers made an explicit connection between the moderate character of that opposition and the Barbadians'
longstanding fears of servile revolt. That connection was reserved for the
Jamaica Assembly in the crisis that immediately preceded the American Revolution. In December 1774, that body formally petitioned the British Crown
to "become a mediator between your European and American subjects" and
persuade the British Parliament to abandon its claims to bind the colonies by
legislation.[49]

Such claims, the Jamaica Assembly announced in reiterating a well-devel-
oped tradition of British colonial political thought, represented a profound
violation of the settlers' identities and inheritances as English people. Declaring
that "the settlers of the first Colonies, but especially of the elder Colonies of
North America, as well as the Conquerors of this Island, were a part of the
English people in every respect equal to them, and possessed of every Right and
Privilege at the time of their emigration, which the people of England, were
possessed of, and irrefragably, to that great Right of consenting to the Laws
which should bind them," it asserted, as "the first established principle of the

---

[48] Ibid., 17–18.
[49] Alleyne, *Letter to the North American*, 12; *The Humble Petition and Memorial of the Assembly
of Jamaica to the King's most Excellent Majesty in Council* (Philadelphia, 1774), 8.

constitution," that "the people of England have a right to partake, and do partake of the Legislation of their country, and that no laws can affect them, but such as receive their assent, given by themselves, or their representatives," and argued that by this principle "no one part of your Majesty's English subjects, either can, or ever could legislate for any other part." Demanding, "as a guarantee of" the "just rights" of their constituents, "on the faith and confidence of which, they have settled, and continue to reside in those distant parts of the empire, that no laws" should "be made and attempted to be forced upon them, injurious to their rights, as Colonists, Englishmen, or Britons," the assembly asked the king "to avert that last and greatest of calamities [for English people], that of being reduced to an abject state of slavery, by having an arbitrary government established in the Colonies."[50]

By acknowledging in its petition that, notwithstanding its endorsement of the position of the resisting colonies in North America, Jamaica was too "weak and feeble" ever to offer any physical "resistance to Britain," the Jamaica Assembly implicitly confessed to the whole world that its own settler population had already effectively reduced the colony to that "abject state of slavery" which it sought to avoid. In contrast to the continental colonies, the assembly confessed, Jamaica's "very small number of white inhabitants, and its peculiar situation from the encumbrance of more than two hundred thousand slaves," had put it in a condition in which its proud settler population could no longer fully act like free-born English people. Rather than standing up for their rights in the tradition of independent English people, settler Jamaicans, like their own despised dependents, could do no more than to petition "humbly" for them. By this confession, the assembly called attention to the degree to which in the West Indies the institution of chattel slavery, broad in its extent and deep in its entrenchment, had functioned to creolize settler identities as free-born Britons, and powerfully raised the question of to what extent peoples so dependent on the parent state for protection against their own enslaved population could maintain credible claims to such an identity.[51]

If their dependence on Britain for defense against their own slaves and foreign powers set clear limits on West Indian settlers' capacity to defend their rights against the new metropolitan measures of the 1760s and 1770s, the era of the American Revolution was nonetheless a period of marked expansion of representative government throughout the British West Indies. Between 1766 and 1768, the organization of civil government in the four ceded island colonies of Dominica, Grenada, St. Vincent, and Tobago brought representative assemblies to each of those colonies in the late 1760s, and the Virgin Islands acquired an assembly in 1773. In pursuit of the objective of gaining more centralized control over the colonies, metropolitan officials, to be sure, never intended for these assemblies to acquire the extensive powers enjoyed by those in the older colonies, and in the case of the Ceded Islands, they immediately followed the

---

[50] *Petition and Memorial of the Assembly of Jamaica*, 4, 7.
[51] Ibid., 3.

establishment of civil government by an executive order extending to them – without local consent – the export duty voted by the Barbadian and Leeward Islands assemblies a century before. Asserting the right of their constituents not to be taxed without their formal consent, however, the new assemblies in the Ceded Islands aggressively opposed this imposition, and when the Grenada settler Alexander Campbell brought suit against this tax in London courts, Lord Mansfield in 1774 ruled in Campbell's favor. In the landmark case of *Campbell vs. Hall*, Mansfield affirmed Campbell's contention that the Crown could not tax colonies without their consent *after* it had formally extended civil government to them. This ruling nullified the export duty throughout the Ceded Islands, the legislatures of which adamantly refused all subsequent efforts to persuade them to grant such a duty.[52] Thoroughly familiar with the constitutional pretensions of their counterparts in the older islands, the legislators in these new colonies used the power of the purse to secure the same authority, which the Crown, preoccupied with the war against the revolting continental colonies, did remarkably little to discourage, even cashiering Governor Valentine Morris of St. Vincent for his efforts to hold the St. Vincent Assembly in check.[53]

As for the older West Indian colonies, the era of the American Revolution proved to be a time for the preservation and extension of the legislative authority of their assemblies, which showed their intellectual affinity with the revolting colonies by stubbornly resisting Crown efforts to diminish in any way their authority over provincial affairs and by endeavoring to consolidate that authority at every turn. Even as a major slave revolt in Jamaica in 1776; slave unrest in several other colonies; and the French capture and occupation of Dominica, Grenada, and St. Vincent during the late 1770s were demonstrating their dependence on Britain for their defense, if not their very survival, the assemblies went toe-to-toe with royal governors over most of the old issues that had traditionally roiled metropolitan–colonial relations, refusing to surrender any authority over taxation, the disposition of public revenue, the appointment of revenue officers, the supervision of public works, the tenure of judges, their own legislative integrity and privileges, or their control over the local militia.[54]

Resolutely "determined to preserve their rights and privileges exclusive of the prerogative" and "to control all matters affecting their internal affairs, without interference from London," assemblies throughout the islands defied governors seeking to implement Crown directives that they regarded as subversive of colonial rights. In the process, they categorically denied Crown contentions that the colonial constitutions were "wholly founded upon the King's

[52] Bryan Edwards, *The History, Civil and Commercial, of the British Colonies in the West Indies*, 2 vols. (Dublin, 1793), vol. 1, pp. 350–59, provides a contemporary account of these developments.

[53] Selwyn H. H. Carrington, *The British West Indies during the American Revolution* (Dortrecht, the Netherlands: Foris Publications, 1988), pp. 141–50. See also, Andrew Jackson O'Shaughnessy, *An Empire Divided: The American Revolution and the British Caribbean* (Philadelphia: University of Pennsylvania Press, 2000), pp. 186–87, 193.

[54] Carrington, *British West Indies during the American Revolution*, 130–31.

commission" and cited provincial custom and their constituents' inherited rights as English people as the legitimate basis for their civil polities. If this debate had been going on for more than a century by the mid-1770s, it carried, for settler West Indians, a new urgency as a result of the constitutional discussions produced by the metropolitan challenge to colonial autonomy over internal governance that preceded the American Revolution. If, in these contests, "Barbados was the least tractable of all the islands," in virtually every colony the assembly stood its ground and was successful "in nearly every clash of authority." At the height of the American Revolution, the recalcitrance of the assemblies produced "a virtual stalemate between the islands and the civil governors," leaving the metropolitan government with no choice during the last stages of the war but to recall those governors – John Dalling of Jamaica and James Cunningham of Barbados – who had been most intransigent in upholding prerogative claims. A similar fate would probably have befallen Governor William Burt of the Leeward Islands had he not died before Crown officials could act. As in the case of David Parry, who in 1783 succeeded Cunningham as governor of Barbados, their replacements "went out authorized to concede every thing which" their predecessors "had fought so stubbornly to preserve." If, as one historian has remarked, the assemblies "*had* robbed the Crown of a portion of its executive authority" during the war, "imperial authorities [immediately thereafter] showed their willingness to acquiesce in the loss."[55] If the West Indian assemblies thus "doggedly guarded their [colonies'] constitutional and political rights" throughout the American War for Independence, they showed little sign of being willing to relinquish them in the immediate post-war era.[56] When Bryan Edwards published his two-volume *History, Civil and Commercial, of the British Colonies in the West Indies* in 1793, he gave special attention to "their constitutional establishments, internal governments, and the political system maintained by Great Britain toward them." An immigrant to Jamaica who served in the Jamaican Assembly throughout the era of the American Revolution and later returned to Britain, where he was elected to Parliament in 1793, Edwards offered a view of the West Indian–British relationship that located the origins of representative government in the colonies in the original settlers' inherited rights as English people, stressed the autonomy of colonial governments over local affairs, denied metropolitan claims "for the unconditional supremacy of the mother country," and was thoroughly compatible with – and represented an extension of – the constitutional argument North Americans developed in the 1760s and 1770s before they opted to withdraw from the British empire.[57]

[55] Ibid., 140, 160, 181; Spurdle, *Early West Indian Government*, 210, 214; O'Shaughnessy, *An Empire Divided*, 185–86, 195.

[56] Carrington, *British West Indies during the American Revolution*, 137.

[57] Edwards, *History, Civil and Commercial, of the British Colonies in the West Indies*, vol. 1, pp. v, 355.

Drawing upon a century and a half of West Indian experience, Edwards endeavored, like James Wilson, Thomas Jefferson, John Adams, and other North American writers in the mid-1770s, to lay out a theoretical foundation for a division of authority within the empire that would leave provincial governments at liberty to exert maximum control over matters concerning their internal polities. Contrary to the contention of many metropolitans, Edwards argued "that the prerogative of the crown in arranging the system of colonial establishments" for the empire was not "unlimited" and could never override, "in the smallest degree, the claim of the British colonists in America to a British constitution," specifically the claim, made by the earliest English colonists and frequently acknowledged by the Crown itself, to "the great and important" right "of assenting to all laws by which they were to be bound." "To say that a limited monarch, in a free state, may govern any part of the dominions of such a state in an arbitrary and tyrannical manner," Edwards declared, was "absurd." Constitutionally unable to "prescribe, any form of government incompatible with the principles of the British constitution, to any colony or territory whatever, whether acquired by conquest or settlement," the Crown, Edwards argued, had no choice but to assimilate each new colony to British traditions of government, putting each "on the same footing" as Britain itself with, as Edwards said in the case of the Virgin Islands, "the establishment of a perfect civil government," at the center of which would be a representative assembly, "and constitutional courts of justice among them," and leaving each to develop its own provincial constitution that, while "its parentage and principles" were emphatically British, would in "its outward form" invariably be "modified and regulated by various unforseen events, and local circumstances" so as to become peculiarly its own.[58]

Denouncing the British Parliament's claim in the Declaratory Act of 1766 to *"the power of binding the colonies in all cases whatsoever"* as "a system of perfect unqualified tyranny" that had no place in the "liberal system of self-government" that had emerged in the empire over the previous two centuries, Edwards pointed out that, "from first to last," the British Parliament had "consented that the king should govern his subjects in America (so far at least as related to their internal concerns) as he governed his subjects in Ireland, by parliaments of their own." "Incapable from their situation of being admitted to a participation with the people and peers of Great Britain in the British legislature, the colonists," he explained, established "legislatures of their own, which" were "subject to the king of Great Britain" but not "to the lords and commons; to whom they are not subjects, but *fellow* subjects with them to the same sovereign." Thereafter, these "provincial parliaments or colonial assemblies ... being thus established and recognized," Edwards observed, "constantly copied ... the example of the parliament of Great Britain" in "their formation, mode of proceeding, and extent of jurisdiction within their own circle," with the result that, as was the case with the British Parliament, there were "no

[58] Ibid., 1: 172, 358–59, 441; 2: 323, 326.

concerns of a local or provincial nature to which" their authority did not
extend. With the North Americans of the mid-1770s, he acknowledged that
Parliament could exercise "a constitutional, superintending, controuling
power" over matters of general concern to the whole empire, but he contended
that it could not interpose "in the concerns of internal legislation, and all other
matters to which the assemblies are competent." "With powers so extensive and
efficient," he declared, "these assemblies must necessarily be sovereign and
supreme within their own jurisdiction, unobstructed by, and independent of
all controul from without."[59]

Edwards took pains to challenge the idea, circulated by Sir William Blackstone and various metropolitan spokesmen during the 1760s and 1770s, that
absolute sovereignty over the empire had to reside in the British Parliament or
any other institution. "Inasmuch as all *'entrusted'* authority is necessarily
accountable," he wrote, it could not therefore be "*'absolute* and *despotic.'*
The truth is," he declared in taking a cue from his predecessors in North
America, "that this despotic and unlimited power is reserved by the people in
their own hands (not to be resorted to indeed, but in the last extremity) and it
never was the intention of any society of free agents, from the creation of the
world to this day, to delegate to any man or body of men, an absolute and
despotic authority in all cases over them." Because the English government was
"a *limited* government," it seemed to Edwards "a gross and palpable contradiction and paradox to say, that a *limited* government can possess *unlimited*
authority. If it be asked, by what limits its authority is restrained?," he continued, "I answer, by those ancient, fundamental, unwritten laws, which in the
act of settlement, are called THE BIRTHRIGHT OF THE PEOPLE." Based on
"a system of principles transmitted down to us from time immemorial, and
established into common rights at the price of the best blood of our ancestors,"
this inheritance, Edwards said, included, "the rights of personal liberty and
private property, the mode of trial by jury, the freedom of worshipping our
Creator in what manner we think best, a share in the legislature, and various
other rights, coeval with the government; which if the legislature should wan-
tonly abrogate or subvert, they would be guilty of tyrannical and unfounded
usurpation, and the people would be justified, by the laws of God and nature, in
resuming into their own hands (in the last resort, I admit) the trust which has
been thus violated and abused."[60]

The growth of anti-slavery sentiment in Britain during the half-century after
1780 would provide West Indian settler communities with many additional
occasions to reiterate similar sentiments by linking their own rights and liberties to their autonomy over their own provincial affairs.[61] If Parliament had no
jurisdiction over such matters, it would be powerless to act against slavery, the

---

[59] Ibid., 2: 327, 328–29, 331–32, 343, 346 note.
[60] Ibid., 2: 340–41.
[61] Christopher Leslie Brown, *Moral Capital: Foundations of British Abolitionism* (Chapel Hill:
    University of North Carolina Press, 2006), is the fullest discussion of the origins of anti-slavery.

most significant component of West Indian society as it had been structured since the 1650s. Although trade restrictions had many precedents in parliamentary legislation for the regulation of economic life in the broader empire, West Indian legislatures, with the help of the powerful West Indian lobby, an association of merchants, absentees, and others highly invested in the Atlantic trade in sugar and slaves, were able to stave off the abolition of the slave trade for twenty years between the founding of the Society for the Abolition of the Slave Trade in Britain in 1787 and Parliament's abolition of the trade in 1807.

As demands for the abolition of slavery itself expanded through the 1820s, however, and led, first, to metropolitan insistence on the amelioration of slavery within the colonies in 1823, and, when that failed, to the consideration of parliamentary legislation to abolish slavery throughout the empire, West Indian legislatures again put up stubborn resistance on the grounds that such measures infringed on their liberty "to regulate their particular social order[s]," their right to be governed by no legislation that did not have their formal consent through their own legislatures. Even after they had lost this fight with Parliament's passage of an emancipation act in 1833, they continued during the five-year apprenticeship period before ex-slaves were to secure their full freedom to resist or subvert metropolitan directives on the grounds that it was, as the Jamaica Assembly phrased it in traditional terms, "the undoubted birthright of Her Majesty's subjects of this island to have and enjoy all and every of the same rights, privileges and immunities as their fellow subjects in England, and that no law or enactment affecting their lives or fortunes, their peace or happiness, is of any force or effect or can legally be acted upon by any authority in this island, unless such an enactment shall have been sanctioned by the people themselves through their representatives in Assembly."[62]

When the British Parliament in 1838 passed an act to permit Jamaican governors to regulate penal institutions without the approval of the assembly, that body simply nullified it by ceasing all legislative activity and refusing to provide funds for any public purposes. This "deliberate defiance" led the British ministry to propose a bill to suspend the Jamaica Assembly for five years and empower the governor and council to take over all legislative business in Jamaica. Although the bill passed by a very narrow margin, the ministry soon rescinded it, thereby admitting the incapacity "of the British government to overrule" a "local legislature by a Parliamentary act." Thereafter, as Samuel J. and Edith F. Hurwitz have observed, metropolitan authorities could not impose "a program of domestic reform on Jamaica or any other colony that was ruled by a 'representative' government. Thereafter," the Hurwitzes add, "the British Government might demand, but it was the local legislature that would ultimately decide."[63]

---

[62] Samuel J. Hurwitz and Edith F. Hurwitz, *Jamaica: A Historical Portrait* (New York: Praeger, 1971), pp. 105, 134–35.
[63] Ibid., 135–36.

After full emancipation, however, the exclusionary white establishments in many of the islands found themselves in an increasingly anomalous position. Reluctantly, most of them gave way to demands from independent people of mixed race for full civil rights, but the restiveness of ex-slaves, their resistance to supply labor to plantations, and their demands for a public voice made it more and more difficult for the old establishments to continue to govern effectively in a political society in which all the population was free but continued to be governed by a small majority of whites, still the only inhabitants to enjoy British liberty in its fullest sense. Never had the exclusionary nature of British liberty in its colonies been more starkly revealed than it was in the West Indian colonies after emancipation. In Jamaica, the white establishment became ever more fearful of how it might deal with a massive uprising of the excluded, restive, and, for the most part, impoverished population who now had to be governed without the aid of slavery. Following an uprising by disgruntled ex-slaves at Morant Bay in early October 1865, whites essentially lost both faith in their capacity to govern in their own interest and their urge to liberty. Although Governor Edward Eyre quickly put down the rebellion with a military force and thereby prevented it from spreading beyond the bounds of a single parish, this episode dramatically raised the specter of a massive uprising of the majority black population, the slaughter of whites, and the expropriation of their property. In its last act as a free British legislature, the Jamaica Assembly, hoping to prevent future rebellions and "to close off political channels that might be used at a future time for the benefit of the masses," abolished itself on December 22, 1865, less than three months after the rebellion – after almost 200 years of existence.[64]

This action set the stage for the conversion of Jamaica into what had come to be called a Crown colony government, which vested authority entirely in an appointed governor and council. Perhaps using the Quebec model of 1763 to 1791 as a model, British authorities had already developed this form of colonial governance in the West Indies for the colonies acquired during the Napoleonic Wars: St. Lucia, Trinidad, and British Guinea, none of which had been permitted to establish legislative governance. Jamaica's surrender of its legislature and of the British right to consensual governance marked the beginning of a constitutional revolution in the West Indies. Although the Atlantic islands of Bermuda and the Bahamas retained their legislatures, most of the old West Indian colonies rapidly agreed to follow the Jamaican example, abandoning their assemblies and accepting Crown colony governance. Of all the old West Indian colonies, only Barbados managed to retain its legislature. Elsewhere settler establishments had opted to give up their own liberty rather than to share it with the descendants of their former slaves, and by the early 1870s, only the deeply embedded common-law legal tradition with its emphasis on the rule of law remained as an artifact of the British liberty the early settlers had transplanted to the island colonies.

---

[64] Ibid., 145–51, provides a succinct account of these events.

3

"Era of Liberty"

The Politics of Civil and Political Rights in Eighteenth-Century Ireland

James Kelly

INTRODUCTION

The liberties of the kingdom of Ireland and of the Protestant population that constituted its political nation were central to political discourse in Ireland in the eighteenth century. This is attributable primarily to the perception of much of that political nation that they were entitled for historical, ethnic, and religious reasons to possess the same rights and liberties as Englishmen. Indicatively, they legitimated their claim by reference to rights granted by the Crown to the first generation of English settlers in Ireland, and were prone during the late seventeenth and early eighteenth centuries to describe themselves as "of English blood born in Ireland." They did, to be sure, embrace a more distinctively Irish identity in the course of the eighteenth century,[1] but this development did not dilute the esteem in which they held the English constitution, or their conviction that as subjects of the same Protestant royal house and residents of the kingdom of Ireland they were entitled to enjoy the same liberties. The main problem they encountered in realizing this aspiration was that the British governing elite instinctively conceived of Ireland in colonial terms, and was disinclined as a consequence to acknowledge the Irish Parliament's legislative autonomy or to extend the same liberties to Irish Protestants that were possessed by Englishmen. This situation ensured that the aspiration of Irish Protestants to possess equal constitutional and civil liberties provided one of the main themes of both Anglo-Irish and domestic Irish politics in the eighteenth century. At the same time, Irish Protestants did not press their claims in an uncompromising manner. Conscious of their minority status within Ireland, and of the vulnerability of their ascendancy to challenge from the Catholic population, they contrived to safeguard their position by approving a distinct body of discriminatory legislation – the Popery

---

[1] See D. W. Hayton, "Anglo-Irish attitudes: changing perceptions of national identity among the Protestant ascendancy in Ireland, *ca.*1690–1750," *Studies in the Eighteenth Century*, 17 (1987), pp. 145–57.

Laws – limiting the economic, political, and religious liberties of Catholics. There was thus an inherent contradiction in the manner in which Irish Protestants sought liberty for themselves and refused to extend it to others, but they justified it by the particularities of their situation. This contradiction explains why they did not seek to emulate the American colonists, whose situation was seen to resemble their own, and pursue political as distinct from "legislative independence" in the 1770s and 1780s. However, the Protestant elite in Ireland was presented with a more serious challenge in the 1790s, when elements of the Protestant middle class, largely excluded from the political process, and an invigorated Catholic interest were inspired by the example of revolutionary France to press a vision of *liberté* that was more radical and egalitarian than that which emerged out the crucible of religious and political discourse of the seventeenth century to shape eighteenth-century Irish Protestant conceptions of liberty. As a result, the limits of the tradition of Protestant liberty were exposed, and many among the Protestant elite embraced a more overtly ideological conservatism. Politically, this development contributed to the decision of the Irish Parliament to vote for its own abolition in 1800, but because it resulted in the integration of Britain and Ireland in the United Kingdom from 1801, it did not signal the end of an "era of liberty" as the constitutional and civil liberties (the crucial right of self-government excepted) transmitted and extracted from Britain over previous centuries were not only retained, but extended by the embrace of democracy in the nineteenth century.[2]

THE HISTORICAL BACKGROUND

The transmission of British ideas of liberty to Ireland is more complex than it is in many of Britain's North American, antipodean, African, and Asian dependencies because of the longer history of English involvement in that jurisdiction. It is helpful for this reason to explore the historical background, both to provide a context for the debates about liberty that took place in the eighteenth century, and to identify why key rights and liberties – of which the right to make law is the most important – were not available in Ireland on the same terms as they were in England.

The English presence in Ireland can be said to have commenced with the Anglo-Norman incursion of the late twelfth century, and it was associated from virtually its inception with an attempt to extend existing systems of English law, government, and administration. One of the most enduring was the decision of King John in 1210 to order that English (common) law should apply in the lordship of Ireland.[3] Since the lordship for long embraced only part of the

---

[2] The phrase "era of liberty' was employed by Henry Flood in a speech to the Irish House of Commons in October 1765 (Birr Castle, Rosse Papers, F/21).

[3] Sean Duffy, *Ireland in the Middle Ages* (Dublin: Gill and Macmillan, 1997); Geoffrey Hand, *English law in Ireland 1290–1324* (Cambridge: Cambridge University Press, 1967); A. G. Donaldson, *Some Comparative Aspects of Irish Law* (Cambridge: Cambridge University Press, 1957).

island, the adoption of English law proved prolonged, and it was still incomplete at the beginning of the seventeenth century, when the attorney general, Sir John Davies, famously commented that the king's writ could not be said to extend fully to "two thirds of that countrey" and that the "jurisdiction of his ordinary courts doth not extend into whole parts."[4] Davies might have presented matters more positively, given the advances that were made in extending royal power during the sixteenth and early seventeenth centuries.[5] He might also have made more of the fact that Ireland possessed a parliament, which had a tradition of law-making extending back to the early fourteenth century,[6] and which was so firmly rooted by the end of the fifteenth that Henry VII directed his Lord Deputy, Edward Poynings, to secure approval for what became one of the most enduring and important restraints on Irish political liberties – Poynings' Law.[7] Ratified in 1494, this law stipulated that the Irish Parliament could only meet when authorized to do so by the monarch, and that all legislation must have the prior approval of the Irish and English Privy Councils.[8]

While Poynings' Law mirrored the conviction in England that the maintenance of royal authority necessitated the imposition of restrictions on the liberties of the Irish Parliament, the task was greatly complicated by the English Reformation, since, as well as adding a divisive religious dimension, it was an important consideration in the Tudor monarchy's initiative to extend and tighten its control over what in 1541 became the kingdom of Ireland. This effort proved long and costly, but it had largely been achieved by the demise of Elizabeth I in 1603, whereas the attempt to convert Ireland to Protestantism foundered badly. The introduction of a cadre of loyal New English officials did provide the Protestant Church of Ireland with a community of worshippers, and its official status was confirmed when it became the established church. However, it singularly failed to win over either the native Gaelic population or the descendants of the Norman settlers (the Old English) for whom counter-reformation Roman Catholicism not only better satisfied their spiritual needs, but also equipped them with a vigorous anti-Protestant ideology, with the result that Irish society

[4] Sir John Davies, *A Discoverie of the True Causes Why Ireland Was Neuer Entirely Subdued, nor Brought Under Obedience of the Crowne of England, Untill the Beginning of His Maiesties Happie Raigne* (London, 1612), p. 7; see also Hans Pawlisch, *Sir John Davies and the Conquest of Ireland: A Study in Legal Imperialism* (Cambridge: Cambridge University Press, 1985).

[5] See S. G. Ellis, *Ireland in the Age of the Tudors, 1447–1603: English Expansion and the End of Gaelic Rule* (London: Longmans, 1998); N. P. Canny, *Making Ireland British 1580–1650* (Oxford: Oxford University Press, 2001).

[6] H. G. Richardson and G. O. Sayles, *The Irish Parliament in the Middle Ages* (Philadephia: University of Pennsylvania Press, 1964). The first statute dates from 1310: *The Statutes at Large Passed in the Parliaments Held in Ireland 1310-1800* (20 vols, Dublin, 1789–1800), i, 1–3.

[7] An act that no parliament be holden in this land until the acts be certified into England (10 Henry VII, chap 4).

[8] See James Kelly, *Poynings' Law and the Making of Law in Ireland, 1660–1800* (Dublin: Four Courts Press, 2007), pp. 8–14; R. D. Edwards and T. W. Moody, "The history of Poynings' Law part 1, 1494–1615," *Irish Historical Studies*, 2 (1940–1), pp. 415–24.

was soon firmly cleaved on religious lines.[9] As was the case elsewhere in early modern Europe, this division proved acutely destabilizing, but its impact was heightened in Ireland because it combined with the aspirations of the New English to achieve cultural hegemony and economic dominance to permit them to acquire enormous influence and power, and progressively to assign the Catholic Gaelic and Old English to a subordinate and essentially inferior position.[10] This goal took several generations, but it can conveniently be tracked in the acquisition by the New English of ownership of the bulk of the kingdom's land.

Various schemes to introduce settlers through formal plantations in the sixteenth and seventeenth centuries paved the way for the creation of an aristocratic order, comparable to that in other parts of Europe. Having acquired possession of an estimated 41 percent of the land by 1640, this percentage rose sharply to circa 78 percent as a result of the draconian Cromwellian confiscation of the 1650s and had increased further to circa 86 percent by the early eighteenth century.[11] It is important to note that although these massive transfers in landownership were made possible by the military eclipse, first, of the traditional clans, and, second, of the Old English urban and rural elites, most of the land that passed into the possession of New English landowners was legally forfeit because of the treasonable conduct of its erstwhile occupants. This explains why a minority of Catholic landowning families successfully negotiated the conquest and colonization of the sixteenth and seventeenth centuries, and why others were able, by recourse to the legal system, to secure the reversal of losses. This is not to suggest that their rights were not confined, as members of the Gaelic and Old English interests encountered restrictions on their right to worship, barriers to their capacity to purchase land, limitations on their freedom of movement, and so on, but they were not barred per se from sitting in Parliament, owning property, appealing to the courts, or from practicing their religion. Significant liberties were intermittently withdrawn, and others whittled away, as the New English extended their control, but other than their experience at the hands of Cromwellians in the 1650s, there was no deliberate (and certainly no successful) attempt in the seventeenth century to deprive the Catholic population as such of access to fundamental English liberties.[12]

---

[9] Colm Lennon, "The Counter-Reformation" in Ciaran Brady and Raymond Gillespie (eds), *Natives and Newcomers: Essays on the Making of a Colonial Society, 1534–1641* (Dublin: Irish Academic Press, 1996), pp. 75–92; S. A. Meigs, *The Reformations in Ireland: Tradition and Confessionalism, 1400–1690* (New York: St Martin's Press, 1997).

[10] Canny, *Making Ireland British 1580–1650*, passim; Aidan Clarke, *The Old English in Ireland, 1625–42* (London: McGibbon and Kee, 1966).

[11] Raymond Gillespie, *Seventeenth-Century Ireland* (Dublin; Gill and Macmillan, 2006).

[12] For perspectives see R. Dudley Edwards, "Church and state in the Ireland of Míchél Ó Cléirigh, 1626–41" in S. O'Brien (ed.), *Measgra in gCuimhne Mhíchél Ó Cléirigh* (Dublin: Assisi Press, 1944), pp. 1–20; idem, "The Irish Catholics and the puritan revolution" in Franciscan Fathers (ed.), *Fr Luke Wadding Commemorative Volume* (Dublin: Clonmore and Reynolds, 1957), pp. 92–118; T. C. Barnard, *Cromwellian Ireland: English Government and Reform in Ireland 1649–1660* (Oxford: Oxford University Press, 1975).

At the same time, in addition to the rights to which they were assured by reason of their access to the common law, and the economic, social, and political influences they accrued as a consequence of their expanding political and economic power, the New English aspired to put a political system in place consistent with what they believed themselves entitled as loyal subjects. Based on the options to which recourse was made in the early and mid-seventeenth century, there were three possibilities. The first, replicating in broad terms that existed in the medieval lordship, was to entrust the responsibility to the settler population; this was the option resorted to during the reign of James I when the New English elite provided reasonably stable, if partisan administration.[13] The second, which was the preference of Charles I, was to vest the direction of Irish affairs in an English lord lieutenant or lord deputy; this option proved highly unpopular when Thomas Wentworth, Lord Strafford, pursued it during the 1630s.[14] The third option was a legislative union, which the Protectorate attempted during the 1650s when it opted to administer Ireland from Westminster.[15] Significantly, each of these options failed to meet the aspirations of the New English. They had the least difficulties, inevitably, with the system of administration resorted to during the reign of James I, for, although Parliament met only once, in 1613–15, it still offered the best prospect of their being in a position to shape the law in Ireland according to their design and needs.

The New English were in a strong moral position when they asserted their entitlement to possess a parliament with real powers both because it was the English practice and because Ireland possessed a venerable parliamentary tradition.[16] The support forthcoming for the idea from senior members of the judiciary in England in 1613 was also encouraging,[17] although the fact that by the mid-1630s the legislative initiative of the Irish Parliament had been fundamentally compromised by Thomas Wentworth's ingenious recourse to Poynings' Law to confine the Irish Parliament to considering bills that emanated from the Irish Privy Council gave some cause for pause. Wentworth's scheme was so effective that Charles, Lord Lambert, observed dolefully: "if

---

[13] See Aidan Clarke, "Pacification, plantation and the Catholic question, 1603–23" in T. W. Moody, F. X. Martin, and F. J. Byrne (eds.), *A New History of Ireland, iii* (Oxford: Oxford University Press, 1976), pp 187–232; John McCavitt, *Sir Arthur Chichester, Lord Deputy of Ireland 1605–16* (Belfast: Institute of Irish Studies, 1998).

[14] Hugh Kearney, *Strafford in Ireland, 1633–41: A Study in Absolutism* (Manchester: Manchester University Press, 1959).

[15] Patrick Little, *Lord Broghill and the Cromwellian Union with Ireland and Scotland* (Woodbridge: Boydell Press, 2004); idem, "The first unionists?: Irish protestant attitudes to union with England, 1653–9," *Irish Historical Studies*, 32 (2000), pp 44–58; Brian P. Levack, *The Formation of the British State: England, Scotland and the Union, 1603–1707* (Oxford: Oxford University Press, 1987).

[16] See Sayles and Richardson, *The Irish Parliament in the Middle Ages*, passim; Brian Farrell (ed.), *The Irish parliamentary tradition* (Dublin: Gill and Macmillan, 1973).

[17] P. H. Kelly (ed.), "Sir William Domville, A disquisition touching the great question whether an act of parliament made in England shall bind the kingdom and people of Ireland . . .," *Analecta Hibernica*, 40 (2007), p. 19.

Poynings' Law be so understood as that parliament can do nothing but pass bills, that is scarce a parliament."[18] This restriction was unacceptable, as Lambert's troubled tone testifies. The unhappy experience of Irish members of Parliament (MPs) at Westminster in the 1650s ensured there was also little support for a legislative union, and it was thus hardly surprising that the Protestant community in Ireland was to the fore in welcoming the restoration of the monarchy in 1660.[19] They did so in the hope that it would pave the way for a parliamentary assembly with proper powers, and this consideration, when set against the backdrop of the 1634–5 and 1640–1 parliaments and the unsuccessful attempt to plot a way forward during the 1640s,[20] provided the context for the preparation by Sir William Domville, Charles II's attorney general for Ireland, in 1660 of a treatise on the "great question whether an act of parliament made in England shall bind the kingdom and people of Ireland."[21]

Domville's treatise was the second of the three major commentaries on the legislative powers of the Irish Parliament written in the seventeenth century that made a case for legislative independence.[22] Unlike Richard Bolton, who preceded him and accepted that England's title to Ireland was founded on conquest,[23] Domville denied that Ireland had been conquered; he interpreted the historical record to indicate that the kings and bishops of Ireland had submitted voluntarily to Henry II, and that in a reciprocal gesture of recognition the king had acknowledged their entitlement to the same liberties as his English subjects, of which the right to make law was preeminent. Based on this acknowledgement, and on the fact that Henry bestowed Ireland as a distinct kingdom on his son, John (1167–1216), and on his broader assertion of the antiquity of Ireland, Domville constructed a strong argument.[24] It had limited influence on the course of events, however, because Irish Protestants were not disposed publicly at this moment to press for legislative independence. They had good strategic and political reasons for this stance, and because these had an enduring influence on the way they made their case for political liberty, it is appropriate to consider them briefly at this point.

---

[18] Quoted in Aidan Clarke, "The history of Poynings' Law 1615–41," *Irish Historical Studies*, 18 (1972–3), p. 218.

[19] T. C. Barnard, "Planters and policies in Cromwellian Ireland," *Past and Present*, 61 (1973), pp 31–69; Aidan Clarke, *The Prelude to Restoration in Ireland* (Cambridge: Cambridge University Press, 1999).

[20] For the 1640s, see Micheál Ó Siochrú, *Confederate Ireland, 1642–49: A Constitutional and Political Analysis* (Dublin: Four Courts Press 1999), pp. 71–2, 77–9, 92–3, 110–12; idem, "Catholic confederates and the constitutional relationship between Ireland and England" in Ciaran Brady and Jane Ohlmeyer (eds), *British Interventions in Early Modern Ireland* (Cambridge: Cambridge University Press, 2005), pp. 207–29; Kelly, *Poynings' Law*, pp. 12–4.

[21] Kelly (ed.), "Sir William Domville, A disquisition."

[22] The others were written by Sir Richard Bolton and William Molyneux.

[23] For an excellent consideration see P. H. Kelly, "'Sir Richard Bolton and the authorship of the Declaration ... (1644)," *Irish Historical Studies*, 35 (2005–06), pp. 7–14.

[24] See the introduction to Kelly (ed.), "Sir William Domville, A disquisition," pp. 20–25.

Of all the factors that guided Irish Protestants in their political decision-making for the duration of their ascendancy in Ireland, the most crucial was their awareness of their minority demographic status and their consciousness of their vulnerability in the event of a Catholic resurgence. The 1641 Rebellion, which exerted the same formative influence on the thinking of Irish Protestants as the Marian persecution and the Gunpowder Plot did in England, was the key event in this respect.[25] An estimated 12,000 Protestants fell victim to the insurgents when they targeted the Protestants settlers in their midst in the winter of 1640–41. It was substantially fewer than the number of royalists and confederate Catholics that fell victim to Oliver Cromwell's Roundheads between 1649 and 1651, but Irish Protestants were unable to view matters in this balanced fashion. They accepted implicitly Sir John Temple's inflated claim that the number of Protestant victims may have numbered 300,000 and, conceiving of themselves as a chosen people surrounded by an intransigently Catholic population committed to their extirpation, they were resolved neither to forget their forbears nor to relax their guard. With this revolution in mind, they instituted an annual commemoration at which they recalled the events of 1641 as a reminder of the fate that awaited them if circumstances permitted.[26] Their sensitivity on this point was reinforced by their consciousness of the fact that even with the significant addition to their number attributable to the Cromwellian land settlement and in-migration, they constituted less than 20 percent of the population.[27] Their sense of vulnerability was certainly compounded by the knowledge that both the Irish and the Old English had not only not come to terms with their religious and economic marginalization, but also aspired actively to overturn the Cromwellian confiscation and to restore the Catholic faith to an ascendant position.[28]

Prompted by these considerations, MPs and peers acceded during the 1660s to the active involvement of both the Irish and the English Privy Councils in the preparation of law even though it contravened their own legislative ambitions. As a result, all the legislation admitted to the statute book between 1661 and

---

[25] See, generally, David Cressy, *Bonfire and Bells: National Memory and the Protestant Calendar in Elizabethan and Stuart England* (London: Wiedenfeld and Nicolson, 1989); M. Perceval-Maxwell, *The Outbreak of the Irish Rebellion of 1641* (Montreal: McGill-Queen's University Press, 1994).

[26] James Kelly, "'The Glorious and immortal memory': Commemoration and protestant identity, 1660–1800," *Proceedings of the Royal Irish Academy*, 94C (1994), pp. 25–9; T. C. Barnard, "The uses of 23 October and Irish protestant celebrations," *English Historical Review*, 106 (1991), pp. 889–920.

[27] K. S. Bottigheimer, *English Money and Irish Land: The Adventurers in the Cromwellian Settlement* (Oxford: Oxford University Press, 1971); Toby Barnard, *A New Anatomy of Ireland: The Irish Protestants, 1649–1770* (London: Yale University Press, 2003).

[28] L. J. Arnold, *The Restoration Land Settlement in County Dublin, 1660–1688: A History of the Administration of the Acts of Settlement and Explanation* (Dublin: Irish Academic Press, 1999); David Dickson, *Old World Colony: Cork and South Munster, 1630–1830* (Cork: Cork University Press 2005); Breanda'n O' Buachalla, *Aisling ghe'ar: na Sti'obhartaigh agus an t-aos le'inn* (Baile Atha Cliath: An Clóchomhar, 1996).

1666 took its rise at the Irish Council rather than with Parliament. Because this legislation included landmark measures reinstating the Church of Ireland as the established church in Ireland, and an Act of Settlement, which affirmed them in possession of the bulk of the country's land, it was clearly in the interest of Irish Protestants to cooperate.[29] That said, they were not merely passive receptors of the decisions of others, as they demonstrated by their active input into the Act of Settlement and their insistence on a supplemental Act of Explanation.[30]

More importantly for the future, they evolved a form of proto-legislation known as heads of bills that was consistent with the letter of Poynings' Law. In practice, no act admitted to the Irish statute book in the 1660s began as a heads of bill, but this was less important in the long term than the acknowledgement of the right of both houses of Parliament to initiate measures in this form, subject to the approval of both the Irish and the English Privy Councils, because it afforded them direct say in the process of making laws that they were not permitted in the 1630s. Yet, while it is apparent in retrospect that this was an important step toward the liberties to which Irish Protestants believed their entitlement, they had achieved nothing that was not reversible, and the failure of Charles II to convene a further parliament during the remainder of his reign and of James II to do likewise during his briefer rule underlined the weakness of their position during the Restoration era.

Meanwhile, Irish Protestant liberties continued to fall behind those available to subjects of the Crown in England. This development is exemplified by the decision of the Westminster legislature in 1679 to provide parliamentary sanction for the customary right of habeas corpus, but the ratification at Westminster of mercantilist regulations that confined Ireland's right to export and to trade with Britain's imperial dependencies was more obviously burdensome.[31] The Glorious Revolution set Irish Protestants at a further disadvantage, because there was no Irish equivalent to the English Declaration of Rights of 1689, which enshrined the sovereignty of Parliament and authorized the election of the representatives of the people, regulated the royal prerogative, confined the potential for royal despotism by restricting the capacity to maintain a standing army, and provided for the right of the subject to bear arms.[32] It might have been worse. The deposition of James II was the occasion for a further phase of conflict, as Catholics (Jacobites) rallied to James' standard and contrived between 1688 and 1690 to maintain him on the throne of Ireland in the hope that it would assist him to regain the English Crown. While in

---

[29] For the most recent consideration of the 1661–6 Parliament, see Kelly, *Poynings' Law*, pp. 18–46; 17 and 18 Chas II, chap 6 (Act of Uniformity); 14 and 15 Chas II, sess 4 chap 2 (Act of Settlement).

[30] Kelly, *Poynings' Law*, pp. 29–32, 37–41.

[31] See C. A. Edie, "The Irish Cattle bills: study in restoration politics," *Transactions of the American Philosophical Society*, n.s., 50 (1970), pp. 5–66; L. M. Cullen, "Economic trends, 1660–91" in Moody et al. (eds), *A New History of Ireland*, iii, pp. 399–401.

[32] 1 William and Mary, sess. 2, chap 2; Lois G. Schwoerer, *The Declaration of Rights, 1689* (London: Johns Hopkins University Press, 1981).

Ireland, James authorized the convening of a parliament – the so-called Jacobite Parliament – in 1689, which amply demonstrated the extent of Catholic hostility to Protestantism and the land settlement of the 1660s. Had James prevailed, the form of government that would have been put in place in Ireland would, given his avowed preference and the inclination of Irish Catholics, in all likelihood have followed a Catholic and absolutist model, which must have destroyed the embryonic system of parliamentary government and political liberty identifiable in late seventeenth-century Ireland. This possibility was not lost on Irish Protestants, who shared the conclusion of Protestants across Europe that the evident increase in religious intolerance in the 1680s was a product of the rise of political absolutism.[33] Their own experience during the same decade certainly convinced them that Catholicism and absolutism were hand in glove, and that self-interest demanded that they take appropriate steps to ensure Catholics were not in a position even to attempt to regain power if the Protestant interest in Ireland was to enjoy the fruits of Protestant liberty that the Glorious Revolution came to emblemize.

ESTABLISHING PROTESTANT LIBERTIES, 1690–1740

Because their memory of 1641 was so apocalyptic, the minority Protestant community (both Presbyterian and Church of Ireland) in Ireland was less traumatized by the experience of Jacobite rule between 1689 and 1691 than it might otherwise have been. The episode had an abiding impact, nonetheless, and, convinced that their delivery from "Popery, slavery, arbitrary power, brass money and wooden shoes,"[34] as a popular Protestant oath memorably summarized their fate, was attributable to the providential intervention of William of Orange, they were determined to erect appropriate barriers. The implications of this determination for the Protestant community was not without irony, given their perception that English officials were responsible for depriving them of their rightful liberties, but the conviction that Catholic doctrine was incompatible with the tradition of Protestant liberty they valorized eased their concerns on this point. Most Protestants in Britain as well as Ireland were in agreement on the necessity of disempowering Catholics militarily, religiously, politically, and economically, and that they could best do this, not by depriving them of access to the law, land, parliament, or religion by means of sweeping prohibitions, but by restricting and regulating their ability to operate in these spheres. Their approach, in other words, following the example historically pursued in England where Catholics were a religious minority, was to confine and to limit their access to the political and legal process, to confine their freedom to

---

[33] One consequence of this was the emergence of a vigorous literature on toleration. See John Marshall, *John Locke, Toleration and Early Enlightenment Culture* (Cambridge: Cambridge University Press, 2006), and the review thereof by J. I. Israel in *English Historical Review*, 122 (2007), pp. 1042–4.

[34] Hugh Staples (ed.), *The Ireland of Sir Jonah Barrington* (London: Peter Owen, 1968), p. 214.

practice their religion, and to limit their opportunity to prosper economically. In order to be able to do this, they had to be in a position to shape the law, which, in the first instance, meant building on the shaky foundations laid in the 1660s.

Their overwhelming support of William of Orange was no guarantee that Irish Protestants would be entrusted with the right to make laws in the aftermath of the Glorious Revolution. Some in England, apprehending a Catholic rebellion in the future and the emergence of "jealousies" that must in time drive a wedge between Britain and the Protestant interest in Ireland, favored a legislative union. This was seen to possess advantages for all parties, including the English settler in Ireland, who would not "lose his birthright or [the] privileges he had before in the legislative power of England."[35] This argument had limited appeal, however, not only because the mood of the moment, as exemplified by the Declaration of Rights, favored parliamentary government, but also because there were powerful financial and administrative reasons for pursuing this option.[36] Irish Protestants, for their part, were not of one mind on the way forward. At its most basic, the issue exposed tensions within their ranks between those who maintained that they were entitled a priori to the same liberties as subjects of the Crown resident in England and those whose outlook was shaped by the realization that, since they were utterly dependent on Britain for protection, they should continue to adopt the essentially deferential stance they had taken in the 1660s. By implication, the latter were more accepting of restrictions on their entitlement to make laws, limitations to their individual liberties, and constraints on their freedom to trade because that was the price of sustaining a harmonious connection with the larger Protestant communion in England.

Guided by these crucial considerations, Irish Protestant opinion received the decision to convene a parliament in 1692 with a mixture of expectation and wariness. They welcomed the renewal of parliamentary government as an acknowledgment of their right to participate in the making of laws for the kingdom of Ireland, but they were suspicious of ministerial intentions and quietly determined to ensure that they were allowed real and substantive power. To this end, they refused openly to cooperate with the Irish executive unless their "sole right" to approve the raising of revenue was recognized. In so doing, they were asserting their entitlement to the right to be free from taxation by royal decree enshrined in the English Declaration of Rights, although ministers, who sought to uphold the royal prerogative, were reluctant to concede the point.[37] As a result, the 1692 session had to be prorogued prematurely, and it was not until 1695 that a compromise was reached whereby in return for their cooperation in

---

[35] Considerations concerning Ireland in relation to England and particularly in respect of an union (National Archives of Ireland, Wyche papers, 2nd series, no. 143).

[36] For the financial issue see Charles Ivar McGrath, *The Making of the Eighteenth-Century Irish Constitution: Government, Parliament and the Revenue 1692–1714* (Dublin: Four Courts Press, 2000).

[37] James McGuire, "The parliament of 1692" in D. W. Hayton and Thomas Bartlett (eds), *Penal Era and Golden Age: Essays in Eighteenth-Century Irish History* (Belfast: Ulster Historical Foundation, 1979), pp. 1–31; Kelly, *Poynings' Law*, pp. 60–9.

voting a sufficient sum to pay for the government of the kingdom, MPs were facilitated to initiate legislation in the form of heads of bills. They shared the power of initiating legislation with the Irish Privy Council, which was the *fons et origo* of a substantial proportion of bills during the 1690s, but their acceptance then of the law-making role of the Privy Council was less crucial for the future than the explicit recognition of the right of Parliament to do likewise.[38]

This arrangement was possible because the ruling Protestant elite in Ireland was also able to ensure that the majority Catholic interest was subject to a battery of discriminatory regulations known collectively as the Penal Laws.[39] The implementation of this legislation was not something that ministers desired as much as they required financial legislation, but it was more than symbolically significant that among the enactments of the Irish Parliament in 1695 was a measure prohibiting Catholics (other than those deemed sufficiently trustworthy to be permitted a license to do so) from bearing arms. Some thirty years later, in 1728, when the coping stone was added to the penal law edifice by the formal removal of their right to vote, Catholics were subject to a panoply of religious, economic, legal, and political restrictions and restraints that fundamentally confined their civil and legal rights but did not trespass on their still more fundamental entitlement to own property, to practice their religion, to acquire legal knowledge and to practice as a chambers attorney, and to carry on in business.[40] Moreover, the Irish Parliament's action was not unprecedented; it followed in the footsteps of the Westminster legislature, and still more discriminatory codes elsewhere. The key difference was that whereas in most jurisdictions those who were subject to such restraints were religious or ethnic minorities, Catholics comprised the majority of the population in Ireland. The Protestant elite in Ireland was acutely aware of the demographic imbalance, but it was so persuaded that it was justified in securing the Protestant constitution in church and in state that it did not hesitate to also penalize Presbyterians by making it a requirement in 1703 that they must receive the sacrament of the Eucharist according to the rights of the Church of Ireland if they took public office.[41] The attitude of mind that informed and guided the Protestant elite at this time is exemplified by Henry Maxwell (1669–1730), MP, a squire from county Down and the author of a number of political tracts; he justified the privileging of Protestants on the grounds that since they were "naturally the offspring of the people of England," that was their entitlement.[42]

[38] Kelly, *Poynings' Law*, pp. 69–79.

[39] See Maureen Wall, *The Penal Laws, 1691–1760* (Dundalk: Dun Dealgan Press, 1976); James Kelly, "The ascendancy and the Penal laws" in J. R. Bartlett and S. D. Kinsella (eds), *Two Thousand Years of Christianity and Ireland* (Dublin: Columba Press 2006), pp. 133–54.

[40] Ivar McGrath, "Securing the Protestant interest: the origins and purpose of the penal laws of 1695," *Irish Historical Studies*, 30 (1995–6), pp. 25–46.

[41] J. C. Beckett, *Protestant Dissent in Ireland, 1687–1780* (London: Faber and Faber, 1948).

[42] [Henry Maxwell], *An Essay towards an Union of Ireland with England* (London, 1703); D. W. Hayton, "Henry Maxwell, MP, author of *An Essay towards an Union of Ireland with England* (1703)," *Eighteenth-Century Ireland*, 22 (2007) pp. 28–63.

Although the introduction of restrictions targeted at Catholics and Presbyterians, combined with the application of a strict code of regulatory censorship
that penalized political or religious opinions incompatible with those of the
dominant Protestant elite,[43] helped to ease Protestant anxieties, it was not a
precondition for a more vigorous assertion by Irish protestants of their entitlement to the same constitutional liberties and civil rights as Englishmen. This
assertion was justifiable on its own terms, but it was encouraged in the late
1690s by the perception, articulated in 1698 by Bishop William King, that
"their liberties and privileges [were] being invaded."[44] King was prompted to
make this observation by the apprehension that the Westminster Parliament
aspired to assert its controversial claim to make law for Ireland, rather than by
what he elsewhere denominated "the great abuse of Poynings' Law." King
referred to Poynings' Law in this manner because, he maintained tendentiously,
the right assumed by the Irish Privy Council "to put bills" arising with the Irish
legislature "in form was contrary to the meaning of the act" that "speaks
nothing of the Privy Council but the Council of the realm."[45] Stephen Ludlow,
the MP for Dunleer, was still more strident; he deemed the alterations made to
bills arising in the Irish Parliament so egregious he counselled in 1709 that MPs
should, as a matter of course, refuse to admit all amended legislation to the
statute book. It was only by "exert[ing] the power of a negative ... so often as
the Queen and Council should exert their power of altering a bill" that MPs
would be enabled "to hinder Poynings' Law from doing all the mischief that it
might do."[46] This position was too confrontational for all but a minority of
legislators; the majority did not believe the matter to be of such significance, but
the greater readiness to address these issues publicly pointed to the growing
strength of feeling on the constitutional liberties of Ireland.

There was greater unanimity, certainly, among peers and MPs, and among
the Protestant population at large, on the question of Westminster legislating
for Ireland. The point at issue here, William King observed trenchantly in 1698,
was "whether the people of Ireland be slaves or freemen [and] whether they be
more the subjects of England than the people of England are the King's subjects."[47] Nearly two decades later, King, now archbishop of Dublin, was still
more explicit: Any attempt "to bind our liberty, property or conscience by laws
where we have no representatives and where the dependence of Ireland is not
concerned I take to be against the constitution or fundamental maxims of our
nations."[48] The problem for King and others who shared this outlook was that
it collided with political sentiment in England, which, as expressed by the

---

[43] James Kelly, "Regulating print: the state and the control of print in eighteenth-century Ireland,"
Eighteenth-Century Ireland, 23 (2008), pp. 142–74.

[44] King to Annesley, 19 May 1698 (Trinity College Dublin (henceforth TCD), King papers, Ms
750/1 ff. 232–3).

[45] King to Weymouth, 28 Mar. 1707 (TCD, King papers, Ms 750/2 f. 108).

[46] Quoted in Kelly, *Poynings' Law*, pp. 153–4.

[47] As in note 44.

[48] King to Annesley, 3 July 1714 (TCD, King papers, Ms 750/4 f. 176).

House of Commons in June 1698, was "to preserve and maintain the dependence and subordination of Ireland to the imperial crown of this realm."[49] This had long been the preferred strategy in England, but it was rarely affirmed so explicitly, and it might not have been articulated on this occasion but for the intervention of William Molyneux with the classic eighteenth-century statement of the entitlement of Irish Protestants to possess "the like freedoms with the natural-born subjects of England, as being descended from them."[50]

Molyneux's articulation of the claim of Irish Protestants that they were entitled to the same rights as their English equivalents was grounded on the existence of an ancient Irish constitution, avowed and recognized by Henry II. Echoing the argument made nearly forty years previously by his father-in-law, William Domville, Molyneux contended that:

The laws and liberties of England were granted, above 500 years ago, to the people of Ireland upon their submission to the Crown of England, with a design to make them easy to England, and to keep them in the allegiance of the King of England.[51]

Like Domville (and Bolton), Molyneux drew heavily on historical and legal precedents to sustain his contention that Ireland was not a dependent colony in the manner of the Crown's dependencies in North America but an independent kingdom linked with England by a shared allegiance to a common monarch.[52] He broke new ground in invoking the seminal doctrine of natural rights promoted by his "excellent friend" John Locke, whose *Two Treatises of Government* (published in 1689) justified the deposition of James II on the grounds that he had lost the trust of the English people because of his failure to protect their rights, property, and lives. This argument was also appealed to in Ireland, most famously by Archbishop King in his seminal work, *The State of the Protestants*, which went to four editions in the 1690s, but King's work was less significant in 1698 than Molyneux's adaptation of Locke's thesis to suggest that "the natural right to consent to government meant that no one nation could have an exclusive right to dominate another."[53] It was a conclusion that resonated strongly in Ireland, where public resentment at what was perceived as the condescending attitude of English ministers elevated the issue of "consent" into a potent political issue. Bishop King tirelessly iterated his position that to "be taxed and bound by laws to which I am no party I shall reckon myself as much a slave

---

[49] *Journal of the House of Commons, 1697–9*, vol xii (London, 1803), p. 337.

[50] William Molyneux, *The Case of Ireland's Being Bound by Acts of Parliament in England, Stated* (London, 1698), p. 20.

[51] Ibid., pp. 171–2.

[52] Ibid., p. 148; Ian McBride, "The common name of Irishman: Protestantism and patriotism in eighteenth-century Ireland" in idem and Tony Claydon (eds), *Protestantism and National Identity: Britain and Ireland, c. 1650–1850* (Cambridge: Cambridge University Press, 1998), pp. 243–4.

[53] P. H. Kelly, "Perceptions of Locke in eighteenth-century Ireland," *Proceedings of the Royal Irish Academy*, 89C (1989), p. 20.

as one of the grand seignor's mutes."[54] Others were so alarmed by the suggestion that England aspired to legislate directly for Ireland that, like Molyneux,
they concluded that the only way to bring this intolerable state of affairs to a
close and to ensure parity between the subjects of the two kingdoms was to
conclude a legislative union.[55] Such a union was not to be because England did
not want it, but it is a measure of how galling Irish Protestants had come to
perceive their position that Molyneux invoked what Ian McBride has termed
his "second line of defence against England's claim to govern Ireland by right of
conquest"; in this defence he avowed that England's insistence that Ireland had
been conquered was applicable only to "the *antient race* of the *Irish*" and that
"the *English* and *Britains*," as participants in the conquest, "retain'd all the
freedoms and immunities of *Free-born* subjects."[56]

Interestingly, the latter was not among the objectionable passages singled out
by the Westminster House of Commons' committee appointed to review Molyneux's text; its focus was on what it termed "the bold and pernicious assertions"
that purported on behalf of the king's subjects in Ireland "to shake off their
subjection to and dependence on this kingdom."[57] The committee identified
thirty-two such passages, which justified their decision to formally recommend,
and for MPs to conclude that the book was "of dangerous consequence to the
Crown and People of England by denying the authority and parliament of
England, to bind the kingdom and people of Ireland; and the subordination
and dependence that Ireland hath, and ought to have upon England."[58] These
were stern words, and their impact was reinforced by the accompanying statement that the preservation of "the wealth and power" of England demanded
that steps be taken to discourage the burgeoning Irish woollen manufacture.
The committee recommended that Ireland should concentrate on promoting
linen production, which complemented rather than competed with English
economic interests.[59]

This was a dismissive response to a tract that, based on its enduring popular-
ity (it was reprinted on eight occasions in the course of the eighteenth century),
has justifiably been described as the "manual of Irish liberty."[60] Be that as it
may, the political upper hand at this moment lay firmly with London, and
ministers repeatedly highlighted this fact by refusing to extend to Ireland civil

---

[54] King to Bishop Lindsay of Kildare, 13 May 1698 (TCD, King papers, Ms 750/1). It is significant
    that the reference to enslavement, made by King, was echoed by a Cork merchant, Christopher
    Crofts, who observed of the woollen act, "had they made an act to have hanged us all, it had
    been better to die martyrs than live as slaves" (Dickson, *Old World Colony*, p. 127).

[55] James Kelly, "The origins of the Act of Union: an examination of unionist opinion in Britain
    and Ireland, 1650–1800," *Irish Historical Studies*, 25 (1987), pp. 240–4.

[56] McBride, "The common name of Irishman," p. 244; Molyneux, *The Case of Ireland*, p. 19.

[57] *Commons Journal* (England), xii, 336.

[58] Molyneux, *The Case of Ireland*, p. 150; *Commons Journal* (England), xii, 326, 331.

[59] *Commons Journal* (England), xii, 338; P. H. Kelly, "The Irish woollen export prohibition act of
    1699: Kearney revisited," *Irish Economic and Social History*, 7 (1980), pp. 22–44.

[60] McBride, "The common name of Irishman," pp. 244–5.

liberties that were available in England. This disposition was amply manifested during the 1690s, when the English Privy Council denied several attempts by the Irish Parliament to introduce habeas corpus, and the Council Board continued this practice by rejecting, in 1703, 1705, 1707, 1709, and 1710, further bills "for better securing the liberty of the subject."[61] The English protection against military tyranny was likewise denied to Ireland by the refusal, in 1696, to agree to an annual mutiny bill. And, in 1701, the English Act of Settlement, which established a Protestant succession, agreed to implement a number of important provisions aimed at countering royal influence – judges commissions were now on good behavior rather than the will of the Crown, and certain office and pension holders were precluded from sitting in Parliament – that were not deemed appropriate to extend to Ireland.[62]

Irish Protestants were understandably disappointed by the failure to apply equivalent regulations in Ireland, but the discontent this failure caused was modest by comparison with the impact of the curtailing of established liberties, particularly when, as was the case with the Declaratory Act approved at Westminster in 1720, it diminished the standing of their Parliament. There were two points at issue at this time. The first was the appellate jurisdiction of the Irish House of Lords, which had long been disputed by the British Upper House, so it was not entirely surprising that the act affirmed the supremacy of the British House of Lords. This measure was objected to in Ireland, but opposition was articulated in far stronger terms to the accompanying affirmation of the entitlement of the Westminster legislature to make law for Ireland, because it negated Irish claims that their Parliament was the sole body entitled to make law for the kingdom of Ireland.[63] Peers protested that because Ireland was a "distinct dominion, and no part of the kingdom of England, none can determine concerning the affairs thereof, unless authorized thereto by the known laws and customs of this kingdom," but the decision had been made.[64] The angry mood was highlighted by the publication of new editions of William Molyneux's *Case* in 1719, 1720, and 1725 and by the entry of Jonathan Swift into the lists in defense of Irish liberties, most notably in the fourth Drapier's letter, in which he invoked Molyneux's citation of John Locke's contractual argument in support of political liberty for the kingdom of Ireland.[65]

The provisions of the Declaratory Act certainly represented a major setback to the aspiration of Irish Protestants to legal and constitutional equality with England insofar as it statutorily affirmed Irish dependency, and it is for this reason that the measure has been portrayed as the culmination of a trend that brought about a diminution in Ireland's status from that of kingdom to that of

---

[61] Kelly, *Poynings' Law*, pp. 74, 79, 81, 108, 112, 145.

[62] Act of Settlement: 12 and 13 William III, chap 2.

[63] Isolde Victory, "The making of the Declaratory Act (1719)" in G. O'Brien (ed.), *Parliament, Politics and People* (Dublin: Irish Academic Press, 1987), pp. 9–29.

[64] *A Collection of the Protests of the Lords of Ireland* (London, 1771), pp. 49–51.

[65] Kelly, "Perceptions of Locke in eighteenth-century Ireland," p. 25.

colony over the three decades following the Glorious Revolution.[66] Significantly, this is not just a historiographical conclusion. The description of Ireland
as a colony by an Irish peer resident in England in 1720 indicates that it was
also the contemporary perception.[67]

If this description suggests that the efforts of Irish Protestants to secure the
constitutional and individual liberties that were emblematical of the Glorious
Revolution had failed spectacularly, and that they were farther away than ever
from attaining the elusive goal of equality with England, the practical reality
was not so disagreeable. It is notable, for example, that Westminster used the
power it had arrogated by the Declaratory Act to make law for Ireland spar-
ingly, and rarely with a seriously restrictive intent. More importantly insofar as
the exercise of power in Ireland is concerned, the continuing disinclination of
the king's representative – the lord lieutenant – to reside in Ireland for the
duration of his appointment meant that much of the practical day-to-day business of administering the kingdom and managing Parliament was delegated to
the leaders of the Irish Protestant political nation. They had already been conceded a direct say in what law was made by the "compromise" reached in 1695,
but Lord Rochester's inauguration of a tradition of vice-regal nonresidence in
1701 permitted them to assume a still more important role. This development
was formally acknowledged by the appointment of individuals from within the
Irish elite to head the church, judiciary, and the revenue and, in the absence of
the lord lieutenant, to oversee the Irish administration, as a result of which
figures like William Conolly, Alan Brodrick, and Marmaduke Coghill became
influential in their own right.[68] Moreover, it did not end there. Once George I
was securely established on the throne, and the prospect of a contested succession or, worse, a Catholic monarch faded, the need to maintain control of
Parliament allowed individuals of ability like William Conolly to accrue enormous power both as an officeholder and a parliamentary manager. Indeed,
when in the wake of the Wood's halfpence dispute, the lord lieutenant sought
to vest still further responsibility for the management of Parliament in an Irish
politician, Conolly was transformed from a parliamentary manager into an
"undertaker," in which capacity he and his successors assumed a leading
role both in constructing a Commons' majority and in securing approval for
necessary legislation.[69] This development was a signal one that confirmed
the centrality of the Irish political elite to the smooth operation of the Irish

[66] Patrick Kelly, "Ireland and the Glorious Revolution: from kingdom to colony" in Robert
Beddard (ed.), *The Revolutions of 1688* (Oxford: Oxford University Press, 1991), pp. 163–90.

[67] Perceval to Dering, 5 Mar. 1620 (British Library, Egmont papers, Add. Ms 47029 ff. 22–5).

[68] See Patrick McNally, *Parties, Patriots and Undertakers: Parliamentary Politics in Early Hanoverian Ireland* (Dublin: Four Courts Press, 1997).

[69] There is a large literature on this subject: see R. E. Burns, *Irish Parliamentary Politics in
the Eighteenth Century, 1714–60* (2 vols., Washington, DC: Catholic University of America
Press, 1989–90), and McNally, *Parties, Patriots and Undertakers*. The most recent, and finest,
contribution is D. W. Hayton, *Ruling Ireland, 1685–1742: Politics, Politicians and Parties*
(Woodbridge: Boydell Press, 2004).

Parliament and the efficient administration of the kingdom, and they were gratified by the attendant power and influence it brought them. Moreover, it assisted, and was assisted by, the assumption by the Irish Parliament, and by the House of Commons in particular, of a dominant role in the making of law.

Following on the inauguration during Queen Anne's reign of a meeting of Parliament every two years, the legislature became an increasingly important vector of Irish Protestant ambition during the early Hanoverian era. This development is best demonstrated by reference to the growth in the amount of law that was made, which rose from 84 enactments during the reign of William and Mary to 131 during the reign of George I.[70] But it is still more clearly revealed by the increased percentage of measures that originated as heads of bills in the House of Commons and by the parallel fall, from 19 percent during the reign of Queen Anne to 8 percent during that of George I, in the percentage of legislation that took its rise at the Privy Council. Moreover, this trend intensified following the House of Commons' rejection of a bill to combat riot in 1730 simply because it arose at the Council; as a result, the percentage of Privy Council bills to reach the statute book contracted to a modest 2.6 percent during the reign of George II. By the end of this reign, the Privy Council's law-making function was more symbolic than real; it was maintained solely to uphold the royal prerogative and to preclude Parliament convening without prior authorization.[71]

The eclipse of the Privy Council as a law-making body necessarily resulted in a significant transfer in influence from the executive to the legislature, which was responsible for an impressive body of law in the decades that followed. It did so within the parameters of Poynings' Law, which meant that the British Privy Council continued to scrutinize every item of legislation emanating from the Irish Parliament and was at liberty to use its extensive powers to respite and amend Irish bills to ensure the legislation that was admitted to the Irish statute book was both compatible with British law and acceptable to British national and imperial interests. What this meant in practice was that 19 percent of the bills received at the British Council Board during the reign of Queen Anne were never returned, and that 69 percent of the public and 54 percent of the private bills were returned in an amended form (only 17 percent were forwarded without amendment).[72] The percentage respited during the reign of George I fell to 14 percent, but the rise in the proportion that were amended to circa 75 percent indicates that, notwithstanding the eclipse of the Irish Privy Council as a source of law, Poynings' Law continued to act as a very real brake on the liberty of the Irish Parliament.[73]

Significantly, Irish opinion was broadly content to operate within the constraints of Poynings' Law in the early and mid-eighteenth century, perhaps

[70] See Irish Statutes; Kelly, *Poynings' Law*, p. 159.
[71] Kelly, *Poynings' Law*, pp. 126, 145, 199.
[72] Kelly, *Poynings' Law*, pp. 145–6.
[73] Kelly, *Poynings' Law*, pp. 210, 217.

because the constraints were applied with a measure of flexibility, even though the restrictions Poynings' Law imposed on the liberties of the Irish Parliament to make law were very real. The most compelling evidence of this contentment is provided by the fact that parliamentary approval was routinely forthcoming for bills returned from Whitehall with extensive amendments. Most of these measures did not, to be sure, engage with sensitive constitutional issues, but it is noteworthy also that there was no sustained criticism of Poynings' Law. Indeed, there was a palpable willingness, particularly manifest during the 1730s and 1740s, when the political milieu was at is most stable, to follow British commentators in extolling the virtues of the constitution and in praising it as better than any other known to man, as a commentator writing in the influential *Universal Advertiser* made clear:

The excellence of our legal and truly admirable constitution chiefly consists in the due distribution of power to every branch of the legislature, which forms that glorious political balance, not to be found in any other government.[74]

Jasper Brett, a Church of Ireland clergyman based in county Down, was no less enthusiastic. Writing in 1721, he observed: "Tis indeed the great happiness of a people to live under a government where the prerogative of the prince and the liberties of the people are duly tempered." And pointing to the fact that "the people of these nations have the comfort to live under the most mild and just government that ever was known to mankind," he exulted openly in the fact that it was "a government in short, which all the subjects of Europe envy, and none but a wanton people would find fault with."[75]

PUSHING THE FRONTIERS OF LIBERTY, 1740–1789

The contentment to which Jasper Brett's intervention bears witness provides a useful insight as to why politicians in Ireland were satisfied to strive to push the frontier of opportunity within the existing political system rather than press for new and elusive liberties during the early Hanoverian era. This tendency was encouraged by a "shift in the language of political discourse in Ireland" during the 1720s from the rights-based rhetoric of the 1690s and early eighteenth century to the language of "Country Whiggery, which assimilated political difference into the paradigm conflict of patriotism and corruption."[76] Stimulated by the hostile reaction to the enactment of the Declaratory Act and the confrontation over Wood's halfpence (1724–5), it was accelerated by serious economic problems in the late 1720s, which prompted Jonathan Swift and other influential commentators to call on the population to stop blaming

---

[74] Universal Advertiser, 5 Feb. 1754.
[75] Jasper Brett, *The Sin of With-Holding Tribute by the Running of Goods, Concealing Excise etc . . .* (Dublin, 1721), p. 11. See Patrick Walsh, "*The sin of with-holding tribute*, contemporary pamphlets and the professionalisation of the revenue service in early eighteenth-century Ireland," *Eighteenth-Century Ireland*, 21 (2006), pp. 48–65.
[76] Kelly, "Perceptions of Locke in eighteenth-century Ireland," p. 26.

England for Irish economic ills and to embrace a culture of improvement.[77] This recommendation was not incompatible with the continuing pursuit of constitutional and civil liberties, of course, but the greater willingness to acknowledge that "England is the principal kingdom, and Ireland an accessory to it" was indicative of a reluctance to do so in the obstructive manner that characterized the response to the national bank proposal in 1720–21.[78] Moreover, this attitude was fostered, during the 1730s and 1740s, by the success of the undertaker system not only in ensuring that a substantial corpus of law amenable to the interests and aspirations of Irish protestants continued to be ushered onto the statute book, but also in satisfying the more immediate needs of many within as well as on the fringes of the political elite for power and preferment. The resulting consensus was at its strongest during the ascendancy of Henry Boyle, who was the chief undertaker for two decades from 1733, when Irish politics were ostensibly more quiescent than they were at any point in the eighteenth century.[79]

In reality, personal and factional rivalries ensured that politics was never uneventful, but the skilful way in which Boyle neutralized or bought off potential challengers ensured that potentially disruptive constitutional issues rarely surfaced. This situation was highlighted in the late 1740s when the political elite rallied to negate the threat posed by Charles Lucas, who was the *deus ex machina* of a popular attempt to reform the oligarchical Dublin Corporation.[80] Significantly, Lucas chose to go into exile to avoid sanction, and it is no coincidence therefore that the major political crisis of the mid-eighteenth century, and indeed of the undertaker system – the money bill dispute of 1753–6 – was fundamentally a power struggle within the political elite rather than a contest between two different political visions.[81] It could not be confined within these parameters, however, not least because it took place against the background of a major expansion in the public sphere. This expansion largely accounts for the appeal by Boyle and his lieutenants to the rhetoric of patriotism, but however one assesses his motives, the exchanges that characterized the dispute transformed domestic politics. Moreover, it was conducted in the language of country whiggery, modernized, and updated to embrace recent developments in Britain, though overtly political in its expression. As such, it encouraged calls,

---

[77] James Kelly, "Jonathan Swift and the Irish economy in the 1720s," *Eighteenth-Century Ireland*, 6 (1991), pp. 7–36; Patrick Kelly, "The politics of political economy in mid-eighteenth-century Ireland" in S. J. Connolly (ed.), *Political Ideas in Eighteenth Century Ireland* (Dublin: Four Courts Press, 2000), pp. 105–29.

[78] Michael Ryder, "The Bank of Ireland, 1721, land, credit and dependency," *Historical Journal*, 25 (1982), pp. 557–82. The quoted words, which are by Archbishop Synge, are considered in Kelly, *Poynings' Law*, p. 199.

[79] See Burns, *Irish parliamentary politics*, ii, 13–95 and Hayton, *Ruling Ireland*, Chapter 8.

[80] For Lucas see Sean Murphy, "Charles Lucas" in *Oxford Dictionary of National Biography* (60 vols, Oxford: Oxford University Press, 2004), vol. 34, pp. 665–9.

[81] See Eoin Magennis, *The Irish Political System, 1740–65: The Golden Age of the Undertakers* (Dublin: Four Courts Press, 2000), pp. 62–110; Declan O'Donovan, "The money bill dispute of 1753" in Bartlett and Hayton (eds), *Penal Era and Golden Age*, pp. 55–87.

directed at the Irish administration, not only to combat corruption but also to protect and extend "the libertys of the people."[82] As a result, when Boyle turned his back on his popular support base and made what was perceived as a base deal with the Irish administration, which brought the money bill dispute to a conclusion, he was execrated by the politicized public. By contrast, the British government was simply relieved that the dispute was over; its priority with respect to Ireland, a priority defined influentially by Robert Walpole as *quieta non movere*, was orderly government at all costs. The problem the British government encountered in the aftermath of the money bill dispute was that while there was agreement within the Protestant nation as to the superior merits of the British Constitution, the augmented ranks of those who pursued a patriot political agenda were convinced that those in power had compromised the integrity of that constitution. More seriously, many believed that if corruption was not combated and the constitution restored to its pristine purity, the liberties of the population must be endangered.

This conviction had a visible influence on political discourse from the late 1750s. Manifest initially in the willingness of a small nucleus of patriots to agitate issues such as Poynings' Law and the pension list, the impact of this group increased in the early 1760s when their ranks were augmented by the addition of forceful voices such as Henry Flood and Charles Lucas. The latter was particularly critical of Poynings' Law. It was, he maintained in an address to the lord mayor and freeholders of Dublin, responsible for the prevailing corrupt system and incompatible with the "ancient constitution" because its implementation was "left to the arbitrary determination of one or two servants of the Crown'"[83] Henry Flood was even more passionate. Speaking in the House of Commons in October 1765, he compared the situation of Ireland to that of the American colonies, and, embracing the rhetoric of the British Whigs who perceived that George III was embarked on a campaign to undermine the liberties secured by the Glorious Revolution and to revert to the despotism of the discredited Stuarts, he alleged that the Irish administration was embarked on a similar policy "to rob and enslave."[84] Flood invoked the disproportionate response to agrarian violence in support of his contention that "we have relinquished the civil power, abandoned magistracy and thrown ourselves into the arms of the military." This was profoundly to misjudge the motives of both the Crown and the Irish administration, but Flood and others of like mind were convinced that "ministers" aspired to overturn "the finest, the

---

[82] For the most recent considerations see Bob Harris, *Politics and the Nation: Britain in the Mid-Eighteenth Century* (Oxford: Oxford University Press, 2002), Chapter 5; M. J. Powell, *Britain and Ireland in the Eighteenth-Century Crisis of Empire* (Basingstoke: Palgrave, 2003), Chapter 2; Jacqueline Hill, "Allegories, fictions and feigned representations: decoding the money bill dispute, 1752–56," *Eighteenth-Century Ireland*, 21 (2006), pp. 66–88; Kelly, *Poynings' Law*, p. 201.

[83] [Charles Lucas], *An Address of Charles Lucas MD to the Right Honourable the Lord Mayor, the Aldermen, Sheriffs, Commons, Citizens and Freeholders of Dublin* (Dublin, 1765), p. 4.

[84] Speech by Henry Flood, Oct. 1765 (Birr Castle, Rosse papers, F/21).

fullest, most ancient and best attested national compact, which any nation has to boast of as the ground of its constitution":

We set out in the thirteenth century in every constitutional right equal to Britain, in some superior. We are now in the decline of the eighteenth century, but, alas, how different. In Henry VIII's time, where our declension commences, our judges were made dependent on the Crown and their tenure changed into a tenure at will instead of being for life, as they were originally. Our parliament at the same, according to the construction of that act [Poynings' Law] which seems prevalent, was made dependent on a dependent council ... The era of liberty, the [Glorious] Revolution came. But instead of an era of liberty to this unfortunate country, as it was to Great Britain, it forms the second grand point of its declension. Since that time, we have seen one House of parliament deprived of its judicature, and both, so far as a declaration of another body has validity, deprived of their independence and divested of their supremacy. We hoped that the reign of a patriot prince [George III] would restore to us the independence of our judges ... We hoped that the favourable period was on the wing for which we had long waited with patience and resignation. And what do we now hear of – an aggravation of everything grievous, and annihilation of our parliamentary rights, a deprivation of the last and most precious jewel remaining to us after former usurpations and an accumulation and completion of all that is ignominious and servile.[85]

This was as doubtful an interpretation of Irish history as it was of the aims and motives of George III and his ministers, but the perception of "the decay of liberty" was as compelling to Irish patriots as it was to British Whigs and American colonists, and it provided them with powerful motivation.[86] Their priority was to restore the "ancient constitution," and to this end they repeatedly invoked the rising civil establishment list on the grounds that it was incompatible with political liberty, and urged greater financial probity and responsibility in all areas of expenditure; they also supported the creation of a civilian militia to diminish the need for a large standing army and advocated the reduction in the duration of parliaments to seven years. They were largely unsuccessful in inducing changes in policy though the duration of parliaments was set at eight years in 1768, but, as in England and the American colonies, the appeal of patriotism increased in the late 1760s and early 1770s in response to what was seen as an intensifying threat to political liberty.

In the case of Ireland three events coalesced to generate this impression. The most immediate, and significant, was the appointment of George, Lord Townshend, to head the Irish executive in 1767. Townshend did not come to Ireland with a blueprint for reform, but he did aspire to augment the army to assist with Britain's increased imperial commitments in the aftermath of the Seven Years' War. However, meeting only with obstruction, he resolved to dispense with the services of the undertakers and assumed personal responsibility

---

[85] Ibid.
[86] See Bernard Bailyn, *Ideological Origins of the American Revolution* (Cambridge, MA, Belknap Press of Harvard University Press, 1967); J. W. Derry, *English Politics and the American Revolution* (London: Dent, 1976).

for constructing a working Commons majority. In so doing, Townshend threatened the power base and ambition of a generation of undertakers. He also contrived to antagonize the patriot interest when he prorogued Parliament in response to the refusal of MPs in December 1769 to approve a Privy Council money bill.[87] Perceiving Townshend's actions as apiece with the Westminster Parliament's refusal to accept the legitimacy of the decision of the freeholders of Middlesex in electing John Wilkes, which was followed closely in Ireland, and the attempt to enforce disagreeable policies on the American colonists, the more outspoken patriots concurred with the analysis of their British and American equivalents that the king's ministers were embarked on a plan to undermine political liberties throughout the empire.[88] They offered little hard evidence to support this conclusion, but it had a palpably radicalizing impact on political debate. This impact was clearly in evidence in the House of Commons in 1771, when it was alleged, in response to the introduction at the British Privy Council of amendments to the main supply bill, "that no less than the right of parliament, the constitution of this kingdom [was] at stake; [for] if we consented to the altering a money bill, there was an end of parliament."[89]

Their predilection for inflated rhetoric notwithstanding, patriot MPs and peers pursued Lord Townshend using largely familiar arguments and tactics. The attitude out of doors was more assertive. Convinced that the liberties secured by the Glorious Revolution were under threat from a "despotic and tyrannical" ministry, political activists took full advantage of the increased freedom of political expression that flowed from the diminution in the closeness with which the authorities monitored print to articulate a distinctly more radical message.[90] One of its loudest and most interesting voices was Edward Newenham, a keen supporter of Wilkes and the American colonists, whose wordy commentaries proffered an idealized vision of the balanced Protestant constitution in which the liberties of the people were protected by responsive MPs. As a representative of the freeholders of county Dublin from 1776, Newenham demonstrated how an MP could reflect the interests of the electorate on national as well as local issues, but while his model of active representation corroborated radical Whig belief in the potential of a reformed electoral and representative system, and seemed to demonstrate how endangered liberties could be restored, few were tempted to follow his example.[91] Indeed, more

---

[87] See Thomas Bartlett, "The Townshend administration, 1767–72" in Bartlett and Hayton (eds), *Penal Era and Golden Age*, pp. 88–112.

[88] See James Kelly, *Edward Newenham, 1734–1814: Defender of the Protestant Constitution* (Dublin: Four Courts Press, 2004), p. 58 ff.

[89] Quoted in Kelly, *Poynings' Law*, p. 304.

[90] The commitment to "the freedom of the press" is exemplified by the observation of Lord Mornington in 1783 that "any invasion of the liberty of the press, while restrained within just bounds, would, in my apprehension, be detrimental to the liberty of the subject" (James Kelly (ed.), *Proceedings of the Irish House of Lords, 1771–1800* (Dublin: Irish Manuscripts Commission, 2008], vol. 1, p. 163).

[91] Kelly, *Sir Edward Newenham*, Chapter 4.

shared the conventional view, articulated by Charles Agar, the Archbishop of Cashel, who explicitly rejected Newenham's vision of a member of Parliament as a tribune of the people:

To contend that parliament was restricted, and bound to obey whatever popular opinion and clamour might dictate without doors, was abetting the revolutionary principle of the times; for no reflecting mind could conceive a case where the people after making their election were justified in controuling their legislators without implying a dissolution of all government. The right of election belonged to the people, but legislation, unfettered legislation, belonged to the parliament.[92]

Agar made this remark in 1800, when the political atmosphere had become still more confrontational, but his observation was no less pertinent in the 1770s. Indeed, based on the proceedings of the Irish Parliament in the years between Townshend's recall in 1772 and the outbreak of war in North America in 1775, it is apparent that the traditional caution that guided Irish peers and MPs when constitutional and electoral matters were at issue continued to act as a brake on their ability to press successfully for change.

Matters might have continued thus, but for the war of American independence, since it not only provided Irish Protestants with an inspiring example, but also enabled those of a reformist outlook to seize the political initiative. They were assisted certainly by the magnitude of the problems Britain experienced as a consequence of the war, and by the weak leadership provided in England by the prime minister, Lord North, and, in Ireland, by the lord lieutenant, the Earl of Buckinghamshire. This weakness was symbolized by the failure of the Irish administration to control the Volunteers – a civilian militia established to compensate for the depletion in the number of troops on the military establishment caused by their deployment overseas. As the epitome of the Whig ideal of the citizen soldier, the Volunteers engaged at the outset in the noncontroversial business of maintaining law and order, but when the Westminster Parliament dashed public expectations in 1778 by declining to agree to a generous liberalization of Ireland's right to trade they were quickly politicized. They took up and, using tactics such as nonimportation agreements borrowed from the American colonies, they vigorously agitated the various economic, constitutional, and legal restrictions that had long confined the liberties of the kingdom of Ireland.[93] Inevitably, there were some within the Protestant political nation who contended that this was a "most dangerous and improper time ... to excite dissention or discontent between the two countries," but the caution that had long discouraged a majority of Irish Protestants from pressing sensitive political issues momentarily eased, and the government was compelled to yield.[94] The concession in 1780 of what was known colloquially as "free trade" empowered Irish merchants to trade on the same terms as their English equivalents both

---

[92] Kelly (ed.), *Proceedings of the Irish House of Lords*, vol. 3, p. 476.
[93] James Kelly, "The politics of Volunteering, 1779–93," *Irish Sword*, 22 (2000), pp. 139–56.
[94] Kelly (ed.), *Proceedings of the Irish House of Lords*, vol. 1, p. 66.

within and without the empire, while the still more momentous concession of "legislative independence" in 1782 ensured the removal of the restrictions that had long corralled the kingdom's legislative authority. Specifically, it resulted in the repeal of the Declaratory Act, which restored the appellate jurisdiction to the House of Lords and precluded Westminster legislating for Ireland, and the amendment of Poynings' Law, as a result of which the Irish Privy Council was shorn formally of the entitlement to initiate, amend, and veto legislation, and the British Council of the right to amend and veto bills referred to it that arose with either House of the Irish Parliament. In addition, an annual mutiny act, a habeas corpus act, and the alteration of the terms on which judges held their commissions meant that Irish Protestants now possessed virtually the same rights and liberties as "free-born Englishmen."[95] They did not secure approval for a Bill of Rights in the tradition of that ratified at Westminster in 1689, but the kingdom of Ireland now possessed to all intents and purposes what Henry Flood, in 1782, stated was its entitlement – "a similar constitution with England."[96]

Because these landmark constitutional and commercial reforms coincided with the unprecedented level of freedom of expression permitted by the relaxation in state censorship that had taken place since the 1750s,[97] the liberties available to the Protestant subjects of Ireland were greater in the autumn of 1782 than they had been at any point in Irish history. The fact that the legislature deemed it appropriate at this moment to ease considerably the restrictions under which Roman Catholics lived, worked, and worshipped was also of significance, not least because Ireland in the 1780s exceeded England in its willingness to accommodate Catholic aspirations. However, the circumstances that made this concession possible were not to endure. Eighteenth-century Ireland remained fractured along denominational lines, and although there were some among the Protestant elite who at the time believed in the possibility of forging what Henry Grattan in 1782 termed an "Irish nation" that transcended confessional allegiance, they were a minority.[98] Indeed, they were unable other than momentarily to overcome the fundamentally sectarian divisions that shaped Irish society, for when the issue of broadening the base of the electoral and representative system to extend political liberty was agitated in 1783–4 by the same Volunteers who had spearheaded the campaigns for the reform of the commercial and constitutional relationships with Great Britain, the inherent sectarianism of the Irish ruling elite was soon in evidence. Many among their number had made it explicit in 1778 and in 1782, when major

---

[95] R. B. McDowell, *Ireland in the Age of Imperialism and Revolution, 1760–1801* (Oxford: Oxford University Press, 1979); James Kelly, *Henry Flood: Patriots and Politics in Eighteenth-Century Ireland* (Dublin: Four Courts Press, 1998), pp. 311–24.

[96] *The Parliamentary Register, or History of the Proceedings of the Parliament of Ireland* (17 vols, Dublin: Porter, Byrne and Porter, 1782–1801), vol. 1, pp. 388–9.

[97] Kelly, "Regulating print," pp. 165–6.

[98] See James Kelly, *Henry Grattan* (Dundalk: Dun Dealgan, 1993), pp. 3, 17; idem, "Interdenominational relations and religious toleration in late eighteenth-century Ireland," *Eighteenth-Century Ireland* 3 (1988), pp. 39–67.

measures of Catholic relief were being debated, that they were willing to permit Catholics every civil and religious right consistent with the maintenance intact of the Protestant Constitution. Their commitment to this position was underlined in 1783 and, again, in 1784, when differences on the question of enfranchising Catholics fatally divided the reform movement. This division reflected the deeply held conviction not only that the admission of Catholics to the constitution would compromise its Protestant character, but also that to do so was inherently dangerous because Catholic doctrine was incompatible with the liberties that were provided for by the Protestant Constitution.[99] As a result, the attempt in the mid-1780s to complement the reform of the Anglo-Irish connection with the internal reform of the political system was stillborn.

The defeat of reform signalled the end of the liberal moment spanning the late 1770s and early 1780s. Its failure, and the development a few years later, in response to a surge in agrarian discontent aimed at inhibiting the payment by the Catholic population of tithes to the clergy of the Church of Ireland, of an ideology of "Protestant ascendancy" fostered the reanimation of more traditional sectarian politics. For the advocates of "Protestant ascendancy," personal and sectional security as well as political and religious principles demanded the maintenance intact of the Protestant Constitution.[100] Because they conceived of Catholicism, for historical as well as religious reasons, as uniquely despotic and repressive, they did not believe it could ever be otherwise; what they failed to acknowledge also in the heady days of the 1780s, when Irish Protestants basked in the optimistic afterglow of legislative independence, was that they had reached the limit of the liberties achievable within the parameters of the existing political system.

CONTESTING LIBERTY, 1789–1800

It was not apparent in the immediate wake of the outbreak of the French Revolution, as the public struggled to come to terms with the implications of events in France, that the Whig language, which had long provided the vocabulary of political discourse in Ireland, had a rival. This lack of awareness can be attributed to the fact that it coincided with the brief invigoration of Irish patriotism, which had lost impetus and direction during the mid-1780s. In the aftermath of the constitutional crisis generated by the incapacitation of George III in the winter of 1788–9, the patriots formed a quasi-political party – the Whig Club, which sought to promote the agenda of patriotism. This effort was highlighted by the club's aim, which was "to preserve the constitution of the realms as settled by the Revolution in Great Britain and Ireland in 1688 and

[99] James Kelly, "Parliamentary reform in Irish politics, 1760–90" in David Dickson et al. (eds), *The United Irishmen* (Dublin; Lilliput Press, 1993), pp. 74–87.

[100] James Kelly, "The genesis of Protestant ascendancy: the Rightboy disturbances of the 1780s and their impact upon Protestant opinion" in O'Brien (ed.), *Parliament, Politics and People*, pp. 93–127.

re-established in Ireland in 1782."[101] To this end, the Whigs in the early 1790s resisted efforts by the Irish administration to augment its powers to deal with civil disorder on the grounds that it was nothing less than an attempt, Lord Portarlington explained in the House of Lords, to deprive the population of "the benefits" of the "free constitution" they had secured in 1782 by augmenting the patronage available to the Irish administration. More generally, the Whigs targeted the manner in which the administration utilized the extensive patronage at its disposal to reward its supporters and punish its critics as "corrupt" and "unconstitutional" for the simple reason that these tactics "must in the end totally destroy the balance of the constitution" by making Parliament answerable to the king's minister and "subversive of the liberties of the people."[102] In order to prevent such evils, the Whigs promoted place, pension, and responsibility bills, and contended that in their absence "we are exposed to many dangers against which the wisdom of England has fortified her constitution." They had the satisfaction of witnessing the admission of appropriate measures to the statute book, which eased their fears on this point, but it did not give them the political boost they desired. In an important pointer to the future, they were roundly criticized by the Irish administration, which accused them of seeking to "decide questions by clamour," and by committed reformers, who disapproved of their agenda as unacceptably elitist and disappointingly moderate.[103]

The latter perception came increasingly to prevail in popular circles as the example of the French Revolution encouraged a host of middle-class activists, Catholic, Protestant, and Presbyterian, to conclude that root and branch reform was possible, and that the inspiring example of France had more to offer them than, by comparison, the timorous tinkering favored by the Whigs. For these interests, the French vision of "*liberté*" had far greater resonance than the concept of English "liberty" to which the Whig Club explicitly appealed and the intrinsically, and increasingly, conservative vision articulated by the expanding ranks of defenders of the British political system in the 1790s. The potent linkage of *liberté* with *equalité*, when set beside the still more pregnant implications of religious toleration, also exposed the elitism of the rhetoric of Protestant "liberty" that had dominated discourse in Britain and Ireland since the late 1680s. The effect of this exposure was reinforced, moreover, by the appropriation by political radicals of the Lockean concepts of consent and "fair and equal representation," manifested in the observation in the *Northern Star* newspaper in March 1792 that "there can be no security for liberty in any country that is not fairly represented."[104] The United Irishmen made this point still more emphatically when, having promulgated the ideal of "a people united in the fellowship of freedom" in a circular letter in December 1791, they

---

[101] Kelly (ed.), *Proceedings of the Irish House of Lords*, vol. 2, p. 228.
[102] Kelly (ed.), *Proceedings of the Irish House of Lords*, vol. 2, pp. 104, 154–5, 1790.
[103] Ibid., vol. 2, 104, 192.
[104] Nancy Curtin, *The United Irishmen: Popular Politics in Ulster and Dublin, 1791–1798* (Oxford: Oxford University Press, 1994), p. 15; *Northern Star*, 10 Mar. 1792.

explicitly identified this vision with "a parliament the express image of the people, [and] ... civil, political and religious liberty."[105]

Given the entrenched resistance to parliamentary reform among the political elite in Ireland, it was unsurprising that the United Irishmen and other reform-minded interests looked enviously to revolutionary France. Reified in propaganda as the "temple of universal liberty," the proponents of reform were stimulated by its example to believe that they could achieve the Lockean vision of their most interesting propagandist, William Drennan, which, had it been implemented, would have given Ireland one of the more inclusive representative systems in Europe.[106] This vision is noteworthy because the interest in events in France shown by political activists was replicated by much of the politicized population, for whom the "tree of liberty" became a potent symbol of hope. Describing two remote parishes in county Cork in the 1790s, Roger O'Connor, a well-connected United Irishman, observed that the public reading of newspaper reports of "the French debates" had transformed the population into "politicians," who "talked of liberty and equality [and] appointed a day to plant the tree of liberty."[107] It was thus easy for the United Irishmen, who were skilled and innovative users of print, to promote their argument that true liberty demanded that the representative system be reconstructed on fair and equitable terms.[108] Indeed, the United Irishmen successfully cultivated the impression among the population at large that they were the true evangelicals of liberty and that their opponents were a despotic junto committed to preserving an elitist system that perpetuated the politics of self-interest and elite privilege. This point is well illustrated by the card published to promote the memory of William Orr, a United Irishman from county Down, who was executed in 1797 for attempting to suborn members of the military; held up by radicals as a victim of "British tyranny," he had, they maintained, made the ultimate "sacrifice" in the cause of "liberty."[109]

Paradoxically, the opponents of the revolution in Ireland also appealed to the rhetoric of liberty, only in their case in support of the political status quo. Guided by the traditional Whig idealization of a constitution of Crown, lords, and commons, and the conviction that mass participation in politics was a recipe for chaos, they claimed that the democratic thrust of the French Revolution was fundamentally incompatible with the balanced system of government epitomized by the limited monarchy brought into being by

---

[105] Curtin, *The United Irishmen*, p. 21, citing a "Circular letter from the Society of United Irishmen of Dublin," 30 Dec. 1791.

[106] Curtin, *The United Irishmen*, pp. 26, 36.

[107] Cited in Dickson, *Old world colony*, p. 459.

[108] James Kelly, "Political print, 1700–1800" in Raymond Gillespie and Andrew Hadfield (eds), *A History of the Book in Ireland, 1550–1800*, volume iii (Oxford: Oxford University Press, 2005), pp. 215–33; Curtin, *The United Irishmen*, pp. 174–201; Kevin Whelan, *The Tree of Liberty* (Cork: Cork University Press, 1996), pp. 65–77.

[109] Memorial card to William Orr, 1797 (National Archives of Ireland, Rebellion Papers, 620/36/36). It is reproduced in Dickson, *Old World Colony*, p. 466.

the Glorious Revolution. Memorably aspersed by one of their number as "demonarchy,"[110] the revolution was routinely condemned as the epitome of "anarchy and democracy" that sought to obliterate "all distinctions" and to empower "a few of the rabble to dictate to all the property of the nation," and portrayed as a dangerous experiment by "desperate and designing enthusiasts," who had no regard for what one moderate voice termed "the happiness of the people, which is, or ought to be, the ultimate end of all government."[111] Such sentiments were troubling enough when the revolution was contained within French frontiers, but once the revolutionaries had taken on themselves to disseminate, what the Earl of Westmeath in January 1793 termed "the flagitious effects of their abominable and impracticable doctrines," it posed a direct challenge to the order that the political elite in Ireland was committed to uphold. In an attempt to rally support behind the Crown, Westmeath pointedly called on "all who prefer loyalty to rebellion, religion to atheism, industry to idleness and real liberty to the most abject slavery that ever vilified or disgraced mankind to unite in the most ardent effusions of loyalty" to George III.[112] Thus alerted to the options, conservatives found it easy once conflict commenced in February 1793, not only to portray the war as "just and necessary," but also to depict it as a struggle for "the preservation of the constitution of these kingdoms" and for "your liberty, property and religion."[113] Clubs and associations along the lines of those established by John Reeves in England "for preserving liberty and property against republicans and levellers," devoted to the preservation of "real liberty" and the security of "our excellent constitution" against "subversion," proliferated.[114] Inevitably, their rhetoric grew shriller as the war intensified. By 1794, *liberté* was being dismissed as "that demon of discord" and a mask for French tyranny, while in 1795 France was portrayed in the speech from the throne opening Parliament as posing a threat to European civilization, as well as to the values British and Irish Protestants extolled:

It threatens nothing less than the entire subversion of the liberty and independence of every state in Europe. An enemy of them all, it is actuated with a peculiar animosity against these kingdoms, not only as the natural protection of the balance of power in Europe, but also, because, by the possession of a legal, humane and rational freedom, we seem to reproach that false and spurious liberty, which, in reality, is an ignominious servitude, tending to extinguish all good arts to generate nothing but impiety, crime, disorder and ferocious manners, and to end in wretchedness and general desolation.[115]

---

[110] Richard Musgrave, *A Letter on the Present Situation of Public Affairs* (London, 1794). The word, which is an invention, is a compound of "democracy" and "anarchy."

[111] "Common Sense to the late Volunteers of Ireland in opposition to the nonsense and sedition of the Society of United Irishmen," *Freeman's Journal*, 18 Dec, 1792; "To the Dublin Society of United Irishmen," *Freeman's Journal*, 20 Dec. 1792. See also *Freeman's Journal*, 11 July 1793.

[112] Kelly (ed.), *Proceedings of the House of Lords*, vol. 2, p. 299.

[113] Ibid., vol. 2, pp. 329, 330.

[114] *Freeman's Journal*, 15, 27 Dec. 1792, 3 Jan. 1793; Alan Blackstock, *Loyalism in Ireland, 1789–1829* (Woodbridge: Boydell Press, 2007).

[115] *Freeman's Journal*, 5 Apr. 1794; Kelly (ed.), *Proceedings of the House of Lords*, vol. 2, p. 533.

Hostile characterizations of this ilk were easily embraced because of the established tradition of Francophobia within the political elite.[116] But it is still more significant that the intensity of feeling that informed such comment was fueled by genuine antipathy to "the wild theories" that underpinned the revolution: "French policy is the destruction of all order and rank in society, the promise of unlimited liberty to the mob," one commentator observed disdainfully.[117] Such perceptions were reinforced by the contention that since democracy and anarchy were identifiable, a system of government based on numbers rather than property was not only incompatible with Britain's limited monarchy, but also lacked the balance that was one of the British Constitution's great strengths. The Lord Chancellor, Lord Clare, made the point clearly in 1797, when he observed, à propos of the United Irishmen's plan of reform, that:

By representing population alone, without respect for property, the object was to elect a democratic House of Commons, which would be too strong for the correction of the other branches of the constitution, and in the monstrous formation of the third estate, seal the destruction of the other two.[118]

Others were no less perturbed by the destructive implications of "French principles" for "our government, our morals, our religion, and our lives"[119] and overly prone, as a consequence, to applaud the virtues of their own constitution, which was described, in terms redolent of earlier decades and without a murmur of dissent, in the House of Lords on the eve of the 1798 Rebellion, as simply "the best constitution that ever blessed a free and happy people."[120]

This view was widely endorsed across the British Isles, but it possessed a particular significance in Ireland because the demand for constitutional and political change raised the critical issue of easing the denominational barriers that excluded Catholics from participating in the political process. The United Irishmen accepted the necessity of such action once Wolfe Tone had produced his influential *Argument on Behalf of the Catholics of Ireland*, but many still entertained severe reservations, on the traditional, but still compelling, grounds that the extension to Catholics of political liberties was intrinsically incompatible with the Protestant Constitution brought into being by the Glorious Revolution. Thus when, in 1793, the British government judged it propitious to enfranchise Catholics, the Lord Chancellor, Lord FitzGibbon, made clear his view that it was highly ill-advised because it must endanger both "our connexion with Great Britain and the maintenance of a protestant establishment in Ireland" upon which the rights and liberties of Protestants in Ireland depended. FitzGibbon's contention that history demonstrated both that

---

[116] Gerard O'Brien, "Francophobia in later eighteenth century Ireland" in David Dickson and Hugh Gough (eds), *The French Revolution* (Dublin: Irish Academic Press, 1991), pp. 40–51.

[117] *Freeman's Journal*, 15 July 1794.

[118] Kelly (ed.), *Proceedings of the Irish House of Lords*, vol. 3, 119.

[119] Ibid., vol. 3, p. 118.

[120] Ibid., vol. 3, p. 293.

Catholic doctrines were fundamentally incompatible with Protestant liberties and that Protestants could not safely admit Catholics to political power because they were committed to the extirpation of Protestants constituted a powerful argument in support of the status quo:

The page of history does not furnish a single instance in which Protestants and Papists have agreed in exercising the political powers of the same state; and so long as the preposterous claims of the court of Rome to universal spiritual dominion over the Christian world shall be maintained, it is utterly impossible that any man who admits them to exercise the legislative powers of a Protestant state with temper and justice.[121]

FitzGibbon, inevitably, supported his conclusion that Protestants could expect only "persecution and proscription" at the hands of Catholics by reference to the much traversed history of anti-Protestant atrocity. But he also invoked the claim, frequently made by Catholic champions, that their doctrines were unchanging, to warn that there must soon be a repeat of the horrors of the winter of 1641–2 in Ireland if Protestants did not take appropriate steps to protect their constitution in church and state and resist all demands for change that would in any way weaken it.

This was an alarmist analysis, but it struck a chord with Irish Protestants, who needed little persuasion that there was a direct connection between religious and political systems. As articulated by the lord chief justice of the Court of Common Pleas, Lord Clonmell, in 1793, Presbyterianism could be equated with republicanism, Catholicism with "a despotic monarchy," and Protestants with a "limited monarch and universal freedom." Few were quite so categorical, but the implication that "the best rights of the people" could only be assured within the existing Protestant constitution was inescapable.[122]

It was a short step from this position to the conclusion of the Earl of Westmeath that the authorities were fully entitled to embrace what he euphemistically termed a "manly and decided conduct" to defend the constitution against its enemies. Few of a conservative disposition had any difficulty legitimating such tactics when, in the mid-1790s, the United Irishmen responded to the denial by the British and Irish authorities of their efforts to reform the electoral and representative system by adopting a revolutionary strategy. The authorities had previously demonstrated a readiness to resort to such tactics in the 1780s, when the challenge was less formidable, and it is hardly surprising as a result that the response in the 1790s was more forceful, or that it resulted in the erosion of liberties that had been painstakingly acquired. One of the first casualties was the liberty of the press; this liberty had been weakened by a number of prosecutions in the 1780s that had forced the closure of a number of radical newspapers; in the 1790s the authorities were still more assertive; they sought initially to browbeat printers and newspaper proprietors into compliance by imposing record fines and lengthy jail sentences, and when these measures

---

[121] Ibid., vol. 2, p. 360.
[122] Ibid., vol. 2, 420–1, 469.

proved insufficient to cow their most radical critics they turned a blind eye on the illegal destruction of printing presses by the forces of the Crown before empowering grand juries to seize and destroy presses they deemed seditious.[123] Parallel with these actions, the rights of the subject were curtailed by the suspension in 1796 of habeas corpus,[124] and by the imposition of military law, which, as well as providing for the suspension of trial by jury, allowed for the forcible billeting of the army on the population in the cause of a policy of forcible disarmament. Justified on the grounds that it was the only practical way to combat the threat of mass insurgency, it permitted significant human rights abuses as well as the partisan administration of justice. It was accentuated, moreover, by the encouragement of loyal Protestants to join the Orange Society, a para-military force whose activities served both to weaken insurgency in certain areas while encouraging it in others.[125]

There were, to be sure, a number of voices in both houses of Parliament who regarded the erosion of liberties with visible dismay. They shared the reservations of the liberal peer, Lord Moira, who observed in February 1798 that he would not make "the existence of a Society of United Irishmen, however culpable or misled they may be, a pretext for the suspension of civil government and for laying the country prostrate under a military force. Tyranny could only reason thus."[126] However, such voices were actively decried by a majority, which was content, in the face of an accumulating tide of atrocity, to justify extraordinary measures in order "to check the licentiousness of the times."[127] Lord Blayney expressed this sentiment clearly; when "its existence is not only threatened, but its overthrow [is] presumed upon," government was morally obliged to take whatever steps were required to protect and to preserve the constitution, he observed baldly in February 1798.[128]

This was a slippery slope, of course, and it is clear that it did result in the perpetration by the forces of the state and their para-military allies of abuses before and atrocities during the rebellion. Moreover, sanctions were seldom forthcoming, as Parliament ratified indemnity acts with little hesitation. This action was consistent with the position articulated by Lord Blayney, and the comparable justification provided by Lord Glenworth that the draconian Insurrection Act was necessary "to preserve the very {insert – word omitted} essence of th[e] constitution." It also gave legitimacy to the essentially spurious argument, frequently resorted to by those in positions of influence, that the excesses

---

[123] Kelly, "Regulating print," pp. 169–72.

[124] Significantly, this was recommended in 1794 on the grounds that "the liberty of every individual" was subservient to "the safety of the state" (*Freeman's Journal*, 31 May 1794).

[125] See Nancy Curtin, "The magistracy and counter-revolution in Ulster 1795–98" in Jim Smyth (ed.), *Revolution, Counter-Revolution and Union: Ireland in the 1790s* (Cambridge: Cambridge University Press, 2000), pp. 39–54; R. B. McDowell, *Ireland in the Age of Imperialism and Revolution*, pp. 519–93.

[126] *Speech of Lord Moira in the Irish House of Lords, 19 Feb. 1798* (Dublin, 1798).

[127] Kelly (ed.), *Proceedings of the Irish House of Lords*, vol. 3, p. 13.

[128] Ibid., vol. 3, p. 266.

attributable to the forces of the state were justified by the equally poor record of insurgency.[129] In truth, little justification was required once rebellion broke out in the summer of 1798; the fact that it featured what was interpreted as an attempt to target Protestants for assassination was sufficient to ensure that there were many willing and ready to defend both the necessity and the legitimacy of the hard-line security measures that were taken before, during, and after the rebellion.

The 1798 Rebellion also paved the way for the acceptance of the argument, articulated by Lord Clare in the decisive debate in the House of Lords on February 10, 1800, that "the only solid and lasting foundation of peace and security for their [Protestant] religion, laws, liberty and prosperity [lay in] an entire and perfect union with England."[130] The former solicitor general, Lord Carleton, went further; speaking in the same debate, he maintained that a legislative union offered a solution to the conundrum of how to accommodate the conflicting demands of Catholics and Protestants:

To the Catholicks, union promises a security for permanent religious toleration, and a chance of extension of temporal rights and privileges. To the Protestants, guaranteed and lasting pre-eminence of their religion, with a preference, though not an exclusive claim to influence and power. To both, protection of the civil liberty, their persons, their property, and the fostering interposition of an imperial legislature to heal their differences, calm their animosities, and by a wise, systematic, and steady conduct, to prevent the renewal of calamities which must again occur, if those causes which heretofore occasioned them are suffered to exist.[131]

It is apparent from this statement that Carleton perceived an Anglo-Irish union as an escape from the contention and bitterness that, in the aftermath of the rebellion, were widely seen as the most debilitating legacy of the 1790s. It is also apparent that Carleton was seriously misreading men and their motives if he believed that a legislative union would restore inter-communal harmony since he evidently envisaged that Catholics would accept a situation in which they continued to possess fewer rights and liberties than Protestants. This was not to be, of course, with the result that the Act of Union did not, as Lord Kilwarden confidently forecast, put an end to "the contests for power and superiority" that were the main obstacles he identified in the way of the restoration of "civil society," but merely bought a brief respite as both sides adjusted to the new political context.[132]

---

[129] Ibid., vol. 3, p. 23.
[130] *The Speech of the Right Hon. John, Earl of Clare, Lord High Chancellor of Ireland in the House of Lords ... on Monday, February 10, 1800* (Dublin, 1800).
[131] *The Speech of the Right Hon. Lord Viscount Carleton, Lord Chief Justice of the Court of Common Pleas in the House of Lords of Ireland on Monday, the 10th of February, 1800* (Dublin, 1800), pp. 26–7.
[132] *The Speech of the Right Hon. Arthur, Lord Kilwarden, Lord Chief Justice of the King's Bench ... as Delivered in the House of Lords of Ireland on Monday, the 10th of February, 1800* (Dublin, 1800), p. 8.

Be that as it may, the abolition of the Irish Parliament was a seismic event in Irish history as well as in Anglo-Irish relations, so much so that it reverberates to this day. It was no less momentous at the time, because it brought about the abolition of the institution that was both the focus and the epitome of the efforts of the Protestant nation in the seventeenth and eighteenth centuries to obtain the constitutional and civil liberties to which it believed it was entitled, and the visible expression of the kingdom's aspiration to possess the right to make its own laws free from interference. In voting for its abolition, Irish Protestants not only demonstrated the depth of their unease in the aftermath of the 1798 Rebellion, but also that when obliged to choose between a society in which political and civil liberties would be available to all (which in practice meant admitting Catholics to power) or confining access to liberty to Protestants, they opted for the latter. In so doing, they manifested their continuing adherence to a position their forbears had taken at the beginning of the century, and the strength of their conviction that the principles of liberty enshrined in the Glorious Revolution were such as only Protestants were equipped to enjoy.

CONCLUSION

The eighteenth century concluded in Ireland with two antipathetic power blocs, each claiming that they were guided in their political aspirations by a desire to realize a political vision at the center of which was liberty. On the one side were those (precluded access to the liberties secured by the Glorious Revolution) who had embraced the rhetoric of liberty and equality as defined and described by the French Revolution in the 1790s, who were committed to broadening the representative base so they could gain access to the political process. Indeed, transmogrified in the 1820s into a mass Catholic movement, they were enabled through public and political pressure to lay the foundation of modern democratic politics in Ireland.[133] They were opposed in this attempt, as they had been in their previous efforts to be allowed access to the political process, by a Protestant interest, whose definition of liberty was forged in the crucible of the struggle that had taken place between the king and Parliament in the seventeenth century and that bore the imprint of the still older and more bitter religious battles engendered by the Reformation. They believed that Catholics could not be admitted to participate in the political process because they adhered to views, political as well as religious, that were fundamentally incompatible with Protestantism and liberty as they defined it. This conviction shaped Irish Protestantism as it contrived in the course of the early and mid-eighteenth century to achieve, and in the late eighteenth century to protect its deeply held commitment to a tradition of liberty. It is a measure of the conviction with which such opinions were held that the loss of the ideological battle over

---

[133] Fergus O'Farrell, *Catholic Emancipation: Daniel O'Connell and the Birth of Irish Democracy 1820–30* (Dublin: Gill and Macmillan, 1985).

Catholic empowerment symbolized by the concession of Catholic emancipation in 1829 did not lessen the conviction, expressed as late as 1868, that the maintenance of "our Protestant institutions" is the "foundation and safeguards of the liberty we possess."[134] By then it was already apparent that the combination of mass nationalism, resurgent Roman Catholicism, and demography meant that the preservation of Protestant privileges could not be long sustained. Yet even at the height of the Penal Laws, when it would have been a *non sequitor* to mention Catholics and "liberty" in the same sentence, there were some who perceived that it was inherently implausible to define the access to political rights on denominational grounds. Writing in 1713, on the occasion of the publication of a new edition of Sir John Temple's influential account of the 1641 Rebellion, an anonymous observer noted simply that the Irish had the same entitlement to "recover their liberty from the English as ... the Indians theirs from the Spaniards."[135] Few outside the Catholic communion could have thought in those terms then, and most Irish Protestants would have been appalled by the very thought. Yet the fact that the observation was offered constitutes a useful reminder that those who seek liberty for themselves can equally readily justify their refusal to others.

This is hardly an unexpected conclusion. It was thus across the British empire throughout its long history, and it can be traced in Ireland from the intervention of the Anglo-Normans in the twelfth century. Moreover, it is striking, for all the rhetoric and ink devoted to demonstrating that the English (later British) imperial enterprise was about transmitting liberty, just how reluctantly and conditionally it was extended. This is particularly well manifested in the Irish case by the constraints placed on the authority of the Irish Parliament to make law and by the unwillingness to extend civil rights like habeas corpus. It is for this reason that, it can be argued, responsibility for transmitting the principles and institutions of liberty to Ireland rests more with those Englishmen who settled in Ireland rather than with their political masters in England. This is not to suggest that they were invariably resistant; the introduction of the common law was at royal behest; the establishment of an Irish Parliament was also a monarchical initiative, and the Anglicization of the country economically, culturally, and religiously that was pursued in the sixteenth and seventeenth centuries was also promoted from the center. However, a host of other civil, religious, and economic liberties had to be extracted and, as instanced by the example of the right to make law, which dominated political discourse in the eighteenth century, were frequently only secured after a determined effort.

To be sure, the settlers in Ireland, no more than the settlers elsewhere in the British empire, were still less disposed to confer liberty on those they had displaced. To some extent, this was a natural outcome of the fact that they were the beneficiaries of conquest, and the appropriation of the land of the country, and this foundation naturally left a legacy of suspicion and animosity

---

[134] Lord Oranmore to 4th Earl of Rosse, 25 Aug. 1868 (Birr Castle, Rosse papers).
[135] National Library of Scotland, Fleming of Wigtown papers, Ms 20773 ff. 18–9.

that cautioned against, when it did not simply make such actions impossible. It was certainly made less likely in Ireland because of the enduring character of confessional antipathy, and it is a measure of the depth and pervasiveness of religious animosity that it vitiated, when it did not simply neutralize, the otherwise enduring commitment of Irish Protestants to the principles and institutions of British liberty. Yet, it is noteworthy that these principles and institutions were perceived as having a pertinence and value that extended beyond the settlers, for once the Catholic interest lost faith in the possibilities of a Stuart succession and the absolutist monarchy with which they were identified, they not only came to terms with British liberty but also came to embrace many of its key elements. This process was interrupted for a generation, arguably, by the allure of French *liberté*, but once it was apparent that this allure promised more that it could deliver, and the revolutionaries were defeated in the major ideological struggle that racked Europe between 1793 and 1815, the way was clear for the fuller embrace of British liberties within the constitutional framework created by the Anglo-Irish union. As a consequence, when Irish nationalism finally achieved autonomy for the island of Ireland at the beginning of the twentieth century, it was deemed congenial to locate the governmental, administrative, and legal systems that would apply in the new state within a tradition that was intrinsically British. The process whereby this had come about was prolonged and complex. Indeed, it can ultimately be traced back to the twelfth century, but the similarities of the Irish and British traditions of law and government, and the comparability of the civil and political rights enjoyed in both jurisdictions today, bear witness to the successful transmission to Ireland of British ideas of liberty. More specifically, the fact that the Irish Constitution provides for a bi-cameral legislature that possesses enough echoes of its more exclusive eighteenth-century predecessor suggests also that the eighteenth century's preoccupation with the principle and practice of liberty has also had an enduring legacy.

4

Liberty and Modernity

The American Revolution and the Making of Parliament's Imperial History

Eliga H. Gould

To Britons during the three centuries covered by this volume, Parliament was the great palladium of British liberty. Although rhetoric did not always match reality, the House of Commons served as the final bastion of representative government in both England and (after 1707) Scotland, the Lords and Commons together guaranteed the personal and property rights of both rich and poor, and Parliament was a mainstay of the English common law. Within Britain's settler empire, by contrast, Parliament's history as a guarantor of liberty was more ambiguous. As Victorian imperialists never tired of noting, libertarian reforms such as Catholic emancipation in Ireland, the suppression of the African slave trade, and, eventually, the abolition of slavery in the West Indies all would have been impossible without forceful intervention from Westminster. Yet these same writers recognized that the theoretically unlimited authority that Parliament claimed over the British empire as a whole was potentially inimical to British liberty as it was practiced in the colonies of settlement. In the words of the nineteenth-century English historian F. W. Maitland, Parliament's imperial sovereignty was boundless in theory but limited in practice: Although free to govern the empire as they saw fit, members of Parliament "habitually" refrained "from making laws of a certain class and [had to] suspect that if [they] made such laws they would not be obeyed."[1]

For the most part, historians have taken the first half of Maitland's formulation as the defining feature of Parliament's imperial authority. In many ways, though, Maitland's qualification about limits is more revealing. In particular, his words remind us of three basic principles that informed the relationship between liberty and sovereignty throughout the settler empire's 300-year history. First, for as long as the British government was responsible for governing colonies of settlement, Parliament had not one history but two, with its history

---

[1] F. W. Maitland, *The Constitutional History of England*, ed. H. A. L. Fisher (Cambridge: Cambridge University Press, 1963; orig. pub., 1908), p. 339.

as an imperial sovereign differing in important respects from its history as a national sovereign in Britain. Second, the main difference between these two histories was that in the colonies of settlement – including the colonies that became the United States – British settlers assumed that their own assemblies fulfilled the same legislative functions in a provincial setting that Parliament did in Britain, and most viewed the assemblies, not Parliament, as the first line of defense for their own rights and privileges. Finally, although not as well developed as its metropolitan history, Parliament's history as an imperial sovereign was sufficiently well known in Maitland's day to shield the settler empire, in all but the most extraordinary moments, from the unlimited powers that Britons took to be an indispensable part of Parliament's role as a guarantor of liberty in Britain. From the standpoint of constitutional theory, Parliament's sovereignty was unlimited – even by its own enactments – and reached into the most distant corners of the British empire. In terms of Westminster's actual powers, history showed that reality was more complex.

If these points appear less obvious today than they did to the Victorians, that is probably because the historical consciousness that informed Maitland's thinking was not much older than the crisis that preceded the American Revolution. There was, to be sure, a general awareness throughout the seventeenth and eighteenth centuries that English settlers in the colonies carried all the rights of Englishmen with them, including the right to be governed by assemblies in which they were directly represented. In the years before the revolution, some colonists also posited the existence of an "imperial constitution," one that could be invoked to resist metropolitan interventions such as the Navigation Laws that Parliament first enacted during the 1650s, the Declaratory Act that affirmed Parliament's supremacy over Ireland in 1721, and the Sugar Act of 1733, which created an early precedent for parliamentary taxation.[2] Yet insofar as the settler empire had a constitutional history before the American Revolution, that history was largely a history of provincial confrontations with the Crown. On the eve of the Stamp Act crisis, most British politicians seem to have assumed that imposing parliamentary taxes on the king's American subjects would be an "unexceptional" thing to do, as the *London Chronicle* insisted in 1765.[3] Nor, according to John Adams, was the grasp of history in America much better. "We have been afraid to think," wrote Adams of the colonists' ignorance of their rights vis-à-vis the British Parliament in 1765. "We have felt a reluctance to examin[e] into the grounds of our privileges, and the extent in which we have an indisputable right to demand them, against all the power and authority on earth."[4]

[2] Jack P. Greene, *Peripheries and Center: Constitutional Development in the Extended Polities of the British Empire and the United States, 1607–1788* (Athens: University of Georgia Press, 1987), p. ix.

[3] Eliga H. Gould, *The Persistence of Empire: British Political Culture in the Age of the American Revolution* (Chapel Hill: University of North Carolina Press, 2000), p. 110.

[4] John Adams, *A Dissertation on the Canon and Feudal Law* (1765), in C. Bradley Thompson, ed., *The Revolutionary Writings of John Adams* (Indianapolis: Liberty Fund, 2000), p. 30.

For the British colonies that became the United States, the knowledge of imperial history that Adams regarded as vital to preserving British liberty within the settler empire ceased to matter once Congress declared independence in 1776. In metropolitan Britain and the remaining colonies of settlement, however, the American Revolution served as a crucial moment of historical awareness, one that left people across the political spectrum with a much clearer sense of how far and in what ways Parliament could (and could not) legislate for British subjects elsewhere in the empire. Because the revolution began in response to Parliament's attempt to fund the 10,000 regulars that remained in North America at the end of the Seven Years' War, this new sense of history was partly about the military and fiscal bureaucracies that had sustained Parliament's metropolitan sovereignty since the Glorious Revolution and whether those institutions should (or could) play a comparable role in extending Parliament's authority over the wider empire. But the American Revolution also forced the British to contemplate, practically for the first time in their history, the difficult question of whether there existed any constitutional limits to the imperial authority of the British Crown and Parliament. For this reason alone, the revolution marked a beginning of sorts in the history of the British empire, albeit a beginning substantially different from the one that the revolution inaugurated for the British colonies that became the United States.

Of the principles that underlay their "matchless constitution," probably none mattered more to the British than the doctrine of parliamentary sovereignty. In the oft-quoted words of Blackstone's *Commentaries on the Laws of England* (1765–69), Parliament's authority was "transcendent and absolute," so much so that it could not be "confined ... within any bounds." Here, wrote Blackstone, was where the constitution entrusted "that absolute despotic power, which must in all governments reside somewhere."[5] As the settlement that accompanied the Glorious Revolution of 1689 showed, this "despotic power" was so absolute that Parliament had the final say in determining the rights and privileges of the other two pillars of the British constitution, the Church of England and the British Crown. Although neither was quite as subservient to Parliament's wishes as Blackstone's words suggested, George I and his heirs could not have occupied the British throne during the eighteenth and nineteenth centuries without Parliament's decision in the Act of Settlement (1701) to settle the Crown on the German House of Hanover, nor would the religious liberties of their British subjects have been as secure without parliamentary enactments such as the Toleration Act of 1689, which abolished the Anglican monopoly on public worship in England, and Westminster's various interventions – despite clauses to the contrary in the Anglo-Scottish Treaty of Union (1707) – in the internal affairs of the Church of Scotland. As its history suggested, Britain was a parliamentary monarchy in every sense of the phrase, affording its people both

[5] William Blackstone, *Commentaries on the Laws of England*, ed. Stanley N. Katz, 4 vols. (Chicago: University of Chicago Press, 1979; orig. pub., 1765–1769), vol. I, p. 156.

the political liberty to participate in local and national politics and the civil liberty to conduct their affairs without fear of unjust interference.

Given the unlimited nature of its authority in Britain, British writers in the decades before the American Revolution generally assumed that Parliament had the same powers over the rest of the empire, including Ireland, the East India Company, and the American colonies. As Blackstone himself conceded, however, this authority was occasional and extraordinary, which meant that a colony had to be "particularly named" in an act of Parliament for the act to be legally binding on its inhabitants.[6] To encourage and support what Blackstone called the "maritime state," Parliament had periodically legislated for the colonies since the Restoration of Charles II in 1660, confining the transportation of "enumerated" colonial goods to British ships, authorizing the Crown to establish vice-admiralty courts in colonial ports, and regulating what the Royal Navy could (and could not) do in American waters. Yet the purpose of this legislation was to clarify and regulate the power of the Crown, not to take a direct role in colonial governance.[7] Speaking of the administration of Britain's "distant plantations in America," Blackstone made almost no mention of Parliament, writing instead that each colony had a governor who acted as the king's "representative or deputy," local "courts of justice" for which the appeal lay to the king in council, and an assembly that, with the king's consent, could "make laws suited to [its] own emergencies."[8] Although the Crown could not fulfill any of these functions in ways of which Parliament did not approve, responsibility for most matters of colonial governance was in the hands of the king and the Privy Council.

Because Parliament's involvement in colonial affairs was so minimal before the 1760s, the system that Blackstone described left British Americans free to view the consolidation of parliamentary sovereignty in Britain as a bulwark of their own political and civil liberties. As an indication of the prevalence of such attitudes, colonial leaders often claimed the same rights and privileges for assemblies in the colonies as those that the House of Commons possessed in Britain. "In the Constitution of the Government of New York," wrote Cadwallader Colden during the 1740s, the governor, council, and assembly had the same powers as "the King, Lords and Commons" in England. In a report to the Board of Trade in 1726, Sir William Keith, governor of Pennsylvania, made the same observation, noting that many colonial politicians believed – mistakenly, in Keith's view – that "they represented the King, Lords and Commons of Great Britain within their little districts."[9] As all but the most

---

[6] Ibid., vol. I, 100–102, 105.

[7] Ibid., vol. I, 405–409.

[8] Ibid., vol. I, 105.

[9] Sir William Keith, "A Short Discourse on the Present State of the Colonies in America" (1726), and Cadwallader Colden, "Observations on the Balance of Power in Government" (c. 1744), both in A. F. Madden and D. K. Fieldhouse, eds., *Select Documents on the Constitutional History of the British Empire and Commonwealth*, 8 vols. (Westport, CT: Greenwood Press, 1985–2000), vol. II, pp. 275, 277.

ardent proponents of this imperial constitution admitted, there were important differences between would-be parliaments in the colonies and the British Parliament at Westminster. New York's "Council and General Assembly," wrote Colden, resembled their metropolitan counterparts only insofar as "the very great odds in [their] Circumstances will admit."[10] If parallels between Parliament and the assemblies were inexact, however, the notion that such parallels existed commanded broad support in America. With few exceptions, British governors who wished to succeed in the colonies had to master the art of cultivating provincial legislators, while the officials who staffed customhouses and colonial vice-admiralty courts soon learned that real power in British America resided in the assemblies, not the Board of Trade or Parliament. To claim that Britons in America were entitled to the same legislative rights as their fellow subjects in Britain was, in many ways, to describe how the administration of the British empire actually worked.

The result was an imperial constitution in which the assemblies had much of the responsibility for colonial governance. In matters of religion, the British government made clear that it expected the colonies to extend the same civil liberties to Protestants in America that Protestants enjoyed in Britain, yet the Toleration Act only applied to Protestants in England, which meant that even in Congregational New England, where Anglicans were a small and, in places, a beleaguered minority, colonial assemblies had the final say in deciding how much freedom to give dissenters living under their jurisdiction.[11] Although the right to own slaves was widely viewed as an affront to civil liberty as it was understood in England, Parliament took a similarly hands-off approach to the slaveholders who dominated assemblies in the West Indies and the southern colonies on the North American mainland. According to the brutal codes that helped entrench slavery from the late seventeenth century onward, colonial masters had broad and, in some circumstances, unlimited rights over their bondsmen and -women, all of which were anathema to metropolitan norms and customs. As Chief Justice Mansfield wrote in deciding the celebrated *Somerset* case case in 1772, slavery was "odious" and could only be supported by "positive law," which England lacked, yet Mansfield readily conceded that chattel servitude was "authorized by the laws and opinions of Virginia and Jamaica."[12]

If anything, the autonomy of Britain's colonies was even more conspicuous in areas that directly affected Britain's standing in Europe, including, significantly, war and defense. Despite the Royal Navy's expanding presence in American waters from the late seventeenth century onward, each colony

---

[10] Ibid., 277.
[11] Carl Bridenbaugh, *Mitre and Sceptre: Transatlantic Faiths, Ideas, Personalities, and Politics, 1689–1775* (New York: Oxford University Press, 1962), pp. 65, 123, 131–132; Patricia U. Bonomi, *Under the Cope of Heaven: Religion, Society, and Politics in Colonial America* (New York: Oxford University Press, 1986), pp. 156, 162, 182–183.
[12] *Somerset v. Stewart*, 20 How. St. Tr. 1 (1772). See also Eliga H. Gould, "Zones of Law, Zones of Violence: The Legal Geography of the British Atlantic, circa 1772," *William and Mary Quarterly*, 3rd ser., 60 (2003): 471–510.

retained its own military capacity, with the power to embody the militia, the power to raise and dispatch provincial soldiers, and the power to commission private ships of war. In some colonies – notably Quaker-dominated Pennsylvania – this autonomy gave Americans the freedom *not* to take part in Britain's struggles with its European rivals. In other colonies, Americans did participate, but on their own terms. During the eighteenth-century wars with France and Spain, British American privateers had a well-deserved reputation for smuggling and piracy while also playing a key role in securing Britain's naval supremacy over its rivals in the West Indies. Despite a similar record of independence and, at times, insubordination, provincial soldiers from New England performed equally vital services in the North Atlantic, seizing the French citadel at Louisbourg in 1745 and spearheading the removal of nearly 10,000 French Acadians from modern-day Nova Scotia and New Brunswick in 1755. Even after the British government began sending large numbers of regular soldiers to America during the Seven Years' War, the colonies remained important, semi-autonomous participants in the imperial war effort. In 1759 and 1760, nearly a third of the 50,000 British land forces in America consisted of provincial soldiers, all commissioned and paid by their respective governors and assemblies.[13]

In some ways, of course, the political liberty that this imperial constitution conferred on Britain's overseas colonies was less complete than it seemed. As would become clear during the debates over colonial taxation, the fiscal powers that Parliament began to exert in the colonies after 1763 represented a logical extension of the sovereignty that Charles II had allowed Parliament to claim over the Crown's Atlantic empire when it renewed the Navigation Laws at the Restoration. By the mid-eighteenth century, British Americans were no longer free to wage war against other European powers without Britain's consent, their laws were increasingly subject to metropolitan scrutiny, and they had to make at least a show of obeying the Navigation Laws. More ominous still, although British ministers did not generally insist that the colonists acknowledge the full range of Parliament's authority, there was little sense in Britain that either the colonists or their assemblies possessed rights that Westminster could not unilaterally revise when and if it saw fit. Although this did not mean that Parliament actually had the power to compel Britons in America to comply with its wishes, the imperial constitution that developed in the colonies during the first half of the eighteenth century rested, at most, on what Edmund Burke would call a British policy of "salutary neglect," not a shared sense of British imperial history comparable to the historical consciousness that governed relations between the Crown and Parliament in Britain.[14]

---

[13] See Gould, *The Persistence of Empire;* Fred Anderson, *Crucible of War: The Seven Years' War and the Fate of Empire in British North America, 1754–1766* (New York: Alfred A. Knopf, 2000).

[14] Speech of Edmund Burke, Esq., on Moving His Resolutions for Conciliation with the Colonies, March 25, 1775, in Francis Canavan and E. J. Payne, eds., *Select Works of Edmund Burke: A New Imprint of the Payne Edition*, 4 vols. (Indianapolis: Liberty Fund, 1999; orig. pub., 1874–1878), vol. I, p. 235.

Even so, the question of Parliament's sovereignty might not have become a central issue in metropolitan–colonial relations but for one innovation: the decision to keep a standing army of 10,000 British regulars in North America at the end of the Seven Years' War. As had been evident since the European wars against Louis XIV, the advent of a standing army transformed the British Constitution in profound ways, leading to the creation of onerous new taxes and to borrowing on a scale that was unprecedented in British history. Well into the eighteenth century, people in Britain and Ireland worried that the king's ministers might use the patronage of this military-fiscal state to fashion a parliamentary version of the royal absolutism that had allegedly been the Stuarts' objective before 1688, but it was also clear that the same military and fiscal bureaucracies that had strengthened the informal powers of the British Crown made it difficult (if not impossible) for either the king or his ministers to govern without the fiscal consent of Parliament.[15] By the time of the American Revolution, the fears occasioned by this transformation were far less pronounced than they had once been while the British public seemed increasingly comfortable with the results. Indeed, most British politicians – including the principal opposition groups in Parliament and many self-styled patriots in the British press – regarded Britain's military and fiscal bureaucracies as natural instruments of modern governance, and a surprising number viewed them as mainstays of their own liberty.[16]

Within metropolitan Britain, the result was to confirm one of the central premises of Whig historiography, which attributed the perfection of Britain's modern constitution to the demise of a system of direct military service based on feudal tenures and to the subsequent dependence of the Crown on Parliament for military subsidies. Blackstone, for one, largely endorsed this view of Britain's modern history in the *Commentaries*.[17] Although his well-known Tory sympathies made it difficult for him to embrace "the fashion of keeping standing armies" in times of peace, Blackstone conceded that the old feudal tenures had been inimical to individual liberty, and he accepted that the militia was only useful as an institution for home defense.[18] Given the absence of viable alternatives, a system of military obligation whereby most people fulfilled their duties through the payment of parliamentary taxes appeared to be the only

---

[15] For the Augustan debate over credit and military professionalization, see especially J. G. A. Pocock, *The Machiavellian Moment: Florentine Political Thought and the Atlantic Republican Tradition* (Princeton, NJ: Princeton University Press, 1975), pp. 423–61.

[16] For a fuller discussion, see Eliga H. Gould, "Fears of War, Fantasies of Peace: British Politics and the Coming of the American Revolution," in Eliga H. Gould and Peter S. Onuf, eds., *Empire and Nation: The American Revolution in the Atlantic World* (Baltimore: Johns Hopkins University Press, 2005), pp. 19–34.

[17] Blackstone, *Commentaries*, vol. IV, pp. 400–436. For ancient constitutionalism generally, see J. G. A. Pocock, *The Ancient Constitution and the Feudal Law: A Study of English Historical Thought in the Seventeenth Century: A Reissue with a Retrospect*, 2d ed. (Cambridge: Cambridge University Press, 1987).

[18] Blackstone, *Commentaries*, vol. I, p. 401; vol. IV, pp. 411–431.

way to reconcile the military needs of the Crown and the civil liberties of the subject. Somewhat reluctantly, Blackstone concluded that, because of this reality, a professional army had become "lastingly ingrafted into the British constitution," with the benefits more than covering the costs:

[U]pon the whole it is doubtless much better for the crown, and also for the people, to have the revenue settled upon the modern footing rather than the ancient. For the crown; because it is more certain, and collected with greater ease: for the people; because they are now delivered from the feodal hardships, and other odious branches of the prerogative.[19]

Crucially for the looming debate over Parliament's authority in America, this rendition of Britain's recent history placed the army at the very center of Parliament's consolidation of its constitutional position vis-à-vis the Crown in England. According to Blackstone, the determining event in the creation of Britain's "modern" system of military finance was Parliament's abolition in 1661 of the English feudal tenures that had given successive monarchs independent, though uncertain, powers of taxation. In exchange, Parliament settled undisputed command of the English militia on Charles II and his successors, along with a "more certain" revenue based on the land tax, customs, and excise. The constitutional history of England and, after 1707, Britain was thus a story of the substitution of an orderly system of parliamentary taxation for a prerogative-based system of personal military service, making it possible to accommodate more recent innovations such as a standing army and a perpetual revenue. Speaking of the Crown's powers vis-à-vis Parliament, Blackstone observed:

The stern commands of prerogative have yielded to the milder voice of influence: the slavish and exploded doctrine of non-resistance has given way to a military establishment by law; and to the disuse of parliaments has succeeded a parliamentary trust of an immense perpetual revenue.

It was incumbent on the subjects of such a regime to "guard against corrupt and servile influence." Yet it was equally clear that the modern symbiosis between the Crown and Parliament had made it possible for "good Englishmen" to be loyal to the Crown without fear of compromising their own liberty.[20]

The question was whether the same kind of symbiosis was possible for English men and women who happened to live in America. In particular, could Parliament extend Britain's modern system of military and fiscal obligations to the colonies without destroying the political and civil liberty that was the system's chief rationale? This was a question that the British ought to have found deeply interesting, but few bothered to ask it before Parliament took the fateful step of enacting the Stamp Act in 1765. Although the resort to coercive measures after 1768 aroused metropolitan fears that Whitehall was

---

[19] Ibid., vol. I, 408, 322.
[20] Ibid., vol. I, 326.

establishing a "martial police" in America, a broad cross section of the British public – in Parliament as well as without – accepted the need for a peacetime establishment of 10,000 regular soldiers to defend the colonies.[21] Indeed, many Britons viewed the army as the only way to place "persons of ability and disinterestedness" in charge of a range of provincial matters, including the management of Indian relations west of the Appalachians, the control of potentially disaffected subjects in the two Floridas and Canada, and the maintenance of public order in the older colonies along the Atlantic seaboard.[22] While partly a response to the territorial extent of Britain's new possessions in America, this consensus also reflected the same unwillingness in a colonial setting to accept a system of political obligation based on personal military service. Even after Parliament repealed the Stamp Act in 1766, few people in Britain questioned the advisability of a standing army in America.[23]

Nor were Whitehall's plans to finance the additional costs of this establishment with a colonial revenue any more controversial. Although a few members of Parliament – notably the West Indian planter and London alderman William Beckford – challenged Westminster's right to tax the Americans, the parliamentary debates of the mid-1760s revealed broad support for the course of reform charted by the king's ministers.[24] As Thomas Whately argued in what amounted to the government's official explanation of the Stamp Act, the growing costs of imperial defense, the perpetual nature of the public debt, and the disproportionate burden that both placed on "the Consumption of the Poor" in Britain made it inconceivable that the colonists who benefited from the army's presence in North America should not assume some of the expense.[25] In anticipation of colonial objections to being taxed without their explicit consent, the defenders of the new taxes insisted that modern history showed that only the British Crown and Parliament – the lower house of which, according to Whately, "virtually" represented Britons throughout the British Atlantic – had the authority to correct this imbalance.[26] Although Parliament was strengthening its own military and fiscal capacities, it was doing so on the assumption that the most effective way for British colonists to fulfill their wider military and political obligations – and in so doing to safeguard their political

---

[21] Gould, *The Persistence of Empire*, 11–116.

[22] See *An Examination in the Value of Canada and Guadaloupe, With an Impartial Account of the Latter* (London, 1761), p. 5.

[23] The parliamentary language of the major opposition groups provides a number of particularly striking examples of this shift. Although the various allies of William Pitt and of Newcastle and the Marquess of Rockingham opposed direct parliamentary taxes in America, the more general danger posed by a standing army in the colonies is notably absent from their rhetoric.

[24] P. D. G. Thomas, *British Politics and the Stamp Act Crisis: The First Phase of the American Revolution, 1763–1767* (Oxford: Clarendon Press, 1975), pp. 55–7, 61, 85–100.

[25] [Thomas Whately,] *The Regulations Lately Made concerning the Colonies, and the Taxes Imposed upon Them, Considered* (London, 1765), pp. 56–7. See also [Whately,] *Remarks on the Budget; or a Candid Examination of the Facts and Arguments Offered to the Public in that Pamphlet* (London, 1765), p. 6.

[26] *The Regulations Lately Made*, pp. 40 and 101–4.

and civil liberties – was through the payment of parliamentary taxes to support professional soldiers.

If the British public initially seemed unaware that the Stamp Act might have other, less positive implications, one person who did grasp its larger significance was the former governor of Massachusetts, Thomas Pownall, whose influential *Administration of the Colonies* first appeared in 1764.[27] Although his analysis changed substantially over the course of the work's four subsequent editions, Pownall never departed from the contention that only the British king and Parliament acting together possessed the authority necessary to administer Britain's overseas empire in an equitable and judicious manner. In the first three editions, the last of which appeared in 1766, Pownall appeared to endorse the view of the imperial constitution that was common in America, writing that responsibility for the administration of the colonies belonged "by right" to the Crown and the provincial assemblies.[28] Because Parliament had so effectively circumscribed the king's capacity for independent action in England, however, the colonies had achieved a "measure of independency" that threatened Britain's standing as the preeminent maritime power in Europe. Under Britain's post-1689 constitution, a "royal America" was, for all intents and purposes, an independent America.[29] According to Pownall, the only way out of the "present crisis" was for Parliament to convert the occasional military grants that Whitehall had raised in individual colonies during times of war into a perpetual revenue based on a general stamp duty.[30] By strengthening Parliament's administrative powers, an American revenue would create common imperial institutions that could be used to regulate the divergent, localized interests of Britain's far-flung colonies and dependencies.[31]

In subsequent editions, Pownall denied the novelty of Parliament's innovation on the grounds that in agreeing to the Navigation Acts in 1661, Charles II had effectively "participated" his sovereignty over the colonies with the other two estates of the realm.[32] Before the Restoration, Pownall contended, the colonies had been "distinct communities" bound – like the "counties palatine" of Durham and Chester – to the person of the king "upon the principles of foedal [sic] sovereignty."[33] By assuming jurisdiction over colonial trade, Parliament had effectively "annexed" the colonies to the English body politic, though

---

[27] [Thomas Pownall,] *The Administration of the Colonies* (London, 1764). Pownall published four subsequent revisions in 1765, 1766, 1768, and 1774, the last two with the expanded title *Wherein Their Rights and Constitution Are Discussed and Stated*.

[28] *Administration*, 1st edn., 1764, p. 31; 2d edn., pp. 32–3.

[29] Ibid., 2d edn., 1765, pp. 29–30. The concept of a "royal America" is the subject, most recently, of Brendan McConville, *The King's Three Faces: The Rise and Fall of Royal America, 1688–1776* (Chapel Hill: University of North Carolina Press, 2006).

[30] Pownall, *Administration*, 1st edn., 1764, pp. 30–2, 67–8.

[31] Ibid., 2d edn., 1765, pp. 90–1.

[32] Ibid., 4th edn., 1768, p. 139.

[33] Ibid., pp. 138–9. I assume that by "foedal" Pownall meant "feudal" rather than "foederal."

with the provision that they were "not yet united parts of the realm."[34] Pownall acknowledged the inherent contradictions in this formulation, conceding that in order to allow for the continued exercise of political liberty in the colonies, the House of Commons would eventually have to give British subjects in the most "extreme and remote parts" of the empire the right to send representatives to participate in its deliberations.[35] Until that happened, however, "the various and mutual interconnections of the different parts of the British dominions" – which Pownall attributed to the increasingly global scale of seaborne commerce and land and sea warfare – justified keeping the colonies strictly subordinate to the British Crown and Parliament on the same terms as the metropolitan kingdom of Great Britain.[36]

As Pownall's words suggest, the British reforms that preceded the American Revolution depended on an understanding of history that emphasized the "modernity" of parliamentary taxation and military finance. Initially, Americans challenged the new measures on similar grounds, with the abstract question of Parliament's legal authority playing a strictly secondary role. Although John Adams left no doubt that Parliament had overstepped its rights by taxing the colonies for revenue, most colonists affirmed that British Americans owed the same allegiance to the Crown as the king's metropolitan subjects, including a due "subordination" to what the Stamp Act Congress, in its declaration of October 19, 1765, called "that august body, the parliament of Great Britain."[37] In his celebrated *Letters from a Pennsylvania Farmer* (1768), John Dickinson explicitly recognized Parliament's supremacy over colonial trade, writing that anyone "who considers these provinces as states distinct from the *British Empire*, has very slender notions of *justice*, or of their *interests*."[38] As Americans made clear, preserving their liberty depended, in part, on Britain's recognition of their right to be taxed by assemblies in which they were directly represented (and by no other legislative body), but they were careful to avoid directly challenging Parliament's authority. "True it is," wrote Massachusetts assemblyman James Otis of the Stamp Act in 1764,

---

[34] Ibid., p. 140.

[35] Ibid., pp. xiv–xv, 173–5.

[36] Ibid., pp. 140, 163. In the latter passage, Pownall wrote: "[B]y the various and mutual interconnections of the different parts of the British dominions, throughout the Atlantic, and in America; by the intercommunion and reciprocation of their alternate wants and supplies; by the circulation of their commerce, revolving in an orbit which hath Great Britain for its center . . . there does exist, in fact, in nature, a real union and incorporation of all these parts of the British dominions, *an actual system of dominion*; which wants only to be avowed and actuated by the real spirit in which it moves and has its being . . . ."

[37] Declaration of the Stamp Act Congress (October 19, 1765), in Jack P. Greene, ed., *Colonies to Nation, 1763–1789: A Documentary History of the American Revolution* (New York: Norton, 1975; orig. pub., 1967), p. 64.

[38] [John Dickinson,] *Letters from a Farmer in Pennsylvania, to the Inhabitants of the British Colonies* (London, 1768). All quotations are taken from the 1903 imprint, ed. R.T.H. Halsey, New York.

that from the nature of the British constitution, and also from the idea and nature of a supreme legislature, the parliament represents the whole community or empire, and have [sic] an undoubted power, authority, and jurisdiction, over the whole; and to their final decisions the whole must and ought to peaceably submit.

In conceding this point, Otis hoped that Parliament would reciprocate by demonstrating the same "tenderness ... towards large provinces" in America that it had customarily "shown to the customs of particular cities and boroughs" in England, but he saw no meaningful difference between Westminster's metropolitan authority and the authority that it theoretically possessed in America.[39]

What the colonists and their British supporters refused to concede was that the historical condition of modernity required Parliament to use these powers to tax the subjects of the Crown's overseas colonies for revenue. In his 1769 reply to William Knox's *State of the Nation*, Edmund Burke denied that the cost of defending the colonies would impoverish the British nation without a permanent American revenue.[40] Noting the prosperity that even the most distant regions of England and Scotland had attained since the Glorious Revolution, Burke argued that Britain owed its present international stature to the combination of a flourishing commerce with its colonies and the most efficient, least burdensome system of taxation in Europe.[41] In the colonies, on the other hand, the scarcity of hard currency, the tendency to value land in kind, and an uneven system of taxation that seemed in some places – notably New England – to be based on the remnants of England's feudal tenures all militated against attempting to raise any kind of parliamentary revenue, whether based on internal or external taxes.[42] Given this reality, wrote Burke, Britain already taxed the colonies as fully as could be expected by monopolizing their trade through the Navigation Laws.[43] Rather than using Parliament's limited powers over the settler empire to attempt the impossible, the government should heed the principles of wise administration and allow the colonies to contribute indirectly what they could never supply in direct subsidies.

Although Burke wrote as a member of Parliament, albeit one with close ties to his native Ireland and the colonies, Americans shared many of his views, including those pertaining to the regulation of colonial trade. As Benjamin Franklin told the House of Commons in 1766, "the sea is yours": "You maintain by your fleets, the safety of navigation in it, and keep it clear of pirates; you may have therefore a natural and equitable right to some toll or duty on

---

[39] [James Otis], *Considerations on Behalf of the Colonists* (London, 1765), pp. 9–10.

[40] [Edmund Burke,] *Observations on a Late State of the Nation* (London, 1769), in Paul Langford, ed., *The Writings and Speeches of Edmund Burke*, 8 vols. (Oxford: Oxford University Press, 1981), vol. II, pp. 175.

[41] Ibid., 147–154.

[42] Ibid., 166–7.

[43] Ibid., 195, 192–5.

merchandizes carried through that part of your dominions."[44] In its declaration of October 19, 1765, the Stamp Act Congress made the same point, noting that because "the trade of these colonies ultimately centre[s] in Great Britain," Americans already contributed "very largely to all the supplies granted there to the crown."[45] Although Americans eventually came to question whether it was possible to acknowledge Parliament's right to regulate their external trade while disputing its right to tax for revenue, there was no question about the role that the colonies indirectly played in sustaining Britain's maritime supremacy. "Britain owes much of her well-being, her riches and her power, to her American colonies," wrote the author of the prize-winning entry in an essay competition that the College of Philadelphia sponsored in 1765. "From the commodities of America, chiefly manufactured in England and conveyed through innumerable channels of trade to every quarter of the globe, Great-Britain acquires immense wealth, keeps up a spirit of industry among her inhabitants, and is enabled to support mighty fleets, great in peace and formidable in war."[46]

While acknowledging Britain's maritime authority, Americans denied that there was any need for Parliament to take a more active role in military affairs on the North American mainland. Drawing on the recent history of Britain's wars with France and Spain, American writers argued that the growth of standing armies and permanent revenue systems in Europe had made little impression on the way that Britons and Anglo-Americans waged war in the colonies. Instead, an abundance of able-bodied men skilled in the use of firearms and accustomed to the demands of irregular warfare enabled colonial assemblies to supply the ordinary needs of defense through local militias and temporary levies. Because these forces were paid by colonial legislatures, they were not directly analogous to the feudal levies that the Crown had used as a precedent to raise troops and revenues without Parliament's approval before 1660. Nonetheless, they were almost as independent of Parliament's authority as the medieval array, and they served on the same limited terms, freeing the sparsely populated and cash-poor colonies from the prohibitive costs of supplying a standing army through permanent taxes.[47] As Rhode Island's governor Stephen Hopkins observed during the Stamp Act crisis, Britain's colonies in America had been settled entirely "at the expence of the planters themselves," and until

---

[44] "Examination of Benjamin Franklin" (Feb. 13, 1766), in John Almon, ed., *A Collection of Papers Relative to the Dispute between Great Britain and America, 1764–1775* (New York: Da Capo Press, 1971; orig. pub., 1777), p. 73.

[45] "Declaration of the Stamp Act Congress," in Greene, ed., *Colonies to Nation*, p. 64.

[46] *Four Dissertations on the Reciprocal Advantages of a Perpetual Union between Great-Britain and her American Colonies* (London, 1766), 17–18.

[47] See, for example, [William Bollan,] *The Mutual Interest of Great Britain and the American Colonies Considered* (London, 1765), p. 11; James Otis, *The Rights of the British Colonies Asserted and Proved* (London, 2d edn., 1765), p. 98; [Stephen Sayre,] *The Englishman Deceived, A Political Piece: Wherein Some Very Important Secrets of State Are Briefly Recited, and Offered to the Considerations of the Public* (London, 1768), pp. 34–5.

the Seven Years' War, they had been left "to the protection of heaven and their own efforts." History, therefore, did not justify using Parliament to tax them without their consent.[48] In the words of another opponent of the new measures:

If a standing force be necessary in these colonies, it must be for the purpose of the civil magistrate, *viz.* preserving peace, and executing justice. But as our several colonies have a compleat legislature [sic] subordinate to that of Great-Britain, which has a power of forming militias, raising troops, &c. and as they ought to be the best judges of their own wants, it would seem natural to leave the affair of regular troops to their own option, to be raised and paid as they shall find most convenient, or not to be raised at all, unless it be requisite.[49]

As part of this alternate history of the British empire, American writers argued that during each of Britain's modern wars with France, the colonies had readily and effectively fulfilled their military obligations to the Crown by raising provincial regiments for limited periods of service in specific theaters of operation. Despite serving almost entirely at the pleasure of colonial governors and assemblies, these troops had proved decisive on a number of occasions, most notably in 1745, when the capture of Louisbourg on Cape Breton Island by a force of New England provincials helped compel France to return its extensive conquests in the Netherlands at the peace of Aix-la-Chapelle (1748). According to the Massachusetts clergyman Amos Adams, the "success of the New-England arms" during the 1740s proved to be the "*single* equivalent for all the conquests of France" and Louisbourg "the price that purchased the peace of Europe."[50] "It is presumed," concurred Maryland's Daniel Dulany in 1765, "that it was a notable Service done by *New England*, when the Militia of that Colony reduced *Cape Breton*," in the process "enabl[ing] the *British Ministers* to make a Peace less disadvantageous and inglorious than They otherwise must have been constrained to submit to."[51] If the demands of modern warfare had forced the government to create a permanent army and centrally administered revenue in Britain, those same demands fostered a very different set of needs in America. In a diverse, extended polity like the British empire, history suggested that military power ought to be distributed among the assemblies of the empire's distant provinces.

Although the main purpose of this history was to refute the sense of inevitability that informed British thinking about the parliamentary taxation, it ultimately led Americans to clarify their thinking about the relationship

---

[48] [Stephen Hopkins,] *The Grievances of the American Colonies Candidly Examined* (London, 1766), pp. 38–9.

[49] *The Necessity of Repealing the American Stamp-Act Demonstrated* (London, 1766), pp. 12–3.

[50] Amos Adams, *A Concise Historical View of the Difficulties, Hardships, and Perils which Attended the Planting and Progressive Improvements of New England* (London, 1770), p. 49. See also *A Brief Review of the Rise and Progress, Services and Sufferings, of New England, Especially the Province of Massachuset's Bay* (London, 1774).

[51] [Daniel Dulany], *Considerations on the Propriety of Imposing Taxes in the British Colonies for the Purpose of Raising a Revenue, by Act of Parliament*, 2d ([London], 1766), p. 20.

between parliamentary sovereignty and individual liberty in the colonies. In Daniel Dulany's account of the history of Britain's expansion, for example, the rise of representative bodies throughout the medieval dominions of the English Crown followed a familiar pattern, according to which the Anglo-Norman practice of levying periodic "extrafeudal" contributions had yielded to the more regular system of granting formal supplies in legislative councils.[52] Where British writers saw in this history a justification for extending Parliament's sovereignty over the wider empire, Dulany used it to prove that Englishmen living outside metropolitan England had always retained the right of taxation through local assemblies. Indeed, according to Dulany, the right of the king's subjects not to be "taxed without their consent" in the Anglo-Norman empire was so absolute that, during parliamentary elections, "writs were ... directed even to women, who were proprietors of land in *Ireland.*"[53] Far from being an aberration that the British Crown and Parliament needed to rectify, wrote Dulany, the continued existence of colonial assemblies with a "regular, adequate, and constitutional authority to tax" the inhabitants of their respective provinces was essential for maintaining the liberty of Britons who did not live in Britain proper.[54]

No text played a more important part in this reshaping of Britain's imperial history than John Dickinson's *Letters from a Farmer in Pennsylvania.*[55] Although Dickinson found the entire business of raising a parliamentary revenue in America indefensible, the Stamp Act struck him as particularly dangerous because its goal was to create a tax "that would execute itself."[56] Quoting David Hume's history of England, Dickinson noted that "an equitable administration" had been impossible in metropolitan England before the creation of an "established council or assembly [that] could protect the people," if necessary by withholding supplies from the Crown if gentler means did not suffice.[57] By attempting to establish a perpetual colonial revenue that would be beyond the control of any assembly in America, Parliament was threatening to deprive the colonies of the very conditions that had rescued England from the chaos and tyranny that had characterized Britain's own feudal past. Once their assemblies ceased to enjoy even the "puny privileges of French parliaments," warned Dickinson, Americans would gradually lose the freedom to manage the other subsidiary functions of local government. In a direct reply to Thomas Pownall, he observed:

When the "charges of the administration of justice," – "the support of civil government;" – and "the expences of defending protecting and securing" us, are provided for, I should be glad to know upon what occasion the crown will ever call our assemblies together.

[52] Ibid., 6.
[53] Ibid., 7.
[54] Ibid., 9.
[55] Dickinson, *Letters from a Farmer in Pennsylvania.*
[56] Ibid., 21.
[57] Ibid., 88.

Some few of them may meet of their own accord, by virtue of their charters: But what will they have to do when they are met? To what shadows will they be reduced? The men, whose deliberations heretofore had an influence on every matter relating to the liberty and happiness of themselves and their constituents, and whose authority in domestic affairs, at least, might well be compared to that of Roman senators, will now find their deliberations of no more consequence than those of constables. – They may perhaps be allowed to make laws for yoking of hogs, or pounding of stray cattle. Their influence will hardly be permitted to extend so high as the keeping roads in repair, as that business may more properly be executed by those who receive the public cash.[58]

The aspect of the present crisis that Dickinson found most alarming was the way that conditions in Britain appeared to be driving Parliament's destruction of colonial liberty. Drawing on the modern history of Britain's relations with Ireland, Dickinson noted the ease with which provincial taxes that were ostensibly levied in order to pay the army and meet the costs of government could become yet another source of patronage for a corrupt ministry at Westminster.[59] When the government taxed British subjects in Britain, Parliament's concern for the liberty and welfare of its constituents tended to mitigate the effects of such venality, but few of its members had direct ties to the king's British subjects in America, which meant that Parliament had little incentive "to contradict a minister who should tell them, it was become necessary to lay a new tax."[60] As Dickinson wrote in an especially telling passage:

Has not the parliament expressly avowed their intention of raising money from us for certain purposes? Is not this scheme popular in Great-Britain? ... Will not every addition thus made to our taxes, be an addition to the power of the British legislature, by increasing the number of officers employed in the collection? Will not every additional tax therefore render it more difficult to abrogate any of them? When a branch of revenue is once established, does it not appear to many people invidious and undutiful, to attempt to abolish it?[61]

Far from safeguarding the liberty of Britons everywhere, as Whig historians in Britain liked to claim, the modern institutions of the British military-fiscal state had created a deeply self-referential parliamentary culture at Westminster, one that was inimical to the exercise of political liberty in the colonies of settlement.

Driven by this conflict between parliamentary sovereignty and colonial liberty, Americans eventually embraced a confederated model of the British empire. Despite his explicit disavowal of any notion of the colonies as distinct states, Dickinson, for one, based much of his argument on the idea that Americans' dependence on Britain's king and Parliament meant that they

[58] Ibid., 87–100.
[59] Ibid., 102–8.
[60] Ibid., 102.
[61] Ibid., 128.

needed to be especially jealous of their rights and liberties. As he noted toward
the end of the *Letters*:

Machiavel employs a whole chapter in his discourses, to prove that a state, to be long
lived, must be frequently corrected, and reduced to its first principles. But of all states
that have existed, there never was any, in which this jealousy could be more proper than
in these colonies. For the government here is not only mixt, but dependant, which
circumstance occasions a peculiarity in its form, of a very delicate nature.[62]

For many of Dickinson's compatriots, the only way to protect colonial liberty from the "peculiar" threat of parliamentary despotism was to reconstitute
the settler empire as a confederation of sovereign states bound together only by
allegiance to the same Crown. Because most Britons traced Parliament's imperial sovereignty to the Restoration of Charles II, Americans who held such
views could argue that rather than attempting to destroy the British empire,
they were returning it to its first principles. In the words of Edward Bancroft,
an American-born physician resident in London, England's original title to
America had been vested in the person of Queen Elizabeth, which meant that
the colonies had never been "annexed to the Realm" but had always been
bound to Britain simply as "appendages" of the Crown of England.[63] In
1774, Thomas Jefferson employed a similar idea of an ancient imperial constitution, calling on George III to "resume the exercise of his negative power"
by checking the pretensions of Parliament to an imperial sovereignty over the
other "states" of the English-speaking Atlantic.[64] As Jefferson's choice of words
suggested, Americans still hoped to avoid an irreparable breach by crafting a
British history that could reconcile the interests of province and metropole.
Increasingly, however, it seemed that the only certain way to safeguard the
liberty of Britons in America was for the colonies to become independent states.

In terms of the subsequent history of the British empire, this challenge to
Parliament's imperial authority had two far-reaching consequences, both of
which eventually became entrenched in the constitution of the settler empire.[65]
The first and most immediately apparent of these was to force Britain to defend
Parliament's imperial sovereignty in stark and unyielding terms, far more so
than had been the case before the reforms of the 1760s. By declaring the

---

[62] Ibid.

[63] [Edward Bancroft,] *Remarks on the Review of the Controversy between Great Britain and the
Colonies* (London, 1769), pp. 15 and 40. As evidence for this assertion, Bancroft noted
that Virginia had proclaimed Charles II "King of *England, Scotland, France, Ireland*, and
VIRGINIA … long before his Restoration; and that he actually reigned in that Colony a considerable time before he was King in *England*" (p. 41).

[64] [Thomas Jefferson,] *A Summary View of the Rights of British America* (London, 1774), pp. 28,
40–2.

[65] The argument here follows Eliga H. Gould, "A Virtual Nation: Greater Britain and the Imperial
Legacy of the American Revolution," *American Historical Review*, 104 (1999): 476–489. See
also Gould, *The Persistence of Empire*, pp. 181–214.

Americans to be in open rebellion in 1775, the British government not only committed Britain to eight years of global war, but it also affirmed what remained, at least in theory, Parliament's boundless imperial authority into the twentieth century. For the colonies that remained part of the British empire, Parliament retained the unlimited rights upon which its defenders had insisted during the 1760s and 1770s, including the right to impose new constitutions on what became the British provinces of Upper and Lower Canada in 1791, the right to force British planters in the West Indies to accept the end of slavery during the 1830s, the right to protect the rights of aboriginal peoples in the South Pacific, and the right to intervene repeatedly in the affairs of the East India Company, often in the face of stiff opposition from the company's white servants. Although not all of these issues involved contentious questions of taxation and military finance, each brought the British Parliament into conflict with the legislative rights of colonial assemblies and legislatures in the wider empire, and there was no question that Parliament had the legal right to do as it saw fit.

Yet this was not the whole story. Because the constitutional history that the Americans and their British sympathizers helped fashion before the revolution was, at least initially, about how to protect the liberty of British subjects within the settler empire, the American Revolution carried another, more important lesson about the practical limitations on Parliament's imperial authority. Although the conventions of both British and American history tend to cast the Declaration of Independence as a permanent and unbridgeable moment of separation between the two English-speaking empires, new connections soon developed between the British empire and the former colonies, whether through formal exchange based on immigration, commerce, and diplomacy or through the less formal circulation of news and literature. In Canada and the West Indies, in particular, British settlers remained well aware – sometimes keenly so – of the fate of liberty in the United States, and they continued to insist on many of the rights that their erstwhile fellow subjects had claimed before 1776. During the 1780s and 1790s, it was not unusual for British governors in the West Indies to blame political difficulties, in part, on the influence of "Americans" in the colonial assemblies, and such connections lasted even longer in British North America. As the *Montreal Gazette* warned during the provincial crisis that eventually produced the Durham Report (1841), "Americans prior to their Revolution ... addressed themselves patiently and calmly to the Imperial Parliament, and when it turned a deaf ear to their complaints, they appealed to arms."[66] Mindful of the American example, leaders in both Britain and the colonies responded to problems of imperial governance with what one modern historian calls a "mixture of principle and

---

[66] Quoted in D. George Boyce, *Decolonisation and the British Empire, 1775–1997* (New York: St. Martin's Press, 1999), p. 34.

pragmatism," the effect of which was to secure "British sovereignty while offering scope for colonial rights."[67]

Nor were the lessons of the American Revolution purely negative. During the final quarter of the nineteenth century, more than a few Britons thought they saw in the American union a model that could serve as a vehicle for turning a settler empire still nominally subject to Parliament's unlimited authority into a more perfect federal union of equal polities (and legislatures). Although the American Civil War demonstrated the fragility of imperial federations that spanned vast distances, U.S. history also suggested that such a union, if it could be adapted to the particular circumstances of the British empire, might hold the key to reconciling the metropolitan desire for imperial unity with the rise of responsible government in Canada, Australia, and the other colonies of settlement. In the words of a recent history of this quest for a Greater Britain, the American Republic was for metropolitan Britons "a site of both powerful desire and nightmarish visions of the future." "The advocates of Greater Britain looked across the Atlantic"; there, they thought they saw "the future of the empire."[68]

Despite Parliament's theoretically unbounded sovereignty, the American Revolution's most enduring legacy for the subsequent history of the British settler empire was a heightened awareness of the limitations that history imposed on Parliament's capacity for colonial government. If only because no legislative or judicial body in the British empire – including Parliament itself – could limit the metropolitan legislature's authority, the British never formally abandoned the notion that Parliament's imperial powers were as limitless as the powers that it possessed in Britain. Just the same, the trauma of the American Revolution left "in the English mind a doubt, a misgiving," as the Cambridge historian J. R. Seeley would observe in 1883.[69] As F. W. Maitland reminded his students at Cambridge, Britain's loss of the thirteen American colonies "did not lead to any abandonment of the general principle" of parliamentary sovereignty, including Parliament's "right or power to impose taxes," yet the powers that "the sovereign body" actually possessed and could realistically hope to exercise were limited.[70] Significantly, the constitutional history of the post-1783 British empire was largely the history of a return to the principles on which the empire was being governed when Blackstone published the first volume of the *Commentaries* in 1765. Insofar as there was a bulwark of Parliament's imperial sovereignty in the revolution's aftermath, that bulwark was once again the Navigation Act, which Lord Sheffield famously called the "guardian" of Britain's strength and prosperity.[71] In the Declaratory Act of

---

[67] Ibid., 42.

[68] Duncan Bell, *The Idea of Greater Britain: Empire and the Future of World Order, 1860–1900* (Princeton, NJ: Princeton University Press, 2007), pp. 233, 235.

[69] J. R. Seeley, *The Expansion of England* (Boston: Little, Brown, and Company, 1900), p. 17.

[70] Maitland, *The Constitutional History of England*, pp. 338–339.

[71] John Holroyd Lord Sheffield, *Observations on the Commerce of the American States*, rev. ed. (New York,: A. M. Kelley, 1970; orig. pub., 1784), p. 2.

1778 and the Canada Act of 1791, Parliament disavowed the policy of levying taxes for revenue, and the British army, which for a brief period had looked as though it would become the engine of constitutional change within the wider empire that it had been in metropolitan Britain, ceased to be a matter of widespread controversy.

To a greater degree than is sometimes realized, the terms on which Parliament continued to maintain its sway over Britain's empire were thus the ones that had been laid down by moderate Whigs like Edmund Burke and, before they declared their colonies to be independent states, the Americans themselves. The main difference was that those terms now reflected the indisputable lessons of history. As Burke made clear in his *Speech on American Taxation* in 1774, Parliament's sovereignty over the British dominions of the Crown was, and by right ought to be, legally boundless, yet the only way to nurture and maintain that sovereignty was by avoiding measures that history had shown were impossible to enforce. "I am not here going to enter into the distinctions of rights," insisted Burke, "I hate the very sound of them."

Leave the Americans as they antiently stood, and these distinctions, born of our unhappy contest will die along with it . . . . Be content to bind America by laws of trade; you have always done it. Let this be your reason for binding their trade. Do not burthen them by taxes; you were not used to do so from the beginning. Let this be your reason for not taxing. These are the arguments of states and kingdoms. Leave the rest to the schools; for there only they may be discussed with safety.[72]

Here was theory of British imperial government based not on abstract principle or on the theoretical certainty of legal charters, written constitutions, and parliamentary enactments, but on the fluid and often contradictory lessons of history. For a devotee of custom such as Burke, the sovereign right not to act was as much an expression of Parliament's imperial supremacy as the positive right to legislate. Had the history of Parliament's failure to intervene in imperial governance been available to his audience only a decade before, the greater British history of which that history formed such an important part might conceivably have followed a different path.

---

[72] Speech of Edmund Burke, Esq., on American Taxation, April 19, 1774, in Canavan and Payne, eds., *Select Works of Edmund Burke*, vol. I, p. 215.

5

Federalism, Democracy, and Liberty in the New American Nation

Peter S. Onuf

British subjects in the provinces that would form the United States of America shaped their societies in the image of the metropolis. As they adapted to their distance from Britain and to distinctive environmental conditions, colonists understood that provincial societies deviated from the metropolitan standard. Sometimes, their "exceptional" circumstances – most notably, the extraordinary availability of productive land – worked to the advantage of the generality of white householders: This was "the best poor man's country," characterized by what Benjamin Franklin described as a "happy Mediocrity."[1] Yet, as provincial patriots were acutely aware, their provinces were also fundamentally defective and incomplete. That ultimate authority lay elsewhere underscored this incompleteness, for in both a symbolic political sense and in a very real economic sense, Anglo-Americans depended on the metropolis. Far from being "terminal polities," autonomous and independent in fact if not theory, the American provinces were fragmentary projections of metropolitan power and interest. Without the imperial connection, Anglo-Americans would not have developed a sense of provincial or transprovincial, "continental" identity; without metropolitan markets these provinces – and, of course, their successor states – would not even exist.

Provincial Americans first conceived of the British empire as an inclusive transatlantic political community in which all subject-citizens enjoyed equal rights.[2]

---

[1] Franklin, "Information to Those Who Would Remove to America," Sept., 1782, in Phillip B. Kurland and Ralph Lerner, eds., *The Founders' Constitution*, 5 vols. (Chicago: University of Chicago Press, 1987), vol. 1, p. 531; James T. Lemon, *The Best Poor Man's Country: A Geographical Study of Early Southeastern Pennsylvania* (Baltimore: Johns Hopkins University Press, 1972). On American exceptionalism see Jack P. Greene, *The Intellectual Construction of America: Exceptionalism and Identity from 1492 to 1800* (Chapel Hill: University of North Carolina Press, 1993).

[2] David Armitage, *The Ideological Origins of the British Empire* (New York: Cambridge University Press, 2000); Richard Koebner, *Empire* (Cambridge, U.K.: Cambridge University Press, 1961).

Long before Thomas Jefferson and his congressional colleagues claimed a "separate & equal station … among the powers of the earth," provincials claimed membership in an empire of equals.[3] But equality did not mean independence. To the contrary, patriotic provincials cultivated an exaggerated sense of their Britishness, imaginatively identifying with their overseas countrymen, incorporating an idealized metropolis in their provincial worlds, and muting the differences that marked their inferiority. Lacking their own true capital cities, distant Creole elites domesticated, or "Americanized," the British metropolis. As events would show, incorporation in the empire on equal terms was a patriotic fantasy, crucial for energizing resistance but impossible to reconcile with the realities of imperial governance: An actual representation in Parliament, patriots soon recognized, would be less likely to Americanize the metropolis than to suck rustic provincials into the vortex of imperial corruption. Nor, by 1776, would Americans welcome the kind of incorporation in a reformed imperial state that Adam Smith proposed in *The Wealth of Nations*, with the equalization of tax burdens as well as political power.[4] Instead, patriots embraced a conception of their rights at the highest level of abstraction. The "liberty" they invoked was impeccably English in its genealogy, but it was ultimately incompatible with any continuing connection with Britain, even when imperial federalists such as John Adams sought to Americanize George III by removing *him* from the metropolis and incorporating him in their own provincial constitutions, as "king of the Massachusetts, king of Rhode Island, king of Connecticut, &c."[5]

That the American fantasy of incorporation should ultimately turn to, and then against, royal authority points to the peculiar history of British liberty in post-colonial America. New state constitutions boldly asserted provincial self-sufficiency and completeness, making their peoples the source of legitimate authority and thus denying the transcendent and equalizing British imperial identity that had inspired patriot resistance. State "sovereignty" did not represent the logical culmination of the resistance movement, but rather the unintended consequence of its failure.[6] In practice, the states never exercised full sovereign powers, instead improvising and then constitutionalizing collective security arrangements that left them with less actual authority than they had enjoyed before the imperial crisis. Nor, as Jack Greene shows, did the revolution resolve the continuing tension between the metropolitan center and

---

[3] Declaration of Independence, July 4, 1776, in Merrill Peterson, ed., *Thomas Jefferson Writings* (New York: Library of America, 1984), p. 19.

[4] Nicholas Onuf and Peter Onuf, *Nations, Markets, and War: Modern History and the American Civil War* (Charlottesville: University of Virginia Press, 2006), pp. 216–18.

[5] John Adams, "Novanglus," March 6, 1775, in *The American Colonial Crisis: The Daniel Leonard-John Adams Letters to the Press, 1774–1775*, ed. Bernard Mason (New York: Harper & Row, 1972), p. 208.

[6] On the invention of state sovereignty see Peter S. Onuf, "Thomas Jefferson, Federalist," in Peter S. Onuf, *The Mind of Thomas Jefferson* (Charlottesville: University of Virginia Press, 2007), pp. 83–98.

provincial periphery.[7] To the contrary, the new federal system reinforced the position of the states as members of a continental union that was supposed to secure their rights and interests.

"Nationalists" like Pennsylvania's James Wilson might argue that sovereignty *"resides* in the PEOPLE, as the fountain of government," not in the state governments that were their creatures.[8] Geopolitical imperatives, efficient administration, and interdependent economic interests all worked toward the "consolidation" of authority in an "energetic" central government. But fears of metropolitan despotism were reflexive for most post-revolutionary Americans.[9] Whenever they mobilized politically, thus translating the fiction of popular sovereignty into reality, they acted locally, usually in ways that strengthened local and state governments.[10] Ironically, the Federalists' success in ratifying the new federal constitution reinforced these tendencies: For subsequent opponents of centralized authority, the ratifying conventions confirmed the original and plenary authority of the peoples of the respective states; construed strictly, with due deference to the Bill of Rights and the Eleventh amendment, the new central government could only exercise well-defined, delegated powers.[11] Wilson's notion that sovereignty "resides" in the people may have helped Federalists overcome attachments to state governments in the ratification struggle, but that same idea would authorize mobilization against the new federal government and revive the pretensions of sovereign states in later years.

The British empire had been "federal" in practice, but unitary in theory, as all Britons acknowledged their allegiance to the British sovereign in exchange for his protection.[12] Independent Americans raised federalism to the level of fundamental principle, grounding provincial liberties – or state rights – on the sovereignty of the people, made manifest in new constitutions that defined the states as territorial entities and proclaimed their political self-sufficiency.

---

[7] Jack P. Greene, *Peripheries and Center: Constitutional Development in the Extended Polities of the British Empire and the United States, 1607–1788* (Athens: University of Georgia Press, 1986); Greene, "Colonial History and National History: Reflections on a Continuing Problem," *William and Mary Quarterly*, 3rd Series (hereafter WMQ) 64 (2007), 235–50; roundtable (David Armitage, Eliga H. Gould, Michael Zuckerman, Kariann Yokota, Adam Rothman, Robin L. Einhorn), 251–80; "Elaborations" (by Greene), 281–86.

[8] Gordon S. Wood, *The Creation of the American Republic, 1776–1787* (Chapel Hill: University of North Carolina Press, 1969), pp. 530–32, quotation at 530.

[9] Peter S. Onuf, "Federalism, Republicanism, and the Origins of American Sectionalism," in Edward L. Ayers et al., eds., *All Over the Map: Rethinking Region and Nation in the United States* (Baltimore: Johns Hopkins University Press, 1996), pp. 11–37.

[10] Edmund S. Morgan, *Inventing the People: The Rise of Popular Sovereignty in England and America* (New York: Norton, 1988).

[11] The significance of the Eleventh amendment is demonstrated persuasively in Douglas Bradburn, *The Citizenship Revolution: Politics and the Creation of the American Union* (Charlottesville: University of Virginia Press, 2009).

[12] Greene, *Peripheries and Center*; Andrew C. McLaughlin, "The Background of American Federalism," *American Political Science Review* 12 (1918), 215–40. On the sovereignty question see Allison LaCroix, *A Well-Constructed Union: An Intellectual History of American Federalism* (Cambridge, MA: Harvard University Press, forthcoming).

Yet this constitutional articulation of a radically decentered post-imperial regime stood in counterpoint to the realities of federal state formation and to the continuing appeal of the imperial vision that had inspired revolutionary patriots.[13] The ongoing dialectic of center and periphery, the tension between national aspirations and state rights, would shape the history of British conceptions of liberty in post-colonial America.

In *Democracy in America*, Alexis de Tocqueville emphasized the fundamental contradiction between the modern principle of "equality" and the survival of the "liberty" that had flourished under the pre-revolutionary old regime. The ascendancy of the equality principle and of the democratic rule it authorized pointed toward the leveling of distinctions and the concentration of power. The "passion" for equality "tends to elevate the humble to the rank of the great; but there exists also in the human heart a depraved taste for equality, which impels the weak to attempt to lower the powerful to their own level and reduces men to prefer equality in slavery to inequality with freedom." The great challenge for modern liberty-lovers was not to "reconstruct aristocratic society," but "to make liberty proceed out of that democratic state of society in which God has placed us." The new United States, the first democracy in the modern world, offered grounds for hope. "That nation possessed two of the main causes of internal peace," Tocqueville argued: "[I]t was a new country, but it was inhabited by a people grown old in the exercise of freedom." Simply put, Americans were "free" from the time of their first settlements, long *before* they proclaimed their equality; by contrast, Europeans would only *become* equal when the old regime was thoroughly demolished by powerful new states. For Tocqueville, the anatomist of political modernity, American democracy was "exceptional": The passion for equality was tempered by "aristocratic" survivals, by a democratic determination to uphold individual and corporate rights and to sustain the rule of law. By diffusing power, American democrats seem to have avoided their despotic destiny.[14]

When revolutionaries "invented the people" they also invented sovereign state-republics. These states were the basic, irreducible building blocks of the union that revolutionaries formed to make war against the empire that had spurned them. For Jefferson, the Declaration of Independence was most significant "as the fundamental act of Union of these States," not for its much better-remembered recapitulation of social contract theory.[15] Independence thus simultaneously affirmed the integrity of the sovereign states and created a union that stood between those states and "the powers of the earth," thus effectively curbing their sovereignty. The net result of this tension was to

---

[13] For a comprehensive account of federal state activity see Brian Balogh, *"A Government Out of Sight": The Mystery of National Authority in Nineteenth-Century America* (New York: Norton, 2009).

[14] Alexis de Tocqueville, *Democracy in America*, trans. Henry Reeve and Francis Bowen (Ware, UK: Wordsworth Editions, 1998), 29, 61, 362.

[15] Minutes of the Board of Visitors, University of Virginia, March 4, 1825, in Peterson, ed., *Jefferson Writings*, 479.

multiply venues for political action as well as occasions for conflicts over fundamental issues, expanding the scope of popular participation and hastening the progress of what we call "democratization." Yet this familiar, enduringly popular national narrative obscures the simultaneous strengthening of property rights (including the rights of slaveholders) and corporate privileges that seem decidedly "undemocratic" to modern critics. I will argue instead that the new regime's federal character gave rise to a self-consciously "democratic" movement that synthesized and promoted these apparently conflicting impulses. Democracy in America grew out of the collaboration of patriot elites and politicized masses in response to British threats to their liberties. Yet if the specter of metropolitan domination gave Americans a "common cause," anxieties about its revival subsequently played a crucial role in the ideological polarization of early party formation. Struggles over the distribution of power in the new federal regime in turn defined what Americans understood by "aristocracy" and "democracy."

ARISTOCRATS AND DEMOCRATS

Of the revolutions Robert R. Palmer surveyed in his magisterial *Age of the Democratic Revolution*, the American was the most distinctive. Only with the French Revolution did revolutionaries mobilize popular resistance against "aristocrats" who monopolized power and privilege and begin to describe themselves as "democrats."[16] In retrospect, the American Revolution could be seen as democratic, for colonial resistance leaders had articulated the theory of popular sovereignty and promoted the broad political participation that characterized Palmer's age. But when Americans broke from the empire, "democracy" still carried pejorative connotations of anarchy and mob rule that patriot leaders were anxious to suppress. It was George III, "the royal brute of Great Britain," who withdrew his protection from loyal American subjects who were determined to *uphold* the law and to vindicate their own rights *under* law. Independent America would defy dire ministerial predictions of anarchic disorder, Thomas Paine insisted in *Common Sense*, because "in America the law is king."[17] Any acknowledgment that the *demos*, or people, constituted a distinct social order with its own interests – for instance, in redistributing wealth – would destroy the illusion

[16] Robert R. Palmer, *The Age of the Democratic Revolution*, 2 vols., *The Challenge, The Struggle* (Princeton, NJ: Princeton University Press, 1959–64). For an appreciation of Palmer's achievement see Peter S. Onuf, "Democrazia, rivoluzione e storiografia del mondo contemporaneo" ("Democracy, Revolution, and the Historiography of the Modern World"), *Contemporanea: Rivista do storia dell '800 e dell '900* X (2007), 149–55.

[17] Thomas Paine, *Common Sense* (Philadelphia, 1776), reprinted in Bruce Frohnen, ed., *The American Republic: Primary Sources* (Indianapolis: Liberty Fund, Inc., 2002), pp. 179–88, quotations at 188. Neo-Whig historians emphasized the centrality of legal and constitutional issues in the resistance movement. See particularly John Phillip Reid, *Constitutional History of the American Revolution*, 4 vols. (Madison: University of Wisconsin Press, 1987–93).

of a shared commitment to the rule of law. Americans wanted to be recognized as a civil people capable of sustaining law and preserving order without the props of royal authority. Their quarrel was with the British king and a distant, unresponsive, imperial legislature, not with the "better sort" in their own midst, particularly once Loyalists – the first un-Americans – were neutralized or driven into exile.

Cross-class solidarity retarded the class-consciousness – the acute awareness of unequal access to privilege and power – that energized later, professedly "democratic" revolutions.[18] Commitment to home rule did not preempt serious struggles over who ruled at home, but these struggles often focused on establishing broadly acceptable and inclusive legal regimes under state constitutions. Popular sovereignty, the foundational, legitimating premise of American constitutionalism, subsumed class differences and erased civil inequalities. In fact, class differences were all too apparent during and after the revolution, when war-weary and cash-strapped farmers evaded and resisted onerous burdens imposed by state governments. Yet even when embattled fiscal conservatives railed against "popular licentiousness" and warned of imminent anarchy, they did not unleash a wholesale assault on "democracy."[19] These representatives of the people did not want to challenge the wisdom and integrity of their constituents by deploying tendentious language redolent of class conflict. At the same time, the term itself was losing some of its sting. As constitution-writers rejected traditional conceptions of mixed government, in which distinct social orders exercised power and claimed privileges, the only branch of the British Parliament that could serve as a model for Americans was the more-or-less popularly elected House of Commons, the "democratical" branch.[20]

The promiscuous use of anti-democratic language by ruling elites seeking to restrain popular excesses could only be counter-suggestive, bringing back bad memories of earlier constitutional conflicts. If "*democracy* carried no particular inspiration" in the founding era, as political theorist John Dunn suggests, "it held little or no immediate menace."[21] More positive connotations of the term would be fully expressed only when a centralizing national elite threatened provincial liberties by subverting or compromising the authority of state constitutions. Even then, Palmer shows, the American apotheosis of democracy finally depended on developments in France.[22]

---

[18] For a history of popular mobilization that substantiates this point see Benjamin L. Carp, *Rebels Rising: Cities and the American Revolution* (New York: Oxford University Press, 2007).

[19] Wood, *Creation of the American Republic*, 409–13 and passim.

[20] For a good discussion of republicanism and democracy, see Holly Brewer, *By Birth or Consent: Children, Law, and the Anglo-American Revolution in Authority* (Chapel Hill: University of North Carolina Press, 2005), pp. 13–16.

[21] John Dunn, *Democracy: A History* (New York: Atlantic Monthly Press, 2005), pp. 71–84, quotation at 80.

[22] Palmer, *Age of the Democratic Revolution*, vol. 1, pp. 13–20; idem, "Notes on the Use of the Word 'Democracy,' 1789–1799," *Political Science Quarterly* 48 (1953), 203–26.

In their assault on the old regime, French revolutionaries who identified "aristocrats" as their most powerful and insidious enemies began to call themselves "democrats."

Unlike their American predecessors, French revolutionaries did not seek recognition as a "civilized" state, but instead effectively withdrew their own recognition of hostile monarchical regimes and sought to foment radical change across Europe. Unlike the Americans, the French did not seek to suppress consciousness of class differences, but instead banished or executed class enemies as successive regimes redefined the boundaries of French nationhood. The ideological clarity of the binary oppositions of aristocracy and democracy, old regime and new (and, not coincidentally, of old world and new) were powerfully appealing to the emerging Democratic-Republican opposition to Federalist administrations in the 1790s.[23] The French Revolution taught oppositionists not only to think of themselves as democrats and their opponents as aristocrats, but also to reinterpret their own revolution as the *first* great democratic revolution. French successes abroad thus provided a crucial spur to a political mobilization that Jefferson and his followers prayed would redeem their own revolution. Jeffersonians persuaded themselves that aristocratic elements had not been fully purged at the founding and that the American Revolution was therefore not yet complete.[24]

Democratic ideology galvanized the growing opposition to federalism, enabling Jeffersonian Republicans to demonize the administration and forge a continental alliance of disparate dissident factions. Republicans were fearfully forward-looking, most concerned about the shape of things to come, particularly about challenges to traditional provincial liberties that buttressed their own right to rule. The new language of aristocracy and democracy universalized these putative threats to local authority, paradoxically enabling Republicans to challenge Federalists on their own ground as "artificial" aristocrats with illegitimate, neo-imperial ambitions. The Republicans' French-inflected political sociology pitted Anglophiliac "aristocrats" and "monocrats" against the great patriotic mass of the "people," leveling distinctions on both sides. Imported categories profoundly distorted

---

[23] Palmer, *Age of Democratic Revolution*, vol. 2, pp. 509–46. American historians have recognized the central importance of foreign policy conflicts in precipitating party formation in the "first party system" but have exaggerated the significance of republican ideology in this articulation. See particularly John R. Howe, Jr., "Republican Thought and the Political Violence of the 1790s," *American Quarterly* 19 (1967), 147–65; Richard Buel, Jr., *Securing the Revolution: Ideology in American Politics, 1789–1815* (Ithaca: Cornell University Press, 1972); and Lance Banning, *The Jeffersonian Persuasion: Evolution of a Party Ideology* (Ithaca: Cornell University Press, 1978). Banning significantly shifted his interpretative focus away from republican and toward federal themes in his brilliant *The Sacred Fire of Liberty: James Madison and the Founding of the Federal Republic* (Ithaca: Cornell University Press, 1995).

[24] Peter S. Onuf, *Jefferson's Empire: The Language of American Nationhood* (Charlottesville: University of Virginia Press, 2000), pp. 80–108.

American realities. Republican ideologues depicted Federalists as an emergent continental aristocracy, discounting their own leaders' impeccable – indeed, often superior – social credentials.[25] Conjuring up memories of the American Revolution, they justified a massive mobilization against the federal government, reinforcing their own regional power base in the South and launching a "democratic" assault on Federalist rule in the North.

Jefferson never retreated from the highly ideological understanding of political conflict that he embraced in the 1790s, even when he resumed correspondence with his old friend John Adams during his retirement. In 1813 Jefferson famously extolled the claims of "natural aristocracy" or meritocracy over those of "an artificial aristocracy founded on wealth and birth, without either virtue or talents," and utterly dependent on the patronage of a corrupt, engorged state apparatus. Yet, as Adams astutely noted, Jefferson did not really have a quarrel with "aristocracy" as such, which he failed to recognize in its myriad forms. From Adams's perspective, his old coadjutor was making the case for local, landed, and well-established elite rule – that is, for aristocracy. But Jefferson juxtaposed the "democracy" of the southern (slaveholding) states to "aristocratic" Massachusetts and Connecticut, where "a traditional reverence for certain families ... has rendered the offices of the government nearly hereditary in those families." The old regime would survive in New England, Jefferson lectured his good-natured – and surely incredulous – friend as long as "your strict alliance of church and state" survived; by contrast, Jefferson's Bill for Religious Freedom and the abolition of entail and primogeniture that he initiated "laid the axe to the root of Pseudo-aristocracy" in Virginia.[26]

In this exchange with Adams Jefferson looked back with satisfaction on his own achievements: Invidious comparisons between New England and Virginia were always a tonic for him. But the faith in democracy's ultimate triumph that Jefferson embraced in the 1790s was shadowed by profound anxiety.[27] He recognized that "aristocracy" was a formidable force,

[25] TJ alluded to Hamilton's dubious genealogy in a letter to George Washington, March 23, 1792, in Peterson, *Jefferson Writings*, 1000–1001: "I will not suffer my retirement to be clouded by the slanders of a man whose history, from the moment at which history can stoop to notice him, is a tissue of machinations against the liberty of the country which has not only received and given him bread, but heaped it's honors on his head." In a letter to P. S. Dupont de Nemours, Jan. 18, 1802, ibid., 1101, TJ cast aspersions on Hamilton's "contracted, English, half-lettered ideas."

[26] TJ to John Adams, Oct. 28, 1813, in Peterson, ed., *Jefferson Writings*, 1306–8. On Adams and aristocracy see Richard Alan Ryerson, "John Adams, Republican Monarchist," in Eliga H. Gould and Peter S. Onuf, eds., *Empire and Nation: The American Revolution in the Atlantic World* (Baltimore: Johns Hopkins University Press, 2005), pp. 72–92, esp. 81–85.

[27] For a provocative elaboration of these themes, see Ronald L. Hatzenbuehler, *"I Tremble for My Country": Thomas Jefferson and the Virginia Gentry* (Gainesville: University of Florida Press, 2006).

reflecting deep-seated tendencies in human nature itself that never could be fully suppressed.[28] Even where the "axe" had been laid to the root, the aristocratic impulse could take on new, more insidious forms that a complacent citizenry might not be virtuous or vigilant enough to discern. For Jefferson the immediate source of danger was always, by definition, "foreign," whether in the form of "British influence" or the encroachments of a federal judiciary that would prepare the way for neo-imperial consolidation. Jefferson's democratic ideology thus offered a persuasive, comprehensive explanation of political conflict that externalized threat and displaced responsibility. The worst that could be said about self-professed democrats is that they became absorbed in their own "pursuits of happiness" and therefore were insufficiently alert to ambient dangers. Tribunes of the people such as Jefferson who constantly harped on these dangers were, of course, beyond criticism – and oblivious to their own class interest. In the blinding glare of democratic ideology, Jefferson and his followers could not recognize the aristocratic impulses that had driven them toward revolution.

Revolutionary patriots were advocates of provincial liberties and assembly privileges long before they refashioned themselves as "democrats" in the party battles of the 1790s. The "rise of the assemblies" constituted the Anglo-American version of the "aristocratic resurgence" that R. R. Palmer chronicled throughout the pre-revolutionary Atlantic world. As they co-opted or neutralized royal governors and appointed councillors, provincial legislators self-consciously modeled their "little Parliaments" after the metropolitan prototype. Their "quest for power" necessarily depended on cultivating – or "treating" – local constituents, but the ideological rationale for patriot resistance to royal authority was less democratic than corporatist.[29] Parliamentary privilege underscored the growing gap in wealth and status between Anglicizing Creole elites and the mass of modest freeholders: Conducting their business in secret with immunity from arrest, assemblymen constituted a class apart, a temporary aristocracy. The deepening imperial crisis countered this tendency to accentuate social distinctions as patriot leaders sought to rally popular support for more broadly defined provincial interests. Drawing inspiration from "country" opposition to "court" corruption in the metropolis, patriot elites began to

---

[28] "The terms of whig and tory belong to natural, as well as to civil history." TJ to John Adams, June 27, 1813, in Lester Cappon, ed., *The Adams-Jefferson Letters: The Complete Correspondence Between Thomas Jefferson and Abigail and John Adams*, 2 vols. (Chapel Hill: University of North Carolina Press, 1959), 1:335. See also TJ to Henry Lee, Aug. 10, 1824: "Call them therefore liberals and serviles, Jacobins and Ultras, whigs and tories, republicans and federalists, aristocrats and democrats or by whatever name you please, they are the same parties still and pursue the same object. The last appellation of aristocrats and democrats is the true one expressing the essence of all." Thomas Jefferson Papers, American Memory, http://memory.loc.gov/cgi-bin/query.

[29] Jack P. Greene, *The Quest for Power: The Lower Houses of Assembly in the Southern Royal Colonies, 1689–1776* (Chapel Hill: University of North Carolina Press, 1963); idem, "Political Mimesis: A Consideration of the Historical and Cultural Roots of Legislative Behavior in the British Colonies in the Eighteenth Century," *American Historical Review* 75 (1969), 337–60.

argue that their provinces were themselves corporate entities, with "constitutions" that must be secured against encroachments by royal prerogative or an overreaching British legislature.

In a lightly governed, overextended imperial polity, the corporatist impulses that distinguished European aristocracies both from centralizing monarchical states and from the great mass of ordinary, unprivileged folk worked toward the identification of patriot elites and their constituents. The process of political and then military mobilization had democratizing consequences, as elites recognized that concessions on a broad range of policy issues – most notably taxation – constituted the "price of Revolution."[30] But the patriot appeal was always to the "people" as a whole, in a corporate sense that transcended class interest and identity. This expansive conception of colonies as corporate entities was first elaborated in the provincial histories that proliferated in the pre-revolutionary decades and then subsequently deployed in the constitutional forensics of the imperial crisis.[31] In the logic of social contract theory, so memorably epitomized in the second paragraph of the Declaration of Independence, individual persons "endowed by their creator with certain inalienable rights" came first and the "people" followed. But Jefferson reversed the historical sequence: The patriot conceptions of the people – or, rather, of provincial peoples – came first, as patriot leaders universalized their own claims to corporate privileges, ultimately translating them into the revolutionary language of natural rights. That language authorized the metaphorical killing of the king, thus legitimizing the break with Britain; it also set the stage for the recognition – and, of course, military assistance – of other nations.[32]

The process of what we call "democratization" followed from the articulation and apotheosis of the constitutional claims of colonies as corporate entities. In revolutionary America, "aristocracy" and "democracy" thus were not fundamentally opposed, as they would be for "democratic" revolutionaries – and Republican revisionists like Jefferson – in the 1790s. Quite to the contrary, monarchy was the odd branch out in the American revolutionary reshuffling of constituted authorities and social forces. In subsequent European revolutions, democratic insurgents promoted political centralization and the expansion of executive authority in their struggle against resurgent aristocracy. American "aristocrats" presented a more benign face, particularly when their ranks were purged of loyalist enemies of the people and refreshed by the recruitment of

---

[30] Charles Carroll of Carrollton, quoted in Ronald Hoffman, *A Spirit of Dissension: Economics, Politics, and the Revolution in Maryland* (Baltimore: Johns Hopkins University Press, 1973), p. 210.

[31] On provincial historiography see Onuf and Onuf, *Nations, Markets, and War*, 42–48, and the essays collected in Jack P. Greene, *Imperatives, Behaviors, and Identities: Essays in Early American Cultural History* (Charlottesville: University of Virginia Press, 1992). See also Ed White, *The Backcountry and the City* (Minneapolis: University of Minnesota Press, 2005). On "constitutional forensics," see Reid, *Constitutional History of the American Revolution*.

[32] Armitage, *Declaration of Independence*; Peter S. Onuf, "A Declaration of Independence for Diplomatic Historians," in *The Mind of Jefferson*, 65–80.

popular leaders. Republicanism provided a common ground for anti-monarchical mobilization, sublimating class differences in an ostentatious commitment to the public good. New state constitutions codified the corporate claims of colony-states, grounding them in the putative sovereignty of the very "peoples" they brought into being. Executive power was curbed, "artificial" distinctions among the citizenry were abolished, and the aristocratic-corporatist impulses that had inspired the first generation of patriots were sublimated in a broadly shared commitment to property rights and the rule of law.

FEDERALISM

Provincial resistance to metropolitan despotism deflected aristocratic impulses, leading patriot elites to identify with the "peoples" of their new state-republics. If legitimate authority now derived from the people, not the king, it also devolved from a metropolitan center to provincial periphery. New state constitutions thus represented both the culminating triumph of a protracted struggle to vindicate provincial liberties and the inauguration of a new era of conflict with a reconstituted central government. The duly constituted sovereign states claimed the early advantage over congresses that exercised delegated authority over war and peace, the monarch's uncontested prerogative before the break with Britain.[33]

The dilemma for nationalist reformers was that their efforts to strengthen congress inevitably raised the specter of monarchical revival and metropolitan despotism. Their success was at best mixed. By insisting that sovereignty remained in the people and that governments *at all levels* exercised delegated powers, they neutralized the states' privileged position in the new dispensation; they also argued persuasively that the new federal government would have to operate directly on citizens – and taxpayers – in order to discharge its collective security function effectively.[34] Yet it did not follow that the peoples of the respective states were now blended into a single people, thus redefining the locus of legitimate authority. Contemporaries were less impressed by this sleight of hand than modern scholars: When Patrick Henry asked how the drafters of the Constitution could speak for "We, the *people*, instead of the *states*, of America," he struck a resonant chord. Did the drafters mean to abolish the states? "The tyranny of Philadelphia," he warned, "may be like the tyranny of George III."[35]

[33] Jerrilyn Greene Marston, *King and Congress: The Transfer of Political Legitimacy, 1774–1776* (Princeton, NJ: Princeton University Press, 1987); Peter S. Onuf, *The Origins of the Federal Republic: Jurisdictional Conflicts in the United States, 1775–1787* (Philadelphia: University of Pennsylvania Press, 1983).

[34] Max Edling, *A Revolution in Favor of Government: Origins of the U.S. Constitution and the Making of the American State* (New York: Oxford University Press, 2003).

[35] Patrick Henry speeches, June 5 and 12, 1788, in Jonathan Elliot, *The Debates in the Several State Conventions on the Adoption of the Federal Constitution*, 2nd ed., 5 vols. (Philadelphia, 1836–59), vol. 3, pp. 44, 314.

Federalist overreach was counter-suggestive, reviving memories of imperial despotism. Advocates of the new Constitution were better advised to leave theoretical issues alone and to argue instead that the real threat to the states came from the union's critical condition, not from a more energetic and effective central government. A "more perfect union" would protect its member states from internal as well as external threats.[36] That the states would be more secure under the new dispensation was surely the sense of most voters in the ratifying conventions, where the people of each state exercised their sovereign authority. Of course, Federalists insisted that this was precisely their intention, that they were truly "federalists," not consolidating nationalists. The form of the new government was the best guarantee of its safety, for the new Constitution was modeled on – and drew legitimacy from – the state constitutions that preceded it.[37]

Opponents of the Constitution played a major role in shaping the new regime.[38] Cecilia Kenyon influentially argued that Antifederalists were "men of little faith" who exaggerated the dangers of neo-imperial "consolidation."[39] But Hamiltonian High Federalists who sought to expand the new federal government's powers through energetic administration and loose construction, blithely ignoring or discounting reassurances to skeptical voters in the ratification campaign, might with equal justice be called "men of bad faith." In view of this subsequent history, Kenyon's characterization seems inappropriate: With many other scholars of her generation, she identified "democracy" with the modern nation-state in its ongoing struggle against reactionary bastions of local privilege. Yet, if Kenyon failed to grasp the links between localism, decentralized authority, and what contemporaries understood as "republicanism" or, later, "democracy," her interpretation of Antifederalist motives illuminates social realities we now overlook. Where local elites embraced the reform movement, "plebeian" elements might challenge their authority, mobilizing against the Constitution in a bid for local control.[40] But, more often, as Kenyon suggested, republicanism suppressed class antagonisms and reinforced local power relations.

---

[36] Cathy D. Matson and Peter S. Onuf, *A Union of Interests: Political and Economic Thought in Revolutionary America* (Lawrence: University of Kansas Press, 1990); David C. Hendrickson, *Peace Pact: The Lost World of the American Founding* (Lawrence: University of Kansas Press, 2003).

[37] Willi Paul Adams, *The First American Constitutions: Republican Ideology and the Making of the State Constitutions in the Revolutionary Era* (Chapel Hill: University of North Carolina Press, 1980); Onuf, "Reflections on the Founding: Constitutional Historiography in Bicentennial Perspective." *WMQ* 46 (1989), 341–75.

[38] Saul Cornell, *The Other Founders: Anti-Federalism and the Dissenting Tradition in America, 1788–1828* (Chapel Hill: University of North Carolina Press, 1999).

[39] Cecilia M. Kenyon, "Men of Little Faith: The Anti-Federalists on the Nature of Representative Government," *WMQ* 12 (1955), 3–43.

[40] Saul Cornell, "Aristocracy Assailed: The Ideology of Backcountry Anti-Federalism," *Journal of American History* 76 (1990), 1148–72; idem, *Other Founders*.

Antifederalist mobilization against ratification of the federal Constitution forged a powerful and enduring link between "aristocracy" and energetic central government in America. Ironically, Antifederalists' anti-aristocratic polemics emerged in the wake of a Loyalist diaspora that purged provincial ruling elites of "aristocratic" elements and of a revolutionary democratization of political participation and office-holding. Far from being "resurgent," aristocracy in America had been definitively routed – or so it appears in retrospect. Yet the Antifederalists played on pervasive, amply justified fears that the revolution might ultimately fail. Enterprising counter-revolutionaries might exploit the crisis of the union to seize and consolidate power on a continental scale, thus destroying republican governments in the states and subverting civil liberties. As it emerged from the revolution's wreckage, a new continental aristocracy would secure its dominance by neutralizing all potential opposition, guaranteeing itself against the popular political mobilization that had toppled the empire. If vigilant voters failed to discern and resist this threat, constitutional reformers would succeed where the king and Parliament had failed.

For Jeffersonians, securing state rights – and the continuing dominance of provincial patriot elites – was not an end in itself, but rather a crucial line of defense against neo-monarchical and neo-aristocratic tyranny and despotism. By calling the Federalists "aristocrats," Antifederalists and their ideological heirs struck a libertarian pose, identifying themselves with the "people" and denying – or projecting – their own political and social aspirations. Their invention of "aristocracy" thus prepared the way for self-consciously embracing "democracy": The Democratic-Republican opposition denied their administration foes any legitimate place in the new regime, defining them as foreigners with aristocratic ambitions while insisting on the fundamental unity of patriotic Americans. Aristocracy in America did not denote a privileged, titled, landed elite that looked to the past for its legitimating pedigree. To the contrary, aristocratic domination was always an immanent threat, perhaps, Jefferson feared, an irrepressible impulse of human nature itself. Federalists and their descendants successfully donned the "pseudo-republican mask" in their ongoing struggle "to warp our government more to the form and principles of monarchy" and "weaken the barriers of the State governments as co-ordinate powers." The aristocrats, Jefferson warned Justice William Johnson in 1823, "are advancing fast toward an ascendancy."[41]

Aristocrats were everywhere in the Democratic imagination. In the 1790s Federalists sought to promote Britain's malign influence as the "paper junto" of bankers and speculators corrupted the people's representatives in Congress.[42] After Jefferson's rise to power in 1801, loose constructionists in the federal judiciary – John Marshall's "subtle corps of sappers and miners" – worked assiduously to "undermine the foundations of our confederated republic."[43]

[41] TJ to William Johnson, June 12, 1823, in Peterson, ed., *Jefferson Writings*, 1472.
[42] Onuf, *Jefferson's Empire*, 85–93.
[43] TJ to Thomas Ritchie, Dec. 25, 1820, in Peterson, ed., *Jefferson Writings*, 1446.

And during the Missouri controversy, aristocratic Restrictionists who despaired "of ever rising again under the old division of whig and tory, devised a new one, of slave-holding, & non-slaveholding states."[44] For Jefferson, resurgent aristocracy always threatened the union, and, just as "monocrats" and aristocrats promoted a more energetic central government, democrats rallied to state rights and a broad diffusion of power. "The true barriers of our liberty in this country are our State governments," Jefferson told the French ideologist Destutt de Tracy in 1811: "Seventeen distinct States, amalgamated into one as to their foreign concerns, but single and independent as to their internal administration, regularly organized with legislature and governor resting on the choice of the people, and enlightened by a free press, can never be so fascinated by the arts of one man, as to submit voluntarily to his usurpation."[45] Democratic self-government at the local level, Jefferson's "ward republics," would provide the best defense against foreign influence and aristocratic reaction.[46]

The Jeffersonian understanding of the aristocratic threat continued to resonate throughout the antebellum era. British efforts to "consolidate" authority in a strong central government and reduce the American colonies to subject provinces provided the interpretative paradigm for opponents of national banks, protective tariffs, and internal improvements.[47] Henry Clay might call his ambitious design for federal state-building "the American System," but Democratic critics knew that its animating spirit was, in fact, un-American; Andrew Jackson played on the same theme in his campaign against the "monster" Bank of the United States and the pernicious influence of foreign shareholders.[48] Democrats focused obsessively on the equal distribution of benefits under the federal system. Policies that affected different sections and sectors of the economy unequally were presumed corruptly redistributive. Commerce must be protected against political interference, Democratic free traders insisted, "beyond the reach of any combined or corrupted majority in a central or consolidated Congress."[49] Beneficiaries of such unequal policies were "artificial," unnatural "aristocrats" in the Jeffersonian sense, privileged by a corrupt government and therefore enemies of the people.

The testimony of Adam Smith and the classical economists against mercantilist state policies gave the Democrats' ongoing struggle against "consolidation" an up-to-date, liberal gloss. Liberalism in turn reinforced the link among democracy, equal rights, and the decentralization of authority in the American

---

[44] TJ to Albert Gallatin, Dec. 26, 1820, ibid., 1448.

[45] TJ to Destutt de Tracy, Jan. 26, 1811, ibid., 1245–46. See the extended discussion on TJ and Destutt in Onuf and Onuf, *Nations, Markets, and War*, 225–39.

[46] Onuf, *Jefferson's Empire*, 119–21.

[47] Onuf, "Federalism, Republicanism, and the Origins of American Sectionalism."

[48] For a sympathetic history of Jeffersonianism and Jacksonianism, see Sean Wilentz, *The Rise of American Democracy: Jefferson to Lincoln* (New York: Norton, 2005).

[49] "Cotton Manufacture," Nov. 27, 1833, in Condy Raguet, ed., *The Examiner, and Journal of Political Economy; Devoted to the Advancement of the Cause of State Rights and Free Trade*, 2 vols. (Philadelphia, 1834–35), vol. 1, p. 139.

federal system. An aristocratic ruling class would emerge only when the people ceased to be vigilant and their supposed representatives were therefore free to promote their own interests. Yet liberal – or libertarian – strictures on the abuses of power were not equally salient at all levels of government. Indeed, effective resistance to the consolidation of power in a strong central government presupposed strong state governments that could command the people's loyalty.[50]

The enduring "Spirit of 1776" made Americans reflexively suspicious of metropolitan government, but it also authorized popular political – and military – mobilization in defense of republican self-government. When liberty was threatened, Jefferson told Destutt, citizens would "rise up on every side, ready organized for deliberation by a constitutional legislature, and for action by their governor, constitutionally the commander of the militia of the State." The preservation of liberty was a function of a *balance* of power within the federal union, not its transcendence or negation. "Regularly formed into regiments and battalions, into infantry, cavalry and artillery," armed citizens "trained under officers general and subordinate, legally appointed, always in readiness, and to whom they are already in habits of obedience." Jefferson's "democratic" conception of an empowered people was not, in this case, directed at a properly foreign foe in the name of collective security. Instead, he contemplated military measures against a "single State" so "fascinated by the arts of one man" – Napoleon Bonaparte would have been the exemplary figure – "as to submit voluntarily to his usurpation," or "be constrained to it by any force he can possess."[51] Presumably the same logic would apply if more than one state submitted to the "usurpation" of its liberties, as at the Hartford Convention of 1814, or when a majority of states captured the federal government and turned its power against the liberty-loving remnant.[52]

Jefferson's legendary faith in democracy was predicated on an absurdly exaggerated estimate of the potential power of citizen-soldiers in the "strongest Government on earth."[53] But what is crucial here is that "democracy" for Jefferson was a fighting faith, defined against the ubiquitous threat of resurgent "aristocracy." The Enlightened liberal fantasy of a peaceful, post-mercantilist world "governed" by free, non-coerced exchange inspired Jefferson and likeminded colleagues. Yet he recognized that the torturous path toward the end of history would be drenched in "rivers of blood," and – given that the aristocratic impulse to dominate was "natural" – that destination might never be reached.[54] Jefferson and his followers became conscious of themselves as "democrats" in

[50] Onuf and Onuf, *Nations, Markets, and War*, 187–218, 251–56.
[51] TJ to Destutt de Tracy, Jan. 26, 1811, in Peterson, ed., *Jefferson Writings*, 1246.
[52] Onuf, *Jefferson's Empire*, 121–29.
[53] TJ, First Inaugural Address, March 4, 1801, in Peterson, ed., *Jefferson Writings*, 493.
[54] TJ to John Adams, Sept. 4, 1823, in Cappon, ed., *Adams-Jefferson Letters*, 2:596. On war and peace in Enlightenment and post-Enlightenment thought, see David A. Bell, *The First Total War: Napoleon's Empire and the Birth of Warfare as We Know It* (Boston: Houghton Mifflin Harcourt, 2007).

their never-ending struggle against putative "aristocrats," not through a radical or systematic critique of their own social worlds. Aristocrats were always foreigners, distant – and sometimes, more ominously, not so distant – enemies of liberty and local self-government. By contrast, local leaders were "natural aristocrats" who could command the reflexive loyalty of fellow citizens well "trained ... in habits of obedience." Of course, Jefferson knew that his neighbors were not nearly as deferential as he told Destutt, but this was less a measure of his obtuseness than of the power of democratic ideology: The visionary democrat overlooked a great deal.

Antifederalists and their Jeffersonian successors sought to constitutionalize state rights and to secure the traditional liberties of state citizens. This might mean the authority of neighbors impaneled in juries, or the right to participate in local self-government in incorporated towns, cities, or counties. But it also meant security of property, including rights in enslaved human beings. In a strict Jeffersonian sense, aristocracy was abolished. Certainly the aristocratic antecedents of the corporatist impulse were suppressed as republicanized corporate forms proliferated. The states themselves were corporate entities, inviolable, irreducible, and foundational components of the new federal regime, "persons" under the new constitutional dispensation. In the new nation, democracy and federalism were inextricably linked: They defined one another. The "rise of democracy" thus did not lead to agrarian laws and the redistribution of property. To the contrary, the fixation of professed democrats on threats to local, state, and regional rights and interests from a revitalized, "aristocratic" central government secured the property claims of fictive corporate persons as well as private individuals and led to the progressive concentration of wealth.

CORPORATIONS

Jefferson and his fellow revolutionaries may have "laid the axe" to its roots, but new forms of "aristocracy" flourished on American soil, threatening the success of the republican experiment. Perhaps Jefferson had mistaken roots for branches, and pruning away primogeniture and entail had simply cleared the way for more luxuriant growth. Patriots who mobilized against the monopoly privileges of corporations such as the East India Company in the name of free trade and equal rights were also baffled. Far from disappearing, Pauline Maier shows, corporations proliferated.[55] Freed from the taint of court privilege, the republicanized corporate form could now be deployed to serve a widening range of public (and eventually private) purposes. Significantly, state legislatures, responding to broad popular pressure for infrastructural development, took the lead in the new wave of incorporations. As long as they could be seen as instruments of the people's will, corporations were compatible with

[55] Pauline Maier, "The Revolutionary Origins of the American Corporation," *WMQ* 50 (1993), 51–84.

republican government. But the people's representatives were vulnerable to corruption and the corporate form could be abused – as unsuccessful supplicants could so clearly see. "Monopoly," like "aristocracy," could thus emerge in new and insidious "pseudo-republican" forms.[56]

A caricature of the old regime dominated the post-colonial political imagination of republican ideologues, particularly as the French Revolution clarified the supposedly fundamental conflict between "democrats" and "aristocrats." Yet because the most ardent Republicans were also Federalists who did *not* see the "people" or "nation" as a single transcendent whole, but instead as distinct peoples embodied in their respective state-republics, their "old regime" was displaced to an emerging national political arena and projected into the future – obscuring local structures of power and privilege, if not making them altogether invisible. The state governments were "the wisest conservative power ever contrived by man," Jefferson told Destutt, because they protected American liberty from aristocratic encroachments. But federalism also naturalized multiple corporate identities, facilitating the very forms of association that John Taylor of Caroline found so frightening. Revolutionary Americans may have rejected British conceptions of "virtual representation," but in doing so they developed an acute sense of their own corporate rights, in towns, parishes, counties, and provinces.[57] These incorporated entities now derived their authority from the sovereign people, not the king, but they could claim a kind of virtual "personality" and constitutionally protected rights. Now that the "people" exercised sovereign authority, Americans could abstract "personality" from actual persons.

One of the Revolutionaries' leading grievances was the Crown's decision to ban the formation of new counties and towns that would incorporate groups of people into collective bodies that could govern themselves and claim representation in provincial governments. Instead of creating unequal privileges, these corporations enabled settlers in newly developed areas to enjoy equal rights with their fellow colonists. British imperial reformers became convinced, however, that the colonists' claims to corporate rights under their colonial "constitutions" amounted to *imperium in imperio*, a "solecism" in politics utterly incompatible with parliamentary "sovereignty."[58] Only the British sovereign could create corporations, and they in

---

[56] For an illuminating study of the politics of monopoly privilege in New York, see Brian Murphy, "The Politics Corporations Make: Charters, Coalitions, and the Formation of State and Parties in New York, 1783–1850," Ph.D. diss. (University of Virginia, 2008).

[57] On the importance of corporate rights for political mobilization in longer-established provinces of the British empire, see Elizabeth Mancke, *The Fault Lines of Empire: Political Differentiation in Massachusetts and Nova Scotia, ca. 1760–1830* (New York: Routledge, 2005), esp. pp. 1–28.

[58] Daniel J. Hulsebosch, "Imperia in Imperio: The Multiple Constitutions of Empire in New York, 1750–1777," *Law and History Review* 16, (1998), 319–79, at 337–44. See also Hulsebosch, *Constituting Empire: New York and the Transformation of Constitutionalism in the Atlantic World, 1664–1830* (Chapel Hill: University of North Carolina Press, 2005).

turn were limited to the enactment of by-laws that did not encroach on the sovereign's authority. Yet, even as the new constitutional orthodoxy took hold in ministerial circles, colonists constitutionalized their corporate claims, insisting that Parliament could not encroach on their rights – including the right to form corporations. State legislatures thus resumed the process of incorporation after independence. New conceptions of popular sovereignty resolved the imperial reformers' logical conundrum: If ultimate authority was not located in a single place – the king-in-parliament – it could be exercised through multiple jurisdictions, all deriving authority from the people and all, therefore, in some sense "sovereign." Because they were federal in their original formulation, the Revolutionaries' popular sovereignty claims facilitated a new distribution of authority in the independent United States. The federal dimension of the new regime was equally apparent *within* as well as *among* the states, for new state constitutions recognized the rights of the corporate entities that created them and that they in turn created.[59]

Revolutionary Americans were hostile to monopolies that operated to their commercial disadvantage, to vast land grants to royal favorites that denied them access to the continent's riches, and to the plague of Crown appointees or "placemen" who descended on them to implement the ministry's misguided reform measures. But hostility to monopoly did not mean rejection of the corporate form: Even as patriot polemicists waged war against the East India Company, they defended the corporate rights of colonies with similar legal pedigrees; nor did Americans eschew neo-mercantilist policies of their own after independence.[60] Far from eliminating large land grants, revolutionary governments depended on syndicates of speculators to privatize public lands; for their part, settlers demanded law and order, good titles, and progress toward self-government – "rights" that could only be fulfilled through association and incorporation. Nor did popular mobilization against British placemen, the prototypical "aristocrats" who continued to haunt the American political imagination long after 1776, signify rejection of Jefferson's "natural aristocracy." In every case, corrupt, despotic, and illegitimate forms of rule stood in opposition to their republican antitypes. The genius of republicanism was not to level all distinctions by eliminating all vestiges of the colonial old regime in the name of citizens' equal rights. To the contrary, the new regime released the energy of an enterprising people by protecting property rights and promoting the proliferation of corporate entities that facilitated local

---

[59] The fullest elaboration of the constitutional debate can be found in John Phillip Reid, ed., *The Briefs of the American Revolution: Constitutional Arguments between Thomas Hutchinson, Governor of Massachusetts Bay, and James Bowdoin for the Council and John Adams for the House of Representatives* (New York: New York University Press, 1981). For extended commentary on the relation between the sovereignty problem and federalism, see LaCroix, *A Well-Constructed Union*.

[60] John E. Crowley, *The Privileges of Independence: Neomercantilism and the American Revolution* (Baltimore: Johns Hopkins University Press, 1993).

self-government, civic betterment, eleemosynary initiatives, diverse forms of religious worship, and the pooling of capital.[61]

Rallying against metropolitan despotism enabled Revolutionary Americans to purge themselves of corruption, externalize threats to their liberties, and to invent an "old regime" against which to define themselves. But popular sovereignty also gave new legitimacy to old corporate forms. Deriving their authority from the sovereign people, these corporations – beginning with the colony-provinces themselves – no longer had to trace their origins to royal charters, customary practices, or historical precedents. Claiming inviolable rights under the new dispensation, corporations gained a kind of legal "personhood" that was not only compatible with citizens' equal rights but provided crucial sites for its civic and social expression.

Americans could impute personality to corporations that did not create a privileged class, but instead served collective interests. At first, special legislative acts guaranteed that corporations would serve some clearly defined public purpose, whether in dispensing charity, promoting the advancement of knowledge, or developing economic infrastructure.[62] Judgments about which enterprises deserved the people's patronage proved increasingly controversial, however, pointing the way toward general incorporation. A New York act of 1811 led to the incorporation of hundreds of business enterprises; by the 1830s and 1840s, most other states had followed suit.[63] As fictive persons under the law, corporations could accumulate, invest, and disburse property under terms that protected both shareholders and the general public. Under the principle of limited liability, corporate personality was distinct from the personalities of incorporators. Americans thus eventually overcame the Revolutionaries' aversion to the corporate form, notwithstanding widespread anxieties about resurgent "aristocracy" and the protracted conflicts that shaped civil society in various states. Corporations proliferated when they came to be seen as artificial persons that the sovereign people themselves authorized.

General incorporation marked the culmination of a generally neglected process of "democratization" that made corporate personhood universally accessible. The conventional narrative of democratization focuses on the enfranchisement of actual persons who struggled to overcome traditional exclusions based on property-holding, religion, ethnicity, race, and gender. But the "democracy" that antebellum Americans embraced was conceptualized in corporate terms, beginning with patriots' claims of equal rights *for their colonies* in the imperial crisis.

---

[61] On the release of energy see James Willard Hurst, *Law and the Conditions of Freedom in the Nineteenth-Century United States* (Madison: University of Wisconsin Press, 1984). On "developmental corporations" that enjoyed widespread community support see John Majewski, *A House Dividing: Economic Development in Pennsylvania and Virginia Before the Civil War* (New York: Cambridge University Press, 2000), pp. 12–58.

[62] Oscar Handlin, *Commonwealth; A Study of the Role of Government in the American Economy: Massachusetts, 1774–1861*, rev. ed. (Cambridge, MA: Harvard University Press, 1969).

[63] W. C. Kessler, "A Statistical Study of the New York General Incorporation Act of 1811," *Journal of Political Economy* 48 (1940), 877–82.

The new republics revolutionaries created were also corporate entities: By definition, a republic's citizens were equal, but it was also true – as frustrated "nationalists" who promoted proportional representation discovered – that all republics, as self-governing communities, were equal to one another. The "equality" of the states may have seemed – and may still seem – an absurd fiction: Were Delaware and Virginia in any meaningful sense equal? But the same questions could be raised about the putative equality of citizens. In what sense was Jefferson, the "natural aristocrat," equal to his humble (nonslaveholding) neighbors?

It was only by an act of political imagination, by abstracting claims of individuals from their concrete circumstances, that citizens could be seen as equals. Civic equality was a potent and empowering fiction, crucial to the new regime's legitimacy and as a spur to the ambitious and enterprising. Humble Americans aspired to a republicanized "gentility," or "respectability," – a leveling up, not down – predicated on the democratization, not abolition, of privilege.[64] That claims to equal rights within the new republics should be accompanied by the exclusion of whole classes of actual persons, and that those exclusions should be seen as "natural," is hardly surprising, for equality was only meaningful within a bounded civic – that is, corporate – context. Nor is it surprising that so many American republicans should so quickly overcome their reflexive aversion to monopoly and privilege in the empire to embrace republicanized corporate forms that presumably served their interests. In a theoretical sense, the abstraction of civic personality from actual persons – who would be treated *as if* they were equal under the law, or at the ballot box – was equivalent to the fiction of corporate personality. As far as the state was concerned, civic equality guaranteed equal opportunity and, implicitly, unequal outcomes; associations of individuals, whether incorporated or mimicking the corporate form of self-government in an informal, extralegal fashion, were instrumental to the achievement of their own goals and, coincidentally, the public good.[65]

Federalism constituted the critical threshold for the "democratization" of the corporate form in antebellum America. Of course, not all associations gained a foothold in the new regime with equal facility: The Democratic-Republican societies raised the specter of *imperium in imperio* in the 1790s, and workers allegedly jeopardized the public interest when they combined to raise wages or improve working conditions.[66] But Americans were predisposed to accept the

---

[64] Richard L. Bushman, *The Refinement of America: Persons, Houses, Cities* (New York: Knopf, 1992).

[65] My argument here is indebted to Marc Harris, "Civil Society in Post-Revolutionary America," in Gould and Onuf, eds., *Empire and Nation*, 197–216. On evolving, increasingly abstract and economistic definitions of the "public good," see Morton J. Horwitz, *The Transformation of American Law, 1780–1860* (Cambridge, MA: Harvard University Press, 1977).

[66] Albrecht Koschnik, "The Democratic Societies of Philadelphia and the Limits of the American Public Sphere, circa 1793–1795," *WMQ* 58 (2001), 615–36; Johann N. Neem, "Freedom of Association in the Early Republic: The Republican Party, the Whiskey Rebellion, and the Philadelphia and New York Cordwainers' Cases," *Pennsylvania Magazine of History and Biography* 127 (2003), 259–90.

proliferation of corporations – and dismiss the problem of *imperium in imperio* – because their revolution was itself a movement to vindicate corporate privileges. The various jurisdictions through which they asserted their right to self-government provided the pattern for subsequent corporations. States, counties, or towns were equal to one another, and because citizens could move freely from one place to the next, they did not command the exclusive loyalty of, or create exclusive privileges for, their populations. Most importantly, federalism gave Americans dual identities as American citizens and, contingently, as citizens of particular states. Yet, paradoxically, the contingent identity of state citizenship – the identity that could be so easily exchanged for another – was foundational, the predicate of political participation.[67]

Far from being exponents of "actual" representation, as debates over their representation in Parliament suggested, Americans eagerly embraced a protean conception of virtual representation. Americans were simultaneously "present" in multiple corporate entities, impersonated by their agents for particular purposes without derogating from their rights as property-owning citizens.[68] And those corporations were themselves "persons" that embodied and expressed the sovereignty of the people. Multiple modes of representation facilitated the transformation of British-mixed government into the more complex American distribution of powers among and within distinct jurisdictions. The break with Britain vindicated corporate rights, grounding them in popular sovereignty and identifying them with the defense of liberty and property. Revolutionaries thus jettisoned the foundational myth of modern British constitutionalism, that the supposedly distinct social orders that constituted the nation were "actually" present, and therefore representing themselves, in the British Parliament. Americans were accustomed to delegating authority to multiple jurisdictions without compromising their claims to equal rights.

The abstraction of civic personality from actual persons promoted the democratization of the electorate as well as the proliferation of corporations. The easy availability of property meant that barriers to voting had always been extraordinarily low in provincial America, and popular participation in the war effort eroded them further: Property requirements based on the notion that a voter should have a minimal "stake in society" seemed increasingly alien and anachronistic. Of course, progress toward universal white manhood suffrage was uneven and intermittent, but its logic was irresistible. Conceptions of natural rights and social contract that were critical to the new regime's legitimacy postulated an original, natural equality that *became civic* through

---

[67] See James H. Kettner, "The Development of American Citizenship in the Revolutionary Era: The Idea of Volitional Citizenship," *American Journal of Legal History* 18 (1974), 208–42, at 211: "The whole point of the [pre-revolutionary] debate was to delineate and defend the prerogatives of the American colonies as though they were homogenous wholes." See also idem, *The Development of American Citizenship, 1608–1870* (Chapel Hill: University of North Carolina Press, 1978); Bradburn, *The Citizenship Revolution*.

[68] My understanding of "personhood" is derived from my brother Nicholas's discussion of "Moral Persons" in Chapter 4 of Onuf and Onuf, *Nations, Markets, and War*.

revolutionary acts of corporate self-constitution. Civic equality could not therefore depend on property: If it did, then property, not people, would be "represented" in the new American governments. Only by abstracting civic personality from the material conditions of actual persons – by distinguishing persons from property – could the revolutionary premise that "all men are created equal" be in any sense meaningful. Secure in their rights, Americans could pursue happiness and accumulate property. Self-governing republicans were liberated from the tyrannical, personal pseudo-authority of supposed social superiors; so, too, was property liberated from a predatory state with unlimited taxing powers.

Popular sovereignty was a potent fiction that promoted the progressive democratization of American electorates, securing civil liberties and property rights and vindicating the corporate claims of communities – and, ultimately, associations and enterprises of all sorts – in a radically decentralized federal regime. The proliferation of fictive, virtual persons abstracted from actual persons (forming distinct, self-conscious social classes) defanged democracy: The *demos* was everybody – and nobody. Individuals might be stripped of (unequal) identities derived from traditional social and political hierarchies, but they were at the same time empowered to forge new identities (as equals) in the rich associational life of churches and civil society, in the marketplace, and in partisan politics.[69] All would be equal under the rule of law. Surely this was a "new order for the ages," an epochal transformation of social and political life that made subjects into citizens.

Yet the state did not wither away under the new dispensation, nor did the supposedly archaic institution of slavery disappear. Quite to the contrary, revolutionary commitments to democracy, federalism, and property rights gave the institution a powerful new lease on life. The abstraction of persons from property that was so liberating for so many white citizens worked the other way for enslaved blacks. Actual persons without civic identity and rights could be treated as if they were not persons at all.

SLAVERY AND FREEDOM

Slaveowning American patriots feared that enforcement of Parliamentary taxation would reduce them to the condition of their own slaves, a "species of property" stripped of civic personhood. In retrospect, their complaints seem grotesquely disproportionate. We can only ask, with ministerial critic Samuel

---

[69] My argument here is indebted to Albrecht Koschnik, *"Let a Common Interest Bind Us Together': Associations, Partisanship, and Culture in Philadelphia, 1775–1840* (Charlottesville: University of Virginia Press, 2007); Johann Nuru Neem, *Creating a Nation of Joiners: Democracy and Civil Society in Early National Massachusetts* (Cambridge, MA: Harvard University Press, 2008). See also John L. Brooke, "Consent, Civil Society, and the Public Sphere in the Age of Revolution and the Early American Republic," in Jeffrey L Pasley, Andrew W. Robertson, and David Waldstreicher, eds., *Beyond the Founders: New Approaches to the Political History of the Early American Republic* (Chapel Hill: University of North Carolina Press, 2004), pp. 207–50.

Johnson: "How is it that we hear the loudest yelps for liberty among the drivers of negroes?"[70] Enlightened planters were embarrassed by their apparent hypocrisy and expressed misgivings about slavery (generally in private); a significant number of Virginians even freed their slaves when private manumissions were legalized in 1782.[71] Yet the institution was not seriously threatened, notwithstanding the loss of large numbers of slaves during the war. The usual explanation is that material interests trumped revolutionary principle, that emancipationist sentiment was "conditional" – and the conditions were never quite right.[72] I suggest instead that the patriots' understanding of British and provincial liberties ultimately strengthened the institution's ideological underpinnings. Democracy and federalism – the plurality of polities through which the "people" expressed their sovereign will – were inextricably linked. By defending the corporate rights of provincial and local governments, patriots sought to secure the liberty and property of all Anglo-Americans, including their property in slaves.

The patriots' genius for generalizing threats to their property is familiar. They were predisposed to see particular taxes as mere incidents in a larger struggle between "liberty" and "power" and to project a "long train of abuses" into the distant future.[73] The movement from the particular to the universal naturalized rights claims and translated "liberties" into "liberty," the same process of abstraction that made "all men . . . equal." When Parliament sought to tax unrepresented Americans, it constructively asserted a dominion over *all* American property. American property claims, therefore, were merely conventional: They existed only at the discretion of the taxing sovereign. By demolishing the fundamental premises of the colonists' common-law constitutionalism and of their identity as Britons, Parliamentary pretensions to sovereignty forced patriots to look to "nature" (and thus to themselves) to vindicate increasingly abstract, nonnegotiable rights claims. American conceptions of slave property followed the same trajectory. In the *Somerset* decision of 1772, Lord Mansfield resolved any lingering ambiguity about the status of slaves in the empire as a whole: Slavery only existed under the positive law of particular plantation colonies and, again, presumably at the pleasure of the British sovereign. As George Van Cleve persuasively argues, slaveholders looked to the new federal union for a new extraprovincial law of slavery. The

---

[70] Samuel Johnson, "Taxation Not Tryanny" (1775), in Donald J. Greene, ed., *The Yale Edition of the Works of Samuel Johnson,* 16 vols. (New Haven, CT: Yale University press, 1977), vol. 10, p. 454.

[71] Eva Sheppard Wolf argues convincingly that slavery in Virginia was "resilient and flexible," accommodating "manumission without being weakened by it." Wolf, *Race and Liberty in the New Nation: Emancipation in Virginia from the Revolution to Nat Turner's Rebellion* (Baton Rouge: Louisiana State University Press, 2006), quotation at 47.

[72] William W. Freehling, *The Road to Disunion,* vol. 1, *Secessionists at Bay, 1776–1854* (New York: Oxford University Press, 1990).

[73] Bernard Bailyn, *The Ideological Origins of the American Revolution* (Cambridge, MA: Harvard University Press, 1967).

general recognition of property rights in human beings was the *sine qua non* of union.[74]

It would take generations before slaveholders claimed that slavery was a "positive good," conformable to nature's design. But, by securing this particular species of property in the new federal union and by mobilizing in defense of property rights generally, slaveholding patriots buttressed the institution against internal and external assaults. And by focusing on the origins of slavery in the slave trade, Americans could blame the British for the institution's development. Jefferson thus asserted in his draft of the Declaration of Independence that George III "has waged cruel war against human nature itself, violating it's most sacred rights of life and liberty in the persons of a distant people who never offended him, captivating & carrying them into slavery in another hemisphere, or to incur miserable death in their transportation thither." The Congress excised this passage, recognizing that Jefferson's absurdly exaggerated projection (and denial) of responsibility would not make a favorable impression on "a candid world."[75] But the logic remained compelling for Jefferson for the rest of his career: All forms of despotism and corruption were ultimately traceable to the evil metropolis.

Jefferson was less concerned about the "crimes committed against the LIBERTIES" of enslaved Africans than about the royal assault on American provincial rights. His specific complaint was that the Privy Council had overturned modest efforts by the provincial assemblies of Maryland and Virginia to tax and regulate slave imports. If *Somerset* made planters anxious about the status of slave property in the empire, these decisions raised equally troubling questions about the authority of the provincial legal regimes that Mansfield claimed were the source of property rights in slaves. Provincial governments that had the authority to define slaves as property should be able to regulate imports, Jefferson reasoned, and that same authority would in turn enable them to take further steps toward the institution's amelioration and even its ultimate eradication.[76] But a king who had "prostituted his negative for suppressing every legislative attempt to prohibit or to restrain this execrable commerce" in human beings now offered freedom to slaves who would murder their masters. The servile insurrection initiated by Lord Dunmore's infamous proclamation of March 1775 showed why it was so essential for self-governing Virginians to be absolutely secure in their property rights, including their property in slaves.[77]

---

[74] George Van Cleve, "Somerset's Case and Its Antecedents in Imperial Perspective," *Law and History Review* 24 (2006), 1–45; idem, "A Slaveholders' Union: The Law and Politics of American Slavery, 1770–1821," Ph.D. dissertation (University of Virginia, 2007). See also Don Fehrenbacher, *The Slaveholding Republic: An Account of the United States Government's Relations to Slavery* (New York: Oxford University Press, 2001).

[75] The quotations from TJ's draft of the Declaration in this and the next paragraph are taken from Peterson, ed., *Jefferson Writings*, 22.

[76] On amelioration see Christa Dierksheide, "The Amelioration of Slavery in the Anglo-American Imagination, 1780–1840," Ph.D. diss. (University of Virginia, 2009).

[77] Woody Holton, "Rebel Against Rebel: Enslaved Virginians and the Coming of the American Revolution," *Virginia Magazine of History and Biography* 105 (1997), 157–92.

Slave property had to be protected throughout the new American union because slaves could be used as tools against the lives and liberties of their masters. "Are our slaves to be presented with freedom and a dagger?" Jefferson asked his old friend Adams in 1821 when anti-slavery forces sought to ban slavery in the new state of Missouri.[78] Any effort by the central government – imperial or federal – to interfere with slavery in any state, old or new, harked back to the king's betrayal of his loyal American subjects. By the same logic, any reform of the institution had to begin within the slaveholding states and be fully compatible with their rights as self-governing republics.

Jefferson's primary commitment as a revolutionary republican and as a self-professed "democrat" was to the vindication of the corporate rights of self-governing communities, not to natural rights claims that could only be fulfilled within civic contexts.[79] The fundamental link between federalism and democracy – between the rights of communities and the civic equality of citizens – was most conspicuous in the elaboration of his ideas about "ward-republics" during his retirement. "It is by dividing and subdividing these republics from the great national one down through all its subordinations," Jefferson told Joseph C. Cabell, "until it ends in the administration of every man's farm by himself; by placing under every one what his own eye may superintend, that all will be done for the best." Here the federal principle that inspired the revolutionary generation was made explicit and taken to its democratic extreme: Every citizen was sovereign over his own domain, equal in his rights to his fellow citizens. "Division and subdivision" protected citizens in their equal rights, obliterating the civic inequalities of the old regime. By contrast, "the generalizing and concentrating all cares and powers into one body ... has destroyed liberty and the rights of man in every government which has ever existed under the sun."[80] But the fulfilment of the American Revolution's democratic promise would bind citizens together and empower them, even as it secured their respective rights. As Jefferson explained to Samuel Kercheval, "the whole is cemented by giving to every citizen, personally, a part in the administration of the public affairs."[81]

Jefferson's democratic "patriarch" exercised authority over household dependents, including the human beings he claimed as property.[82] Far from setting slavery on the "road to ultimate extinction," the American Revolution thus provided the peculiar institution with powerful new institutional and ideological props. The "slaveholders' union" secured slave property within and among the states, guaranteeing the rendition of fugitives and preempting federal policies that might in any way jeopardize slaves' value. The Constitutional ban

[78] TJ to Adams, Jan. 22, 1821, in Cappon, ed., *Adams-Jefferson Letters*, vol. 2, 570.
[79] This theme is elaborated in Ari Helo and Peter Onuf, "Jefferson, Morality, and the Problem of Slavery," in *The Mind of Jefferson*, 236–70.
[80] TJ to Joseph C. Cabell, Feb. 2, 1816, in Peterson, ed., *Jefferson Writings*, 1380. For a further discussion of TJ's federalism see Onuf, *Jefferson's Empire*, 109–46, esp. 119–21 (ward republics).
[81] TJ to Samuel Kercheval, July 12, 1816, ibid., 1399–1400.
[82] TJ playfully described himself as a "patriarch" in a letter to Angelica Schuyler Church, Nov. 27, 1793, in Peterson, ed., *Jefferson Writings*, 1013.

on the foreign slave trade – delayed until 1807 – did not impinge on the domestic trade, nor did it block the addition of foreign territory (and foreign slaves) to the union or the migration of masters and slaves to new territory. The states enjoyed the plenary authority over slavery that Jefferson sought to vindicate, and some of them even used it to dismantle the institution – as Jefferson suggested they would. But state sovereignty more often worked the other way, to consolidate slavery's domination; further, as the Missouri crisis revealed, the corollary conception of state equality called into question congressional authority over the status of slavery in territories and new states and raised the unsettling possibility that states might reverse course, introducing slavery where it had once been banned.[83]

Jeffersonians feared that the concentration or "consolidation" of authority would destroy their liberties and reduce them to slavery. Yet, if the state governments were the "true barriers of our liberty," they were also the true bastions of racial slavery, and the democratic devolution of authority to local governments and ultimately to slaveowners themselves reinforced the link between liberty and slavery. Over the course of the antebellum decades, revolutionary conceptions of democracy, federalism, and property rights worked to perpetuate the peculiar institution and promote its expansion.[84] Democratic ideology also obscured and mystified power relations: Proponents of democracy's (and slavery's) "manifest destiny" thus invoked nature and providence in celebrating the westward spread of settlement.[85] In the process, slavery itself was naturalized, if not for most Americans as a "positive good," then at least as the inevitable concomitant of the union's seemingly inexorable expansion to the South and West.[86] Slavery's hold was strengthened by increasingly sentimental conceptions of domesticity and of the household domain within which paternalist slaveholders reigned supreme, and by the waning authority of natural rights thinking, particularly in the South.[87]

---

[83] Van Cleve, "A Slaveholders' Union."

[84] I am indebted to these important recent works: Brian Schoen, "The Fragile Fabric of Union: The Cotton South, Federal Politics, and the Atlantic World, 1783–1861," Ph.D. diss. (University of Virginia, 2004); Craig Hammond, *Slavery and Freedom in the Early American West, 1790–1820* (Charlottesville: University of Virginia Press, 2007); Adam Rothman, *Slave Country: American Expansion and the Origins of the Deep South* (Cambridge, MA: Harvard University Press, 2005).

[85] On the mystification of state power see Peter Onuf and Leonard Sadosky, *Jeffersonian America* (Oxford: Basil Blackwell, 2002).

[86] Even northern opponents of slavery acknowledged the institution's suitability in plantation regions. See Matthew Mason, *Slavery and Politics in the Early American Republic* (Chapel Hill: University of North Carolina Press, 2006).

[87] I develop the domesticity theme in "Domesticating the Captive Nation: Thomas Jefferson and the Problem of Slavery," in Thomas Knock and John Milton Cooper, eds., *Democracy and Race: Jefferson, Lincoln, and Wilson* (Charlottesville: University of Virginia Press, forthcoming). I am indebted to Michael McKeon, *The Secret History of Domesticity: Public, Private, and the Division of Knowledge* (Baltimore: Johns Hopkins University Press, 2005). For a brilliant account of the history of natural rights in America see Mark Hulliung, *The Social Contract in America: From the Revolution to the Present Age* (Lawrence: University of Kansas Press, 2007).

The ascendancy of slavery in antebellum America would not go unchecked or unquestioned. Conceptions of equal rights, particularly when grounded in Christian conviction, could inspire principled opposition to the institution. But, as Matthew Mason persuasively argues, widespread opposition to the "slave power" only emerged in response to geopolitical considerations: in Federalist New England in the wake of Jefferson's "Revolution of 1800" and in areas bordering on the slave South after the War of 1812, when slavery threatened to expand beyond its "natural sphere."[88] Concern about the condition of slaves was predicated on anxieties about slaveholders' dominance of the union. Critics of the slave power recognized that the institution did not emerge naturally in Anglo-America, but was instead the artificial creation of law and politics: Governments at all levels played a crucial role in the expanding empire of slavery. And slaveholders, not manufacturers, were the chief beneficiaries of the federal government's protection, as John Quincy Adams told Congress in 1833: "[I]t is the superabundantly, the excessively protected interest of the south, which revolts at the feeble and scanty protection of the laws enjoyed by the north, the centre, and the west."[89]

Slaveholders exploited revolutionary ideology to buttress racial slavery: federalism, property rights, and democracy themselves raised formidable barriers to outside interference with the institution, whether from meddling abolitionists in the former British metropolis or from their fellow travelers in the North. Slaveholders could self-righteously invoke Jefferson's conception of an "aristocratic" and "monocratic" old regime that had threatened the liberties of revolutionary patriots and that – in insidious new "pseudo-republican" forms – still threatened succeeding generations. Anti-slavery, Mason shows, could only gain traction when the same charges could be turned against the slave power, when embattled New England Federalists began decrying "Virginia influence" and Southern planters could be described as the real "aristocrats." Disenchanted critics could see through the mystifying paradoxes that sustained slavery in the land of freedom. As one writer noted, where the supposedly "aristocratic" principles of Federalism were "cherished in Virginia, slavery is less prevalent, and of course where democracy is strongest, slavery is more prevalent."[90]

Notwithstanding their ostentatious posturing as libertarian anti-statists, slaveowners dominated the machinery of state power in the new nation and used it to promote their peculiar institution. Northerners increasingly saw these slaveowners as "aristocrats," imagining them as (relatively) few in number, ruling slaveless white majorities in the South through corruption and deception

---

[88] Mason, *Slavery and Politics in the Early Republic*. See also Leonard L. Richards, *The Slave Power: The Free North and Southern Domination, 1780–1860* (Baton Rouge: Louisiana State University Press, 2000).

[89] "Report of the Minority of the Committee on Manufactures," Feb. 28, 1833, in *Niles Weekly Register* (Baltimore) 64 (May 25, 1833), 215. For further discussion see Onuf and Onuf, *Nations, Markets, and War*, 278–80.

[90] *Newburyport Herald*, Sept. 10, 1813, quoted in Mason, *Slavery and Politics in the Early Republic*, 47.

and threatening to extend their despotic dominion across the entire union. If "aristocracy" was again linked to metropolitan power and threats to the people's liberties, the image of the slaveholder-aristocrat also focused obsessively on brutal abuses of personal power. Anti-slavery polemics thus challenged Southern pretensions to civility, Christianity, and domestic tranquility.

Northerners who resisted the slave power also raised fundamental questions about what liberty meant in America, emphasizing the radical disjunction between slavery and freedom that seems so conspicuous to us today. As they began to reconceive the meaning of American nationhood, belligerent Yankees articulated a new framework for the definition of citizenship, rights, and responsibilities. In enforcing this new vision on a reconstructed union, Lincoln and his allies rejected the "democracy" of Jefferson and his ideological heirs and demolished the federal union within which it had flourished. Lincoln's apotheosis of the nation marked the end of the post-colonial period of American history. Of course, libertarian suspicions of concentrated power persisted, but Americans now had their own, home-grown metropolis. Their rights and liberties might still be defined against the abuses of concentrated power, but Americans now relied on the nation for protection and security. And as they moved beyond their habitual post-colonial fears of recrudescent British imperial power, they could begin to celebrate the legacy of liberty they shared with Britain. And so they could belatedly fulfill the provincial fantasy of identity with the metropolis that had driven the patriot fathers to declare their independence.

6

Liberty, Order, and Pluralism

The Canadian Experience

Philip Girard

In any attempt to explore how ideas about liberty were received, articulated, and implanted in British North America (later Canada), that congeries of seemingly mismatched colonies and commercial territories perched on the northern reaches of the continent, a preliminary difficulty presents itself: Canadian historians have traditionally not used the concept of liberty as an organizing device. As observed recently in striking fashion by Michel Ducharme:

La liberté n'a jamais été abordée par les historiens comme le principe qui fonde la légitimité des relations de pouvoir et des rapports sociaux au Canada. Plus encore, la liberté, sous quelque forme que ce soit, n'a jamais été à la base d'aucune interprétation historique.[1]

Three sets of interactions have traditionally dominated the study of Canadian history: French–English relations, first in an imperial, then in a domestic setting, dominated by the idea of military, political, and cultural conflict; domestic–imperial relations, dominated early on by a preoccupation with the achievement of colonial autonomy and the road to nationhood; and Canadian–American relations, dominated by the desire to explain and justify the existence of the northern nonrebelling colonies.[2] In none of these has the idea of individual liberty been seen as a motive force. In fact, quite the contrary: Canadian historians, both French and English, trying, as historians of most

---

[1] "Liberty has never been approached by historians as the legitimating principle upon which political and social relations in Canada are founded. Moreover, liberty, in whatever form, has never been the basis of any exercise in historical interpretation." Michel Ducharme, "Aux fondements de l'État canadien: La liberté au Canada de 1776 à 1841" (PhD dissertation, McGill University, 2005), p. 17.

[2] A fourth set of interactions, those between Euro-Canadians and native peoples, has only been addressed in any depth more recently; liberty is a theme addressed more openly in this literature, as will be seen later.

I thank Shirley Tillotson for comments on an earlier version of this chapter. All errors remain my own.

countries have traditionally done, to justify the legitimacy of their nation, have always written with a wary eye on the republic of liberty to the south. The need to emphasize the distinctiveness of the Canadian experience from that of its southern neighbor has meant that liberty, the watchword of revolutionary America, was almost off-limits in Canadian historical discourse. Instead, Canadian historiography until the 1960s saw the emergence of a conservative paradigm in which a preoccupation with order – that is, the "peace, order and good government" referred to in Canada's Constitution, the British North America Act 1867 – was promoted as the leitmotiv of Canadian history. There were, to be sure, distinct versions of Canadian history written by those of French and English origin, but they tended to proceed in parallel insofar as the conservative thesis was concerned.[3]

With the advent of the Quiet Revolution in Quebec and the youth-oriented social revolution of the 1960s, historians became more interested in the role of liberalism in Canada's past, and political scientists and sociologists joined the fray. The Hartz thesis of fragment societies identified Canada as a liberal society with a "Tory touch" provided by the Loyalists, thus justifying the apparently greater role of the public sphere in the affairs of the northern country. This argument was highly influential for some time, but in some ways it provided a way of maintaining the conservative thesis, depending on how strongly the Tory touch was emphasized.[4]

But this renewed interest in liberal*ism* in Canada's past did not give rise to much discussion of liber*ty* as such. The study of liberalism led to the study of the liberal state and the emergence of a school of thought interested in state formation. The manifesto of this school may be deduced from the title of a ground-breaking collection of essays by its adherents: *Colonial Leviathan: State Formation in Mid-Nineteenth-Century Canada.*[5] The emphasis in this work is on the gap between liberal promise and liberal performance. By and large these scholars see the state as using liberal ideas to oppress vulnerable classes in the interests of dominant classes and the state itself, while denying or ignoring the emancipatory potential of liberalism.

---

[3] For English Canada, the work of S. F. Wise, conveniently accessed in the collection edited by A. B. McKillop and Paul Romney, *God's Peculiar Peoples: Essays on Political Culture in Nineteenth-Century Canada* (Ottawa: Carleton University Press 1993), is perhaps most representative, although the oeuvre of Donald Creighton is also fundamental, especially his *The Commercial Empire of the Saint Lawrence 1760–1850* (Toronto: Ryerson Press 1937). For French Canada, Lionel Groulx, *Histoire du Canada français depuis la découverte*, 2 vols. (Montreal: Fides, 1960). Ducharme, "L'État canadien," contains a summary of the historiography at 17–48.

[4] Louis Hartz, *The Founding of New Societies* (New York: Harcourt, Brace & World, 1964), applied to Canada by Gad Horowitz, "Conservatism, Liberalism, and Socialism in Canada: An Interpretation" *Canadian Journal of Economics and Political Science* 32:2 (May 1966). See also H. D. Forbes, "Hartz-Horowitz at Twenty: Nationalism, Toryism, and Socialism in Canada and the United States" *Canadian Journal of Political Science* 22:2 (1987).

[5] Allan Greer and Ian Radforth, eds., *Colonial Leviathan: State Formation in Mid-Nineteenth-Century Canada* (Toronto: University of Toronto Press 1992).

This analysis has been carried further by Ian McKay. In an influential article published in 2000, McKay proposed that Canada should be understood as "a project of liberal rule in northern North America" and "essentially a liberal empire, not a nation, and [speaking of the period before 1940] not a democratic state."[6] Distinguishing liberalism from capitalism, democracy, and modernity, MacKay emphasized three of its components: individual liberty (understood as political and civil liberties), equality, and property, or rather the individual's right to hold property. In his view, a liberal order in which the protection of property would be the dominant imperative was implanted in eastern British North America in the 1840s and became hegemonic from coast to coast by the end of the century, successfully replacing "antithetical traditions and forms that had functioned for centuries and even millennia with new conceptions of the human being and society." McKay was careful to frame his proposal as a "reconnaissance of Canadian history," rather than speaking in essentialist terms. The achievement of the liberal order was a contingent and contested process of a quasi-revolutionary nature, not the unfolding of a predetermined plot line.

In accounting for the fact that liberty has largely been missing in action in Canadian historiography, one must also note the discipline's longstanding tendency to insularity. It did not matter that the revolutionary notion of liberty was swirling all about the Atlantic world in the late eighteenth and early nineteenth centuries: Canadian historians were convinced that all that fuss had little to do with their work.[7] *God's Peculiar Peoples*, the title of a collection of essays by S. F. Wise, one of Canada's best-known post-war historians, sums up this approach. According to Wise and his colleagues, Canadians had been bequeathed a "contradictory heritage" best understood "in terms of muted conservatism and ambivalent liberalism, of contradiction, paradox and complexity."[8] Occasional attempts by historians such as Donald Creighton to paint Canadian history in bold colors, as in *The Commercial Empire of the Saint Lawrence 1760–1850*, achieved popular success but tended quickly to become easy targets for later historians. Canadian history was a story of how the remnants and rejects of various empires and revolutions had found that they had enough in common to demand home rule from Britain, achieved it, and then joined in a closer union and spread across the northern half of the continent, but still remained loyal enough to the mother country to defend her in

---

[6] Ian McKay, "The Liberal Order Framework: A Prospectus for a Reconnaissance of Canadian History" *Canadian Historical Review* 81 (2000), 630.

[7] An exception is F. Murray Greenwood, *Legacies of Fear: Law and Politics in Quebec in the Era of the French Revolution* (Toronto: University of Toronto Press for the Osgoode Society 1993); Greenwood argued that fear of possible disloyalty by Quebec's *habitant* population after the French Revolution transformed Quebec society from one organized primarily along class lines to one riven by ethnic division.

[8] "Liberal Consensus or Ideological Battleground: Some Reflections on the Hartz Thesis" in Canadian Historical Association *Historical Papers 1974*, 13.

two horrific wars in the twentieth century. There was a kind of delicious improbability about it all, which meant that emergent trends in European or American history were seen as vaguely interesting but not all that relevant.

This tendency to insularity meant that the rise of the Atlantic World school of history, beginning with the work of Gordon Wood, J. G. A. Pocock, and Bernard Bailyn, remained, if not unnoticed, on the edges of Canadian history until recently. In fact, it has tended to be political scientists and sociologists who most enthusiastically incorporated the insights of this body of scholarship into their own work, but their affinity for model-building and vast generalization has not always endeared them to historians.[9]

McKay's proposed liberal order framework has the potential to address both of these traditional, and inter-related, problems: to reinsert the theme of liberty into Canadian history, and to reinsert Canadian history into the mainstream of the West, the Atlantic World, and the Enlightenment. Conceived with the goal of integrating the fragmented and balkanized literature on Canadian history that has emerged in the last few decades, the liberal order framework has attracted an enormous amount of attention in Canada. A recent book entitled *Liberalism and Hegemony: Debating the Canadian Liberal Revolution* brings together a dozen stimulating responses to McKay's work.[10] A number of the essays raise a concern that I share and will pursue in this chapter. They note that there is a lot about property but not much about liberty in McKay's liberal order framework.[11] The questions posed by the contributors to this volume prompt me to adopt McKay's concept of Canada as a liberal empire but to recast it by asking what kinds of liberty found a place within it (or not). Unlike McKay, I cannot permit myself the luxury of starting in the 1840s, and must consider this question over the *longue durée*.

THE EMERGENCE OF BRITISH NORTH AMERICA

A brief account of the spread of the British presence north of the thirteen colonies is necessary to set the stage for this inquiry. In the late sixteenth century the British joined the fishermen of southern Europe in exploiting the cod fishery off the coast of Newfoundland, and they made a half-dozen attempts to create chartered colonies on the island between 1610 and 1638, all of which failed. For the next century or so the English government treated Newfoundland "not

---

[9] Much of this work is collected in Janet Ajzenstat and Peter J. Smith, eds., *Canada's Origins: Liberal, Tory, or Republican?* (Ottawa: Carleton University Press 1995). See also the work of sociologist Stéphane Kelly, *Les fins du Canada selon Macdonald, Laurier, Mackenzie King et Trudeau* (Montreal: Boréal 2001).

[10] Jean-François Constant and Michel Ducharme, eds., *Liberalism and Hegemony: Debating the Canadian Liberal Revolution* (Toronto: University of Toronto Press 2008).

[11] E.g., the contributions by Jeffrey McNairn, "In Hope and Fear: Intellectual History, Liberalism, and the Liberal Order Framework"; Elspeth Heaman, "Rights Talk and the Liberal Order Framework"; and Robert McDonald, "'Variants of Liberalism' and the Liberal Order Framework in British Columbia."

as a colony but rather a seasonal fishing station to be used solely for the benefit of the west of England fishery" and governed the island by a system of naval justice.[12] Nonetheless, permanent settlement slowly developed, followed by the gradual establishment of a traditional colonial infrastructure: the appointment of a governor and permanent resident magistrates in 1729, the creation of a supreme court in 1792, and the extension of representative government in 1832. By the Treaty of Utrecht in 1713 France gave up all territorial claims in Newfoundland, although it retained certain fishing rights on the northwest coast, as well as Île Royale and Île St-Jean in the Gulf of the St. Lawrence. It also gave up claims to the drainage basin of Hudson Bay, known as Rupert's Land, which had been given by a royal charter of Charles II to the Hudson's Bay Company in 1670.

By the same treaty France gave up its colony of Acadia on peninsular Nova Scotia. Its French Catholic population would be ruled by an English governor and council sitting at Annapolis Royal until 1749, when the seat of government shifted to newly founded Halifax. Settlement of the colony under British auspices then began in earnest, but included many Irish (both Catholic and Protestant) and German- and French-speaking Protestants. The Nova Scotia government deported the Acadians in 1755 as a result of concerns about their loyalty during the Seven Years' War and regranted their lands, mostly to New England settlers now known as Planters. Many Acadians had already fled to Île St-Jean, from which they were in turn deported after the fall of Louisbourg (Île Royale) in 1758. Some remained in hiding and some returned after an amnesty in 1764, but those Acadians who returned to the region established themselves mainly in that part of Nova Scotia that would become the new province of New Brunswick in 1784 after a large influx of Loyalists settled there. The Seven Years' War saw the final demise of French power in North America with the fall of New France and Île Royale and their cession, along with Île St-Jean, to Britain by the Treaty of Paris 1763, and the transfer of Louisiana (then including a large part of the Mississippi Valley) to Spain. The British renamed Île Royale as Cape Breton Island and returned the entire population of Louisbourg to France. Île St-Jean, renamed Prince Edward Island in 1799, was divided in 1767 into large estates that were distributed by lottery among veterans and those having some claim on the Crown. These proprietors were required to settle their lands with tenants, and Prince Edward Island was thus unique among the English-speaking colonies in its heavily unequal land distribution and its development of a large tenant population.

The arrival of the Loyalists in 1783–85 added a significant English-speaking presence to the outpost of Planter Nova Scotia. A small Loyalist influx led to

[12] Jerry Bannister, *The Rule of the Admirals: Law, Custom, and Naval Government in Newfoundland, 1699–1832* (Toronto: University of Toronto Press for the Osgoode Society 2003) at 31. There are good reasons for including or excluding Newfoundland, which remained a separate dominion until 1949, from this survey, but I have decided to include it.

the erection of Cape Breton as a colony separate from Nova Scotia (it would be re-annexed in 1820), and a larger one to the separation of Upper and Lower Canada in 1791. Immigration from both the United States (before 1815) and Britain (after 1815) soon made Upper Canada the demographic anchor of English-speaking British North America. Some Loyalist immigration to Lower Canada's eastern townships occurred, and Montreal and Quebec City retained sizeable populations of English merchants, later augmented by Irish immigrants, but the basic character of Lower Canada remained French and Catholic.

Exploration in the northwest led to British claims being extended as far as the Pacific and the Arctic Ocean, but settlement would not begin until the mid-nineteenth century. In 1792 Spain ceded its claims to the west coast to Britain. The North West Company established some trading posts in the northern interior of what was then called New Caledonia in 1805–06, but the fur trade was not exploited with any vigor until the merger of the North West Company with the Hudson's Bay Company in 1821 and the grant to it of an exclusive trading license. In 1849 the Hudson's Bay Company was also granted the proprietorship of Vancouver Island on condition that it promote colonization, while interest in settling the mainland quickened after the discovery of gold in 1858. A separate mainland colony named British Columbia was established, only to be merged with Vancouver Island in 1866. Few treaties with the native peoples were entered into in British Columbia, in contrast to the western plains, where large areas were the subject of treaties prior to their settlement in the late nineteenth century. The plains and the sub-Arctic territory to the north of them remained under the control of the Hudson's Bay Company and unsettled until after Confederation, when the area, known as the North West Territories, was transferred to the new dominion. The one exception was a small agricultural colony at Red River south of Lake Winnipeg established in 1812. The Red River colony (also known as Assiniboia) developed as a largely Métis settlement and, after some initial armed resistance to the establishment of Canadian authority, became the center of the province of Manitoba when it joined Canada in 1870.[13]

The four colonies of Ontario, Quebec, New Brunswick, and Nova Scotia united into the new Dominion of Canada in 1867, an event referred to as Confederation. The new federal state was to have "a Constitution similar in Principle to that of the United Kingdom," but was still in fact and law a colony. The British-appointed governor general could reserve bills duly passed by the federal parliament "for the Signification of the Queen's Pleasure," and legislation receiving the governor general's assent could be disallowed by the Queen in Council within two years of its passage. Only very gradually did full Canadian autonomy emerge: Finally in the Statute of Westminster 1931 the British government admitted the legislative equality of the dominion parliaments with that at Westminster and agreed that the latter would not pass any legislation for a

---

[13] The Métis were (and are) a distinct people born of the mixing of aboriginals and those of European (primarily French) origin in the seventeenth and eighteenth centuries.

dominion except at its own request. Meanwhile, the remaining British North American colonies joined Canada: Manitoba in 1870, British Columbia (1871), Prince Edward Island in 1873, Alberta and Saskatchewan in 1905 (carved out of the North West Territories), and Newfoundland (now officially known as Newfoundland and Labrador) in 1949.[14]

From this brief review a few salient facts emerge that are relevant to our inquiry. The first is that early Canada was a place of remarkable cultural diversity, one home to peoples (especially the French Canadians, native peoples, and the Irish) who were definitely marked as Others in metropolitan society. An Anglican clergyman observed in the 1780s that his neighbors in Nova Scotia's Annapolis Valley were "a collection of all nations, kindred, complexions and tongues assembled from every quarter of the globe and till lately equally strangers to me and each other."[15] The future rebel William Lyon Mackenzie described an Upper Canadian election crowd in 1824 as containing "Christians and Heathens, Menonists and Tunkards, Quakers and Universalists, Presbyterians and Baptists, Roman Catholics and American Methodists; there were Frenchmen and Yankees, Irishmen and Mulattoes, Scotchmen and Indians, Englishmen, Canadians, Americans and Negroes, Dutchmen and Germans, Welshmen and Swedes, Highlanders and Low-landers...."[16] And these accounts do not reckon with the French-Canadian presence in Lower Canada (the *canadiens*, as they were known) and the growing Acadian and Gaelic-speaking presence in the Maritimes. After 1815 British immigration began in earnest and by mid-century the British-born and their immediate descendants formed a majority of the Canadian population, but the imperial relationship and domestic institutions were shaped by the earlier and more complex cultural landscape.

Some of these peoples had their own conceptions of freedom and liberty, distinct from those shared by the British. The *habitants* of Lower Canada manifested a strong sense of social solidarity even though they formed largely self-sufficient peasant households. They valued their independence and resisted seigneurial and clerical exactions whenever they could.[17] The degree of freedom enjoyed by members of the First Nations was astonishing to early Europeans, both French and British, and was to some extent absorbed by both during the fur trade era.

---

[14] Three northern territories have not yet acceded to provincial status, although each has its own assembly: Yukon (carved out of the North West Territories in 1898), Nunavut (created in 1999 as a distinct homeland for the Inuit), and the remainder of the North West Territories, which is a single political unit in spite of its plural title.

[15] Quoted in J. M. Bumsted, "The Cultural Landscape in Early Canada," in Bernard Bailyn and Philip D. Morgan, eds., *Strangers within the Realm: Cultural Margins of the First British Empire* (Chapel Hill and London: University of North Carolina Press 1991), p. 383.

[16] Quoted in David Murray, *Colonial Justice: Justice, Morality, and Crime in the Niagara District, 1791–1849* (Toronto: University of Toronto Press for the Osgoode Society 2002) at 14.

[17] Alan Greer, *Peasant, Lord and Merchant: Rural Society in Three Quebec Parishes, 1740–1840* (Toronto: University of Toronto Press 1985).

The second fact of note is that the northern colonies did not have particularly strong commercial or cultural ties with each other; indeed, the patterns of settlement along the border with the United States meant that cross-border ties were often more important than those with other British North American colonies. Most inhabitants of the Maritime provinces felt more at home in New England than in Upper Canada, while inhabitants of the latter province were often more familiar with developments in Michigan, Ohio, and New York than in the Maritimes or Quebec. The free movement of people, capital, and ideas across the Canada–U.S. border meant that Canada's British-oriented understanding and practice of liberty always existed in a dialectic with their U.S. counterparts.[18]

Thirdly, the northern colonies of North America all dated from the post-1688 period, from a time when the Crown-in-Parliament was conceived as the fountainhead of sovereign power in Britain itself and in the empire. At a cultural level, the ideology of the Glorious Revolution struck deep roots in English-speaking Canada, where it was constantly referenced and memorialized.[19] At a constitutional level this meant, as Elizabeth Mancke has observed, that "[Canadian] colonists could not claim a constitutional autonomy from Parliament and an allegiance to the Crown alone in the way the people in the older colonies did."[20] And unlike New England, which essentially carried on its own foreign policy by the eighteenth century, all the lightly populated northern colonies understood that they were dependent on British military and naval protection. Nonetheless, this dependency did not translate into an acceptance of all imperial demands, and could co-exist with a robust defense of personal liberty. When the Planters settled the former Acadian lands, for example, they negotiated a ten-year exemption from impressment. They later built on this agreement so as to give complete control over impressment on land to the civilian authorities; as a result, as has recently been argued, Nova Scotians "enjoyed a degree of freedom from

---

[18] See generally Jane Errington, *The Lion, the Eagle, and Upper Canada: A Developing Colonial Ideology* (Montreal and Kingston: McGill-Queen's University Press 1987); Sterling Evans, ed., *The Borderlands of the American and Canadian Wests* (Lincoln and London: University of Nebraska Press 2006). Nor did the language barrier prevent American values and developments from having an influence in Quebec: See Yvan Lamonde, *Ni avec eux ni sans eux: le Quebec et les Etats-Unis* (n.p.: Nuit Blanche 1996); Maurice Lemire, *Le mythe de l'Amérique dans l'imaginaire "canadien"* (Quebec: Nota Bene 2003).

[19] Gregory Marquis, "In Defence of Liberty: 17th Century England and 19th Century Maritime Political Culture" *University of New Brunswick Law Journal* 42 (1993), 69–94.

[20] *The Fault Lines of Empire: Political Differentiation in Massachusetts and Nova Scotia, ca. 1760–1830* (New York and London: Routledge 2005), p. 5. Mancke has also pursued this argument in "Another British America: A Canadian Model for the Early Modern British Empire" *Journal of Imperial and Commonwealth History* 25 (1997), 1–36, and "Early Modern Imperial Governance and the Origins of Canadian Political Culture" *Canadian Journal of Political Science* 32:1 (1999), 3–20. It must be observed, however, that the Act of 1778, preventing the imposition of imperial taxes without colonial consent, meant that the British North American colonies were not put to the test in the same way as the thirteen colonies.

impressment that was nearly unprecedented in the British Empire" prior to 1815.[21]

In summary, the cultural diversity of early Canada and the absence of a revolutionary founding moment meant that liberty has been understood in various ways but often involved accommodating the respective liberties of various cultural groups as much as it emphasized the advancement of individual freedom of action. One might say about liberty what W. L. Morton claimed about other rights: The unifying fiction of the Crown "allowed a diversity of customs and rights under law in a way that the rational scheme and abstract principles of republican democracy did not."[22] This chapter attempts to follow that insight in considering the development of both the theory and practices of liberty in Canada.

LIBERTY UNDER THE ANCIEN REGIME IN BRITISH NORTH AMERICA: THE EIGHTEENTH-CENTURY INHERITANCE

Jack P. Greene has observed that "the earliest settlers did not so much bring authority with them across the ocean as a license to create their own authorities."[23] In the British North American context, where structures of authority so often preceded settlement, it would be more accurate to say they brought both. It is true that the common law validated the use of custom, and thus provided a way for settlers legitimately to make their own law long before the arrival of representative institutions. Thus, in the fur trade country north and west of the Great Lakes, a symbiosis of English and native law evolved, especially in the areas of family law, contract law, and criminal law, where the two peoples constantly interacted.[24] In Quebec and Acadia, however, the British had to deal with subject populations, neither of whom had any experience of English law and on whom they could not realistically impose it in the short term. The Quebec Act of 1774 allowed the *canadiens* to keep French law as found in the custom of Paris, and while no such formal guarantee was made to the Acadians, the council at Annapolis Royal in fact applied largely French law in settling disputes between Acadians.[25] Jerry Bannister observes that in eighteenth-century Newfoundland, "[c]ustoms occupied the centre of the island's

---

[21] Keith Mercer, "Sailors and Citizens: Press Gangs and Naval-Civilian Relations in Nova Scotia, 1756–1815" *Journal of the Royal Nova Scotia Historical Society* 10 (2007), 87–113.

[22] "The Relevance of Canadian History," presidential address to the Canadian Historical Association, Queen's University, 11 June 1960, http://www.erudit.org/revue/ram/1960/v39/n1/300442ar.pdf.

[23] " 'By Their Laws Shall Ye Know Them': Law and Identity in Colonial British America" *Journal of Interdisciplinary History* 33:2 (Autumn 2002), 251.

[24] See the references in Philip Girard, "British Justice, English Law, and Canadian Legal Culture," in Phillip A. Buckner, ed., *Canada and the British Empire* (Oxford: Oxford University Press 2008), pp. 256–57.

[25] Thomas G. Barnes, " 'The Dayly Cry for Justice': The Juridical Failure of the Annapolis Royal Regime, 1713–1749" in Philip Girard and Jim Phillips, eds., *Essays in the History of Canadian Law, vol. III, Nova Scotia* (Toronto: University of Toronto Press for the Osgoode Society 1990).

legal culture," but far from being popularly derived, the customary law in question was "constituted and overseen by officials (naval and civil magistrates)" and bereft "of many obligations and processes of accountability."[26]

Newfoundland was somewhat exceptional, however, as it was not officially a colony of settlement. All the eighteenth-century northern colonies of settlement except one were given constitutions that formally provided for the creation of representative institutions, and were understood implicitly to implant the constellation of doctrines aimed at preserving the liberty of the subject known as "British justice." According to jurist Beamish Murdoch, whose *Epitome of the Laws of Nova–Scotia* contained the most comprehensive account of the unreformed constitution of any of the northern colonies, "what are generally esteemed the most valuable portions of British law, have been transplanted into our land, – the Habeas Corpus, – the freedom of the Press – the trial by jury – the Representative Branch of the legislature, – the viva voce examination of witnesses; all those branches of public law . . . we possess."[27] The exigencies of war delayed somewhat the calling of an assembly at Halifax, but it met for the first time in 1758. Prince Edward Island's met in 1773, while the Loyalist colony of New Brunswick saw its first assembly take shape in 1785. Cape Breton was separated from Nova Scotia in 1784, but no assembly was ever called before the island was re-annexed to Nova Scotia in 1820, largely because the population of Acadians and Gaelic-speaking Highlanders was mostly Catholic and thus incapable of voting in any case.

The shock of the American Revolution is often thought to have led the imperial government to draft self-consciously hierarchical constitutions for Upper and Lower Canada when it created them out of the old province of Quebec in 1791.[28] On paper it was so, and in some limited respects, such as the creation of clergy reserves for the support of the Anglican Church and the proposed creation of a landed aristocracy for Upper Canada, the Constitutional Act of 1791 did depart from the constitutions of the Maritime provinces. But in principle the Canadian constitutions of 1791 were no different from theirs. All contained the combination of monarchy, aristocracy (the appointed upper houses of the legislatures), and commons that characterized the constitution of the United Kingdom itself. The constitution of 1791 was, as William Pitt himself said, "intended to give a free constitution to Canada, according to British ideas of freedom,"[29] although in fact it exceeded British ideas of

---

[26] Bannister, *Rule of the Admirals*, 14.

[27] *Epitome of the Laws of Nova-Scotia* (Halifax: Joseph Howe 1832–23), 4 vols., i, 35. This work is explored in Philip Girard, "Themes and Variations in Early Canadian Legal Culture: Beamish Murdoch and his *Epitome of the Laws of Nova-Scotia*" *Law & History Review* 11 (1993), 101–144. On the role of English law generally in Canadian legal culture, see Philip Girard, "British Justice, English Law, and Canadian Legal Culture" in Phillip A. Buckner, ed., *Canada and the British Empire* (Oxford: Oxford University Press, forthcoming).

[28] Greenwood, *Legacies of Fear*, argues that the drafting of the Constitutional Act of 1791 was well under way by the time the French Revolution erupted and was little affected by it.

[29] Cited at Ducharme, "L'Etat canadien," 95.

freedom by granting the vote to thousands of Catholics in both Upper and Lower Canada.

By "British ideas of freedom" Pitt meant those that had taken shape after the Glorious Revolution of 1688 and found canonical form in the *Commentaries* of William Blackstone. Individuals possessed rights to life, liberty, and property that were best guarded by a mixed and balanced constitution, one wherein monarch, aristocracy, and commonalty were all represented, and where none could arrogate excessive power to itself. To quote Beamish Murdoch again: "[T]he strongest form of building was that of the pyramid, having a broad base, and narrowing as it increased in height." Thus, the British Constitution, "consisting of a King or Queen, a House of Lords, and a Commons, gave an apt illustration in politics."[30] The emphasis in this conception of liberty was on the representation of interests rather than individuals, and on the furtherance of commerce and the acquisition of property, but this political ideal of liberty was accompanied by legal notions of liberty embodied in the ideology of British justice.

This understanding of liberty, often referred to as a "court" (as opposed to "country") philosophy, must be distinguished from the classical understanding of liberty that underlay the American, the French, and the first English revolutions. Classical liberty emphasized popular sovereignty and direct participation. It aimed to produce a virtuous and equal citizenry whose independence would be assured by agricultural rather than commercial pursuits. Together, such citizens would arrive at laws and policies that would further the public good. Various terms have been used to distinguish these two conceptions of liberty but, following Ducharme, I will use the adjectives "classical" and "modern" rather than the more familiar "court" and "country" in this discussion. "Classical" has the advantage of recognizing the roots of this version of liberty in classical antiquity, while "modern" acknowledges the relative recency of the concept's emergence and avoids some of the negative connotations associated with the word "court."

The eastern colonies were endowed with constitutions typical of the ancien regime, where, in principle, authority "flowed downwards, through the sovereign's local viceroy, rather than upwards, from elected representatives of the governed."[31] A corollary of this principle was that the imperial parliament remained supreme while colonial legislatures were not of coordinate authority, but an important concession was made in the "celebrated statute of 1778" whereby Britain pledged not to tax colonies having their own assemblies.[32] In practice, the Colonial Office allowed local assemblies considerable

---

[30] Cited in Philip Girard, "'I will not pin my faith to his sleeve': Beamish Murdoch, Joseph Howe, and Responsible Government Revisited" *Journal of the Royal Nova Scotia Historical Society* 4 (2001), 52.

[31] D. G. Bell, "Maritime Legal Institutions under the *Ancien Régime*," in DeLloyd J. Guth and W. Wesley Pue, eds., *Canada's Legal Inheritances* (Winnipeg: University of Manitoba 2001) at 104 (also published in *Manitoba Law Journal* 23 [1996]).

[32] Murdoch, *Epitome of the Laws of Nova-Scotia*, i, 108.

autonomy over their own affairs. The Maritime provinces all abolished primogeniture in favor of partible inheritance in the eighteenth century, for example, and created divorce courts based on Massachusetts models at a time when only Parliamentary divorce was available in England. Local assemblies across British North America erected courts of all descriptions, created land registries, supervised the spending of road money, and passed laws regulating emerging professions and businesses.[33]

Although representatives were elected from a fairly broad franchise to provincial assemblies, elective government at the local level, such as the New England town meeting, was rigorously proscribed.[34] Local government was carried on by appointees of the provincial government, men understood to be trustworthy and, above all, loyal. The governor appointed magistrates to administer civil and criminal law and to act as local government, the earliest being appointed in Nova Scotia (1720), followed by Newfoundland (1729), Quebec (1764), Prince Edward Island (1768), Cape Breton (1785), New Brunswick (1785), Upper Canada (1792), and Assiniboia (1835). With one exception, none of the emergent urban centres of British North America – Halifax, Quebec, Montreal, York (later Toronto), or Hamilton – possessed a city charter until the 1830s. The exception to the rule was Saint John, New Brunswick, settled by Loyalists in 1785. Governor Carleton procured for it a royal charter creating a public corporation styled as "the mayor, aldermen, and commonalty of the city of Saint John," under which six aldermen and six assistant aldermen were elected by the freeholders and freemen of the city to form a common council presided over by the mayor.[35]

Thus, while the settler colonies of British North America soon had representative assemblies, they did not have any experience of elective local government until the mid-nineteenth century. This does not mean that the populace was at the mercy of a ruthless magistracy carrying out central designs. Susan Lewthwaite argues that, when viewed from the perspective of rural people in early Upper Canada, "state-sanctioned authority resembles a jellyfish rather

---

[33] See generally Bell, "Maritime Legal Institutions"; Paul Romney, "Upper Canada (Ontario): The Administration of Justice, 1784–1850"; and F. Murray Greenwood, "Lower Canada (Quebec): Transformation of Civil Law, from Higher Morality to Autonomous Will, 1774–1866," all in Guth and Pue, *Canada's Legal Inheritances.*

[34] On the franchise, the classic work remains John Garner, *The Franchise and Politics in British North America* (Toronto: University of Toronto Press 1969), but Brian Cuthbertson's detailed study, *Johnny Bluenose at the Polls: Epic Nova Scotian Election Battles 1758–1848* (Halifax: Formac 1994), challenges some of his conclusions. In some respects, Canada's Constitution was freer than Britain's: The property qualification (a freehold worth 40 shillings a year in rural areas, or an urban tenancy of at least ten pounds' annual rent) was generally less stringent than in Britain, while in Upper and Lower Canada Catholics could vote and hold office. In Lower Canada, women could vote from 1791 and retained the franchise until 1849.

[35] The English practice was for the common council to elect its own mayor and appoint its own servants, but Saint John varied sharply from this model. The mayor and the corporation's legal officers were appointed by the lieutenant-governor. See T. W. Acheson, *Saint John: The Making of a Colonial Urban Community* (Toronto: University of Toronto Press 1985).

than an octopus."[36] Although political loyalty was de rigueur, magistrates were members of their communities and their own legitimacy rested on an ability to recognize and carry out local wishes. As Mancke's comparative study has shown, the magistrates of Liverpool, Nova Scotia, could be quite clever in appearing to carry out the wishes of Halifax while in fact arranging things to suit local desires. Studies of Upper and Lower Canada have illustrated the tensions inherent in the magistrates' position, "at once accountable to the representative of the Crown who had appointed them and deeply embedded in their communities,"[37] but have also shown them as carrying out their administrative and judicial responsibilities in a way that was both competent, by and large, and responsive to local needs in spite of some occasional and well-publicized scandals.[38]

In Quebec after 1763, the magistrates were the formal engine of local government, but their authority was overlaid on older units of social organization, the parish and the seigneury. Seigneurial courts had disappeared even under the French regime, but until the abolition of their tenure in 1854, seigneurs exercised considerable authority over the lives of their habitants. Parish vestries could be vehicles for the *habitants* to express their wishes in matters beyond the ecclesiastical. They often petitioned for magistrates, noting that they were "si utiles pour maintenir la paix et la tranquilité en et dans la ... paroisse" ("so useful for maintaining peace and tranquillity within the parish") and requested the appointment of particular persons.[39] In Lower Canada, the government relied heavily on the local knowledge represented by parish vestries in making appointments to the commission. In a striking concession to local circumstances, after 1775, the government of Quebec no longer observed either religious or property qualifications in making appointments to the commission. Thus, unlike Ireland, Maryland, and Pennsylvania, Catholics could be and were appointed as magistrates; Jews were initially excluded, but a statute of 1831

---

[36] "Violence, Law, and Community in Rural Upper Canada" in Jim Phillips, Tina Loo, and Susan Lewthwaite, eds., *Crime and Criminal Justice, Essays in the History of Canadian Law,* vol. V (Toronto: University of Toronto Press for the Osgoode Society 1994), p. 373. Undoubtedly there was some regional variation in perceptions of the magistracy. Murray, *Colonial Justice,* portrays a more solid and imposing magisterial presence in Niagara, but it was one of the longest-settled districts of Upper Canada.

[37] Mancke, *Fault Lines;* Murray, *Colonial Justice* at 29; Donald Fyson, *Magistrates, Police and People: Everyday Criminal Justice in Quebec and Lower Canada, 1764–1837* (Toronto: University of Toronto Press for the Osgoode Society 2006), p. 67.

[38] Murray, *Colonial Justice;* Fyson, *Magistrates, Police and People;* Susan A. Lewthwaite, "Law and Authority in Upper Canada: The Justices of the Peace in the Newcastle District, 1803–1840" (PhD dissertation, University of Toronto 2001). On the scandals, see the introduction to Robert L. Fraser, *Provincial Justice: Upper Canadian Legal Portraits from the Dictionary of Canadian Biography* (Toronto: University of Toronto Press for the Osgoode Society 1992). Peter Oliver suggests that they have been overdrawn: "Power, Politics, and the Law: The Place of the Judiciary in the Historiography of Upper Canada," in G. Blaine Baker and Jim Phillips, eds., *Essays in the History of Canadian Law,* vol. VIII: *In Honour of R. C. B. Risk* (Toronto: University of Toronto Press for the Osgoode Society 1999).

[39] Fyson, *Magistrates, Police and People,* at 67.

extending full civil rights to Jews made them eligible, and the first took office in 1833.[40]

Trial by jury was the institution, after representative government, that was most associated with respect for British liberty, and colonial governments duly put in place the machinery to enable it as soon as sufficient numbers of English-speaking residents arrived to make it practicable. Even in Quebec, the principle of *de medietate linguae* was put in place immediately after the Conquest to ensure bilingual grand and petit juries. After some confusion in the wake of the Conquest, the *canadien* population appears to have gradually embraced the jury. As in Quebec, in the colony of Assiniboia trial juries were active long before a representative assembly existed, and appear to have resolved disputes in ways that were equitable and acceptable to the population.[41] Work on the composition of eighteenth-century grand and petit juries in Halifax, and on grand juries in Quebec, on the other hand, reveals that the promise of "peer review" held out by the jury was not always carried out in practice. Grand juries especially were the preserve of leading merchants and citizens, and trial juries, if not quite as unequal in class terms as the English juries studied by Douglas Hay, were "not a representative cross-section of the community."[42] Eligibility gradually broadened on paper in the nineteenth century, but we have as yet no studies of the social composition of juries comparable to those for the eighteenth century.

The arrangements just described relate to political liberty, but economic, personal, and religious liberty may have been more important to the average inhabitant of the northern colonies. Interests in land took many forms in the eighteenth century: Fee simple grants in Nova Scotia, New Brunswick, Upper Canada, and the eastern townships of Lower Canada existed alongside seigneurial tenure in the latter colony, along with widespread tenancy relationships in Prince Edward Island and customary forms of individual and collective property in Newfoundland. Aside from Newfoundland, where agricultural land was a rarity in any case, settlement was generally preceded by survey: Acquiring title by squatting was not the norm, and registry systems were

---

[40] Ibid., at 75.

[41] H. Robert Baker, "Creating Order in the Wilderness: Transplanting English Law to Rupert's Land, 1835–1851" *Law & History Review* 17 (1999), 209–246.

[42] On Quebec, see Donald Fyson, "Jurys, participation civique et représentation au Québec et au Bas-Canada: les grand jurys du district de Montréal (1764–1832)" *Revue d'histoire de l'Amérique française* 55:1 (2001), 85–120. It is important to note that while the *canadiens* were under-represented in grand juries in Quebec/Lower Canada before the 1830s (with 90% of the population, they held only half the positions on grand juries), they were certainly not excluded from this important form of civic participation, as has often been assumed. The quotation is from Jim Phillips, "Halifax Juries in the Eighteenth Century," in Greg T. Smith et al., eds., *Criminal Justice in the Old World and the New: Essays in Honour of J. M. Beattie* (Toronto: Centre of Criminology, University of Toronto 1998) at 166. Douglas Hay, "The Class Composition of the Palladium of Liberty: Trial Jurors in the Eighteenth Century," in J. S. Cockburn and T. A. Green, eds., *Twelve Good Men and True: The Criminal Trial Jury in England, 1200–1800* (Princeton, NJ: Princeton University Press 1988).

established early on (except in Quebec, where they remained controversial) to facilitate land transfers.

Disputes over the terms on which land resources would be made available, however, regularly shook colonial governments, and indicated just how deeply settlers equated the fee simple with liberty. Threats by colonial governments to collect quit-rents regularly troubled the waters and were successfully resisted. A powerful escheat movement emerged in 1830s Prince Edward Island to demand the breakup of proprietorial estates and their distribution to the tenants who worked on them, but imperial support for the proprietors delayed its success until the Island joined Confederation in 1873.[43] The clergy reserves set aside in Upper Canada became a target of sharp complaint as the provincial population grew, while seigneurial exactions during the poor harvests of the 1830s in Lower Canada contributed to the rebellions of 1837–38.[44]

If land represented freedom for the yeoman, did labor represent coercion? In an economy where labor was usually in short supply, one might expect that master and servant law, either received or locally enacted, would be frequently resorted to. Such legislation dated back to 1562 in England and provided for the imprisonment of laborers breaching their obligations, but authorized only fines for their masters. In the Hudson's Bay Company territories, the master and servant law was virtually governmental in nature, but in the colonies of settlement it had much less impact.[45] Many local master and servant statutes were enacted, but the Canadian experience with them was mostly symbolic: "[E]nforcement was sporadic, convictions relatively few, and punishments rarely harsh."[46] The exceptions were Newfoundland, where an authoritarian naval government relied heavily on master and servant law (including corporal punishment) to maintain order and deference, and Nova Scotia, where it was used mainly to discipline blacks.[47] Even though master and servant law was not frequently invoked in the nineteenth century, the criminal sanction was retained until 1877, when the federal Breaches of Contract Act abolished it. And aside entirely from legal forms of coercion, the life of the laborer was generally precarious enough that economic coercion sufficed to maintain order.

The law of personal status illustrated the cross-currents flowing through the Atlantic world during the revolutionary era. The capitulations of Montreal in

---

[43] Rusty Bittermann, *Rural Protest on Prince Edward Island: From British Colonization to the Escheat Movement* (Toronto: University of Toronto Press 2006).

[44] See generally Allan Greer, *The Patriots and the People: the Rebellion of 1837 in Rural Lower Canada* (Toronto: University of Toronto Press 1993).

[45] Russell Smandych and Rick Linden, "Administering Justice without the State: A Study of the Private Justice System of the Hudson's Bay Company to 1800" *Canadian Journal of Law and Society* 11 (1996), 21–62.

[46] Paul Craven, "Canada, 1670–1935: Symbolic and Instrumental Enforcement in Loyalist North America," in Douglas Hay and Paul Craven, eds., *Masters, Servants, and Magistrates in Britain and the Empire, 1562–1955* (Chapel Hill and London: University of North Carolina Press 2004) at 175.

[47] On Newfoundland, see Jerry Bannister, "Law and Labor in Eighteenth-Century Newfoundland," in Hay and Craven, *Masters and Servants*; on Nova Scotia, see Craven in op. cit.

1760 provided that "the negroes and panis [Pawnees, or Native slaves] of both sexes shall remain, in their quality of slaves, in the possession of the French and Canadians to whom they belong; they shall be at liberty to keep them in their service in the colony, or to sell them; and they may also continue to bring them up in the Roman religion." Both Planters and Loyalists brought black slaves to Nova Scotia in the 1750s–80s, where they were bought, sold, bequeathed, and attached for debt as a matter of course, and generated a certain amount of litigation. But the new colony of Upper Canada abolished slavery in one of its earliest statutes in 1792, albeit allowing existing slaves to remain so and postponing the freedom of their children to the age of twenty-five. And the turn of the century saw outright judicial abolition of slavery in Lower Canada and its indirect judicial abolition in Nova Scotia. Only New Brunswick's Loyalist judges upheld the institution as a way of shoring up the hierarchical world order they believed should characterize their new home.[48]

The legal status of native peoples was affected in part by the discourse of anti-slavery, but more importantly by their relative strength in the military calculus at any given point in time. The Royal Proclamation of 1763 aimed to reserve the lands west of the Appalachians for native peoples and marked perhaps the apogee of an imperial policy of ethnocentric paternalism. In Nova Scotia, the ability of the Mi'kmaq to harass settlers led to treaties of friendship in 1760–61, and to an uneasy *pax indigena* until the arrival of large numbers of Loyalists; thereafter they were largely left to their own devices as long as they did not pose a direct threat[49]; a similar position, without the treaties, prevailed in the Hudson's Bay Company territories. In Upper Canada the situation was different as a result of the settlement of the Six Nations there after the American Revolution. Their territories in the Grand River valley were accorded to them in recognition of their role as allies during the revolution, but they ultimately lost a considerable amount of land as a result of unauthorized sales and squatting by white settlers. The leadership of the Six Nations repeatedly contested these acts in court – litigation continues to this day – but to little effect. The disruptions of the American Revolution seriously undermined the economy and sovereignty of the native peoples, and the War of 1812 was the last occasion on which their military prowess proved useful. Subsequently, each colony dealt with its own native people in its own way, and all effectively ignored the protestations of the Colonial Office about the poor treatment of native populations. In theory, native individuals who met the property qualification could vote on the same basis as European settlers in some colonies at least, but this theoretical commitment to political equality did not translate into any

---

[48] See generally Robin Winks, *The Blacks in Canada: A History*, 2d ed. (Kingston and Montreal: McGill-Queen's University Press 1997); D. G. Bell, "Slavery and the Judges of Loyalist New Brunswick" *University of New Brunswick Law Journal* 31 (1982), 9–42; J. Barry Cahill, "Slavery and the Judges of Loyalist Nova Scotia" *University of New Brunswick Law Journal* 43 (1994), 73–136.

[49] John G. Reid, "*Pax Britannica* or *Pax Indigena*? Planter Nova Scotia (1760–1782) and Competing Strategies of Pacification" *Canadian Historical Review* 85:4 (2004), 669–92.

improvement in native welfare. The seeming inability of native people to improve property in the way that liberal theory expected was at the heart of the hostility toward them in settler society.[50]

It was in the family that the hierarchical worldview of the ancien régime was perhaps most evident, as opposed to the "republican" family evolving in the United States. The position of the father was analogized to that of God and the monarch.[51] Divorce was almost nonexistent: Although some of the Maritime colonies had adopted Massachusetts-style judicial divorce in the eighteenth century, only one or two were granted annually throughout the nineteenth century.[52] In Upper and Lower Canada only parliamentary divorce was available, and in Newfoundland before 1949 even that possibility was ruled out. Paternal custody rights remained virtually unassailable even after the enactment of a more liberal Upper Canadian law in 1855.[53]

Freedom of worship was by and large enjoyed by British North Americans, even if some disabilities were attached to being a Roman Catholic or dissenter until the end of the first quarter of the nineteenth century. The timing of British North American settlement, occurring after the Toleration Act 1689, explains the position of dissenters, while demography helps to explain the relatively liberal attitude toward Catholics. The sheer numbers of Roman Catholics in Acadia in 1710 and Quebec in 1760, compared to the British population, meant that any attempt at proscribing Catholic observance was futile, and even formal restrictions on various forms of Catholic civic participation were widely ignored, as we have seen. Indeed, the Catholic Church was itself all but formally established in Quebec as a result of the Quebec Act's legal recognition of its ability to collect tithes.[54] Even outside Quebec, however, some colonies passed bills for the removal of Catholic disabilities that were disallowed by the British government before Catholic relief was recognized in Britain itself. The position of Jews was especially favorable: Some of the initial Crown grants in Halifax were to Jewish men, at a time when significant restrictions existed on

---

[50] Sidney L. Harring, *White Man's Law: Native People in Nineteenth-Century Canadian Jurisprudence* (Toronto: University of Toronto for the Osgoode Society 1998).

[51] Cecilia Morgan, *Public Men and Virtuous Women: The Gendered Languages of Religion and Politics in Upper Canada, 1791–1850* (Toronto: University of Toronto Press 1996).

[52] Kimberley Smith Maynard, "Divorce in Nova Scotia, 1750–1890," in Philip Girard and Jim Phillips, *Essays in the History of Canadian Law,* vol. III.

[53] Constance B. Backhouse, "Shifting Patterns in Nineteenth-Century Canadian Custody Law," in David H. Flaherty, ed., *Essays in the History of Canadian Law,* vol. I (Toronto: University of Toronto Press for the Osgoode Society 1981); cf. Jamil S. Zainaldin, "The Emergence of a Modern American Family Law: Child Custody, Adoption, and the Courts 1796–1851" *Northwestern University Law Review* 73 (1979), 1038–1089; Michael Grossberg, *Governing the Hearth: Law and the Family in Nineteenth-Century America* (Chapel Hill: University of North Carolina Press 1985).

[54] See generally Terrence Murphy and Gerald Stortz, *Creed and Culture: the Place of English-Speaking Catholics in Canadian Society, 1750–1930* (Kingston and Montreal: McGill-Queen's University Press 1993); D. G. Bell, "Religious Liberty and Protestant Dissent in Loyalist New Brunswick" *University of New Brunswick Law Journal* 36 (1987), 146–162.

Jewish landholding in Britain, and the Jewish John Franks held high office by commission in Quebec as early as 1768. Ideas of religious equality rather than mere toleration quickly gained ground in Canada, with the exception of native religions, which did not enjoy the same respect.[55]

The ancien régime constitution may have been based on the conceit that all authority flowed from the sovereign down to the people, but official ideology was constantly countered by colonial practice: "[I]n a world of free land . . . religious pluralism, and a de facto open frontier with the United States, the ideology of deference, dependence and hierarchy was always under challenge."[56] No landed aristocracy as contemplated by the 1791 constitution emerged in Upper Canada, while attempts to preserve Anglican privilege in all the colonies provoked outright resistance more than they inspired deference. Relatively widespread landholding and a similarly generous franchise helped to diffuse power throughout colonial society without, of course, obliterating inequality.

THE INHERITANCE TRANSFORMED: NINETEENTH-CENTURY REFORM

Historians have long parsed the specific grievances that provoked the rebellions in Upper and Lower Canada, leading to responsible government there and in the Maritime colonies.[57] A common theme in all these grievances was the abuse of traditional rights and liberties by the executive branch of government. But, as in the former American colonies, the main problem with the colonial machinery of government was not that the governor held too much power, but rather too little. He had relatively little patronage to dispense and thus could not employ the techniques of "old Corruption" that smoothed the parliamentary wheels in Westminster. Assemblymen could pass whatever legislation they liked, but they became frustrated with the veto exercised by the upper house, which functioned as a combined legislative and executive council until the roles were separated at London's insistence in the 1830s. The executive could frustrate the assembly's measures but could not carry its own, leading to increasing confrontation and stasis in colonial governance, and demands for reform. In Lower Canada the dominance of the assembly by *canadiens* and the upper house by appointees of the British governor gave an ethnic edge to this confrontation that created a more explosive atmosphere than in Upper Canada.[58]

---

[55] Judith and Sheldon Godfrey, *Search Out the Land: The Jews and the Growth of Equality in British Colonial America 1740–1867* (Montreal and Kingston: McGill-Queen's University Press 1995). In spite of the title, the work contains a detailed survey of the growth of equal treatment with regard to Protestant dissenters and Catholics, not just Jews. The situation with regard to Protestant dissenters is more complex than can be dealt with in this brief survey.

[56] D. G. Bell, "Maritime Legal Institutions" at 129.

[57] Greer, *Patriots and the People*; Gerald M. Craig, *Upper Canada: The Formative Years* (Toronto: McClelland and Stewart 1963); Colin Read, *The Rising in Western Upper Canada, 1837–8: the Duncombe Revolt and After* (Toronto: University of Toronto Press 1982).

[58] Phillip A. Buckner, *The Transition to Responsible Government: British Policy in British North America, 1815–1850* (Westport, CT: Greenwood Press 1985).

The mentalités underlying the reform movement have been the subject of some controversy. A traditional Whig worldview was long assumed to be the dominant set of ideas behind the reformers' claims. More recently, following the discovery of the tradition of civic republican thought underlying the American Revolution, some have found the real debate during the 1830s and 1840s to be one between different conceptions of liberty, that is, between civic republicans and liberals, or, in the terms used in this chapter, between classical and modern liberty.[59] Others have insisted on the specifically Irish Whig roots of Upper Canadian reform,[60] while yet others have found the presence of Upper Canada's "late loyalists" crucial. According to Paul Romney, the latter were essentially liberals but developed a form of localism that tended to glorify the role of the provincial assembly, to a point that would have prohibited imperial interference in anything other than navigation and defence. He argues that reformers "pulled back" on the strong version of their thesis in order not to alienate potential supporters, but that in itself suggests that for a majority of the Upper Canadian population, however aggrieved, a maintenance of the British connection was not seriously in doubt.[61]

Exploring the ideological underpinnings of the reform movement is made all the more difficult by the "pragmatic eclecticism with which contemporaries constructed a case."[62] British history; the Bible; and the vocabularies and ideas of Whigs, Tories, and American republicans all combined to form a "broad and rich repertoire" upon which colonial actors drew in speech and writing. Reformers often couched their claims in the language of liberty but "[p]aradoxically, . . . the rhetoric of British liberty was simultaneously both vehicle for making the case for colonial autonomy and means for cementing heartfelt attachment to empire."[63] What is certain is that the currents of ideas flowing through the Canadian body politic began to have much more impact when the diffusion of newspapers in the 1820s to 1840s allowed debate and discussion to proliferate.

---

[59] Ajzenstat and Smith, *Canada's Origins*.

[60] John McLaren, "Reflections on the Rule of Law: The Georgian Colonies of New South Wales and Upper Canada, 1788–1837," in Diane Kirkby and Catharine Coleborne, eds., *Law, History, Colonialism: the Reach of Empire* (Manchester: Manchester University Press 2001); and his "The Rule of Law and Irish Whig Constitutionalism in Upper Canada: William Warren Baldwin, the 'Irish Opposition,' and the Volunteer Connection," in Jim Phillips, R. Roy McMurtry, and John T. Saywell, eds., *Essays in the History of Canadian Law*, vol. X: *A Tribute to Peter N. Oliver* (Toronto: University of Toronto Press 2008). Eighteenth-century Irish Whigs argued for equal status for the kingdom of Ireland instead of the quasi-colonial relationship that then existed; in a similar manner, some Upper Canadian reformers wanted the virtually independent status of the British North American colonies under the Crown to be recognized.

[61] "From Constitutionalism to Legalism: Trial by Jury, Responsible Government, and the Rule of Law in the Canadian Political Culture" *Law & History Review* 7 (1989), 121–174.

[62] Jeffrey McNairn, *The Capacity to Judge: Public Opinion and Deliberative Democracy in Upper Canada, 1791–1854* (Toronto: University of Toronto Press 2000), 12.

[63] Bell, "Maritime Legal Institutions" at 131.

The extent to which public discussion critical of government itself would be allowed was one of the major issues in the reform campaign leading to responsible government. It resulted in a number of politicized libel trials in the 1820s–40s, the most famous of which was the libel trial of newspaperman Joseph Howe of Halifax. But if the role of the jury as a flashpoint in the struggle for local autonomy has been emphasized, its role in the protection of individual liberty has been underexamined. Prior to the 1820s, the yeomen, artisans, and shopkeepers of colonial British North America had shown no great love for the jury. Political figures might laud it in their speeches, but men eligible to serve as jurors often resented the time and expense involved in jury service. Many served grudgingly and absenteeism rates were fairly high. Aside from a few cases of murder or serious crimes, most cases heard by petit juries were routine matters. The creep of summary jurisdiction, far from being resisted, was applauded.[64] In trials with political overtones, however, the jury's role was staunchly defended and jury packing strongly resisted, but several attempts at jury reform to prevent this practice failed in the 1820s and 1830s.

The potential for the jury to protect citizens from oppression was nowhere revealed with more brilliant results than in the trial of Joseph Howe in 1835.[65] Whether he was charged with criminal or seditious libel is still a matter of debate, but his publication of serious charges of malfeasance in office against the Halifax magistracy in its administrative capacity called down on him the wrath of the establishment. Howe specifically appealed to the jurymen to consider their role in defending liberty: "The victim may be bound, and prepared for sacrifice, but an English jury will cast around him the impenetrable shield of the British law."[66] In the Howe trial a petit jury was seen to have protected the accused from the over-reaching and oppressive charges brought by the grand jury, and to have ignored the judge's view that the newspaper articles in question constituted a libel. Howe was fortunate to face a relatively friendly jury. Other newspapermen in British North America were not so lucky. Accusations of packed juries in the trials of those charged in the wake of the rebellion of 1837 gave further ammunition to the reform movement, and jury reform was

---

[64] The work of R. Blake Brown on the nineteenth-century jury in Ontario and Nova Scotia is virtually unique in the Canadian literature: see "The Jury, Politics, and the State in British North America: Reforms to Jury Systems in Nova Scotia and Upper Canada, 1825–1867" (PhD dissertation, Dalhousie University 2005) and his forthcoming book *A Trying Question: The Jury in Nineteenth Century Canada* (Toronto: Osgoode Society 2009). On resistance to jury duty, see his "Storms, Roads, and Harvest Time: Criticisms of Jury Service in Pre-Confederation Nova Scotia" *Acadiensis* 36 (2006), 93–111.

[65] The trial has attracted a large literature. See generally J. Murray Beck, *Joseph Howe*, vol. I: *Conservative Reformer, 1804–1848* (Kingston and Montreal: McGill-Queen's University Press 1982), chap. 9; Barry Cahill, "*R. v. Howe* (1835) for Seditious Libel: A Tale of Twelve Magistrates," in F. Murray Greenwood and Barry Wright, eds., *Canadian State Trials: vol. I, Law, Politics and Security Measures, 1608–1837* (Toronto: University of Toronto Press for the Osgoode Society 1996); Lyndsay M. Campbell, "Licence to Publish: Joseph Howe's Contribution to Libel Law in Nova Scotia" *Dalhousie Law Journal* 29 (2006), 79–116.

[66] Cited in Brown, "The Jury," 73.

one of the first priorities of Reform governments after the achievement of responsible government.

All parties during the reform period invoked liberty, but they did so in different ways. William Mackenzie in Upper Canada and Louis Papineau and the Patriotes in Lower Canada were clearly motivated by classical ideas of liberty and popular sovereignty, while the colonial governments defended the concept of modern liberty as enshrined in the mixed and balanced constitution. Once the Patriote members of the assembly of Lower Canada began boycotting the institution, paralyzing government, it was clear that the impasse could only be resolved in an extra-parliamentary fashion.

In the wake of the 1837 rebellions, the British government sent Lord Durham to Canada to investigate the causes of the rebellions and recommend reforms in governance. He diagnosed two problems, and proposed two solutions. To remedy the complaints of oligarchy leveled at the provincial governments, he recommended responsible government, probably on the advice of the Upper Canadian reformer Robert Baldwin. And to remedy the ethno-political tensions in Lower Canada, he recommended the union of the colonies of Upper and Lower Canada, which was consummated in 1841. The idea of a union was not new, but Durham's motivation for raising it was. In true liberal fashion, Lord Durham can be seen as trying to acculturate *canadiens* in the ideas of modern liberty. Quite literally, they would have to be forced to be free.[67] But to ensure that the *canadiens* would not dominate the assembly of the new united province, they would only be given equal representation with the former Upper Canada, in spite of having a much larger population.

With the defeat of the rebellions, there emerged a more moderate form of reformism within the parameters of modern liberty, one devoted to responsible government, which now had the imprimatur of Lord Durham's report. Although the adoption of responsible government ultimately undermined the mixed and balanced constitution by reducing the monarchical role to a symbolic one and eliminating or emasculating the role of the "few," the reformed colonial governments after 1848 still respected the tenets of modern liberty. They would be judged on how well they protected life, liberty, and property.

Nonetheless, responsible government evolved in British North America in a somewhat distinctive fashion insofar as respect for individual liberties was concerned. The role of the colonial legislature came to be viewed in somewhat mystical terms, as "the only legitimate organ of local sovereignty, . . . the apotheosis of the provincial community in parliament assembled," in Paul Romney's words.[68] With no written bill of rights on the American model, what emerged was a variant of the British political tradition. The possibility of executive tyranny inherent in ministerial responsibility and majority government in Britain was long checked by a set of conventions that respected individual rights, by

---

[67] Janet Ajzenstat, *The Political Thought of Lord Durham* (Kingston and Montreal: McGill-Queen's University Press 1988).
[68] Romney, "From Constitutionalism to Legalism," 163.

and large. Few such conventions inhibited Canadian legislative majorities, which could be checked only by a little-used imperial veto.[69] The provincial legislature itself came to be seen as the guarantor of the rights and liberties of its citizens, and this outlook formed an important strand in the post-confederation provincial rights movement.

MID-CENTURY MOMENTS

The achievement of responsible government unleashed British North America's "moment of mid-century radicalism," when it seemed as if society might be remade to enhance the liberty of the white yeoman farmer, with all offices elective, all monopolies abolished, and all state impositions justified by the strictest test of efficiency and necessity. But the moment passed, leaving much of the larger agenda unenacted. Elective municipal institutions were instituted in Upper and Lower Canada (though not until the 1870s in the Maritimes), but the elective principle was resisted everywhere in the judiciary except for the institution of aldermanic courts in some cities; these possessed a relatively petty jurisdiction and lasted only a generation, being replaced by stipendiary magistrates in cities and towns in the 1860s and 1870s. Universal male suffrage did not emerge quickly, reflecting the reformers' unease with full democracy, although the secret ballot did spread in the 1850s and 1860s. Attempts to break the lawyers' monopoly did not succeed, and far from limiting state powers to spend and borrow, as occurred in the United States, mid-century electorates watched with apparent approval as their governments embarked on an unprecedented campaign of institution building and economic development, including railway building in some cases.[70]

The concern with economic development also led to the transformation of property relations in those two jurisdictions, Lower Canada and Prince Edward Island, where aliberal forms of landholding had prevailed. In Lower Canada the seigneurial system was abolished in 1854, although compensation for the seigneurs was charged on the land in the form of a constituted rent instead of paid out of state coffers. In Prince Edward Island renewed agitation for reform of the tenancy system emerged in the 1860s and was finally crowned with success after the Island entered Confederation in 1873. The British government abandoned the proprietors to their fate, and their appeals against the passage

---

[69] The imperial veto could still be important in particular instances, as in preventing the electors of Prince Edward Island from expropriating the lands of the large proprietors to distribute to their tenantry.

[70] See generally Greer and Radforth, *Colonial Leviathan*, and Philip Girard, "The Maritime Provinces, 1850–1939: Lawyers and Legal Institutions," in Guth and Pue, eds., *Canada's Legal Inheritances* (also published in *Manitoba Law Journal* 23 [1996]). This Canada–U.S. contrast should not be pushed too far, however, in light of William J. Novak, *The People's Welfare: Law and Regulation in Nineteenth-Century America* (Chapel Hill: University of North Carolina Press 1996).

and implementation of the Land Purchase Act would be unsuccessful in the new Supreme Court of Canada, established in 1875.[71]

The abolition of the seigneurial system was part of a larger reorientation of the Quebec legal order that resulted in the Civil Code of 1866, a social constitution that combined bourgeois property relations, freedom of contract, and a newly invigorated commercial law with an enhanced patriarchal vision of the family. The Code, the bilingual product of a joint effort between Anglophone and Francophone codifiers, promoted an ideal of (male) individual liberty and formal equality sharply at variance with that of the nationalist codifiers of the pre-rebellion period, steeped in customary law and seigneurialism. The vision of women, especially married women, contained in the Code was echoed in the English-speaking colonies by the formal legislative exclusion of women from the vote and from such niches in the public sphere as they had found under the ancien régime.[72]

There was no little irony in the treatment of the jury after the achievement of responsible government. The reformers had the chance to alter all those aspects of jury selection and practice that they had earlier found so objectionable, but their reforms, especially in Upper Canada, created a system so complex and expensive that it helped to create a backlash against the jury itself. A determined assault on the jury led mainly by lawyers, decrying the inefficiency of the institution and the ignorance of most jurors, swept Canada in the 1860s and 1870s. Ontario abolished civil juries in 1868 except where a party requested one or the judge so ordered. Jury trials for all civil actions except a few torts involving personal reputation were abolished in Halifax in 1878 and across the province in 1884, and other provinces followed suit. Under pressure from Ontario, the federal government passed the Speedy Trials Act in 1869, which provided for nonjury trials in a wide range of criminal cases, most of them carried out in the new county courts created in all provinces except Quebec.

The jury was under attack everywhere in the common-law world in the latter half of the nineteenth century, as the growth of professionalism and legal formalism rendered it seemingly anachronistic. The possible anti-corporate views of juries were also a factor in their decline, in Canada as elsewhere. What was unique in Canada was the harnessing of the ideology of responsible government to justify reducing the role of the jury. During the reform period both the jury and the legislature were conceived as popular institutions blocked from performing their proper roles by the interference of "irresponsible" members of the executive. All that had now changed. There may have been a time, admitted Attorney General H. W. Smith of Nova Scotia in the course of a debate on a bill

---

[71] Margaret McCallum, "The Sacred Rights of Property: Title, Entitlement, and the Land Question in Nineteenth-Century Prince Edward Island," in Baker and Phillips, *Essays in the History of Canadian Law, vol. VIII.*

[72] Brian Young, *The Politics of Codification: The Lower Canadian Civil Code of 1866* (Kingston and Montreal: McGill-Queen's University Press for the Osgoode Society 1994). See also Lykke de la Cour, Cecilia Morgan, and Mariana Valverde, "Gender Regulation and State Formation in Nineteenth-Century Canada," in Greer and Radforth, eds., *Colonial Leviathan.*

limiting recourse to juries, when juries were needed to protect the liberty of the subject from state oppression. Now, fortunately, Nova Scotia was "governed by the people, and her judges were of the people, and discharged their duties under the solemn obligation of an oath."[73] This view was echoed by Jonathan McCully, a father of Confederation, in 1875: Juries were no longer sacred because "we have now no fears of Star Chamber justice ever again being meted out to us."[74] It would be hard to find clearer statements than these of the idealized role of the provincial legislature in protecting the rights and liberties of its citizens. The pervasiveness of this discourse may be one of the reasons for the virtual absence in Canada of any discussion of the idea of provincial constitutions (even though Part V of the British North America Act 1867 is headed "Provincial Constitutions"): Constitutions are typically about citizens' rights *against* governments, an idea that did not sit well with the provincial governments' self-perception as guarantors of those same rights.

For one particularly disadvantaged population, British North America represented a bastion of liberty at mid-century.[75] As of the 1820s, Canadian authorities refused to return fugitive slaves to the United States, even those who may have committed crimes in the course of their escape. This stance led to the development of the "underground railway," which reached its apogee in the years after the enactment of a much harsher U.S. Fugitive Slave Act in 1850. Some 20,000 blacks are believed to have sought their freedom in Canada in the antebellum years. In southern Ontario, where most of them arrived, they found much racial prejudice and endured various forms of social discrimination. Crucially, however, they derived moral, legal, and practical support from the Canadian government, which resisted all local pressures to discourage black settlements and treated fugitive blacks as having equal rights to white British subjects. In some areas their voting power allowed them to determine elections, and, in 1859, Abraham Shadd was likely the first black to hold political office in North America, when he was elected as a member of the Raleigh Township council in Kent County, Canada West (Ontario).[76] The *Provincial Freeman*, the newspaper begun in 1853 by his daughter, Mary Ann Shadd (later Cary), was the first in North America to be published by a black woman. When a committee in Cincinnati, Ohio, requested information on the treatment of blacks in

[73] R. Blake Brown, "'We have now no fears of Star Chamber Justice': The Decline of the Jury in Nova Scotia," in *A Trying Question*, p. 257.

[74] Ibid.

[75] Fugitive slaves sought what we might call Liberty with a capital "L," but other U.S. groups have sought particular liberties in Canada denied to them at home, from Volstead Act refugees seeking alcohol in Canada during Prohibition in the 1920s, to those evading the draft during the Viet Nam war in the 1960s and 1970s, to those currently seeking same-sex marriage and the legal use of medical marijuana. Some Canadian migrants might be described as seeking greater economic liberty in the United States, while others sought more personal freedom by divorcing there (and then returning to Canada) during the period before 1968, when Canadian divorce laws were highly restrictive.

[76] The first black to hold elected office in a North American urban setting was likely Mifflin Gibbs, who was elected to the city council of Victoria, British Columbia, in 1866.

Canada, the respondents stated that "we are compelled to admit that . . . we have to contend with . . . prejudice against color, though it is unlike that which is so formidable in the United States. There it is bolstered up by law – here it has no foundation to stand upon."[77] The one major exception to this observation was in the field of education, where provincial law in Ontario and elsewhere permitted segregated schools even in areas where black parents would have preferred to send their children to the public school.

Confederation

The union of four of the British North American colonies in 1867 was propelled by a number of economic and political considerations, both domestic and imperial. On the domestic side, the most pressing need was to end the political impasse in the united province of Canada by a divorce that would meet Upper Canadian demands for representation by population and western expansion, and Lower Canadian demands for protection of its language and culture.[78] The Maritimes were ambivalent about Confederation, but with the end of the reciprocity treaty with the United States in 1866, the appeal of access to larger markets in the Canadas could not be denied. London, meanwhile, was concerned about the cost and feasibility of defending its northern colonies. All these factors have been explored in detail, but what might be called the "ideological origins" of Canadian confederation have not been much investigated until recently.[79] Much of the earlier literature on Confederation saw it as a pragmatic exercise in deal making undistinguished by any philosophical or theoretical commitments, while scholarship on post-Confederation developments has been dominated by Dominion–provincial struggles that "obscured or pre-empted thinking about individual rights."[80]

On its face, the British North America Act 1867 does not appear to address individual liberty in any way. The goal of the Union is laconically and vaguely expressed: to "conduce to the Welfare of the Provinces and promote the Interests of the British Empire." The only indirect reference to the rights and liberties of individuals is contained in the preambular statement that the Dominion was

---

[77] S. G. Howe, *Report to the Freedmen's Inquiry Commission 1864: The Refugees from Slavery in Canada West* (New York: Arno Press 1969), p. 101, cited in Sharon A. Roger Hepburn, *Crossing the Border: A Free Black Community in Canada* (Urbana and Chicago: University of Illinois Press 2007), p. 21. The community of the title is the Buxton settlement in Kent County, Ontario, one of the most successful of the North American settlements founded by refugees from slavery.

[78] The equal representation in the assembly of the United Province of Canada, initially favorable to the former Upper Canada (known as Canada West during the Union period), quickly became unfavorable with a strong influx of British immigrants into that part of Canada.

[79] Peter J. Smith, "The Ideological Origins of Canadian Confederation," *Canadian Journal of Political Science* 20:1 (1987), 3–29; Ged Martin, ed., *The Causes of Canadian Confederation* (Fredericton: Acadiensis Press 1990); Phillip A. Buckner, "The Maritimes and Confederation: A Reassessment," *Canadian Historical Review* 70:1 (1990), 1–45.

[80] R. C. B. Risk and R. C. Vipond, "Rights Talk in Canada in the Late Nineteenth Century: 'The Good Sense and Right Feeling of the People'" *Law & History Review* 14 (1996), 3.

to have "a Constitution similar in Principle to that of the United Kingdom." In other words, Canadians would continue to enjoy existing civil and political rights and freedoms: effectively, the blessings of modern liberty, transposed into a federal state. Canadians would continue to do so as British subjects since the Act created no new status of Canadian citizen. In fact, no such status would emerge until the Canadian Citizenship Act of 1946. Thus, claims about individual liberty would continue to be couched in terms of "British justice" until after the Second World War.

One group of Canadians continued to exist on the margins of liberal subjecthood. Authority over "Indians and Lands reserved for the Indians" was vested by the 1867 Constitution in the federal government, and it exercised this power by passing the first comprehensive Indian Act in 1876. The Act provided for a system of registration of Indians living on reserves and those covered by treaties, and set up new elected band councils to replace traditional structures of political authority. Indians registered under the Act lost the vote if they had previously held it and could only regain it by surrendering their Indian status. The underlying premise was that Indians were currently unfit for liberty, both individually and collectively, and should be permitted to "improve" at their own pace under the paternal supervision of white Indian Act bureaucrats until they were ready to join white society. When the anticipated improvement proved too slow in arriving, Ottawa pushed the pace by joining with Canadian churches to promote the idea of residential schools, to which many young aboriginals were consigned with varying degrees of coercion. The ensuing cultural tragedy resulted in class action lawsuits against the federal government and the churches that have only recently been settled.[81]

Federalism would continue to dominate Canadian discussions of liberty and rights until the enactment of the *Canadian Charter of Rights and Freedoms* in 1982, but that does not mean that individual liberty was not prized, valued, or protected. As R. C. B. Risk and R. C. Vipond have noted,

What distinguished Canadian and American approaches to rights in the late nineteenth century was less a commitment to individual rights than a difference in perspective concerning threats to rights. For Canadian lawyers, the principal threat to individual liberty seemed to come not from tyrannical legislatures but from the arbitrary actions of unaccountable executive authority. Steeped in the British tradition, the lawyers took their lessons not from the democratic excesses associated with debt-relieving, paper-money-producing state legislatures, but from the executive abuses associated with the Stuart kings.... In the United States, protecting liberty required placing limits on the power of legislatures. In Canada, protecting liberty meant fostering robust legislatures that would be able to constrain executive power.[82]

---

[81] See the website of the government agency created to deal with the claims, Indian Residential Schools Resolution Canada, www.irsr-rqpi.gc.ca. And see generally J. R. Miller, *Skyscrapers Hide the Heavens: A History of Indian-White Relations in Canada*, 3d ed. (Toronto: University of Toronto Press 2000).

[82] "Rights Talk," 15.

It was, of course, not merely the ancestral memory of Stuart kings that inspired concerns about arbitrary executive power, but the much more recent domestic struggles for obtaining responsible government.

At first glance, this emphasis on the fostering of "robust legislatures" would appear to be misplaced. With the development of political parties and the inculcation of party discipline, the executive was able to control the legislature, rather than the reverse. In the context of a two-party system, the minority could embarrass members of the executive in the legislature and hope to appeal to public opinion, but it could not truly hold them accountable for their actions in between elections. What gave a new lease on life to this debate was federalism itself.

On paper, the British North America Act appeared to give the federal government the upper hand. In the division of powers it gave "all the great subjects of legislation"[83] – trade and commerce; criminal law; and a residual power to legislate for the peace, order, and good government of the country – to the federal government, backed up by a power of disallowance and reservation over provincial legislation. The provincial power over education was subject to a rider whereby religious minorities enjoying by law any "right or privilege" to denominational schools could appeal to the federal government for remedial legislation in case of provincial interference with those rights. And Section 94 allowed the federal government to promote the uniformity of laws regarding property and civil rights in all the provinces. All of these powers suggested that the federal government would be the ultimate guarantor of individual rights and liberties against the possibly arbitrary actions of provincial governments.

This seemingly impressive armory of federal powers ran up against the ideology and practice of responsible government as it had developed in the individual colonies in the 1850s and 1860s.[84] Provincial governments stoutly defended their own autonomy and successfully pushed back against Macdonaldite centralism. They found one of their chief ideologists in the person of David Mills, ultimately minister of justice under Sir Wilfrid Laurier, who absorbed the emerging doctrines of legal liberalism and divided sovereignty from Thomas Cooley's lectures while studying at the University of Michigan Law School. Mills described provincial autonomy as a form of liberalism: Federalism was meant to preserve the "'rights' of the individual provinces from other governments in much the same way as the object of the liberal state was to protect the rights of individuals from overbearing governmental power."[85] The

---

[83] The phrase was that of Sir John A. Macdonald, Canada's first prime minister.

[84] Christopher Moore, *1867: How the Fathers Made a Deal* (Toronto: McClelland & Stewart 1997).

[85] Robert C. Vipond, *Liberty and Community: Canadian Federalism and the Failure of the Constitution* (Albany: SUNY Press 1991), p. 135. The thought of Edward Blake, leader of the federal Liberals in opposition in the 1880s, is also illustrative of this point: see R. C. B. Risk, "Blake and Liberty," in R. C. B. Risk, *A History of Canadian Legal Thought: Collected Essays*, G. Blaine Baker and Jim Phillips, eds. (Toronto: University of Toronto Press for the Osgoode Society 2006).

legal-rhetorical construction of provinces as rights-bearing individuals who should be left alone within their exclusive sphere of authority was enormously successful both within Canada, where it led to the power of disallowance and reservation quickly falling into desuetude, and even more importantly in the Judicial Committee of the Privy Council, which largely adopted it in adjudicating the multitude of federal–provincial disputes that came before it prior to the abolition of appeals in 1949.[86]

British justice and British-style liberty – liberty understood as exercised in a parliamentary tradition and not as a natural right – appealed not just to those of British descent but spread to Francophone Quebec society and to the newly settled West. The long reign of the Liberal prime minister Sir Wilfrid Laurier (1896–1911) coincided with the victory of provincial Liberals in Quebec in 1897 and helped cement the idea that the aspirations of Francophone Quebeckers for liberty and cultural self-determination could be reconciled with the practices and institutions of modern liberty as they existed within Confederation.[87] A striking feature of the settlement of the Canadian West was the extent to which it was carried on as a Toronto- and Ottawa-based enterprise conceived as an extension of the British empire, rather than one pushed forward by the arrival of settlers on the ground.[88] The myth of a uniformly peaceful and law-abiding Canadian frontier has been exploded in the last generation, and injustices in the treatment of native peoples revealed even if native–newcomer relations were less violence-ridden than south of the border.[89] But the creation of the North-West Mounted Police in 1873 and the early extension of British justice in the form of superior and inferior courts seem to have created a relatively stable environment in which thousands of non-British immigrants joined the native and Métis inhabitants in the quarter-century before 1914.

Canadian legal and political thinkers did not expand on the possible tensions between individual liberty and the liberty of self-government, which might lead to the oppression of individuals or minorities by a majority. Rather, they tended to see them as existing "in harmony." According to A. H. L. Lefroy, one of the best-known authorities on constitutional law in the early twentieth century, the constitution "guards the liberty of the subject without destroying the freedom of action of the legislature."[90]

---

[86] John T. Saywell, *The Lawmakers: Judicial Power and the Shaping of Canadian Federalism* (Toronto: University of Toronto Press for the Osgoode Society 2002).

[87] H. Blair Neatby, *Laurier and a Liberal Quebec* (Ottawa: McClelland & Stewart 1973).

[88] Doug Owram, *Promise of Eden: The Canadian Expansionist Movement and the Idea of the West 1856–1900* (Toronto: University of Toronto Press 1980).

[89] For a recent comparative synthesis, see Marian C. McKenna, "Above the Blue Line: Policing the Frontier in the Canadian and American West, 1870–1900," in Sterling Evans, ed., *The Borderlands of the American and Canadian Wests: Essays on the Regional History of the Forty-ninth Parallel* (Lincoln: University of Nebraska Press, 2006).

[90] R. C. B. Risk, "A. H. L. Lefroy: Common Law Thought in Late-Nineteenth-Century Canada – On Burying One's Grandfather," in *A History of Canadian Legal Thought*, 75.

The co-ordinate theory of federalism thus left the protection of individual rights to the federal and provincial legislatures themselves until the enactment of the *Canadian Bill of Rights* in 1960 and, more importantly, the adoption of the *Canadian Charter of Rights and Freedoms* in 1982. One positive feature of this development was the recognition that all individual rights are exercised in a social context, and that some trade-off between them and the public good is always required. This experience is reflected in Section 1 of the *Canadian Charter of Rights and Freedoms*, which "guarantees the rights and freedoms set out in it subject only to such reasonable limits prescribed by law as can be demonstrably justified in a free and democratic society." Another advantage was that when new rights were granted legislatively, they were the product of democratic discussion and debate, and could not be dismissed as the idiosyncratic or illegitimate product of mere judicial interpretation. Thus, the spread of provincial human rights codes across Canada in the 1950s and 1960s was a generally peaceful process that both reflected and entrenched a growing commitment to equality.[91]

The role of property in securing liberty is somewhat schizophrenic under Canadian law. Property did not, and still does not, enjoy formal constitutional protection in Canadian law: In Justice Riddell's pithy summation, "the prohibition 'Thou shall not steal' has no legal force upon a sovereign body."[92] Expropriation by a public authority without compensation is permitted as long as the legislative intent is clear and explicit. In general, Canadian legislatures have been solicitous of the rights of existing property holders, but they have also not hesitated to expropriate, often without compensation, various corporate interests and whole classes of private rights such as riparian rights. Such actions were particularly evident during the initial period of industrial development, from roughly 1870 to 1930.[93] Provincial governments have successfully fended off campaigns to add property to the rights protected under the *Canadian Charter of Rights and Freedoms* by relying on a version of the historic argument about provincial autonomy: Provincial governments must have the ability to protect their citizens by reallocating property when and if that proves to be necessary in the public interest.

The disadvantage of the Canadian model of rights protection was the weak support it provided for the development of a "rights culture." In spite of the continual evocation of the ideals of British justice down to the Second World War, shocking deviations from traditional ideas of fairness in criminal

---

[91] Philip Girard, *Bora Laskin: Bringing Law to Life* (Toronto: University of Toronto Press for the Osgoode Society 2005), chap. 11.

[92] Cited in Jennifer Nedelsky, "Judicial Conservatism in an Age of Innovation," in Flaherty, ed., *Essays in the History of Canadian Law I*, 310.

[93] Christopher Armstrong and H. V. Nelles, *Monopoly's Moment: The Organization and Regulation of Canadian Utilities, 1830–1930* (Toronto: University of Toronto Press 1986); Jennifer Nedelsky, "From Private Property to Public Resource: The Emergence of Administrative Control of Water in Nova Scotia," in Girard and Phillips, eds., *Essays in the History of Canadian Law III*.

procedure, for example, could occur virtually without comment. The Crown appeal from an acquittal, which first appeared in the Criminal Code of 1892, is one such illustration.[94] The decline in the role of the grand jury as a safeguard against overzealous state action is another: London, Ontario, grand juries returned only one verdict of "No bill" in more than 300 indictments submitted to them between 1879 and 1905.[95] It was not until after the Second World War that a more aggressive movement for the protection of civil liberties and human rights led to sufficient disillusionment with the model of legislative protection of rights that a shift to judicial protection via a written bill of rights could be seriously contemplated and promoted.[96]

The Canadian model of rights protection also did not seem to fulfill the promise of individual flourishing supposedly inherent in a liberal society. Economic rights and those enjoyed by prosperous white males generally enjoyed a high degree of protection. The rights enjoyed by women, minorities, native people, and the poor generally did not, although some white women were increasingly offered the benefits of liberal society after the enactment of the Married Women's Property Acts of the 1880s and their admission to the vote in the 1910s (except for women in Quebec, who had to wait until 1940 for the provincial vote). These trends were broadly similar in all Western countries until after the Second World War, however, which suggests that the specific model of rights protection adopted has a rather marginal impact on the lives of most citizens.

One area where the Canadian experience may have some broader resonance internationally is in its recognition of group rights within a constitution strongly committed to individual rights and to equality. The British North America Act of 1867 provided for the protection of the rights of religious minorities to denominational schools with public funding if they had enjoyed such rights "by law" at the time of Confederation or were subsequently granted such rights. Outside Ontario and Quebec these rights were not adequately protected for complex reasons, but in those two provinces they have survived and flourished. The British North America Act also provided for the usage of both English and French in the debates and published Acts of Parliament and the legislature of Quebec, in the courts of Quebec, and in any courts to be established in the future under federal authority. These linguistic rights served as the basis of the Official Languages Act, 1969, which made Canada officially bilingual, and inspired similar legislation in New Brunswick in the same year; both moves were entrenched in the 1982 constitutional amendments. Several other provinces offer governmental services in the "other" official language even though they are not constitutionally obliged to do so. In addition,

---

[94] Discussed in Paul Romney, "From Constitutionalism to Legalism."

[95] Nancy Parker, "Reaching a Verdict: The Changing Structure of Decision-Making in the Canadian Criminal Courts, 1867–1905" (PhD dissertation, York University 1999).

[96] Christopher MacLennan, *Toward the Charter: Canadians and the Demand for a National Bill of Rights, 1929–1960* (Kingston and Montreal: McGill-Queen's University Press 2003).

Quebec's linguistic and cultural distinctiveness is recognized by a variety of arrangements at the federal level that constitute a de facto, if not de jure, form of asymmetrical federalism. The distinct place of native peoples in Canada is slowly being recognized by the settlement of land claims and the spread of self-government agreements.

The layering of various forms of cultural rights on individual rights in Canada suggests that liberal subjectivity does not have to be univocal, and that plural forms of identity – one of the highest forms of liberty – can be accommodated within the liberal tradition.[97] The Canadian experience also suggests that the parliamentary tradition of "modern liberty" is sufficiently flexible to reshape itself in significant ways to accommodate demands for various kinds of freedom, provided citizens are sufficiently aware and engaged to make those demands.

[97] James Tully, *Strange Multiplicity: Constitutionalism in an Age of Diversity* (Cambridge: Cambridge University Press 1995).

7

Contested Despotism

Problems of Liberty in British India

Robert Travers

> I know nothing of the liberty you talk of, I do not understand it; I cultivate my
> land, the Produce maintains my Family; I have several Wives and Children, with
> whom I am happy; what more can I desire?[1]

Thus spoke an imaginary "native" of Hindustan through the unreliable mouthpiece of a committee, elected by the British inhabitants of Calcutta in 1779 to
petition the Westminster Parliament. The petitioners, a motley collection of
East India Company officials, soldiers, sailors, lawyers, and merchants, complained about the effects of the extension of rights in English law to native
inhabitants by British judges of the Calcutta Supreme Court. The court had
erred, they argued, in trying to extend British laws and liberties to Indians; they
urged that if "Liberty with us is real, it is also an artificial Source of our
Happiness, and that other Nations may enjoy a more perfect Felicity than
ourselves, though denied the Freedom we possess." The invented voice of the
native man, secure in his religion, land, and family, exemplified the categorical
distinction between happiness and liberty. The alien complexity of the English
law, premised on a "Spirit of Equality and Independence," would actually
subvert the "real substantial happiness" of Indian society. "Nature and the
Climate were the Legislators of the People of Hindostan," and they had
ordained that "despotic government," with simple, summary laws maintaining
a rigid social and political hierarchy, were the proper forms of rule in India.[2]

---

[1] *Humble Petition of the British Subjects Residing in the Provinces of Bengal, Behar and Orissa,
and Their Several Dependencies* (London, 1780), p. 66. This pamphlet contains both the text of
a petition to the House of Commons, signed by 647 persons (pp. 1–13), and also some lengthier
"observations" on the petition composed by a committee, nominated by ballot from among the
British inhabitants of Calcutta (contemporary Kolkata), to take charge of presenting the petition
to Parliament. The above quote is taken from these "observations."

[2] Ibid., pp. 62–65.

I would like to thank Philip Stern, Peter Marshall, Ken Macmillan, Manu Sehgal, Siraj Ahmed,
Emma Rothschild and all the participants at the conference on "Liberty and Cultural Transmission
in the British Empire" for valuable advice on aspects of this chapter. All mistakes are my own.

Within the same text, however, lurked another, far more threatening image of Indian life, co-existing in sharp tension with the figure of the contented, rural family man. This was the Indian who all too eagerly took advantage of the English law to complain against the authority of the East India Company government and the domineering behavior of the British inhabitants, or who crowded into the Supreme Court with sufficient knowledge of the English language to understand the critical statements of the judges about the oppressive practices of the company, or who then circulated these statements throughout the "Black Town" as "Articles of News." Thus, "the Respect and Veneration which the Natives have heretofore manifested for the Government" was "daily decreasing," and contempt for authority and for "Europeans in general" was diffused throughout Calcutta society.[3] The petitioners referred menacingly to the "late daring tumult" during the Muslim festival of Muharram, when the courthouse and other surrounding houses had been pelted with bricks by an angry crowd and Europeans were beaten and wounded.[4]

The inevitable conclusion, according to the petitioners, unless the English court's jurisdiction was restricted, was not simply "the Loss of these Kingdoms forever," but quite possibly also the "Destruction of the British Subjects residing in these Provinces." This was because "the Disproportion between the governing Power and those governed" was so great that the safety of British authority depended on an "ideal Superiority." This precarious sense of superiority in turn rested on the strict maintenance of social separation and also "the Forms of personal Submission and Respect to Europeans."[5]

The febrile rhetoric of this 1779 petition incorporated a complex analysis of the problem of liberty in British India. The central problem, as the petitioners saw it, was how to maintain their own birthright as free-born subjects of the British Crown, while at the same time maintaining the forms of distinction and hierarchy that underpinned British authority over native subjects in India. Calcutta had long been construed as a British settlement, governed by English laws, though with due allowances made for local circumstances and for the legal norms of indigenous inhabitants. Before 1773, a Mayor's Court and the East India Company's governor and council acting as JPs administered English law to the settlement, while these courts coexisted with other tribunals, such as the "zamindar's court," designed to administer justice to indigenous inhabitants.[6] From 1774, a new, royally appointed Supreme Court, staffed by four British judges from outside the East India Company service, provided a more unified and independent judicial authority for Calcutta, but the petitioners complained that this court had provided both too little English law in some respects and too much in others.

---

[3] Ibid., pp. 44–5, 5.

[4] Ibid., pp. 5, 49. For a recent account of this riot, see P. J. Marshall, "The Muharram riot of 1779 and the struggle for status and authority in early colonial Calcutta," *Journal of the Asiatic Society of Bangladesh*, 50 (2005), pp. 293–314.

[5] *Humble Petition of the British Subjects*, pp. 48, 5, 4, 52.

[6] For a good summary of the early legal history of Calcutta under East India Company rule, see M. P. Jain, *Outlines of Indian Legal History* (2nd edition, Bombay: N. M. Tripathi, 1966), pp. 51–80.

They argued, for example, that the judges had acted tyrannically toward the British inhabitants, denying their "inherent, inalienable, and indefeasible rights" to trial by jury in civil cases and exercising an "uncontrouled Dominion" by their discretionary awards of damages to native litigants. The petitioners invoked the "fundamental law" of England, including the Magna Charta, the "great Charter of English liberties," to defend their right to juries in civil trials.[7] At the same time, the petitioners complained that the judges had been overly officious in other respects in their application of strict English legal forms in regard to property and contract disputes, "when no such Laws could be known, or practiced by Natives or Europeans then residing in the Country, and at a time too, when few or no Persons of legal knowledge were in the Country to assist or advise them." The judges also erred, according to the petitioners, by extending their jurisdiction beyond Calcutta over the other regions of Bengal and Bihar conquered by the East India Company in the 1750s and 1760s. By doing this, the judges had supposedly undermined the company's attempt to preserve a measure of authority for the former provincial governors, the *Nawabs* of Bengal, and also the effort to administer Hindu and Muslim laws through the company's own law courts, or *adalats*.[8]

The judges of the Supreme Court, needless to say, took a very different view of the matter than the petitioners. Appointed by Lord North's Regulating Act of 1773, in an atmosphere of scandal surrounding the apparent abuses of East India Company servants, the judges supposed themselves bound to hear complaints by Indian subjects in Bengal against oppressive British officials and traders.[9] Interpreting their jurisdiction broadly, the judges even deployed writs of habeas corpus to free Indians from the company's custody.[10] The judges' actions provoked angry resistance not only from British settlers in Bengal but also from the East India Company authorities.

Hurriedly responding to the complaints of the British petitioners, Elijah Impey, the chief justice of the Supreme Court, worked hard to counter their imputations in his letters to powerful figures in Britain. He presented the petition as the sour grapes of a British community too long accustomed to exercising uncontrolled power over Indian subjects. He explained to Lord Weymouth (secretary of state for the Southern Department) that the catalyst for the petition was the case of James Creasy, who was fined by the court in January 1779 after two Indian carpenters brought charges of assault, battery, and false imprisonment. According to Impey, Creasy had "kept them [the carpenters]

---

[7] *Humble Petition of the British Subjects*, pp. 4, 39–40. A system of petty and grand juries was already used in criminal trials at the Quarter sessions in Calcutta.

[8] Ibid., pp. 7, 43–48.

[9] The fullest account of the early history of the court is still B. N. Pandey, *The Introduction of English Law into India; the career of Elijah Impey in Bengal 1774–1783* (Bombay: Asia Publishing House, 1967).

[10] For the use of the writ of habeas corpus in India, see Paul D. Halliday and G. Edward White, "The Suspension Clause: English Text, Imperial Contexts, and American Implications," *Virginia Law Review*, 94, 8 (2008), and Nasser Husain, *The Jurisprudence of Emergency. Colonialism and the Rule of Law* (Ann Arbor: University of Michigan Press, 2003), ch. 3.

in Confinement for a Night, had ordered Servants to beat them, and had himself beat them with a Rattan Cane."[11] Creasy had argued in open court that the case should be tried by a jury, but Impey thought that trial by jury in civil cases was impracticable in Calcutta, where the British community was too small to afford regular juries, and too biased in favor of Europeans to judge fairly. If Britons were allowed to sit on juries in civil cases, then "natives might with equal justice" also do so.[12] Meanwhile, limiting the powers of the court with respect to the East India Company government would be simply a "license for the enormities the Court as I understood was intended to suppress."[13]

Impey claimed that it was by no means the wish of British judges to impose English municipal law on Indian society, but rather to judge in cases involving Indians according to the dictates of "natural justice" and local "custom." He held out the prospect that the Supreme Court would discover a kind of Indian common law through its researches into local custom.[14] Meanwhile, he detected in the petition a style of colonial disregard for due authority that was becoming all too prevalent in the British world. By electing a committee to petition Parliament, the British inhabitants were behaving "like your Bill of Rights men in England," and "they talk of their rights being indefeasible like Americans and in case of want of success to follow their example."[15] Whereas the petitioners, like some American patriots, saw themselves as loyal British subjects unfairly placed beyond the pale of British liberty, Impey viewed them as corrupt frontiersmen and unruly adventurers. The liberties they demanded would in effect trample on the rights of Indians; only proper legal scrutiny could strike the proper balance between liberty and authority, and prevent the rights of free-born Englishmen descending into cruelty and license.

The clash in 1779 between the East India Company, the British inhabitants of Calcutta, and the Calcutta Supreme Court was one of the defining moments in the constitutional definition of the emerging British Indian empire. It nicely illustrated the way that constitutional questions became highly charged sites of ethnic identification, which produced competing and often confused notions of Britishness, Englishness, Europeanness, and the "native" character. In these debates, ideas about liberty and despotism were powerful rhetorical tools, hurled about like cannon fire by the various participants. Liberty appeared in the Calcutta petition as both a product of the "European" climate, manners, and customs, and also a particular inherited privilege attached to British (male) bodies, nontransferable to Indians without creating alarming consequences. Liberty was clearly a highly gendered category. The "British inhabitants" of

---

[11] Impey to Lord Weymouth, 26 March 1779, British Library [BL], Additional Manuscripts [Add. MSS] 16,259, fo. 166r.

[12] Ibid., fo. 169r.

[13] Impey to Lord Thurlow, 12 August 1778, BL, Add. MSS 16, 259, fo. 137v.

[14] Robert Travers, *Ideology and Empire in Eighteenth Century India. The British in Bengal* (Cambridge: Cambridge University Press, 2007), pp. 190–1.

[15] Impey to Mr. Kerby, 26 March 1779, BL, Add. MSS 16,259, fos. 181v, 182v.

Calcutta laying claim to liberties under the law were constituted by British men, just as the putative "native" subject was figured as a male householder.

Shadowing notions of liberty, despotism was a highly charged pejorative term used by both sides, often implying arbitrary, tyrannical, and potentially cruel practices of domination. Yet it was also (for the petitioners, at least) an ingrained and unavoidable habit of Asian life, and perfectly compatible with the happiness of native subjects. On the one hand, according to the petitioners, a despotic form of colonial government could itself become a way of upholding the traditional "liberties" of Indians. On the other hand, the judges argued that too expansive a view of British "liberties" on the turbulent frontiers of empire would result in a rapacious and destructive form of despotism.

The immediate outcome of these early disputes about English law reflected the instinct of the imperial parliament, harassed by costly wars in both the Atlantic and Asian spheres of empire, to secure the East India Company government and the British inhabitants of Bengal from the meddlesome interference of the Supreme Court judges. Members of Parliament rallied to defend the British inhabitants from the levelling effects of the court. Edmund Burke argued that the court's imposition of the convoluted and unfamiliar forms of English law on Indian society was itself a form of tyranny. Like the British petitioners, Burke invoked the figure of the servile native to justify his argument. Despotism in India was actually a form of free choice: If the natives preferred "arbitrary and despotic government" over "the beautiful and free system of British legislation, what must be done?" "Men must be governed by those laws which they love," and the government of the few over the many must proceed upon the basis of "consent."[16] Thus, limits on an independent English judiciary in British India could be squared with a reformist Whig's notion of consensual governance.

An amending act of 1781 sharply cut back the jurisdiction of the Calcutta Supreme Court, preventing it from interfering in the ordinary revenue or judicial business of the East India Company government in the interior of Bengal.[17] In Calcutta, Indians would be judged by the standards of their own laws, as interpreted by the British judges advised by Indian law officers, *qazis, muftis,* and *pandits.* Beyond Calcutta, the company would rule supreme through its own networks of law courts (*adalats*), revenue collectors, and military garrisons. Supposedly modeled on the forms of rule inherited from the Mughal empire, the company government had successfully defended its rule of constitutional difference from the encroachments of the English law.

The new judicature act amounted to a resounding rhetorical assertion of the necessity of "despotic" government in India, limiting the power and independence of the Crown-appointed judiciary and the capacity of Indian subjects to claim rights in English law. Yet the meaning of British despotism in India, and

---

[16] Burke's speech to the House of Commons, 27 June, 1781, in P. J. Marshall ed., *Writings and Speeches of Edmund Burke.* Volume 5, *India: Bengal and Madras* (Oxford: Oxford University Press, 1981), pp. 141–2.

[17] 21 Geo. 3, c. 70, discussed in detail in Jain, *Outlines of Indian Legal History,* pp. 143–152.

its effects on both Indian subjects and Britain itself, would long continue to be disputed. Within a few years, Edmund Burke himself was roundly condemning the idea that despotism was in fact the natural form of governance in Asia, elaborating a more expansive vision of the constitutional rights of Indian subjects. The temporary alliance between the British inhabitants of Calcutta and the East India Company government would also prove fragile and short-lived. The British inhabitants were disappointed in their demand for trial by jury in civil cases, and chafed against the company's tight rein on British settlement, commerce, and the freedom of information in India. A growing community of mixed-race Eurasians, officially excluded from the ranks of "natural-born" British subjects, demanded recognition and rights for themselves. Meanwhile, the company's diverse Indian subjects, like those who flocked to the Supreme Court in the 1770s, continued to defy British stereotypes of timidity and servility, challenging the East India Company with their own distinctive conceptions of the rights and obligations of rulers and ruled.

The concept of liberty has not played a prominent role in the historiography of early British rule in India. This lacuna is not especially surprising, given the official consensus among contemporaries that British rule in India was, and should be, a kind of despotism, and given the authoritarian, militaristic ethos of the British Indian "garrison-state."[18] Nonetheless, as the arguments over the Calcutta Supreme Court suggested, British Indian politics in the late eighteenth and early nineteenth centuries was shot through with ideas about liberty, about the nature and scope of liberty, and about the limits of liberty in the context of empire.

That modern historians have often overlooked these debates in part reflects the profound influence of late Victorian categories of "settler" and "dependent" colonies on British imperial history. Victorian thinkers tended to draw stark distinctions between settler colonies, forged in the Atlantic mould of settlers, English laws, and representative assemblies, and the dependent empire, marked by authoritarian rule over nonwhite populations.[19] Thus, India has usually been viewed as the laboratory of a "second British empire," and an empire of conquest rather than settlement, and of imperial despotism rather than colonial liberty. According to John Stuart Mill, in a famous passage of *Considerations on Representative Government*, colonial despotism, meaning a rule of white experts unchecked by elected colonial assemblies, was the best form of rule where a civilized nation like Britain governed "a barbarous or semi-barbarous" people as in India.[20] The emergence of Mill's brand of imperial liberalism in Victorian Britain, with its

---

[18] For the concept of a "garrison state," see Douglas M. Peers, *Between Mars and Mammon. Colonial Armies and the Garrison State in India, 1819–1835* (London: Tauris Academic, 1995).

[19] For a fine recent survey of late Victorian imperial thought, see Duncan Bell, *The Idea of Greater Britain. Empire and the Future of World Order 1860–1900* (Princeton, NJ: Princeton University Press, 2007).

[20] J. S. Mill, "On the Government of Dependencies by a Free State," in *Considerations on Representative Government* (London, 1856), pp. 322–3.

hard-nosed justifications of freedom at home and unfreedom in certain colonies, is now a much-studied aspect of nineteenth-century political thought.[21]

Yet, framing the problem of liberty in British India around the question of "liberalism and empire" is also quite limiting, both in the potential for privileging high theory over more diverse or mundane forms of political language, and also because of the danger of taking teleological, anachronistic, and polarized Victorian conceptions of "free nations" and "dependent peoples" too much for granted. By contrast, tracking changing ideas about liberty in British India suggests how J. S. Mill's distinction between settler and nonsettler colonies was an ideological statement framed at a particular moment, and not a straightforward historical description. There is no question that J. S. Mill's model of two empires grew out of entrenched (and deeply racialized) differences in status and power between British settlers and other subjects of imperial government. But the question of whether parts of India, too, could become settler colonies, or whether certain groups even within Indian society could achieve rights analogous to those of British settlers, remained more open in the late eighteenth and early nineteenth centuries than Mill's account – or ultimately the East India Company and the British state – ever allowed.

Feeding off the rich historiography of ideologies of empire in the Atlantic world, historians of British India have recently begun to ask how India, with its vast population of non-Christian subjects and its massive land-armies made up largely of local recruits, fit into a prevailing eighteenth-century idea of the British empire as "Protestant, commercial, maritime and free."[22] Posing the problem in this way does indeed capture an important strand of contemporary thought, especially as it considered whether the British empire might go the way of Rome, with conquest and despotism overseas leading to corruption and despotism at home.[23] Again, though, there is a danger of taking for granted rather than properly analyzing a set of teleological assumptions about a

---

[21] The classic study was Eric Stokes, *English Utilitarians and India* (Oxford: Oxford University Press, 1959); for the intersections of liberal theory and imperial ideology, see Thomas R. Metcalf, *Ideologies of the Raj* (Cambridge: Cambridge University Press, 1994); for contrasting recent interpretations of liberal political theory in relation to empire, see Uday Singh Mehta, *Liberalism and Empire. A Study in Nineteenth Century British Liberal Thought* (Chicago: Chicago University Press, 1999), which tends to see imperialism as an expression of an authoritarian streak in the abstract heart of liberalism; and Jennifer Pitts, *A Turn to Empire. The Rise of Imperial Liberalism in Britain and France* (Princeton, NJ: Princeton University Press, 2005), which rejects the notion of a necessary imperial trajectory within a liberal tradition of thought and argues for a conscious "turn to empire" among liberal thinkers in nineteenth-century Britain and France. For a recent review essay, see Andrew Sartori, "The British Empire and its Liberal Mission," *Journal of Modern History*, 78, 3 (2006), pp. 623–42.

[22] The phrase is from David Armitage, *The Ideological Origins of the British Empire* (Cambridge: Cambridge University Press, 2000), pp. 195–7; see also P. J. Marshall, *A Free Though Conquering People. Britain and Asia in the Eighteenth Century* (London: King's College, 1981), and my own *Ideology and Empire in Eighteenth Century India*, which was much indebted to Marshall's formulation of the problem.

[23] Marshall, *A Free Though Conquering People*, pp. 6–8.

relatively "liberal" Atlantic tradition of empire, and a relatively "illiberal" Asian one. Some contemporaries wanted, for different reasons, to frame the problem in these stark terms. It remains unclear, however, whether the conquest of India can be considered as an authoritarian turn in an empire that had long been built on the labor of African slaves, which commonly regarded the native inhabitants of the Americas as barbarians and savages, and in which the "liberties" of domestic subjects let alone colonial settlers remained deeply contested.

What in the end was so striking about British political argument in relation to India was not the intense difficulty of justifying a regime of imperial conquest within a political vocabulary built around the concepts of "liberty and property," but rather in fact the apparent plasticity of British conceptions of legitimate authority. One of the most crucial, and underemphasized, features of British political language in the eighteenth century was its flexibility, its ability to adapt itself to many different settings and contingencies, and remain in some way recognizably British. This flexibility was no doubt related to the long history of British and imperial state-formation, the multiple styles of governance and authority exhibited within the British composite monarchy, and the variety of peoples included in the British world long before the conquest of Bengal.[24] There were not two empires in the eighteenth century, but many forms of imperial rule, with many different permutations of anointed, appointed, and elected powers.[25] The problem of incorporating new Indian territories into a diverse imperial constitution was not a shortage of ideas about how to do so, but rather an alarming proliferation of potential models for the new empire. Was the best model Republican Rome, with its tolerance of diverse local laws, or the Rome of the great imperial law-giver Justinian? Should Bengal be governed as a province of the Mughal empire established by the great sixteenth-century emperor Akbar, or as a province of Great Britain?

It was the very plasticity and flexibility of British political language that so alarmed and shocked some contemporaries, who had grown up with a distinct conception of an "empire of liberty," and put their faith in a particular view of the constitutional proprieties inherent in Britishness.[26] Liberty and despotism, descriptive terms heavily freighted with evaluative moral meanings, seemed all too easily to lose their bearings in debates over the new empire. Indeed discussions about India suggested that liberty and despotism did not necessarily refer to neatly distinguished forms of rule, poles apart and comfortably separate. Rather, they often appeared as blurred and overlapping constellations of

---

[24] Joanna Innes, "Governing Diverse Societies," in Paul Langford, ed., *The Eighteenth Century 1688–1815* (Oxford: Oxford University Press, 2002), pp. 103–140.

[25] For a good survey, see Ian K. Steele, "The Anointed, the Appointed, and the Elected: Governance of the British Empire, 1689–1784," in P. J. Marshall ed., *Oxford History of the British Empire. Volume 2, The Eighteenth Century* (Oxford: Oxford University Press, 1998), pp. 105–127.

[26] For eighteenth-century notions of an "empire of liberty," see Jack P. Greene, "Empire of and Identity from the Glorious Revolution to the American Revolution," in ibid., pp. 208–230.

ideas about authority, forming and reforming in different patterns to fit varied contexts.

Liberty and despotism were, after all, two of the most contested and complex political concepts available to eighteenth-century Britons. Liberty could be rooted in languages about English "municipal law," ancient constitutions, common-law rights, and representative assemblies; these approaches might overlap with republican notions of virtue and self-government. But liberty also related to theories of natural jurisprudence, as a fundamental, natural right to "power over one's own actions," a right that was prior to any particular constitutional arrangement.[27] A sense of liberty as a basic security, what we might term civil liberty, was an important element in Scottish enlightenment writings on commercial society. Martha Maclaren has argued that to writers in this tradition, the term liberty "rarely meant much more than the security of the persons and property of the governed under rulers whose right to govern ultimately rested on some form of tacit consent."[28] "By a people's being free," the famous political economist Sir James Steuart wrote in 1767, "I understand no more than their being governed by general laws, well-known, not depending upon the ambulatory will of any man, or any set of men, and established so as not to be changed, but in a regular and uniform way." "Under this definition of liberty," he continued, "a people may be found to enjoy freedom under the most despotic forms of government."[29] In this sense, the highly authoritarian form of the British Indian "garrison state" could appear compatible with the essential rights of individuals to work, trade, and form families under the protections of the law.

Similarly, the idea of despotism, so often deployed in fiercely polemical terms as arbitrary, lawless, and tyrannical, the opposite of and negation of liberty – in effect a form of slavery – also possessed a set of less pejorative connotations derived from the tradition of European absolutism.[30] Absolute authority could also be legal and law-abiding authority, and therefore in some sense compatible with the fundamental, natural rights of subjects. Despite frequently trumpeted stereotypes, despotism was not seen simply as the preserve of Asian potentates. William Blackstone, for example, thought that "absolute despotic power" was

---

[27] Knud Haakonsen, *Natural Law and Moral Philosophy. From Grotius to the Scottish Enlightenment* (Cambridge: Cambridge University Press, 1996), p. 40.

[28] Martha Mclaren, *British India and British Scotland, 1780–1830. Career Building, Empire Building and a Scottish School of Thought in Indian Governance* (Akron, OH: University of Akron Press, 2001), pp. 160–161. For a subtle essay on the theme of liberty in Scottish enlightenment, which warns against overdrawing the lines between republican and jurisprudential ideas of liberty, or between "political" and "civil" liberty, see Dario Castiglione, "'That Noble Disquiet': Meanings of Liberty in the Discourse of the North," in Stefan Collini, Richard Whatmore, and Brian Young, eds., *Economy, Polity and Society. British Intellectual History 1750–1950* (Cambridge: Cambridge University Press, 2000), pp. 48–60.

[29] Sir James Steuart, *An Inquiry into the Principles of Political Oeconomy* (ed. A. S. Skinner, Edinburgh and London, Scottish Economic Society, 1966), pp. 206–7.

[30] R. Koebner, "Despot and Despotism: Vicissitudes of a Political Term," *Journal of the Warburg and Cortauld Institutes*, xiv, 3–4 (1951), pp. 275–302.

an essential feature of the supreme authority in all well-ordered states, a final
bulwark of authority against anarchy, which in England resided in the "sovereign and uncontrollable" power of Parliament.[31] Absolute government was
also seen within some versions of Scottish conjectural history as a necessary
stage in societal development, mediating the transition between feudal lord-
ships and the formation of a modern sovereign state.[32] This, too, was an
important intellectual context for the elaboration of a British "despotism of
law" in India.[33]

Though modern historiography has drawn a sharp distinction between the
Atlantic and Indian Ocean worlds in the early modern period, eighteenth-
century Britons often viewed the different spheres of empire as tied together
by a loose but coherent imperial constitution. As British politicians struggled
to define rights of sovereignty and property over the East India Company's new
empire in India in the 1760s and 1770s, they looked to relevant models from
the Atlantic world. For some observers, like the imperial theorist Thomas
Pownall, the powers of the East India Company were like those that "have
been given to all other colonists and emigrants"; such chartered rights were thus
equally susceptible to abuse in both spheres of the empire, necessitating a more
conscious assertion of metropolitan sovereignty.[34] On the other hand, Atlantic
claims to colonial autonomy could also underwrite the company's claims to
relative independence. Arguing that the company, not the Crown, should have
power to appoint judges in Bengal, Sir George Colebrooke (chairman of the
company's directors) noted that in some proprietary colonies the power of
appointing judges was "lodged in the hands of the proprietors," and that justice
was as well administered in these colonies as elsewhere in the empire.[35]

These debates reflected the common origins of the East India Company's
settlements and other British overseas possessions in the complex tradition of
English corporate government.[36] The company claimed its rights on the basis of
royal and parliamentary charters of incorporation; challenges to the company's
prerogatives seemed, therefore, to affect the "liberties" of other corporations as
diverse as the City of London, the Bank of England, or chartered colonies. The
company had its own form of representative assembly and elective government,

---

[31] Cited in David Lieberman, *The Province of Legislation Determined. Legal Theory in Eighteenth-Century Britain* (Cambridge: Cambridge University Press, 1989), pp. 50–53.

[32] Martha Mclaren, "From analysis to prescription: Scottish concepts of Asiatic Despotism in
Early Nineteenth Century British India," *International History Review*, 15 (1993) pp. 469–501.

[33] For this phrase, see Radhika Singha, *A Despotism of Law. Crime and Justice in Early Colonial
India* (New Delhi: Oxford University Press, 1998).

[34] Thomas Pownall, *The Right, Interest, and Duty of Government as Concerned in the Affairs of
the East Indies* (1st ed. 1773, rev. ed. London 1783), pp. 7–13.

[35] House of Commons Debate, 13 April 1772, *The Parliamentary History of England from the
Earliest Years to 1803 (Cobbett's Parliamentary History)*, (London, 1812–20), vol. 17, p. 469.

[36] The corporate and political character of the East India Company is expertly drawn out in Philip
J. Stern, "'One Body Corporate and Politick': The Growth of the East India Company State in
the Later Seventeenth Century," Unpublished PhD (Columbia University, 2004).

in the Court of Proprietors and Court of Directors in London. Meanwhile, the company's factories in India also shared in the wider fabric of corporate self-government. Since the late seventeenth century, "presidents and councils" had been granted local legislative and judicial powers over the "presidency towns" of Bombay, Madras, and Calcutta, limited by the familiar provision that local laws could not be repugnant to the laws of England. These towns also enjoyed the privileges of chartered municipalities, with mayors, aldermen, and burgesses administering a flexible system of "English law" and local customary justice in mayoral courts. Since 1726, appeals could go led from the mayoral courts to the company councils, and then to the Privy Council, further tying Indian settlements into a wider imperial orbit.[37]

The elaborate constitutional forms of company governance provided many institutional and ideological pressure points for the company's critics in the era of empire building after 1757. The company's authorities in Bengal found themselves in conflict not only with Indian rulers over rights to land and trade, but also with company servants and soldiers who sought to convert military conquests into expansive claims to unrestricted trade and settlement. Keen to rein in what it regarded as the threatening and destabilizing forces of "private" British trade, the company strengthened the powers of local governors in Bengal, establishing a new select committee to circumvent the power of the local council.[38] Robert Clive, in his second governorship in Bengal between 1765 and 1767, made full use of his ample authority, using court martials and expulsions to put down a mutiny of army officers, deporting company servants accused of bribe-taking and other offences, and cracking down on "private" trade in part through strengthening the company's system of monopoly.[39]

These measures soon provoked loud denunciations of a new commercial despotism from angry British traders.[40] The Scottish MP George Johnstone, whose brother was forced out from Bengal by Governor Clive, denounced the "wicked" principles of Clive's government. The system of monopoly, Johnstone argued, "checks the incitements to labour, and produces famine and all the other evil consequences that have followed in Bengal." Clive's policies tended toward "an uncontrouled Direction at home, and an absolute government

---

[37] A. B. Keith, *A Constitutional History of India 1600–1935* (1st ed. 1926, repr. Methuen: London, 1969), p. 43.

[38] B. B. Misra, *The Central Administration of the East India Company (1773–1854)* (Manchester: Manchester University Press, 1959) pp. 66–7.

[39] H. V. Bowen, *Revenue and Reform. The Indian Problem in British Politics, 1757–1773* (Cambridge: Cambridge University Press, 1991), pp. 85–6.

[40] Later imperial historians have tended to favor the company's rhetoric of controlling rapacious British interlopers, and thus the substantial constitutional disputes of these early years of empire in Bengal have often been ignored. Radical, free-trade critics of the company authorities in the 1760s are now finally getting their due; see, for example, Willem G. J. Kuiters, *The British in Bengal 1756–73. A Society in Transition Seen through the Eyes of a Rebel* (Paris: Indes savants, 2002); James M. Vaughan, "The Politics of Empire: Metropolitan Socio-Political Development and the Imperial Transformation of the British East India Company 1675–1775" (Unpublished PhD, University of Chicago, 2009), and Emma Rothschild, *The Inner Life of Empires* (forthcoming).

abroad, which [Johnstone added with feeling] are heard with such applause by a British parliament." By contrast, he argued that the company should "lay your markets free and open," and that the Crown should accept its sovereign responsibilities for Bengal by granting the territories to the company in the manner of "Philadelphia, the most perfect government under the King." Justice should flow from the Crown, via a locally established legislative authority, and the goal should be to establish "one certain system of redressing injuries through that extensive country, and particularly to guard, that no man can be safe, from the nature of your system, in the commission of wrongs."[41]

Johnstone's arguments for opening up Bengal to private British enterprise found support in noted polemics produced in the early 1770s by disgruntled former servants of the company, William Bolts and Alexander Dow.[42] Both, in different ways, argued for the exertion of Crown sovereignty and the extension of select aspects of British law to protect the rights of both Indians and Europeans in Bengal. Bolts saw the chance to encourage commerce by creating a more accountable system of authority, which would incorporate Indians as magistrates in the interior. He discussed "the practicability of making the East Indians happy under the Laws of Great Britain," admitting the difficulty of introducing the "full-blown Oak" of English law given local attachments to Hindu and Muslim laws, but arguing that the "greatest shoot" of the oak, trial by jury, was as well suited to India as to Britain.[43] Meanwhile, Dow argued that "the laws of England, in so far as they do not oppose prejudices and usages which cannot be relinquished by the natives, should prevail."[44] Some of the rhetoric of British free traders, opposed to the restrictive practices of the East India Company authorities, held out the prospect of radical transformations within Indian society from the introduction of a new style of British government. Joseph Price, in a series of published letters addressed to the company governor, Warren Hastings, argued that establishing a true freedom of commerce and a reciprocal trade between Bengal and Britain would not only "multiply the human race" but also "give to millions a taste of liberty and independence."[45]

Yet such arguments did not find much favor among either the company's directors on Leadenhall Street, jealous of their powers and monopolies, and suspicious of the motives of private traders, or among ministers charged with establishing new regulations for the India trade. Lord North's Regulating Act

---

[41] House of Commons Debate, 30 March, 1772, *Parliamentary History of England*, vol. 17, pp. 366–380.

[42] For the impact of these writers at a time of parliamentary scrutiny of the company, see Lucy Sutherland, *The East India Company in Eighteenth Century Politics* (Oxford: Oxford University Press, 1952), pp. 221, 231.

[43] William Bolts, *Considerations on Indian Affairs; Particularly Respecting the Present State of Bengal and Its Dependencies* (3 vols., London, 1772–5), vol. 2, pp. 179–181; this passage is also discussed in Kuiters, *The British in Bengal*, pp. 264–8.

[44] Alexander Dow, *History of Hindustan* (3 vols., London, 1768–72), vol. 3, p. cxliii.

[45] Joseph Price, *Five Letters, from a Free Merchant in Bengal, to Warren Hastings Esq.* (London, 1778), p. 264.

was premised on an elaborate series of compromises with the company, establishing (as a later Parliamentary report described) "Checks and Counterchecks ... in which all the Existing Authorities of this Kingdom had a Share." Parliament appointed members of a new Supreme Council in Calcutta; the Crown appointed judges to a new Supreme Court; and "the Company preserved the nomination of their other Officers."[46] There was no final determination of the disputed question of sovereignty in Bengal (and therefore of the rights to the Bengal revenues) and no comprehensive effort to establish a new system of laws for Bengal, as reformers like Johnstone and Bolts had urged; rather, the territorial authority of the company's council was presumed to carry on as before, under procedures and regulations either inherited from the Mughal empire or newly established by the company.[47]

North's Regulating Act satisfied neither the company's goal to preserve its autonomy from parliamentary interference, nor the radical reformers' aspirations for drastic changes in policy. In its apparent moderation, it did at least insulate North's government from the frequently made imputation that ministers would exploit the extensive wealth and power of the company to overbalance the precarious equilibrium of the British Constitution and finally extinguish British domestic liberty. The Regulating Act also suggested how the preservation of the East India Company as an arm of imperial government, under supervision from domestic authorities, could itself be seen as a very British form of "mixed government," involving "checks and balances" that would guard against abuses of authority.

In the short term, however, North's act tended merely to re-export conflicts over the constitutional shape of the new empire, rather to settle them. While the North American empire lurched toward chaos and collapse, Calcutta became a maelstrom of constitutional and political argument, all too often falling on deaf ears among ministers pre-occupied with troubles in the Atlantic. As American patriots were giving colonial settlers a bad name, the company government decisively consolidated its limits on private British settlement and commerce. New "covenants" barred the company's civilian and military servants from engaging in internal trade, from buying land, or from lending money to Indians. Gradually, a reformed salary structure offered new incentives to resist extracurricular activities. Company monopolies in key commodities such as opium and salt supplied much-needed revenues for the bloated government, as well as excluding private Europeans from these sectors of the economy. In theory, no Britons could enter Bengal without a license, and a licensing system was also established to limit British movement beyond the company's main settlements.[48]

---

[46] Ninth Report of the Select Committee, 25 June, 1783, reprinted in Marshall, ed., *The Writings and Speeches of Edmund Burke*, vol. 5, p. 198.

[47] H. V. Bowen, "India: the Metropolitan Context," in Marshall, ed., *The Eighteenth Century*, pp. 538–9; Travers, *Ideology and Empire in Eighteenth Century India*, pp. 143–4.

[48] P. J. Marshall, *East Indian Fortunes. The British in Bengal in the Eighteenth Century* (Oxford: Oxford University Press, 1976).

Meanwhile, despite consolidating its grip on cotton exports through investing its new tax revenues, the company could defend its fair trade credentials, pointing to a rationalization of the system of internal customs, and its attempts to protect the "natural rights" of Indian merchants from the depredations of company officials.[49]

The question, though, of by what laws, if any, the company's power in Bengal was mediated and limited was still alive and uncertain. Governor Warren Hastings (1772–1785) elaborated a sophisticated if speculative notion of an "ancient constitution" in Bengal by which the company government would be guided. Consisting of a dual system of Hindu and Muslim civil law, and Muslim criminal law, administered by a network of state courts supposedly modeled on the summary forms of Mughal justice, Hastings' "ancient constitution" appeared to suggest that a viable form of absolute, though generally law-abiding, authority existed within the wreckage of the Mughal imperial system. Hastings' critics also embraced the idea of an "ancient constitution," though they tended to argue that the company's voracious appetite for new taxes was actually destroying the remnants of a long-established system of landed private property. At the same time, conflicts between the company government and the Supreme Court in Calcutta raised the question of how the dual system of Crown sovereignty and English law in Calcutta, extending also over the bodies of British subjects in the interior, could co-exist with the revived forms of an Indian "ancient constitution."[50]

One of the most intriguing constitutional proposals of this period emerged from a scheme by Warren Hastings and Elijah Impey to unite the jurisdictions of the Supreme Court and the company's law courts in a single system, with appeals lying in the first instance to a general high court, consisting of the judges and the company's councilors, and then finally to the Privy Council.[51] The proposed high court would also become a local legislative body for Bengal, making regulations for the judicial and administrative systems, advised by indigenous law officers. In a remarkable example of the flexibility of British constitutional thinking, one of the judges, Robert Chambers, suggested a new "Grand Assembly" to act as a parliament for Bengal, made up of three "chambers" – the governor, the council, and the judges. The governor, he proposed, was analogous to the king, the councilors to the Lords, and the judges to the House of Commons. As Chambers' biographer has noted, these proposals

---

[49] Sudipta Sen, *Empire of Free Trade. The East India Company and the Making of the Colonial Marketplace* (Philadelphia: University of Pennsylvania Press, 1998).

[50] These arguments about an "ancient constitution" in Bengal are further explored in Travers, *Ideology and Empire in Eighteenth Century India*, chs. 3–4.

[51] The draft bill is printed in G. W. Forrest, ed., *Historical Documents of British India. Warren Hastings* (2 vols., New Delhi: Anmol Publications, 1985), vol. 2, pp. 300–312. It is discussed in detail in Neil Sen, "Warren Hastings and British Sovereign Authority in Bengal," *Journal of Imperial and Commonwealth History*, 25 (1997), pp. 59–81.

echoed the "hierarchical and oligarchical" notion of government outlined in Chambers' earlier Vinerian lectures at Oxford on English law.[52] Mixed constitutions, it seemed, were adaptable to the distant provinces of Britain's Asiatic empire, even if representative assemblies were not.

While these schemes came to nothing, and appeared to the Supreme Court's enemies to symbolize the excessive judicial activism of the judges, ministers and parliament could not long ignore the unresolved questions provoked by political and legal disputes in Bengal. Parliament's decision in 1781, limiting the power of the Supreme Court and the role of English law, was relatively uncontroversial; but the question of how finally to resolve the relationship between the British state and the company government was one of the most difficult and contentious that any eighteenth-century parliament had to face. As the issue came to a head in 1783–4, the balance of the British Constitution again appeared to be at stake, let alone the well-being of millions of Indian subjects of the empire, and (in the aftermath of American independence) the very future of Britain as an imperial power.

Again, the rhetoric of later apologists for the company's emerging colonial "despotism" may have obscured the depth and extent of differences of opinion about how best to regulate the new empire. While Edmund Burke's tirades against Warren Hastings sometimes made him appear as an uncompromising critic of the Indian empire, he was also a prominent theorist of ways of reconciling the principles of domestic and overseas rule, developing a coherent vision of an empire of the common good.[53] The key to this was his sense (drawing also on the thought of another reformist Whig, Philip Francis) that a viable ancient constitution existed in Bengal, resting on immemorial Hindu rights to landed property and the wise stewardship of the Mughal conquerors. His goal was to restore what he saw as the natural channels of authority and subordination within Indian society, protecting the Indian rajahs, sultans, and landholders from the company's interference, and governing them within a loose imperial federation analogous to the Mughal empire itself.[54]

To secure this goal, Burke was convinced that Parliament, the ultimate guarantor of the common good within Britain and its empire, must assume the obligation of the virtual representation and protection of its Indian subjects. Great Britain had in effect "made a virtual act of union with that country, by which they bound themselves as to the securities of their subjects,

---

[52] See Thomas M. Curley, *Sir Robert Chambers. Law Literature and Empire in the Age of Johnson* (Madison: University of Wisconsin Press, 1998), pp. 253–5.

[53] This line of argument is further developed in P. J. Marshall, "Edmund Burke and India," in R. Mukherjee and L. Subramanian, eds., *Politics and Trade in the Indian Ocean World. Essays in Honor of Ashin Das Gupta* (New Delhi: Oxford University Press, 1998), pp. 250–269.

[54] For this interpretation of Burke's Indian thought, see Travers, *Ideology and Empire in Eighteenth Century India*, pp. 217–221.

to preserve the people in all their rights, laws and liberties."[55] "Liberties" here were not something to be transmitted from Britain to India, but rather a set of indigenous rights to be jealously guarded by the imperial parliament. To this end, Parliament needed to curtail the independent power of the company. Charles James Fox's India Bills of 1783, heavily influenced by Burke's thinking, aimed to effect a kind of parliamentary takeover of the company, with new directors appointed in the first instance by Parliament taking charge of the company's affairs.[56]

The fragility of Fox's administration, and the sense that his attempted takeover of the company could throw undue power and wealth into ministerial hands, undid Burke's hopes for Indian reform. Burke fiercely opposed Pitt's India Act of 1784, which left the powers of patronage and administration in the hands of the company's directors, under the controlling power of a ministerial Board of Control, and he was even more damning about Pitt's decision in 1786 to award the new governor-general, Lord Cornwallis, a discretionary power to override his council. The principle of that bill, Burke wrote, was to "introduce arbitrary and despotic government in India" under the false pretence of "strength and security." Nor did Burke support the statutory provisions that forced returning company servants to publicly declare their incomes, and which made them subject to special tribunals for investigating complaints. Burke pilloried these provisions as further evidence of a new style of arbitrary government, a "full-blown monster of tyranny."[57]

For Burke, the best defense against corruption in India, as in Britain, was maintaining essential freedoms as a bulwark against tyranny: "[A] government by law, trial by jury, and publicity in every executive and judicial concern."[58] Thus, while Burke had opposed the extension of English laws to Indians, he believed that in Calcutta, a British settlement long governed by English law, trial by jury was essential in civil cases, and that even Indians might be allowed to sit on these juries.[59] Instead, the new system of proconsular rule sacrificed "all our prepossessions for the liberty of Britons, and the rights of humanity."[60]

---

[55] Burke's Speech on the Opening of the Hastings Impeachment, 15 February 1788, in Marshall ed., *The Writings and Speeches of Edmund Burke*. Volume 6. *The Opening of the Hastings Impeachment* (Oxford: Oxford University Press, 1991), p. 282.

[56] Courtney Ilbert, *The Government of India. Being a Digest of Statute Law Relating Thereto* (Oxford, 1898), pp. 63–4.

[57] Speech before House of Commons, 22 March 1786, in Marshall, ed., *Writings and Speeches of Edmund Burke*, vol. 6, pp. 66–68.

[58] Ibid., pp. 68–9.

[59] See his comments in the Ninth Report of the Select Committee, 1783, that Parliament had assumed "perhaps a little too hastily" that Indians were not capable of acting as jurors. Marshall, ed., *Writings and Speeches of Edmund Burke*, vol. 5, p. 205.

[60] Speech before House of Commons, 22 March 1786, in Marshall, ed., *Writings and Speeches of Edmund Burke*, vol. 6, p. 71.

Burke's distinction between the "liberty of Britons" and "the rights of humanity" raised again the question of the extent of the "rights" that humanity, beyond the natural-born subjects of the British Crown, could legitimately claim. To defenders of Pitt the Younger's reforms of the Indian empire, the liberties of Britons, the liberties of the company, the system of liberty enshrined in the British Constitution, and also the basic natural rights of Indians had all been judiciously accommodated within the compromise settlement. When Lord Cornwallis issued his famous "code" of administrative regulations in 1793, fixing the land revenue demand in Bengal against the urge of future governments to invade the rights of landed property and reordering the company's law courts, company apologists and government supporters united in self-congratulatory encomiums about the new style of absolute, despotic but legal government.[61] In the new atmosphere of imperial retrenchment during the French Revolutionary wars, British political society was more likely to rally round its Indian empire as a bulwark against the terrifying new threat of a universal French republic.[62] As P. J. Marshall has noted, the growing domestic campaign against Atlantic slavery increasingly cast the Indian empire, where the widespread practice of domestic slavery was often regarded as a relatively mild and inoffensive variant, in a better comparative light.[63]

British India was a vast improvement, thought a very whiggish William Jones, who was busy codifying the Hindu and Muslim laws, from the old arbitrary despotism of the Mughals.[64] Even though the concentration of powers in the company government meant that there was no true "mixed" constitution in Bengal, the rigid separation of the "revenue" from the "judicial" line of the company's service offered some semblance of judicial oversight. As the state and the company forged a new alliance after Pitt's settlement, the questioning by those like Francis and Burke about how "arbitrary" and "despotic" indigenous rulers actually were appeared to be rapidly forgotten. As one of the company's lawyers would later state, in 1824, the British claimed allegiance in India "as better than the Mahomedan usurpation which it has superseded." At the same time, despite the company's "sincerest disposition to protect the person and property of every individual," and "to rule by fixed law, and not by arbitrary despotism," a "foreign dominion like ours cannot

[61] See, for example, John Bruce, *Historical View of Plans for the Government of British India* (London, 1793); and for an account of the new triumphalism, see P. J. Marshall, "'Cornwallis Trimphant': War in India and the British Public in the Late Eighteenth Century," in *Trade and Conquest: Studies on the Rise of British Dominance in India* (Aldershot: Variorum Press, 1993).

[62] C. A. Bayly, *Imperial Meridian. Britain, Empire and the World, 1780–1830* (London: Longman, 1989).

[63] P. J. Marshall, "The Moral Swing to the East. British Humanitarianism, India and the West Indies," in K. Ballhatchet and John Harrison, eds., *East India Company Studies. Papers Presented to Sir Cyril Philips* (Hong Kong: Asian Research Service, 1986).

[64] Garland Cannon, ed., *Letters of William Jones* (2 vols., Oxford: Oxford University Press, 1970), p. 664.

be quite secure in such a comparison upon a question of right with the people we govern as a conquered people, without their choice, their participation, their natural sympathies."[65] Thus individual Indians were in theory more secure than ever before; but their "liberties," in a broader Burkean sense, had been dramatically curtailed as the British despotism of law clawed its way across Hindustan in the period of the Napoleonic wars.

There remains much historical argument around questions of the degree of Indian "agency" in the transition to colonialism in India, about the extent of colonial domination or hegemony, and about the role of "intermediary groups" of Indian merchants and property holders in making strategic alliances with the British.[66] There is no question, however, that the British empire in India saw itself as a rule of conquest, and that Indians (including people of mixed race) were rigorously excluded (at least from the 1780s) from the administrative and deliberative heights of state power.[67] John Shore, governor-general from 1793 to 1796, justifying the rigid subordination of Indians in the administrative system, argued that they were a people "wholly void of public virtue." Nonetheless, even though he considered the native inhabitants as "happier under our administration than they ever were before," with peace, order, and the protection of their "prejudices" and "superstitions," he still "would not argue that this country will remain fifty years longer under our dominion."[68] This sense of foreboding, combined with a strong feeling of the strictly limited attachments between rulers and ruled, suffused the language of high officials.

Therefore, even among the most determined apologists of the new Indian empire, a sense of loss haunted the repeated assertions that the basic rights to life and property were being respected. Some dissenters among British officials bemoaned the lack of efforts to reconcile and incorporate Indians into the system of government. Warren Hastings, scion of an era when some high officials from late Mughal times had survived the cull, denounced blanket attacks on the "native character" by evangelically minded zealots.[69]

Among dispossessed Indian elites, meanwhile, the daring, uncouth, and contemptuous behavior of hat-wearing foreigners caused both a surge of introspection about the decline of virtue within Indian society and also in some circles a strong vein of nostalgia for the lost glories of the Mughal empire. Recently, South Asian historians have begun to explore the complex codes of

---

[65] Opinion of Mr. Spankie before Privy Council, 1824, cited in Peter Auber, *Analysis of the Constitution of the East India Company and of Laws Passed by Parliament for the Government of their Affairs* (London, 1826), pp. 24–5.

[66] For useful introductions to these debates, see Seema Alavi, ed., *The Eighteenth Century in India* (New Delhi: Oxford University Press, 2002), and P. J. Marshall, ed., *The Eighteenth Century in Indian History. Evolution or Revolution?* (New Delhi: Oxford University Press, 2003).

[67] K. Ballhatchet, *Race, Sex and Class under the Raj. Imperial Attitudes and Policies and Their Critics, 1793–1905* (New York: St. Martin's Press, 1980).

[68] *Memoirs of the Life and Correspondence of John, Lord Teignmouth, by his son Lord Teignmouth* (2 vols., London, 1863), vol. 1, pp. 5–6, 285.

[69] Hastings to Lord Moira, 2 December, 1812, BL, Add. MSS 29233, fols. 1–15.

political ethics from the period of the Mughal hegemony, and how these were reinterpreted in the transition to British dominance.[70] Some scholar-administrators found a precarious foothold within the new British regime and continued to argue for their own conceptions of rights and justice. One striking feature of this body of thought, which may have contributed to British fears for the future of their power expressed by those like John Shore, was a sense that the British government had wilfully ignored customs of consultation and negotiation that were built into the flexible system of Mughal imperial authority. "Fixed laws" from this perspective, such as those written down in Lord Cornwallis' regulations, appeared less as a form of emancipation from arbitrary government than as a closing down of avenues of public debate.[71]

An example of this strand of thought comes from perhaps the most famous Persian language history of the eighteenth century, written by the scholar-administrator Ghulam Husain Khan Tabatabai in the 1780s and quickly translated into English. This history was even praised by William Jones, a judge of the Supreme Court and founder of the Asiatic Society, as "an excellent impartial modern History of India ... containing very just Remarks on the Administration of Government and Justice by our Nation, but *sine ira aut odio*."[72] Ghulam Husain did not hide his dismay at the contempt shown by Europeans for Indian society, or the exclusion of Indians of rank from the government. He gave a fascinating account of the British takeover of his own home city of Patna in Bihar. Ghulam Husain claimed he had approached the young British civilian charged with governing the region, George Vansittart, and instructed him of the former practice of Mughal governors of sitting in public "from one-half of each day down to one-third of each night in hearing petitions, and in giving decisions." According to Ghulam Husain, Vansittart replied that "being not accustomed ... to sit in public amongst hundreds of people, nor to listen to complaints ... he could not believe that he would be able to comprehend one-half of them"; but he agreed to receive petitioners '"privately, as he conceived that in the recess and silence of a closet he would be more recollected and better able to give a decision." Vansittart apparently tried his best, but under the rule of strangers, Ghulam Husain complained, the fora of public engagement had

---

[70] Notable recent works include Muzaffar Alam, *The Language of Political Islam in South Asia* (Chicago: Chicago University Press, 2004); C. A. Bayly, *Origins of Nationality in South Asia. Patriotism and Ethical Government in the Making of Modern India* (New Delhi: Oxford University Press, 1998); Rajay Ray, *The Felt Community. Commonalty and Mentality Before the Emergence of Indian Nationalism* (New Delhi: Oxford University Press, 2003); and Kumkum Chatterjee, "History as Self-Representation: The Recasting of a Political Tradition in Bengal and Bihar," *Modern Asian Studies*, 32 (1998), pp. 913–948.

[71] Jon E. Wilson makes this argument forcefully in Chapter two of his recent work, *The Domination of Strangers: Modern Politics in Colonial India 1780–1835* (Basingstoke: Palgrave Macmillan, 2008).

[72] Cannon, ed., *Letters of William Jones*, vol. 2, p. 723.

inexorably atrophied; the British had retreated behind the walls of their council chambers, and forbidding books of regulations had taken the place of reasoned debate between the government and local society.[73]

Ghulam Husain also had interesting words to say about the British domestic government, which ran against the grain of British perceptions that representative government was both unknown among and beyond the comprehension of the despotically inclined peoples of India. He described how, in England, the king could not give an order to the company "without the advice and consent of his Council," made up of "Omrahs, or Great Lords of that land," as well as "the principal inhabitants" of each city and town. Ghulam Husain approved of this system, calling it "an admirable institution," "extremely useful and beneficial." Yet the British had chosen to keep such institutions "among themselves," rather then using similar methods to decide on "what concerns the welfare of these countries."[74] Future generations of Indians would seek ways of penetrating the hard outer shell of British authority, drawing both on the resources offered by models of representative government derived from Britain itself as well as on notions of ethical government and political inclusion recovered from within Indian history.

By the 1790s, in the afterglow of the Pitt and Cornwallis reforms, the problem of liberty in British India appeared to many Britons to have been successfully contained. The essential right of British settlers to be governed under English law was maintained by the flexible jurisdiction of the Supreme Courts in the presidency towns. At the same time, the licensing system and the reserved powers of the company to limit and regulate British settlement were supposed to protect the rights of native subjects as well as the company's monopolies. Despite widespread forms of "domestic slavery," Indians were often presumed to be free subjects rather than slaves, in the sense that individual rights were supposedly protected by the company's police and law courts, operating in accord with the "prejudices" of the Indian inhabitants. In the context of broader changes in imperial politics at the turn of the nineteenth century, the war-time assertion of uncompromising sovereignty at home and abroad, the strengthening of the military arm of government, and the establishment of a series of "neo-absolutisms" overseas, British India did not appear to be out of step with the spirit of the times.[75]

Yet under the surface of the global war effort, the meanings of liberty were changing and hardening in ways that were highly problematic for the British government in India. In Britain, political economists preached the virtues of

---

[73] Ghulam Husain Khan Tabatabai, *The Seir Mutaqherin, Or Review of Modern Times* (ed. and tr. Haji Mustafa, 3 vols., Calcutta, 1789, repr. Lahore: Sheikh Mubarak Ali, 1975), vol. 3, pp. 198–9. For a longer discussion of this text, see Travers, *Ideology and Empire*, pp. 225–9.

[74] Ghulam Husain Khan Tabatabai, *Seir Mutqherin*, vol. 3, pp. 153–4.

[75] For the argument that British imperial policy in the era of global warfare was marked by "a series of attempts to establish overseas despotisms which mirrored in many ways the politics of neo-absolutism and the Holy Alliance of contemporary Europe," see C. A. Bayly, *Imperial Meridian*, p. 8.

free trade to an ever-widening circle of adherents, just as a growing army of evangelicals sought to liberate not only their compatriots but also Britain's overseas subjects from the tyranny of immorality and superstition.[76] Potentially the most threatening development for British authorities in India, however, was the growing international movement of constitutional liberalism.[77] With tangled roots in revolutionary conceptions of popular sovereignty, anti-colonial state formation in the Americas, and national independence movements in post-Napoleonic Europe, new ideas of liberty could potentially strike at the very roots of British imperialism in India.

The implications of the new international context were felt by the governor-general of India soon after the French Revolution. In the French town of Chandernagore, reported John Shore, just up the river from Calcutta, Monsieur Richemont, the leader of "the democratic band," had declared that all religion was abolished by the revolution; to emphasize the point he had proposed giving thanks for French victories to the Hindu mother-goddess Durga, rather than through a conventional recital of the Te Deum. Shore was relieved that political questions were discussed with "tolerable moderation in Calcutta," yet noted that "we have some sturdy democrats among us."[78] In the coming decades, Calcutta and other presidency towns would furnish a fertile ground for new forms of radicalism, as expanding communities of British settlers, mixed-race Eurasians, and English-educated Indians created a vibrant if uneven form of public sphere, chafing against the highly restrictive regulations of the company government, and seeking new forms of enfranchisement in line with the perceived trends of European liberalism.

Newspapermen, regularly persecuted by the nervous company, were among the most vigorous spokesmen of the "sturdy democrats" to whom Shore referred. Charles Maclean, a ship's surgeon who became (as he wrote) 'proprietor of a newspaper and a magazine' in Calcutta, was forcibly deported by Governor-General Richard Wellesley in 1798 after publishing a letter criticizing the conduct of a district magistrate in the *Calcutta Telegraph*.[79] Maclean later

---

[76] For the connections between political economy and evangelicalism, see Boyd Hilton, *The Age of Atonement. The Influence of Evangelicalism on Social and Economic Thought 1785–1865* (Oxford: Oxford University Press, 1986).

[77] For the idea of a "liberal constitutionalist moment" in the early nineteenth century, see C. A. Bayly, "Rammohan Roy and the Advent of Constitutional Liberalism in India, 1800–30," *Modern Intellectual History*, 4, 1 (2007), pp. 25–41. In a similar vein, David Armitage writes of "the first Eurasian rights moment, when conceptions of rights, both collective and individual, first animated movements for independence, autonomy, and liberation across the world." See Armitage, *The Declaration of Independence. A Global History* (Cambridge, MA: Harvard University Press, 2007), p. 107.

[78] Shore to Charles Grant, Bengal, 21 October, 1793, in *Memoir of the Life of Lord Teignmouth*, vol. 1, p. 261.

[79] Charles Mclean, *Affairs of Asia Considered in their Effects on the Liberties of Britain. Letters addressed to the Marquis Wellesley* (London, 1806), p. 106. Official letters relating to this scandal are collected in India Office Records, Asia and Africa Collections, British Library, London, Home Miscellaneous, 537, pp. 289–315.

composed an angry attack on Wellesley's "despotic" administration published in London in 1806. Like earlier eighteenth-century polemicists, Maclean posited the danger of "Asiatic influence" spreading to Britain, "like a vile creeper, which twines itself round the majestic Oak." Interestingly, Maclean looked back wistfully to the lost opportunities of Burkean reform from the 1780s, arguing that Fox's proposed reforms in India were far superior to those of Pitt, and indeed approached the "sublime." Echoing the familiar chants of British colonists, Maclean appealed to his "essential birthrights, the trial by jury, the Habeas Corpus, and the liberty of the press."[80]

Maclean also dwelt on the international contest between liberty and despotism, and appeared to extend his vision of liberty beyond the birthright of British subjects to Asians as well. The whole system of government in Asia, he wrote, was "completely and fundamentally erroneous." If Britons wanted to understand the situation in India after Wellesley's military conquests, they should look to "the actual situation of France and its surrounding tributaries and vassals." Wellesley was compared to Bonaparte, while Maclean styled himself as a modern Cicero, bravely exposing the tyranny and corruption of imperial proconsuls. It would be better, thought Maclean, to admit the inhabitants of India "to all the privileges of the English laws." At present, they were deprived not just of the "benefits of the English laws," but also those of "the law of nations, which we are falsely taught to believe in this country they generally enjoy." The conquest of India went on even while "we proclaim ourselves the defenders, and are so in effect, of the independence of Europe."[81]

Independence here is a key word, and catches the implications for India of what David Armitage has recently termed "the contagion of sovereignty," spreading out from the twin revolutions of America and France.[82] If Maclean could be safely written off as a marginal fire-brand, out of step with the determined imperialism of the French wars, even the company directors were shocked by the high-handed, military authority exercised by Wellesley in India, and its alarming effects on the company's debt.[83] Meanwhile, Maclean saw himself as operating within a coherent tradition of imperial reform, stretching back to Fox and Burke, and pointing to the potential of a vastly different style of empire in India. The relatively unusual setting of Calcutta, which was regarded as a fully British sovereign territory, regulated by Crown courts, English laws, juries in criminal cases, and which generated a notably diverse public of British and Indian newspaper readers, was a crucial laboratory for this kind of imperial radicalism.

---

[80] Mclean, *Affairs of Asia Considered in their Effects on the Liberties of Britain*, pp. 14, 19, 73.

[81] Ibid., pp. 130–1, 170–1, 158, 133.

[82] Armitage, *The Declaration of Independence*, p. 103.

[83] P. J. Marshall, *Problems of Empire: Britain and India, 1757–1813* (London: Allen and Unwin, 1968), pp. 75–6.

The agitations over liberty of the press continued to attract opponents of the company's despotism in the years after the ending of the French wars. The expulsion of the British co-editor of the *Calcutta Journal*, James Silk Buckingham, in 1823, and the promulgation of newly restrictive press ordinances in 1824 signaled the tense standoff between company authorities and radical arguments for free trade, the ending of restrictions on European colonization, free access for missionaries, and new constitutional checks on the company's local authority.[84] In the heat of this battle, Thomas Munro, the company's governor of Madras, composed a startlingly fearful minute, which further marked both the changing meanings of liberty and its increasing terrors for the "garrison state" of British India.[85]

"The tenure by which we hold our power never has been," Munro wrote, "and never can be, the liberties of the people." A free press in India would not spread "useful knowledge" as its proponents hoped, but rather "insubordination, insurrection, and anarchy." This was because "there was no public in India to be guided and instructed by a free press"; yet, still, a free press must of necessity "spread among the people the principles of liberty," including the desire to "establish a national Government." In the absence of a mature Indian "public," this desire would take hold first among the Indian soldiery, who would quickly learn "to compare their own allowances and humble rank, with those of their European officers." Munro outlined the likely results of such an experiment in the onset of a "sanguinary civil war." Drawing on his experience of the Vellore mutiny of the Madras army in 1807, he described how this would begin in the army, before spreading to the many discontented elements of the surrounding populace, including unemployed former administrators and soldiers, and overtaxed village headmen.[86]

Munro's fears about press freedom in some sense echoed those of the British inhabitants of Calcutta from 1779, that the misapplication of liberty would stir Indians into a violent and vengeful mob. But the stakes had now been dramatically raised. Instead of an urban riot and massacre envisaged by the Calcutta residents, Munro foresaw a general uprising in town and country and, above all, the implosion of the very basis of the company's authority, the Indian army, numbering nearly a quarter of a million men. What would effect this change was not the example of English laws and liberties, but a still more dangerous idea of global liberty – amounting in effect to a desire for "national" self-government. For Munro, this was not simply a side effect of a free press; it

---

[84] C. A. Bayly, "Rammohan Roy and the Advent of Constitutional Liberalism," pp. 36–7; Miles Taylor, "Joseph Hume and the Reformation of India, 1819–33," in Glenn Burgess and Matthew Festenstein, eds., *English Radicalism 1550–1850* (Cambridge: Cambridge University Press, 2007), pp. 293–4.

[85] For a detailed discussion of the minute in the context of Munro's career, see Burton Stein, *Thomas Munro, The Origins of the Colonial State and His Vision of Empire* (Oxford: Oxford University Press, 1989), pp. 283–7.

[86] Thomas Munro, *Liberty of the Press in India. A Minute Written by Thomas Munro, 35 Years Ago* (London, 1857), pp. 3, 4, 7.

was its very essence. As a company lawyer put it, "a free press (in the sense of the advocates of a free press, as desired by the friends of a free press in India) would naturally" have taught that "a people ought not to submit to a foreign yoke."[87]

Arguing not just from the uniqueness of Indian circumstances but also within the established conventions of the British and imperial constitution, the company successfully defended its press restrictions in 1824 from an appeal to the Privy Council. Complicating the picture of liberty at home and despotism abroad, one company lawyer noted the elaborate historical and contemporary restrictions on printing and publishing in Britain. Another showed that the Privy Council had only overturned colonial laws where they were "unreasonable" or encroached on royal authority, but not where they were "necessary for the safety and protection of the colony" in matters where the law of England furnished no remedies. He referred to a law from early eighteenth-century Barbados, ratified by the king's council, which authorized a year in prison, pillory, and the loss of an ear for knowingly bidding at auction for an estate beyond the bidder's means. This was "pretty strong," yet the company's attorney argued it was justified by colonial conditions and did not create any essential conflict within the laws of England. Thus, the company continued to appeal to the "ancient constitution" of the British empire, confident in the diversity of imperial legal regimes and the latitude of the concept of legal "repugnance."[88]

While the company could win such important victories, it was facing threats to its established constitution that were louder and more powerful than ever before. Apparently unstoppable rises in military costs, a failed war in Burma in 1825–6, and the gradual atrophying of the company's commercial system, contributed to unprecedented attacks on the company in the runup to a parliamentary review of its charter in 1832–3. The reformed parliament, facing mass petitions for ending the last vestiges of commercial monopoly in the China trade, had little desire to defend the unreformed structures of the company.[89] Recent studies by Miles Taylor of the imperial dimension of the age of reform have shown how diverse and powerful were the pressures for liberalization of the Indian empire.[90] They included radical newspapermen like James Silk Buckingham; provincial merchants and industrialists seeking access to new markets; radical MPs like the former company servant Joseph Hume, a supporter of limited government, a free press, European colonization, and direct

---

[87] Mr. Spankie's opinion, printed in Auber, *Analysis of the Constitution of the East India Company*, p. 25.

[88] Bosanquet's and Spankie's opinions, printed in ibid., pp. 19–23.

[89] P. J. Cain and A. G. Hopkins, *British Imperialism, 1688–2000* (2nd ed., London: Longman, 2002), p. 282.

[90] See especially Taylor, "Joseph Hume and the Reformation of India," and the same author's "Empire and Parliamentary Reform: The 1832 Reform Act Revisited," in Arthur Burns and Joanna Innes, eds., *Rethinking the Age of Reform. Britain 1780–1850* (Cambridge: Cambridge University Press, 2003) pp. 295–311.

representation for India (including potentially by Indians) in Parliament; and Eurasian campaigners for the rights of mixed-race subjects to enter the company's service, to be accorded rights in English law, and to buy and settle lands.[91]

One of the most interesting of these reformers, and at the time among the most famous, was the Bengali intellectual and activist, Raja Rammohan Roy, whose political thought has recently been situated in the global context of constitutional liberalism by C. A. Bayly.[92] Versed in Persian and Arabic, a scholar of Sanskrit and reformer of Hinduism, and a newspaper proprietor in Calcutta supporting liberty of the press and proper forms of mixed or balanced constitutions, Rammohan was (as Bayly has argued) a new style of Indian "public man" and patriot. Like the earlier scholar-administrators of late Mughal Bengal, Rammohan looked not just to the examples of national movements and constitutional governments from Europe and the Americas, but also within ethical traditions derived from Indian history. For example, he posited an ancient form of mixed government in Hindu polities, represented by the division of powers between Rajput warriors and Brahmin priests, and also an indigenous analogy to trial by jury in the system of village tribunals (*panchayats*). He made common cause with the advocates of free European colonization, as well as seeking greater official recognition of the rights of Indians to participate in government. Rammohan was not an advocate of the early separation of India from the British empire, though he envisaged a growing Indian public taking an increasingly prominent role in a more liberal imperial constitution.

The outcomes of this spur of reformism are in some ways similar to the earlier convulsions of the 1770s and 1780s. The imperial establishment was able to buy off the most powerful strands of domestic opposition by strict attention to the financial interests of British taxpayers and merchants, retrenching expenses in India, and allowing private British enterprise fuller access to the Asian trade. At the same time, the imperial state made selective appropriations from the aspirations of reformers. William Bentinck, governor-general of India from 1828 to 1835, was a sincere liberal, with an expansive rhetoric of economic improvement, who sought to incorporate Indians into the imperial government as "responsible advisers and partners in the administration."[93] Above all, Bentinck's abolition of *Sati* (widow-burning) in 1829, and his sponsorship of English-language education, marked him as a reformer. Bentinck also supported opening restrictions on European settlement and investment in India, as a vehicle of "national" uplift, envisioning (as Bentinck's modern biographer has described) "a kind of Indian Canada or United States, where British settlers would give Indians a lead towards 'civil liberty' and 'improvement.'"[94]

---

[91] Christopher Hawes, *Poor Relations. The Making of a Eurasian Community in British India, 1773–1833* (Richmond: Curzon Press, 1996), pp. 133–5.

[92] Bayly, "Rammohan Roy."

[93] Cited in John Rosselli, *Lord William Bentinck. The Making of a Liberal Imperialist 1774–1839* (London: Sussex University Press, 1974), p. 201.

[94] Ibid., p. 199.

Yet what is most striking is how the hopes of some reformers, including Bentinck, for a thorough overhaul of the company's "despotism" were relatively smoothly parried and deflected. If much of the energy for reform grew from the vibrancy of the presidency towns in India, then this was also the reformers' Achilles heel. The bedrock of the Indian empire, as Thomas Munro had emphasized, was not in the coastal enclaves, but up the country, in the garrison towns, markets, and villages of rural India, where the cash-crops that sustained the vast military-bureaucratic machine of the empire were grown. Above all, nothing could be allowed to jeopardize military discipline, though Bentinck's cost-cutting would come close. *Sati* was abolished only after official inquiries concluded that the effects of the measure on military morale would be nugatory.[95] Tax-cutting and the reform of monopolies was limited by the overriding needs of the army. The Charter Act of 1833 was supposed to enable free European settlement of the interior, but the limited attractions of the climate and the stuttering economy, as well as continued restraints imposed by the company, severely limited colonization in practice.[96]

The aborted project of colonization well reflected the mismatch between the reformers' goals in the 1820s and 1830s, and the eventual outcomes.[97] The formal prohibition on non-Christians sitting on juries in presidency towns was lifted.[98] Bentinck also tried to introduce some version of trial by jury into the company's courts by involving Indians of the "respectable" classes more in the company's administration of justice; but Indians were included merely as advisors, at the discretion of the British magistrate, who still enjoyed full powers of determination. Indians and Eurasians were allowed new sources of employment in the company's services, though the higher levels remained a European preserve. Meanwhile, the old jealousies of the British inhabitants, and their desire to preserve their exclusive rights as "Britons," was much in evidence during the loud protects over the so-called "Black Act" of 1836, which made British, European, and American settlers in the interior amenable to the company's courts, without power of appeals to the royal courts.[99] Despite the hopes of some reformers for integrating Britons, Eurasians, and Indians in a common project of liberty and improvement, social life in colonial towns remained as deeply riven by racial distinctions as it had been in the 1770s.

The reformist energies of officials ran less into the expansive demands of radical liberals for making government more accountable to an Indian or multiethnic "public" and more into the authoritarian impulses of an increasingly harsh

---

[95] C. H. Phillips, *The Correspondence of Lord William Cavendish-Bentinck* (2 vols., Oxford: Oxford University Press, 1977), introduction, p. xxvii.

[96] P. J. Marshall, "The Whites of British India, 1780–1830: A failed colonial society?" *International History Review*, 12, 1 (1990), pp. 26–44.

[97] For a more comprehensive analysis, see David Washbrook, "The Two Faces of Colonialism: India, 1818–1860," in A. Porter, ed., *Oxford History of the British Empire*, Volume 3. *The Nineteenth Century* (Oxford: Oxford University Press, 1999), pp. 395–421.

[98] Ilbert, *Government of India*, p. 84; Bayly, "Rammohan Roy," p. 36.

[99] Jain, *Outlines of Indian Legal History*, pp. 318–8, 356–7.

utilitarian outlook, best exemplified by James Mill, historian of British India and a leading player in company politics. As Jennifer Pitts has argued, Mill turned Benthamism into a powerful rhetoric of imperial control. Scottish stadial theory became a stick with which to beat apparently weak-minded, superstitious "barbarians," and a justification for consolidating a narrowly based rule of white experts.[100] Whereas Holt Mackenzie, secretary to the Supreme Government in Calcutta, proposed a large legislative council for India, made up of the governor-general, his council, judges of the Supreme Court, as well as nominated Indians, James Mill argued instead for a smaller body of purely British legislators, guided by the philosophical acumen of a special "law member." Mill's utilitarian planning won out in this case, and did much to energize the new system of legislative self-sufficiency, uniformity, and code-making in Victorian India.[101]

Pitts has suggested how "the erosion of absolutist or ancient regime powers and the partial emergence of the democratic nation state produced pressures and anxieties for liberal thinkers of this period that may have facilitated a turn to empire."[102] Indeed, the utilitarian turn in British Indian rhetoric, and the new disdain in some official circles for "Indian civilization," can perhaps be seen as a direct response to the threat of liberal constitutionalism and demands for increased recognition of an Indian public. Utilitarianism, which had emerged as a radical reformist language in British politics, was turned to defensive, conservative purposes in the Raj. Thomas Macaulay, who was appointed "law member" of the new legislative council in 1833, signaled the utilitarian rationale of company autocracy in a speech to the Commons: "The work of digesting a vast and artificial system of jurisprudence is far more easily performed, by a few minds than by many, by a Napoleon than by a Chamber of Deputies and a Chamber of Peers, by a government like that of Prussia or Denmark than by a government like that of England."[103] The slight deepening of representative government in Britain after the 1832 reform act, and the very gradual spread of representative institutions and "responsible government" in the white settler colonies after 1837, would further consolidate the differences between colonial despotism in India compared with more liberal regimes in some other parts of the empire.

CONCLUSION

The arguments against the transmission of liberty in early British India were constant, powerful, and officially sanctioned. But the meanings imputed to the idea of liberty changed dramatically from the 1770s to the 1830s, and so did the political pressures acting on the British Indian empire. Some free traders of the 1760s hoped that the British conquest of Bengal would lead to the expansion of

---

[100] Pitts, *A Turn to Empire*, pp. 123–32.
[101] Stokes, *English Utilitarians in India*, pp. 175–9.
[102] Pitts, *A Turn to Empire*, p. 14.
[103] Speech of 10 July 1833, cited in Stokes, *English Utilitarians and India*, p. 179.

English legal forms, alongside European settlement and commerce, but they were roundly condemned by the company hierarchy, rejected by many British settlers, and often ignored in Britain. In the 1770s and 1780s, Whig critics of the company government theorized constitutional models for the new empire that appeared compatible with the historical "liberties" of Indians, as well as with the constraints on executive power implied by the British Constitution. But the eventual emergence of a highly authoritarian pro-consular despotism in India was justified as providing insulation for the domestic constitution, protection for the liberties of British settlers in coastal towns, while also respecting the essential natural rights to life and property of Indian subjects. Indians had been rescued from the slavery of Asiatic despotism, so the official argument went; if they were not free in the sense that Britons were free, they still enjoyed certain fundamental natural rights under a colonial rule of law.

While company rule formally lasted until the mutiny/rebellion of 1857, the eighteenth-century settlement of the Indian question proved ideologically fragile. The company was intensely vulnerable to new forms of liberal critique in the early nineteenth century, as a classic exemplar of the old corruption, a tax-and-spend vehicle of unbridled militarism all too eager to silence its critics. Moreover, the presidency towns of India, with their distinct constitutional heritage from eighteenth-century royal charters of justice, combined with segmented, competitive, and vibrant communities of professionals and traders, were natural breeding grounds of reformist ideas, much like the northern industrial towns in Britain itself. Reformers often clamored for similar freedoms as their eighteenth-century forebears, such as basic rights under the British Constitution, or freedom to trade and settle. But the growing assertiveness of Indian and Eurasian communities gave reformist aspirations a newly threatening edge, as did the wider context of constitutional liberalism, especially as it seemed to eat away at the old world of empires in Europe and the Americas.

It is notable that the defenders of company despotism, such as Thomas Munro, for example, made much more of the threat of a "national" revolt than radicals like Joseph Hume or Rammohan Roy. Whereas Munro saw a rapid and direct link between a free press and a mass rebellion in India against foreign rule, British and Indian radicals understood liberal progress and enlightened principles spreading within the framework of a reformed empire, rather than tearing it apart. The patriotism of Rammohan Roy was a distinctively imperial form of Indian patriotism, just as Maclean or Hume, and even Bentinck, seemed to envisage a kind of multi-ethnic national spirit working toward the improvement of India.

Yet the fear of the contagion of liberty among British Indian officials was palpable enough, and especially focused on the army. This helps to explain the consolidation of a "two empires" model in the middle decades of the nineteenth century, drawing a clear constitutional line between "settler colonies" imagined to be steadily proceeding toward political liberty (at least for "white settlers") and "dependent" colonies for whom political liberty was both premature and potentially disastrous. At the same time, liberal radicals in Britain increasingly put their hopes in the settler empire, constructing a genealogy of free coloni-zation linking back to the eighteenth-century Atlantic, and drawing on a Greek model of federated democratic communities. Despite the disastrous effects of settler colonialism on indigenous peoples, Victorian advocates of the empire of settlement often contrasted the virtues of settler democracies with the corrupt-ing effects of despotism in India.[104]

Previously, the constitutional lines between India and the wider imperial constitution had been quite blurred; India had seemed to share in a tradition of legal diversity under the broad umbrella of royal authority. At least in the presidency towns, India could be seen as a kind of settler colony. But new claims on behalf of liberty, not just in Britain or India but also around the world, spurred imperial ideologues to posit a more decisive break between India and the settler empire. The rapid growth of per-capita incomes in settler colonies, and the apparent stagnation of Indian agriculture and industry, made the broad distinction between different stages of civilization appear still more plausible. The mutiny/rebellion of 1857, fulfilling Thomas Munro's worst fears, added urgency to the project of limiting the transmission of liberty, just as it threw the vulnerable community of British settlers back into the embrace of the government.

Eventually, utilitarian theories of liberal imperialism and the "civilizing mis-sion" would themselves create new tensions within the colonial despotism of British India. How could civilizational improvement be measured, and how long would Indians have to wait to be admitted to the family of nations? Indian liberals and nationalists in the late nineteenth century held up the improving pretensions of colonial despotism beside the withering reality of an impover-ished, starving population, and they would feed off a new global movement of national self-determination in the aftermath of the First World War.[105] By this time, a less confident community of British and European settlers was firmly bound to the fortunes of the British government, and earlier visions of a multi-ethnic or creolized Indian public were long forgotten. The problem for the British empire was not necessarily that liberty and empire were always incom-patible; it was that the meanings of liberty, just like the meanings of empire itself, would not stay still.

---

[104] Miles Taylor, "Imperium et Libertas? Rethinking the Radical Critique of Imperialism dur-ing the Nineteenth Century," *Journal of Imperial and Commonwealth History* 19, 1 (1991), pp. 1–23.

[105] Erez Manela, "Imagining Woodrow Wilson in Asia: Dreams of East-West Harmony and the Revolt against Empire in 1919," *American Historical Review* 111 (2006), pp. 1326–1351.

8

"… a bastard offspring of tyranny under the guise of liberty"

Liberty and Representative Government in Australia, 1788–1901

Richard Waterhouse

INTRODUCTION

The establishment of elected governments at the colony and national levels in Australia involved a drawn out process that extended over a century. Throughout the first half of the nineteenth century the Colonial Office resisted the colonial campaigns for responsible government, but from the 1840s it became increasingly compliant to the demands emanating from New South Wales, in particular, for the institution of a bicameral parliament. In the end, British flexibility ensured that representative government at the colonial level as well as the succeeding federal Constitution resulted from peaceful political and constitutional movements rather than from revolution. Australians believed that the adoption of the Constitution meant Australia had ceased to be a set of subservient colonies and become a nation in partnership with Great Britain. Rather than promoting a spirit of independence, federation strengthened the commitment to nationhood within the empire.

Developments in colonial Australia to some extent mirrored those in South Africa and New Zealand. In the course of the nineteenth century colonial elites emerged in all three colonies, leading to campaigns for freedom of the press and responsible government. However, as was the case in India, imperial authorities referred to particular local circumstances, in this case that New South Wales and Van Diemen's Land (Tasmania) were convict colonies, to justify Britain's continued support of the governors' executive and legislative authority and its refusal to establish representative institutions.

In the first section of this chapter I map the distinctive features of colonial government in the convict era, while also tracing the development of the movement for self-government. In the second section I focus on the debates leading to the creation of responsible government in New South Wales, for this was the colony in which the issues surrounding representation and the rights of individuals versus the rights of property were most fiercely debated. In the final section I explore the debates that surrounded the writing of a federal

Constitution, arguing that they reflected a new consensus in favor of democracy, popular sovereignty, and the right of the people to a wide range of individual liberties.

A SINGULAR COLONY

In 1819 a young native-born but English-educated Australian colonist, William Charles Wentworth, published *A Statistical, Historical and Political Description of the Colony of New South Wales and its Dependent Settlements in Van Diemen's Land.*[1] He argued that because the Australian colonies were rich in natural resources, their potential to produce an array of staples was considerable. Yet Wentworth's optimism about the colonies' prospects was tempered by his concern with the absence of both representative institutions of government and a court system that provided for trial by jury. He claimed that British people both at home and abroad only flourished and prospered because of the "superior freedom of ... (British) laws." Their absence in New South Wales (NSW) inhibited the colonies' economic growth, not least because many prospective free immigrants chose instead to move to countries that possessed systems of representative government, most notably the United States.[2] "The colony of New South Wales is, I believe, the only one in of our possessions exclusively inhabited by Englishmen in which there is not at least the shadow of free government," he wrote, "as it possesses neither a council, a house of assembly, nor even the privilege of trial by jury."[3] In the decades that followed, the insistence that Englishmen overseas possessed equivalent political and legal rights to those who remained at home was consistently at the heart of the case put by colonials who favored self-government.

While the system of government established in New South Wales was singular and exceptional, it drew for its constituent parts on British colonial precedent. The commissions issued to the first governor, Captain Arthur Phillip, required him to follow instructions from the Crown but also gave him the power to appoint "necessary" officers, grant pardons to convicts, execute martial law, and to raise and distribute monies. Two acts of 1787 established a criminal court presided over by a judge advocate, assisted by a "jury" of six officers of the king's forces; and a court of civil jurisdiction consisting once again of the judge advocate, in this case assisted by two colonists appointed by the governor. The practice of appointing a naval officer, who presided over a government, lacking an appointed council or an elected council and/or assembly, had a precedent in the colony of Newfoundland. The two court acts of 1787 were necessary because the Crown had no power simply to deny trial by jury. Yet there was also an example for the New South Wales' legal system, for

---

[1] G. and W. B. Whitaker, London, 1819.
[2] Ibid., 161, 399.
[3] Ibid., 164, 173.

juries in Gibraltar were given military membership in 1752.[4] Under these arrangements and following the strong executive authority established by Phillip between 1788 and 1792, the governors of New South Wales were effective enforcers of Colonial Office policy, powerful pro-consuls of a modernizing empire.

The early governors were not altogether opposed to reform, to the transfer of more clearly recognizably English institutions, particularly trial by jury. Hunter and King both pressed Westminster for its introduction, and when Bligh returned to England in 1809 he carried with him a petition signed by more than 800 colonists, asking for trial by jury. The 1810 report on the colony's legal system produced by the newly arrived judge advocate, Ellis Bent, also favored introducing it as standard legal practice. The interest of the colonists in achieving this English right was spurred by their strengthening belief that the coup conducted by the New South Wales Corp in 1808, resulting in the overthrow of Bligh, had left the military with too much power, reflected in the fact that the court martial system of justice included the civilian population.[5]

However, in the first thirty years of the colony, criticisms of other aspects of its system of government tended to come from England rather than the colonists themselves. In 1803 Jeremy Bentham, an opponent of transportation, wrote a pamphlet with the short title of *A Plea for the Constitution*. He argued that the governor of New South Wales possessed authority over the military officers and their men by the Articles of War and the Mutiny Act, while Acts of Parliament bound convicts. However, he claimed that the governor had no legal authority relating to the liberty and property of free settlers and ex-convicts (emancipists).[6] Although the obvious legal solution was the establishment of an advisory body, the early governors were opposed to the creation of a legislative council consisting of either appointed or elected officials (or a blend of both), arguing in Bligh's words that it would cramp the governor and "... cause great trouble in this country ..." by promoting political faction.[7] Nevertheless, English advocates of a council persisted. In 1812 the Select Committee on Transportation argued that the concentration of so much power in the hands of the governor had led to some arbitrary and self-promoting decisions,

---

[4] *Historical Records of New South Wales* (hereafter HRNSW), vol. 1, Part 2, 24; *Historical Records of Australia* (hereafter HRA), First Series, vol. 1, 2–8; Alan Atkinson,"The First Plans for Governing New South Wales, 1786–1787," *Australian Historical Studies*, vol. 24, April 1990, 29, 36; Alan Atkinson, "The Free Born Englishman Transported: Convict Rights as a Measure of Eighteenth Century Empire," *Past and Present*, vol. 144, number 1, 1994, 110. The first four governors were all naval officers.

[5] David Neal, *The Rule of Law in a Penal Colony: Law and Power in Early New South Wales* (Cambridge: Cambridge University Press, 1991), 54, 173–5: HRA, First Series, vol. 4, 48–55, 57–68.

[6] Alan Atkinson, "Jeremy Bentham and the Rum Rebellion," *Journal of the Royal Australian Historical Society*, vol. 64, June 1978, 1–2. The tract was printed but not published because Bentham hoped for a remedial Act of Parliament and he also feared the impact of his argument on the convicts of NSW.

[7] HRA, Series 1, vol. 6, Bligh to Windham, 31 October 1807, 151.

especially in relation to the punishment of prisoners and the granting of land. Even the actions of a wise and even-handed governor were likely to provoke "...opposition and discontent amongst men unused in their own country, to see so great a monopoly of power."[8] Although the committee's solution was the creation of a council, the secretary of state for the colonies rejected this advice, arguing that it would be difficult to find qualified members, that its creation would promote political factions, and that the final result would be a weakening of the governor's authority, a dangerous prospect in a convict society. The Colonial Office view that New South Wales lacked sufficient men of caliber to be granted institutions of responsible government was to persist for a further forty years.[9]

The English advocates of constitutional reform were preoccupied with ensuring that the colonial and British governments were acting legally and constitutionally; they were not much concerned with the rights and liberties of the colonists themselves. But a serious colonial challenge to executive authority was mounted in 1808, when wealthy colonists, led by John Macarthur, combined with the officers of the NSW Corps to overthrow Governor William Bligh in the so-called Rum Rebellion. To justify their actions, they drew on traditional notions regarding the rights of Englishmen, as well as Bentham's argument that governors had no legal jurisdiction over free men. Macarthur, a select group of other wealthy free settlers, and officers of the NSW Corps had profited heavily from their participation in the rum trade. In 1807 Bligh took steps to stamp out the widespread use of rum as both a beverage and currency, banning the use of spirits in payment for grain, food and flour, and re-issuing a previous ban on private stills. In October the government seized two illegal stills, the property of Macarthur and Edward Abbott, an act that Macarthur denounced as "contrary to the laws of the realm."[10] In December colonial authorities ordered the owners of the schooner *Parramatta* to forfeit a bond of £900 for earlier leaving Sydney Cove with an escaped convict on board. Macarthur, a part owner, declared he had abandoned the ship and refused to provide rations for the crew, who were then forced to come ashore in search of food. The judge advocate issued a warrant for Macarthur's arrest, charging him with illegally stopping provisions for the crew. In late 1807, Bligh acted in a manner designed to further alienate not only Macarthur but other wealthy settlers and the officers of the NSW Corps, including one of its most senior officers, Major George Johnston. He directed that houses and buildings constructed within the area of Sydney Town were illegal and were to be removed. Legally Bligh was within his rights, because in 1792 Phillip had declared that the area would remain the property of the Crown. But the properties to be demolished numbered those leased by prominent citizens, including both

[8] C. M. H. Clark (ed.), *Select Documents in Australian History 1788–1850*, two volumes (Sydney: Angus and Robertson, 1950, 1955), vol. 1, 314–5.
[9] HRA, Series 1, vol. 7, Bathurst to Macquarie, 23 November 1812, 674.
[10] HRNSW, vol. 6, 332.

Johnston and Macarthur. Effectively Bligh had created a context in which Macarthur could elevate the issues between the governor and the free settlers to matters of fundamental human rights. Macarthur had learned of Bentham's arguments from discussions with the judge advocate, David Collins, and in 1805 he relied on them when he informed Governor King that local regulations were illegal unless endorsed by Parliament. At his trial, which began on January 26, 1808, he argued against the legality of Bligh's regulations on the same grounds, adding that the governor's actions threatened the liberties, lives, and property of the colonists. In response to Macarthur's direct request Johnston arrested Bligh and declared martial law. "Liberty and Equality reigns (sic) in this colony," Macarthur declared, and in a letter to his wife he wrote:

I have been deeply engaged all this day in contending for the liberties of this unhappy colony and I am happy to say I have succeeded beyond what I expected.[11]

No doubt out of a concern to ensure future governors did not issue orders and regulations that threatened their property, a meeting of colonists held in Sydney on February 8, 1808 resolved that Macarthur carry a list of grievances to England, together with a request for the establishment of a legislative council, consisting of the governor, four officials, and two colonists elected by the magistrates.[12] Perhaps what motivated these men to petition for a legislative council was the influence of a strand of British political ideology that stretched back into the seventeenth century, which emphasized the need to balance monarchy (executive), lords (wise counsel), and commons (democracy and liberty). In the context of NSW it was impossible to replicate this system, but a combination of wise counsel and "democracy" in the form of a blended council might balance the arbitrary powers of governors.[13]

When Macarthur and Johnston arrived in England, they discovered that the English authorities had no sympathy for their grievances, or for their case for reform. Johnston was court martialed and cashiered and Macarthur was prevented from returning to NSW until 1816. In any case, Macquarie, who succeeded Bligh in 1809, was a more careful and seemingly less arbitrary governor, and so the case for legal restraint became less urgent among the free settlers. In their determination to escape from what they considered Bligh's despotic and arbitrary rule, Macarthur and his supporters were, I suspect, more concerned with protecting their property and their right to make their fortunes through trade and the pastoral industry than with the right and freedom to participate in political decision making or assert individual independence through free speech or freedom of the press. Indeed as the emancipists, encouraged by Macquarie, began to flex their economic and political muscles, the Macarthurs and other

[11] Quoted in Atkinson, "Bentham," 7; quoted in Ross Fitzgerald and Mark Hearn, *Bligh, Macarthur and the Rum Rebellion* (Sydney: Kangaroo Press, 1988), 104.

[12] Fitzgerald and Hearn, 6–8. See also HRNSW, vol. 6, 434, 435.

[13] J. G. A. Pocock, *The Machiavellian Moment: Florentine Political Thought and the Atlantic Republican Tradition* (Princeton, NJ: Princeton University Press, 1975), 361–2.

"exclusive" or "pure merino" families became entrenched opponents of the extension of consultative and elected political institutions. It became one of John Macarthur's greatest regrets that, by 1820, what he referred to as a "democratic feeling" had become endemic.[14] In this context the Rebellion hardly marked the beginnings of a campaign for self-government.

Convicts, too, used the rhetoric of liberty. From the beginning they insisted that the authorities acknowledge their legal rights and they constantly aspired to freedom. For them liberty meant the release or escape from captivity, not the establishment of a less authoritarian form of government. Many convicts were aware when their terms of servitude ended, and when the official indents confirming the lengths of sentences sometimes did not arrive they were vociferous in demanding redress. What made the convict system so different from slavery in the Americas was the fact that convicts had clear, defined, and enforced rights in law, and most were freed even before they had finished their prescribed period of punishment. Nor were their children subject to any form of inherited bondage. However, if, like the common people in England, they believed they had rights under the law that protected them from arbitrary power, they were also willing to evade the law when opportunity arose.[15] In the first thirty years of settlement attempted escapes from the colony – either on stolen small vessels or by stowing away on ships – were fairly common, with about one in four succeeding.[16] Planned uprisings also became increasingly frequent in the 1790s and early 1800s, especially with the arrival of large numbers of Irish convicts, some of them political prisoners.[17] The largest insurrection to take place was organized by Irish convicts assigned to the Government Farm at Castle Hill in 1804 and included up to 400 rebels. A local resident, George Suttor, witnessed the encounter between the commander of the NSW Corps, Major Johnston, and the leader of the rebels, Phillip Cunningham. When Johnston asked him what he wanted, Cunningham responded that he wanted "Death or Liberty," but then added more prosaically that the rebels also demanded a ship to take them home. A desire to return to Ireland probably was a greater motivating factor among the rebels then radical ideology. Nevertheless, the uprising was brutally suppressed with most of the leaders slaughtered on the road and others summarily hanged, while other participants were assigned to chain gangs.[18]

---

[14] Fitzgerald and Hearn, 123.

[15] E. P. Thompson, *The Making of the English Working Class* (New York: Vintage Books, 1966), 80.

[16] Grace Karskens, "'This Spirit of Emigration': the Nature and Meaning of Escape in Early New South Wales," *Journal of Australian Colonial History*, vol. 7, 2005, 1–34.

[17] There were also Scottish political prisoners in NSW, most notably Maurice Margarot, one of the "Scottish martyrs," who was suspected but never convicted of inspiring some of the planned uprisings. Governor King claimed Margarot possessed papers containing "... some very elegant Republican Sentiments...." HRA, Series 1, vol. 5, Governor King to Under Secretary King, 14 August 1804, 138.

[18] HRNSW, vol. 5, George Suttor to Joseph Banks, 10 March 1804, 351; Major George Johnston to Lieutenant-Colonel Paterson, 7 March 1804, 348–9.

There were no further rebellions after 1804, and the number of escapes or attempted escapes gradually diminished. As Sydney grew, the convicts created families, and a decent standard of living, achieved from earning wages in "their own time." "Liberty" and "freedom" were now secured through the creation of a culture of defiance and opposition, reflected in a commitment to gambling and drinking, an enjoyment of blood sports and other pre-industrial pastimes, and a refusal to pay the dues of deference. The convicts maintained an oppositional value system that mirrored an English plebeian culture that was most cogently reflected in the words and actions of English merchant seamen.[19] Macquarie encouraged the emancipists, claiming such a policy assisted their rehabilitation, and that in any case they and their children now owned the "...principal part of the property in the Collony..."[20] By the end of the second decade of the nineteenth century the colony was recognized increasingly as a place of opportunity, leading the British government to query its credentials as a site of punishment.

It was in this context that the Colonial Office commissioned J. T. Bigge to examine the regulations of NSW and its dependencies, as well as the operation of its government and courts and the functioning of the convict system. He produced a series of reports that were presented to Parliament in 1822–23. Although Bigge concluded that Macquarie was too lenient in his treatment of convicts and emancipists, he also recommended protection for the legal rights of the latter, a separate judiciary for Van Diemen's Land (Tasmania), and the establishment of a legislative council in NSW – although he did not believe that either colony was yet ready for trial by jury. The Bigge Report and its critique of Macquarie almost certainly determined the governor's successors, Brisbane and Darling, to recreate a more disciplined and controlled society. But the genie was out of the bottle, and the emergence of the emancipists as a powerful economic and articulate political group provided a powerful impetus to the movement for responsible government.

Stimulus to this campaign came with a decision by Judge Barron Field in the Court of Civil Judicature in 1820 that emancipists were not restored "to any Civil Rights of free Subjects, nor put in the capacity to acquire, hold or convey Property..." until their names were included in a general pardon. Such a ruling threatened both the legal rights of the ex-convicts and the colony's economy, because it could not function without their fundamental contribution. In the view of more than 1,300 emancipists and their supporters who signed a petition of protest they now stood as "Convicts attaint without personal Liberty, without Property.[21] The British government acted to restore the legal status of the

---

[19] Richard Waterhouse, *Private Pleasures, Public Leisure: a History of Australian Popular Culture Since 1788* (Melbourne: Longman, 1995), 20–25; Marcus Rediker, *Between the Devil and the Deep Blue Sea: Merchant Seamen, Pirates and the Angle-American Maritime World 1700–1750* (Cambridge: Cambridge University Press, 1987). Men and women who became convicts rubbed shoulders with seamen both in English towns and on the transports.

[20] HRA, Series 1, vol. 10, Macquarie to Bathurst, 22 February 1820, 216.

[21] HRA, Series 1, vol. 10, Petition from the Emancipists, 22 October 1821, 550–54.

emancipists, but the ruling remained as a warning of their precarious hold on the freedoms and property rights that were supposed to be the birthright of Englishmen and stimulated their efforts to strengthen their legal status as free men. What allowed them to articulate their campaign was the appearance in the 1820s of newspapers like the *Australian* and the *Monitor* that were sympathetic to the emancipist cause and provided a foil to the official and censored views that the *Sydney Gazette* had published since 1803.

Some of those who now emerged as political leaders were emancipists. Edward Eagar, transported for forgery in 1811, was secretary to the committee that in 1819 drew up a petition to the Prince Regent, asking for trial by jury. The argument in the petition was that without trial by jury the law was an instrument not of justice but of arbitrary and despotic government.[22] In a subsequent statement he submitted to Bigge, Eagar suggested that the government possessed despotic qualities because of its suppression of free discussion, its arbitrary imposition of taxes, and its abuse of the law. Eagar's solution was to introduce a bicameral legislature, claiming that NSW was entitled to "... all the benefits of the Common Law of England and ... Constitutional representative forms of Government, all epitomes of the parliament of England."[23]

Other leaders of the emancipist cause, most notably W. C. Wentworth and Sir John Jamison, were not ex-convicts, although their associations with convict women and their daughters made them anathema to the exclusives. William was the product of an out-of-wedlock liaison between his father Darcy and the convict Catherine Crowley. He hoped to join the exclusives by marrying Elizabeth Macarthur, but his proposal was spurned by Elizabeth's father, John, of Rum Rebellion fame. And so William became a social and political leader of the outsiders, a member of the "fancy" (a group of plebeians and gentry who organized, supported, and gambled on sporting events) and the de facto and later legal husband of Sarah Cox, the daughter of convict parents. Wentworth was an articulate and wealthy spokesman for the emancipist cause. His publication of his history of 1819 amounted to a first call to arms, and he became the prime architect of the campaign for an elected legislative assembly.

Sir John Jamison's practice of living with convict women earned him the title "old debauchee," and the government house circle shunned him. His profile was lower than Wentworth's and he was more restrained in his demands, focussing his attention on the campaign for trial by jury.[24] In response to this persistent demand, and despite Bigge's reservations, the Colonial Office moved

---

[22] Ibid., Petition by Colonists for Redress of Grievances 22 March 1819, 52–65.

[23] N. D. McLachlan, "Edward Eagar (1786–1866): A Colonial Spokesman in Sydney and London," *Historical Studies Australia and New Zealand*, vol. 10 (May, 1963), 435; John Ritchie, *Punishment and Profit: The Reports of Commissioner John Bigge on the Colonies of New South Wales and Van Diemen's Land, 1822–23; Their Origins, Nature and Significance* (Melbourne: Heinemann, 1970), 111.

[24] *Australian Dictionary of Biography*, vol. 2 (Melbourne: Melbourne University Press, 1967), 582–9; Transcriptions of Missing Despatches 1823–1832, Brisbane to Bathurst, 18 November 1825, Mitchell Library, MS A1267.

slowly to establish trial by jury. In 1828 an act of Parliament allowed plaintiffs
and defendants in civil cases to demand a twelve-man jury of civilians, and in
1833 Governor Bourke extended trial by jury to all criminal cases.[25]

But this was not the limit of the emancipists' demands. Following the arguments set out by Wentworth and Eagar on the right of Englishmen overseas not
to be taxed except by their elected representatives, they campaigned hard for
responsible government throughout the twenties and thirties. Running consistently through the petitions drawn up by the emancipist leaders were the claims
that the colonists possessed the same rights as Englishmen at home, that the
governors' imposition of taxes without the consent of an elected legislature
violated the Magna Charta, and that the Colonial Office had created a unique
situation by its refusal to allow the establishment of a legislative assembly in
NSW, because even the West Indies colonies, with much smaller free white
populations, were allowed this fundamental English right.[26]

The Colonial Office made some concessions, partly because its own legal
advisors had concluded that governors did not have the authority to make laws
on their own authority, but, also, I suspect, in response to the emancipist
campaign. In supporting the 1827 petition Wentworth argued that the situation
in NSW was comparable to America in 1776, and that sort of rhetoric was
likely to cause considerable soul searching in the Colonial Office.[27] In 1823 a
Legislative Council consisting of five to seven members, nominated by the
Crown in consultation with the governor, was established, a majority of whom
could block laws proposed by the governor. All laws passed by the council also
required certification by the chief justice that they did not breach the laws of
England. Those chosen as councillors were always government officials, but an
1828 law that established separate councils in NSW and Van Diemen's Land
also provided that the membership be expanded in each case to include between ten and fifteen councillors, some of whom were to be local residents,
the voices of "popular opinion."[28] But even these concessions did not satisfy
the emancipists and their supporters, who claimed that governors retained the
power and authority to "...go meanwhile to the extent that pride, intolerance
and tyranny can go." The *Australian*, Wentworth's mouthpiece, argued that
because of the failure to establish representative institutions, the white native

[25] Bathurst to Darling, 12 December 1825, HRA, Series 1, vol. 12; "An Act to Provide for the
      Administration of Justice in New South Wales and Van Diemen's Land," in Clark, *Select Docu-
      ments* (ed.), vol. 1, 322–26; Neal, *The Rule of Law*, 184; J. T. Bigge, *Report of the Commis-
      sioner of Inquiry on the Judicial Establishments of New South Wales and Van Diemen's Land*,
      Reprint Edition (Adelaide: Libraries Board of South Australia, 1966), 42–3.
[26] Clark (ed.), *Select Documents*, vol. 1, 321–2 (1825): HRA, Series 1, vol. 13, 51–7 (1827); Series
      1, vol. 18, 399–403 (1836); John Molony, *The Native-Born: the First White Australians*
      (Melbourne: Melbourne University Press, 2000), 149 (1833).
[27] Mark McKenna, *The Captive Republic: A History of Republicanism in Australia 1788–1996*
      (Cambridge: Cambridge University Press, 1996), 19.
[28] Clark (ed.), vol. 1, 318–21, 322–26; A. C. V. Melbourne, *Early Constitutional Development in
      Australia: New South Wales, 1788–1856* (London: Oxford University Press, 1934), 95, 152–61.

born were raised "in utter alienage from the first principles and practice of the British Constitution."[29] And so the colonists were in danger of losing a British heritage based on clearly defined rights and liberties. Finally, emancipists also claimed that, because the exclusives dominated membership of the council, they had become a "factious oligarchy," leaving the emancipists and their children with no political voice at all.[30]

The campaign to establish a representative government failed, at least for the moment, because of the implacable opposition of the British government. The under-secretary of state for the colonies, Henry Howick, argued that if a representative assembly was granted, the emancipists would gain a dominant influence, and that was unacceptable.[31] If the colonists had stood united, the British, aware of the dangers of a second colonial declaration of independence, might have yielded. But the exclusives, led by the quietly articulate James Macarthur, were also implacably opposed to the establishment of a representative government. For them the nominated council was the perfect solution because it gave the exclusives the authority to control the emancipists and provided a check against liberal governors like Richard Bourke (1831–37), who were sympathetic to the emancipist cause. Although convicts now constituted a clear minority, and the vast majority of emancipists were law-abiding colonists, it suited the exclusives to insist that the colony remain populated by unreconstructed criminals, and certainly not yet ready for the free institutions that existed in Great Britain. Perhaps influenced by Hume's view that only educated, property-holding men could fully comprehend "rational liberty" and "rational religion," Macarthur and his supporters argued that property and "rational ... freedom" required protection from the "liberty" proposed by Wentworth and his followers. For this "liberty," by extending political rights to ex-convicts and their children, threatened the existing social order.[32]

However, Wentworth later claimed that he was a Whig, not a democrat, and for him liberty, property, and citizenship were inextricably linked. Governor Darling's assessment of him as a radical democrat, "an American at Heart," was, as events were to show, wide of the mark.[33] But while Wentworth had not yet succeeded in winning the fight for a representative government, along with Edward Hall, the publisher of the *Monitor*, he triumphed in the battle to establish freedom of the press. In response to the critical campaign waged by these newspapers against both the system of government and the manner in which he managed it, Governor Darling (1825–31) sought to enact legislation censoring the press. However, his own chief justice ruled that the proposed law

---

[29] *Australian*, 6 January 1829, 10 February 1830.

[30] HRA, Series 1, vol. 18, 399–403.

[31] J. M. Ward, *Colonial Self Government: The British Experience 1759–1856* (London: Macmillan, 1976), 148.

[32] HRA, Series, 1, vol. 18, Petition of the "free inhabitants" of NSW 13 April, 1836, 392–5; Pocock, *Machiavellian Moment*, 494.

[33] HRA, Series 1, vol. 14, Governor Darling to Sir George Murray, 8 November 1828, 445.

contravened English precedent.[34] I have not come across evidence that Wentworth read John Stuart Mill, whose writings on liberty were in any case still in
the future, but he had succeeded in introducing the colonists to a modern form
of liberty as later defined by Mill, the right to and love of individual independence. Ironically, this form of liberty was achieved in advance of the establishment of representative government.

The response of the British government to rebellions in Canada in 1837 was
to commission what became known as the Durham Report (1839). It marked a
change in British policy, for in his concern to ensure that the Canadians did
not follow the American precedent, Lord Durham recommended conceding
responsible government to them. His scheme involved a division of domestic and imperial responsibilities that was designed to encourage the colonists
to develop an interdependent Canadian/British identity. Self-government, he
argued, would make Canadians more rather than less loyal to the empire.[35]
In NSW the Report became a model for those seeking further constitutional
reform. "The thing has been done in Canada and it can be done here," claimed
the *Atlas*. "If self-government be our right responsible government is incident to
that right. We have not ceased to become Englishmen by becoming colonists."[36] In any case, in the late 1830s the exclusives came to the view that
their interests lay with the emancipists, rather than with a British government
that they now judged did not understand or act in the colony's best interests.
Even the conservative press, led by the *Sydney Morning Herald*, advocated the
establishment of an elected legislative assembly, to ensure that the colonists
controlled their own revenue and the appointment of their own government
officials, which in turn would remove "causes of collision" and, in line with
Durham's views, would result in closer ties between the colony and the
empire.[37]

In 1840, Lord John Russell, the secretary of state for the colonies determined
to cease transportation to NSW. His decision was motivated by a concern with
the cost of transportation, a recognition that there was widespread opposition
to the policy in both England and the colony, an assessment that it did not result
in the reformation of criminals, and was a prelude to the granting of free
institutions.[38] This was followed in 1842 by an act that established a blended
council consisting of thirty-six members, two-thirds of whom were elected and
one-third of whom were nominated by the Crown. The office holding and
voting qualifications prescribed by the act excluded two-thirds of the male
and all female colonists from the franchise and ensured that in the first elections
the large rural property holders triumphed.[39] But not even the wealthy graziers

---

[34] Ibid., Series 1, vol. 13, Chief Justice Forbes to Governor Darling, 8 May 1827, 284.
[35] McKenna, 29–30.
[36] *Atlas*, 28 December 1844, cited in ibid., 30.
[37] *Sydney Morning Herald*, 25 December 1839, 15 June 1840.
[38] Ward, *Colonial Self Government*, 160; John Hirst, *Convict Society and its Enemies* (Sydney:
Allen and Unwin, 1983), 189–217.
[39] Clark (ed.), vol. 1, 335–40.

and merchants were content with this concession, for the fact was that the British government retained control of both the civil list and all revenue from fines, penalties, and the sale of Crown land. The governor also retained authority to prorogue or dissolve the council, while the Crown could still disallow colonial acts at its discretion. The colonists were unanimous in their agreement that this was hardly an even division of responsibilities.

In the years that followed, the campaign for the establishment of a more complete form of representative government was not simply conducted by a now united colonial gentry. The late thirties and early forties witnessed large-scale immigration to NSW with the result that the population doubled. An alternative political leadership reflecting the aspirations of the immigrant working classes emerged, a leadership strongly influenced by Chartist aspirations. These men, too, claimed that they were "the free born children of the British Constitution," but their ambitions centered not just on achieving self-government but on challenging the authority of the Macarthurs and the Wentworths in the process. "If a few antiquated men who live on memory and the fruits of prison labour know not the people," editorialized the radical newspaper, the *Australasian Chronicle*, "how can they govern them? ... they are weighed by the people and found wanting."[40] Such sentiments signaled the commencement of a long campaign for democratic as well as representative government and the emergence of a more radical political culture.

THE CAMPAIGN FOR RESPONSIBLE GOVERNMENT

In 1852, the secretary of state for the colonies, Sir John Pakington, instructed the governor of NSW, and the lieutenant governors of Victoria and South Australia, to require their legislative councils to draft constitutions based on a bicameral system of government. Subsequently Tasmania, Queensland, and Western Australia also adopted constitutions based on this model. Most colonies provided for the election of members of both the lower and upper houses, with a higher property qualification applying for both candidates and electors in legislative council elections, but NSW determined on a nominated upper house. Mostly, the constitutions were adopted with little drama or debate. There was considerable Chartist-inspired unrest in the Victorian goldfields in 1854, culminating in an armed uprising by miners at the Eureka Stockade. But this did not translate into a widespread, popular campaign for a democratic constitution. Neither the squatters nor the urban radicals took much interest in the constitution writing process; the draft constitution was written by government officials and the debate over the document in the legislative council focused on detail rather than principle. The squatters feared that they would lose political power in a bicameral system, but they accepted that, given the new policies emanating from the Colonial Office and the influx of huge numbers of new settlers in the wake of the discovery of gold, a more comprehensive

[40] *Australasian Chronicle*, 29 September 1840.

system of government was inevitable.[41] But in NSW the debates leading to the adoption of the constitution were fierce and protracted as conservatives, liberals, and radicals contested the form that responsible government should take. For this reason, I have focussed the discussion in this section on the constitution making process in this, in any case, the major colony.

The conservatives were led by the large landholders in alliance with prominent public officeholders, including most notably Wentworth, Edward Deas Thomson (the Colonial Secretary), and James Macarthur. In the twenties and thirties opponents had denounced Wentworth as a dangerous radical, but his increasing pastoral wealth and newly formed alliance with the "pure merinos" made him more conservative. Still, there was also a measure of consistency in Wentworth's political ideology because he had always argued that property ownership was a prerequisite of the right to vote or hold office. In past times he had directed his vitriol toward governors and the exclusives, describing the latter as the "yellow snakes of the colony."[42] Now his criticisms were aimed at the Sydney merchants, artisans, and laborers. He denounced the merchants as contributing nothing to the "real wealth of the colony" and working men as "the most vacillating ignorant and misled body of people in the colony."[43] He had once appealed to plebeians for support, but his alliance with the exclusives and his concern with the growing political power of the working classes changed his views and his rhetoric.

The conservatives wanted a society replicating English rank, status, and deference. They belonged to the Church of England and they were instrumental in the establishment of the University of Sydney in 1850, believing that while it had an obligation to provide an education to men of merit from humble families, its main function was to train the sons of the colonial elite to fill "the high offices of state." They revered the English Constitution, which they argued maintained hierarchy, preserved property, and guaranteed their liberty. During the initial discussions over the colony's constitution Wentworth even proposed the creation of a colonial aristocracy whose members would constitute the upper house, an aristocracy that the native-born radical, Daniel Daniehy, derisively and devastatingly referred to as a "bunyip aristocracy." Anticipating its colonial unpopularity and the prospect that the scheme might be seen by the Colonial Office as an attempt to entrench the squatters (large landholders who occupied sheep runs beyond the prescribed limits of settlement) with permanent political power, other conservatives were more tempered in their proposals to institutionalize hierarchy. Macarthur suggested that the new legislative council

[41] Geoffrey Serle, *The Golden Age; a History of the Colony of Victoria, 1851–1861* (Melbourne: Melbourne University Press, 1963, 146–7; J. M. Main, "Making Constitutions in New South Wales and Victoria," 1853–1854, *Historical Studies*, vol. 7, number 28, 373–83.

[42] *Australian Dictionary of Biography*, vol. 2, 582–88.

[43] E. K. Silvester (ed.), *New South Wales Constitution Bill. The Speeches in the Legislative Council of New South Wales on the Second Reading of the Bill for Framing a New Constitution for the Colony* (Sydney: Thomas Daniel, 1853), 29.

consist of members nominated by the governor on the advice of his ministers, while Chief Justice Sir Alfred Stephen argued for a legislative council consisting of nominated government, church, and legal officers together with ten appointed and ten elected "independent gentlemen."[44]

The conservatives nevertheless were committed to the introduction of responsible government. Because they believed that they were entitled to the same rights as Englishmen at home, they objected to the levying of taxes without their consent. They also opposed the Colonial Office's "'despotic" control of the civil list; the British government's refusal to surrender authority over the "wastelands," or the funds raised from their sale; and the subordination of the governor to a Colonial Office, whose officials did not understand the needs and interests of the colony. These grievances were expressed in addresses made by the legislative council, which they controlled, to the Colonial Office, and in petitions drawn up at public meetings that they organized. They also campaigned for responsible government as a means of protecting and extending their own economic prospects. In particular, they feared that the Colonial Office might adopt policies to restrict their access to cheap labor and inexpensive land. The 1847 Orders in Council, which provided fourteen-year leases on land occupied by squatters beyond the prescribed limits of settlement, only partly eased their concerns, for without control of finance, public offices, and the legislative process there remained the risk that future British policies might damage their interests.[45] Finally, they also distrusted and indeed despised democracy, and they sought to safeguard against popular rule by lobbying and legislating to provide high property qualifications for voters and elected office holders, and by perpetuating a gerrymander that left urban areas like Sydney heavily underrepresented. The Election Act of 1842, drawn up by the British Parliament but reflecting the views of the colony's conservatives, not only included relatively high property qualifications but prescribed electoral districts that heavily favored rural at the expense of urban areas. In 1850, when the British government passed the Australian Government Act, which separated Victoria from New South Wales, one consequence was that the electoral boundaries in the latter colony had to be redrawn. The electoral bill drawn up by Deas Thomson with the help of Macarthur maintained the gerrymander, its authors arguing that it was consistent with the Reform Bill of 1832, because it was designed to represent interests and property as much, if not more, than population. To base electorates on population alone, Deas Thomson argued,

---

[44] Ibid., 35, 135; Sir Alfred Stephen, *Thoughts on the Constitution of a Second Legislative Chamber for New South Wales* (Sydney: F. M. Stokes, 1853), 6–8; *Sydney Morning Herald*, 16 August 1853, quoted in Clark (ed.), vol. 2, 341–2.

[45] Clark (ed.), vol. 1, 365–67; D. W. A. Baker, *Days of Wrath; a Life of John Dunmore Lang* (Melbourne: Melbourne University Press, 1965), 75; P. Loveday and A. W. Martin, *Parliament, Factions and Parties; the First Thirty Years of Responsible Government in New South Wales, 1856–1889* (Melbourne: Melbourne University Press, 1966), 10; *Sydney Morning Herald*, 23 October 1845.

would lay "the foundations of republicanism."[46] Similar arguments were later mounted in Victoria in 1857 in opposition to the move to introduce universal manhood suffrage.[47]

For the conservatives, then, nothing could be worse than representation based on population, because they viewed democracy as practiced in the United States as resulting in tyranny, epitomized by lynch mobs in the North and slavery in the South. There was, they claimed, more freedom in NSW than in the United States. They insisted that representative government controlled by the elite guaranteed property and therefore liberty, while "...vile democracy..." produced "...anarchy and confusion..." In the future, Macarthur predicted, Australians would need to determine whether to remain loyal to the principles of English monarchy or develop an appetite for American democracy, and he was confident that "Reason and England will prevail against Democracy and America." Wentworth put it more bluntly when he declared that he wanted a British and not a "Yankee institution." As it turned out Macarthur was wrong, because fifty years later the Australian Constitution blended both English and American constitutional principles.[48]

Because of the gerrymander and the high property qualifications for voting and council membership, the early elections resulted in the return of large numbers of landholding conservatives. But from the mid-forties onward their ascendancy came under increasing challenge from the liberals and, more especially, the radicals. Robert Lowe emerged as the unlikely liberal spokesman. An English barrister, Lowe had come to Sydney in 1842, because his physicians had told him that his eyesight was failing and that he would be blind in seven years. His mission in immigrating to NSW was to accumulate a fortune at the bar and through property investments, before he finally lost his sight. Lowe argued that he shared many of Wentworth's views, including the establishment of a bicameral system and vesting control of revenue, the civil list, and Crown lands in the colonial government. But he also claimed that in monopolizing the land the squatters were retarding the colony's progress, keeping it as nothing more than a giant sheepwalk. "I have been consistent in fighting for liberty," he proclaimed while "the squatters have been consistent in fighting for money."[49] But if he despised the squatters, he also abhorred the Colonial Office and its

---

[46] Peter Cochrane, *Colonial Ambition: Foundations of Australian Democracy* (Melbourne: Melbourne University Press, 2006), 258; Ward, *Colonial Self-Government*, 168; S. G. Foster, *Colonial Improver: Edward Deas Thomson, 1800–1879* (Melbourne: Melbourne University Press, 1978), 109.

[47] Edward Wilson, *An Enquiry into the Principles of Representation: A Reprint of Several Letters and Articles from the Argus Newspaper* (Melbourne: William Fairfax, 1857), i–iii.

[48] Silvester (ed.), 40, 95 135,214; *Sydney Morning Herald*, 28 February 1842, cited in Michael Roe, *The Quest for Authority in Eastern Australia* (Melbourne: Melbourne University Press, 1965), 45.

[49] Quoted in Ruth Knight, *Illiberal Liberal: Robert Lowe in New South Wales, 1842–1850* (Melbourne: Melbourne University Press, 1966), 202.

policies, which had brought "injustice and degradation" to the colony.[50] He objected particularly to the 1847 Orders in Council and to the Colonial Office's proposal in 1849 to re-introduce transportation to NSW, for the latter decision would bring back a system of forced labor and weaken the opportunities for free workers, as well as dim the prospects of responsible government. In short, this policy impinged upon the liberty of the colonists.[51]

Lowe constantly compared the challenges and threats faced by the citizens of NSW with those encountered by the American colonists in the period from 1763 to 1776. He described the English Constitution as "the rock of our freedom..." but also insisted that the English government, in its exercise of colonial policy, was "arbitrary, distant and irresponsible."[52] Because he was influenced by Locke, he did not hesitate in suggesting that if the Colonial Office persisted in imposing "oppressive" and "tyrannical" policies, the English government might once again need to learn the "bloody and expensive lesson of America." "As in America," he proclaimed, "oppression was the parent of independence."[53] Perhaps Lowe was less serious about independence than in playing out a morality tale for the benefit of the Colonial Office.[54] Nevertheless, his arguments fitted within a long English Whig political tradition stretching back to 1688.

The Chartist newspaper, the *People's Advocate*, proclaimed Lowe's election to the council in 1848 by the workingmen of Sydney as representing "the birthday of Australian Democracy."[55] The election revealed that it was not just the issue of land and the role of squatters that divided Lowe from Wentworth. In his victory speech Lowe derided the squatters for their dependence on the British government to secure tenure of their pastoral "runs" and the merchants for what he considered their incompetence. But in proposing an extension of the franchise he valorized the mostly immigrant working classes and argued that they were the colony's best hope for an extension of liberty. I suspect he believed the immigrant workers better understood their rights under the Constitution than the native-born. In any case, he argued that the "popular element" was excluded from power because of the alliance of wealthy landholders and government officials, which dominated the council. Lowe was no democrat, for he did not support universal manhood suffrage. Rather, he believed in extending the franchise to immigrant workers, and thus reducing the political influence of the emancipists and their offspring. In the long run I suspect that Lowe's agenda was probably broader, because he also wanted to extend the vote as a means of breaking the monopoly of membership of the legislative

---

[50] *Sydney Morning Herald*, 23 October 1845.

[51] Ibid., 12 June 1849.

[52] Ibid., 23 October 1845, 18 June 1849.

[53] Ibid., 23 October 1845, 12 June 1849.

[54] Cochrane, 198. For an account of popular constitutionalism as an enduring English ideology see J. Vernon, *Politics and the People: a Study in English Political Culture, c. 1815–1867* (Cambridge: Cambridge University Press, 1993).

[55] *People's Advocate*, 10 February 1848.

council held by the squatters and political nominees. As things stood, he argued, the colonists were losing respect for the legislative council, for, in alliance with the governor, it was "trampling upon the principles of liberty itself."[56]

Between 1848 and 1850, Lowe fell out with and distanced himself from those colonial politicians bent on a more radical agenda, but in the end he acted in a way that unintentionally paved the way for the triumph of the democrats. When he returned to England in 1850 he successfully lobbied the House of Lords to amend the Australian colonies' Government Act to provide that the franchise qualification for occupiers of rental dwellings be lowered from £20 to £10, which was the English qualification. Once again his intention was to increase the electoral power of free immigrants. But in the colonial context the £10 was effectively a household suffrage, with the result that the act considerably strengthened the political authority of the colonial radicals. Depending on whether you were a radical or a conservative, this act led to an increase or diminution of liberty in NSW.[57] In any case, it was a significant step not just toward representative but also toward democratic government.

Politics was transformed in England between the 1820s and 1840s as well organized and successful extraparliamentary campaigns were conducted in favor of the abolition of slavery, parliamentary reform, Catholic Emancipation, and the repeal of the Corn Laws. However, it was Chartism that provided evidence of the extent to which workingmen, in particular, had become committed to the political reform process. The Charter was based on six points: universal suffrage; annual elections; the secret ballot; equal electoral districts; removal of property qualifications for parliamentary candidates; and the payment of members of Parliament. The strategy of the Chartist leaders was to mobilize large numbers of people via the organization of public meetings and parliamentary petitions. While Chartism was modern in its more thorough and carefully organized forms of mobilization, it also reflected ideological continuity, for the movement was a culmination of older traditions of democratic radicalism. Paine had dismissed the notion of an ancient democratic English Constitution and looked for the rights of liberty in natural law. But the Chartists believed in an older tradition of English radical thought, which argued that the Norman aristocracy and its heirs had subverted the Anglo-Saxon democratic constitution. They sought individual liberty through the restoration of the ancient constitution.[58]

Chartism impacted on the radical movement in New South Wales. Henry Parkes, who later served several terms as premier of New South Wales and

---

[56] Robert Lowe, *Speech on the Australian Colonies Bill... June 1850* (Sydney: W. and F. Ford, no date), 12–15.

[57] Cochrane, 162; J. B. Hirst, *The Strange Birth of Colonial Democracy: New South Wales, 1848–1884* (Sydney: Allen and Unwin, 1988), 25; Lowe, 12–15, 28.

[58] Gareth Stedman Jones, *Languages of Class: Studies in English Working Class History, 1832–1982* (Cambridge: Cambridge University Press, 1983); J. Vernon, *Politics and the People*, 298, 306, 315–328.

became a major proponent of federation, attended Chartist meetings in Birmingham before immigrating to Sydney in 1839. In the 1840s he campaigned for responsible government based on universal male suffrage and helped to organize protest movements against the renewal of transportation. In opposing the constitution drawn up by the conservatives in 1853, he revealed himself as belonging to the tradition of popular constitutionalism, for he argued that a constitution with a nominated upper house and which provided for electorates based on interest not population "...was a scheme in violation of the true principles of the British Constitution."[59] Edward Hawksley, who wrote for the Chartist press in England, immigrated to Sydney in 1838 and later became the editor of the *People's Advocate*. In the wake of the revolutions in Europe in 1848, the *Advocate* argued that the "...days of oppression..." were numbered. With the discovery of gold in NSW and Victoria in 1850, leading to the influx of even larger numbers of immigrants from Europe and North America, Hawksley became even more optimistic, predicting wrongly that the Charter's six points would become the basis of the NSW Constitution. In accord with English Chartist traditions, the paper also supported the right of the common people to become small-scale agriculturalists even if that meant dispossessing the squatters of their pastoral leases.[60]

However, not all the radical leaders were influenced predominantly by Chartism. John Dunmore Lang, an immigrant Scottish Presbyterian minister who emerged as the most articulate challenger to conservative hegemony, was inspired by Lockean philosophy, Christian belief, and a dash of popular constitutionalism. "Freedom," he argued, "is the law of nature and the ordinance of God." Almost as an afterthought, he suggested that the Magna Charta, in allowing political equality, universal suffrage, and popular election, had established the basic principles of "manly freedom." He was perhaps the most radical politician of his era, consistent in his commitment to republicanism and in his belief that separation from England was inevitable. "The people, the source of all legitimate power" was a creed from which Lang was never shaken.[61]

The Australian radicals copied not only Chartist ideology but its methods, too. Parkes was instrumental in organizing the Constitutional Association in 1848 with a governing council; an associated newspaper, the *People's Advocate*; a manifesto proclaiming commitment to "...the great immutable principles of universal liberty"; and a reform program including changes to the land laws, responsible government, and extension of the franchise. Its greatest triumph was the organization of the antitransportation campaign in 1849,

[59] David Blair (ed.), *Speeches on Various Occasions Connected to With the Public Affairs of New South Wales, 1848–1874*, by Henry Parkes (Melbourne: George Robertson, 1876), 1, 18, 26–7.

[60] *People's Advocate*, 2 December 1848; 12 March 1853; Andrew Messner, "Contesting Chartism From Afar: Edward Hawksley and the People's Advocate," *Journal of Australian Colonial History*, vol. 1, April, 1999, 62–94.

[61] John Dunmore Lang, *Freedom and Independence for the Golden Lands of Australia; the Rights of the Colonies and the Interests of Britain and the World* (London: Longman, Brown, Green and Longmans, 1852), 47, 54, 67; *People's Advocate*, 17 August 1850.

formed in response to the British's government's plan to resume sending convicts to NSW.[62] Parkes also set up a widespread support network to underpin Lang's successful campaign for election to the legislative council in 1851.[63] For the first time in Australian political history, too, women were mobilized for political purposes. Men like Parkes held mainstream Victorian views on the role of women, assigning them to be the moral guardians of the home while men moved in the public sphere of politics and commerce. Yet in 1851 women became active in the antitransportation movement, with 12,000 of them signing a petition opposing its renewal. In a sense this was consistent with their prescribed roles as moral guardians, for transportation was associated with corruption and depravity. Still, now they were exercising influence through the public rather than the private sphere. Their emerging interest in the wider political context and their public activism was also reflected in their more common attendance at meetings held to celebrate the electoral victories of liberal and radical politicians, and to protest the 1853 Constitution drawn up by the conservatives on the legislative council.[64] With the emergence of a culture of respectability in NSW in the 1840s, a culture largely but not exclusively promoted by a nascent middle class, women saw it as their duty to promote temperance, Sabbatarianism, and opposition to transportation as a way of identifying themselves as a class and expunging the "hated stain" of convictism. Those campaigns inevitably strayed into the public, political arena.[65]

The reasons the Australian Government Colonies Act (1850) attracted unanimous colonial disapprobation were neatly set out in a protest and remonstrance agreed on by the legislative council and forwarded to the Colonial Office in 1851.The protest reiterated that Parliament did not have the right to tax the people of the colony, and that land policy and revenue from land sales and customs duties as well as control of the civil list should be controlled by the colonial legislature as representing the people of NSW.[66]

Earl Grey, the secretary of the state for the colonies, was adamant that, despite the council's remonstrance, there would no concessions. But his successors, Sir John Pakington (1852) and the Duke of Newcastle (1852–54), were more sympathetic to the concerns included in the remonstrance and similar grievances expressed in a second protest letter drafted by Wentworth and adopted by the legislative council in 1852. Even the Colonial Office acknowledged that the situation in NSW had become anomalous, for the British had given a strong measure of constitutional independence to the Canadian Parliament in 1840 and subsequently conceded authority over the Crown lands

[62] Alan Martin, *Henry Parkes: a Biography* (Melbourne: Melbourne University Press, 1980), 51; Michael Roe. *The Quest for Authority in Eastern Australia*, 96.

[63] Terry Irving, *The Southern Tree of Liberty: The Democratic Movement in NSW Before 1856* (Sydney: Federation Press, 2006), 79.

[64] Cochrane, 249, 254, 279–80. 309, 358.

[65] Waterhouse, *Private Pleasures*, 98–101; Henry Reynolds, "'That Hated Stain': The Aftermath of Transportation in Tasmania," *Historical Studies*, vol. 14, October 1969, 19–31.

[66] Clark (ed.), vol. 2, 322–5.

(1847) and the civil list (1851). Moreover, the 1852 draft of a constitution for the Cape of Good Hope colony allowed for an elected bicameral legislature and local control of the civil list.[67] Herman Merivale, now permanent undersecretary at the Colonial Office, had not succeeded in changing Earl Grey's views, but his arguments, that granting representative government to the colonies resulted in fewer tensions between the center and the periphery, carried far more weight with his successors.[68] However, as Pakington acknowledged, the "...extraordinary discoveries of Gold which have lately taken place in the Australian colonies and which may be said to have imparted new and unforseen features to their political and social condition" were the critical developments determining the British government to grant control of customs, Crown lands, and the civil list to the colonies. There was a caveat attached to his concessions, albeit a welcome one, requiring the NSW legislative council to draft a Constitution that provided for a legislative assembly as well as a legislative council. Although Pakington specified that members of the council were to be nominated, Newcastle allowed the colonists to determine whether the councils in NSW and elsewhere should be elected or nominated.[69]

And so, in 1853, a legislative council committee, chaired by W. C. Wentworth, drafted the NSW Constitution, one that was designed to maintain the authority of the conservative pastoralists. Electoral boundaries for the legislative assembly were based on the 1851 Act while the Crown nominated members of the legislative council. To prevent changes that might challenge the conservative ascendancy, the document provided that electoral boundaries could only be altered by a two-thirds majority of the assembly, while the composition of the upper house could only be changed by a two-thirds majority of both houses.

Colonial radicals and liberals who objected to the proposals for a gerrymander and unelected legislative council denounced the enabling bill. Assuming liberty and democracy were inseparable, the *People's Advocate* described it as "...a bastard offspring of tyranny under the guise of liberty."[70] In the end the conservative triumph was short-lived, for the new colonial secretary, Lord John Russell, supported by Merivale, was troubled by the two-thirds clauses that were designed to entrench the conservative landowners in power. And so an additional clause was inserted allowing the colonial parliament to remove the two-thirds clauses by a majority vote.

Despite the gerrymander, by the end of the fifties a series of elections had swept the conservatives from power not only in NSW but elsewhere. The liberals and radicals came to dominate the membership of the lower houses and to use their majorities to enact a democratic and Chartist-influenced agenda. Beginning with South Australia in 1856, all colonies passed legislation

---

[67] Cochrane, 283, 296, 305.

[68] Ibid., 326; Herman Merivale, *Lectures on Colonisation and Colonies* (London: Oxford University Press, reprint edition, 1928), 623.

[69] Pakington to Fitzroy, 15 December 1852, in Clark (ed.), vol. 2, 325–9.

[70] *People's Advocate*, 13 August 1853, quoted in Cochrane, 356.

that provided for manhood suffrage, the secret ballot, an increased number of urban electorates, and triennial parliaments, while most also abolished property qualifications for elected officeholders.[71] Oddly, with the liberals and radicals in power in NSW, the conservatives realized that a nominated upper house was no longer a bastion of conservatism and some began to call for an elected legislative council.[72] In contrast, while an elected upper house remained on the liberal agenda, in practice pragmatic liberals, like Charles Cowper, several times premier in the fifties and early sixties, were content to maintain a nominated upper house, which they now controlled.[73] Ideological concerns had dominated the liberal and radical agendas in the fifties and early sixties, but now that they exercised power their focus switched to maintaining it, even to the extent of abandoning democratic principles.

In the 1860s, the colonies used their new control of Crown lands to pass selection acts, with the intention of turning the large pastoral runs into a multitude of small-scale family-owned agricultural farms. The passage of the selection acts suggested that the liberals and radicals, too, equated liberty and opportunity with the ownership of property. Unlike the squatters, however, they believed that even the "poor man" was entitled to abstract rights and material opportunity.[74] The selection acts were designed to achieve both principled and political ends, establishing a broad-based yeomanry and destroying the authority of the squatters. In response, the conservative landholders lost their faith in responsible government and nostalgically lamented the passing of the old blended council, which one of their leaders described as "the best legislative body that ever existed or will ever exist in this colony."[75]

CULMINATION: AN AUSTRALIAN CONSTITUTION

In the debates about the rights of the male colonists to the same liberties and rights of representation that Englishmen at home enjoyed there is one significant silence. The role and rights of Aborigines under the British and colonial constitutions were rarely discussed. The upper-class early settlers tended to see Aborigines in Rousseauean terms, as childlike creatures of nature who possessed more liberty than themselves. "Liberty has retired from amongst us," lamented Elizabeth Macarthur in 1807, "into the pathless wilds, amongst the poor native inhabitants, who certainly maintain their independence, and have hitherto resisted any infringement on their rights."[76] As far as the Westminster

---

[71] Paul Pickering, "A Wider Field in a New Country: Chartism in Colonial Australia," in M. Sawer (ed.), *Elections, Full, Free and Fair* (Sydney: Federation Press, 2001), 30–4.

[72] In Victoria the elected upper house, protected by high property qualifications for voting and membership, became a bastion of conservatism.

[73] Cochrane, 485.

[74] For a summary of the Selection Acts see Richard Waterhouse, *The Vision Splendid: A Social and Cultural History of Rural Australia* (Fremantle: Curtin University Books, 2005), 24–31.

[75] *Sydney Morning Herald*, 11 September 1862.

[76] Cited in Fitzgerald and Hearn, 77.

government was concerned, British law became the law of the Australian colonies at their founding and all residents, Aborigines included, were considered to be British subjects. Sometimes colonial officials expressed bewilderment and frustration at the persistent Aboriginal refusal to acculturate to English ways and their continued adherence to their own customs and laws. The subjection of Aborigines to English law remained a far from complete process even by the end of the nineteenth century.

What made it easier for politicians in the southern colonies to accept Aborigines as British subjects – and therefore no threat to European hegemony – was the colonists' belief that they were a dying race, most of whom had "...already disappeared from the face of the earth."[77] Precisely because Aborigines were considered to be disappearing and, in any case, because in the judgement of politicians and pastoralists they had failed to make proper use of the land by cultivating it, colonial governments showed no interest in negotiating formal land rights treaties with the indigenous peoples. Rather, policies instigated from the 1870s onward, which involved confining them to reserves and removing their children, further contributed to the marginalization and destruction of Aboriginal communities.[78] New Zealand delegates to a conference on federation in 1890 indicated that the tyranny of distance was one reason why their colony was unlikely to join an Australasian nation-state, but the "'native question'" was another. Australian politicians, a member of the New Zealand Parliament, Captain William Russell argued, had dealt with indigenous peoples "...in a much more summary manner than we have ventured to deal with ours in New Zealand...." To hand over indigenous affairs to a federal parliament dominated by Australians might once again produce "... the difficulties which precluded settlement for years in the North Island...."[79]

The late nineteenth century witnessed a rising tide of popular and "intellectual" racism in Australia, a racism underpinned by theories associated with social Darwinism. Mostly, this was aimed at the Chinese, Indians, and Pacific Islanders, but the assessment of Aborigines as "savages" who lacked the capacity to exercise an "intelligent vote" was used to exclude Aborigines from the vote under the Commonwealth Franchise Act of 1902. Ironically this was the same act that gave the vote to European women. As we shall see, by the 1890s most supporters of an Australian constitution embraced democracy, arguing that liberty, freedom, and democracy were inextricably linked. In terms of their own reasoning in 1902 they deprived indigenous Australians of their liberty.[80]

---

[77] Lang, 77.

[78] For a recent exemplary study of NSW see Anna Doukakis, *The Aboriginal People, Parliament and "Protection" in New South Wales 1856–1915* (Sydney: Federation Press, 2006).

[79] *Official Records of the Proceedings and Debates of the Australasian Federal Conference* (Melbourne: Government Printer, 1890), 126.

[80] Patricia Grimshaw, "A White Woman's Suffrage," in Helen Irving (ed.), *A Woman's Constitution: Gender and History in the Australian Commonwealth* (Sydney: Hale and Iremonger, 1996), 77–97; Pat Stretton and Christine Finnimore, "Black Fellow Citizens: Aborigines and the Commonwealth Franchise," *Australian Historical Studies*, vol. 25, October, 1993, 521–535.

The establishment of a national government in Australia came about in response to the development of a sense of shared interests and purpose among politicians and the wider populace alike. It was not a government born of war because there was little external or internal opposition to the federation movement. Indeed, from the 1840s the Colonial Office encouraged the establishment of a central authority in Australia with jurisdiction over customs, communication, and transport. Beginning in the 1860s, the colonies made their own tentative moves in this direction, culminating in the establishment of the Federal Council in 1883. Its consultative purpose and the refusal of the NSW government to participate restricted its influence. Federation was given impetus in the late 1880s by a growing awareness that the customs duties imposed by individual colonies was harming them all, and by the publication of a British War Office Report on the defense capabilities of the individual colonies, which concluded that they were effectively unable to defend themselves or each other.[81] But federation was not just spurred by a concern to provide a pragmatic response to economic and defense problems. By the eighties and nineties the numbers of native born far exceeded those colonists who were immigrants. Through such organizations as the Australian Natives' Association, those born in Australia articulated their identity as independent Australian Britons, which in turn prompted them to campaign for federation. Only as members of a nation did they believe that they could claim equal status with Britons at "Home."[82] The Victorian liberal politician, Alfred Deakin, neatly summarized the factors giving impetus to federalism when he described them as involving self- interest and sentiment. But his own commitment was shaped largely by a vision of nation. "We cannot forget...," he declared, "that in this country we are separated only by imaginary lines, and that we are a people one in blood, race, religion and aspirations."[83] And so, unlike the campaign for responsible government, which was spearheaded by immigrants, the federation movement was led by the native born.

The initial direction came from the colonial parliaments and their elected members. In a speech at Tenterfield, the veteran politician Henry Parkes, prompted in part by his ambition to be the nation's first prime minister, insisted that the time for federation had arrived, and called for the Federal Conference that was held subsequently in Melbourne in 1890.[84] The 1890 Conference consisted of thirteen delegates, all chosen by their respective legislatures.

---

[81] Neville Meaney, *The Search for Security in the Pacific, 1901–1914* (Sydney: Sydney University Press, 1976), 28.

[82] John Hirst, *The Sentimental Nation* (Melbourne: Oxford University Press, 2000), 29; Helen Irving, *To Constitute a Nation: a Cultural History of Australia's Constitution* (Melbourne: Cambridge University Press, 1999), 31; Bob Birrell, *Federation: the Secret Story* (Sydney: Duffy and Snelgrove, 2001), 144.

[83] *Official Records of the Proceedings and Debates of the Australasian Federal Conference* (1890), 77–78.

[84] Alfred Deakin, *"And Be One People": Alfred Deakin's Federal Story*, with an introduction by Stuart Macintyre (Melbourne University Press, 1996), 27.

Seven representatives from each of the Australian colonies and three from New Zealand, all of them nominated by their respective parliaments, met at the Federal Convention, held in Sydney in 1891. Such a constitution making process suited those conservatives who believed that each colonial parliament was sovereign and for whom confederation was the solution. They were suspicious, too, of "convention made constitutions," believing in "slow organic growth," presumably with the British Constitution in mind. At the bottom of all this lay a residual distrust of democracy, a fear in the words of the Queensland MLC (member of the Legislative Council), Andrew Thynne, of the "...tyrannic exercise of the power of temporary majorities."[85] While such anachronistic rhetoric fitted neatly within the Wentworth tradition, it was at odds with the aspirations of most politicians and the people at large.

The colonists' experiences with democratic government after 1856 meant that by 1890 they were more accustomed to it than during the period when the colonial constitutions were drafted. Replying to the conservatives who favored confederation, Parkes argued that the failure of confederation in the United States had then resulted in a constitution that was a more appropriate model if Australia wished to take an equal place in the family of nations.[86] Moreover, there was growing support for the direct election of convention delegates and for any proposed constitution to be ratified by referendums in each colony. Impetus was provided by two "people's conventions" held at Corowa in 1893 and Bathurst in 1896. At the instigation of John Quick, the Corowa Conference recommended direct elections, a procedure subsequently adopted by four of the six premiers. The convention that met in Adelaide, Melbourne, and Sydney in 1897–98 consisted of delegates elected by the people, and the constitution produced by that convention was subsequently ratified in referendums held in all colonies. The Bathurst Convention amended the 1891 draft to make it more democratic, specifically by providing for the direct election of senators, a proposal subsequently adopted by the official Constitutional Convention. And, finally, the widening popular participation in the movement was reflected in the campaign by influential women's movements, including the WCTU (Women's Christian Temperance Union) and suffragette organizations in promoting federation. In South Australia, where women fought for and won the vote in 1894, they voted for delegates to the 1897–98 Convention and in the referendum on the Constitution, while Catherine Helen Spence also stood unsuccessfully as a delegate. The defeat of suffrage bills in the NSW, Victorian, and Tasmanian upper houses hardened their determination to support federation and gain the vote at the national level, a result that they argued would

[85] *Official Records of the Proceedings and Debates of the Australasian Federal Conference* (1890), 69 (Thomas Playford), 134 (John Cockburn); *Official Records of the Debates of the Australasian Federal Convention*, vol. 1 (reprint edition, Sydney: Legal Books, 1986), 106 (Andrew Thynne).

[86] *Official Records of the Proceedings and Debates of the Australasian Federal Conference* (1890), 44; *Official Records of the Debates of the Australasian Federal Convention* (1891), 27.

surely force the states to also give them the franchise. Female suffrage was new, but the values and rationale behind the campaign to give women the vote was not, for at a time when the campaign for temperance, in particular, was reaching its apex, women argued that their superior moral sense justified their exercise of political influence. Perhaps it was the conservative case put by women that persuaded many male politicians to support their cause, many years before their counterparts in the United Kingdom and the United States were willing to accept female suffrage.[87]

In any case, most politicians embraced the notion that federation was a people's movement and that the constitution should be based on the notion of popular sovereignty. In the 1890s Australian politicians made the same journey that their American counterparts had made in the 1770s and 1780s, discovering both the virtues of representative democracy in a comprehensive form and the location of sovereignty in the people.[88] The 1891 draft specified the constitution as a contract between the states, for it began with the words "Whereas the Australian colonies...have agreed to..." In contrast, Deakin proposed that the constitution begin:

We the people of Australasia, in order to form a more perfect union, establish justice, ensure domestic tranquillity... and ensure the blessings of liberty to ourselves and our posterity to ordain and establish this Constitution.[89]

The words finally adopted were less verbose and did not include the term "liberty," but they did specify that it was the people of the various colonies who had agreed to "...one indissoluble Federal Commonwealth...." In recent years the High Court has specifically ruled that under the constitution sovereignty lies with the Australian people.[90]

Individual rights, liberties, and freedoms were hardly mentioned in the final draft of the Australian Constitution. Section 92 specified that trade within the commonwealth was to be free, while Section 116 prevented the federal government from making any law "...for prohibiting the free exercise of any religion...." When the debate on Section 117 took place at the 1898 Convention there were suggestions to model it on the Fourteenth Amendment to the United

---

[87] Helen Irving, "Fair Federalists and Founding Mothers," in Irving (ed.), *A Woman's Constitution*, 5.

[88] Gordon S. Wood, *The Creation of the American Republic, 1776–1787* (New York: Norton, 1972), 593–615. Politicians also considered that conventions had the pragmatic advantage of bypassing the colonial parliaments, some of which proved slow in taking measures to ensure federation. See G. H. Reid, "The Conference of the Premiers at Hobart," *Review of Reviews*, February 20, 1895, 149–53. The notion of popular sovereignty was probably also used as a rhetorical device to garner support for the federation movement. See Stuart Macintyre, "Corowa and the Voice of the People," in *The People's Conventions: Corowa (1893) and Bathurst (1896)*, *Papers on Parliament*, number 32, December, 1998. 1–12.

[89] Convention Debates (1891), 70.

[90] Mark McKenna, "A History for Our Time? The Idea of the People in Australian Democracy," *History Compass*, vol. 1, January–December, 2003, 3 (http://www.blackwell/.compass.com/subject/history).

States Constitution. Instead the section simply specified that a subject of the Queen resident in any State "...shall not be subject in any other State to any disability or discrimination which would not be equally applicable to him if he were the subject of the Queen resident in such other State."

There were three reasons why rights and liberties were defined in minimal and negative rather than in expansive and positive terms. First, the delegates to the conventions remained admirers and supporters of the English Constitution and English law. They believed their rights and freedoms were protected in common law and constitutional provision was unnecessary.[91] Second, the constitution makers did not want the constitution to provide a blanket provision of equality and liberty because they wished to ensure the legality of existing colonial-level legislation, which discriminated against Asians, Pacific Islanders, and Aborigines; and they also wanted the incoming federal parliament to possess the legal right to pass similar legislation. In opposing the suggestion that Section 117 mirror the Fourteenth Amendment, Henry Bourne Higgins asked rhetorically if the latter "...protects Chinamen, too I suppose, as well as negroes?"[92] In other words, these European Australian delegates were not willing to extend equal rights under the law to all residents. The 1901 Immigration Restriction Act, the first piece of legislation passed under the new commonwealth government, which allowed exclusion via a dictation test in any European language determined by the admitting customs officer, was squarely aimed at potential Asian and Pacific Island settlers.[93] As far as the convention delegates were concerned, liberty was an entitlement restricted to Australians of European descent. Third, many delegates believed that a system of responsible government, in which the ministers were members of Parliament, both houses were elected by popular vote, and constitutional amendments were determined by referenda, not only provided democracy but ensured liberty. Deakin insisted that a close relationship between the executive government and the people was the best guarantee of liberty.[94] In the 1850s, conservatives had equated democracy with tyranny, but, almost without exception, convention delegates now argued that the people could be trusted to ensure that only those committed to the preservation of liberty were elected to Parliament.

Precisely what forms of liberty did these men believe they were defending and entrenching? Although men like Deakin were fairly free in using the term, they were more reticent about defining exactly what the term comprehended. My suspicion is that most subscribed, in perhaps inchoate ways, to a definition of liberty first articulated in Europe in the early nineteenth century, most notably by Benjamin Constant. This notion was transmitted in roundabout and

---

[91] Irving, *To Constitute a Nation*, 162.

[92] *Convention Debates* (1898), 687, quoted in ibid.

[93] Gwenda Tavan, *The Long, Slow Death of White Australia* (Melbourne: Scribe, 2005), 7–8.

[94] *Official Records of the Debates of the Australasian Federal Convention* (Adelaide: Government Printer, 1897), 2–3; *Official Records of the Debates of the Australasian Federal Convention* (Melbourne: Government Printer, 1898), 2477; *Proceedings, People's Convention, Bathurst* (Sydney: William Andrews, 1897), 90–2.

piecemeal ways to Australia and was assimilated into the emerging democratic political ideology. Federationists believed that liberty was protected by a combination of common-law and democratic, representative government. Australians were free to express opinions, choose their own paths of economic opportunity, own and dispose of property, exercise freedom of movement and of religion, associate with other individuals of their choice, exercise some influence on the administration of government, and to be subject to the rule of law, not the arbitrary power of despots.[95]

The Australians drew on the United States Constitution for its federalism and English precedent for the principle of responsible government. Switzerland was the model for determining amendments through referenda.[96] In the 1850s Wentworth and other conservative anglophiles had constantly cited American examples as evidence of the dangers of democracy. But the debates in the conventions in the 1890s indicated not only that Australians had embraced democracy but also that the United States was now the exemplary model for democratic federalism. The initial draft of the constitution compiled by Sir Samuel Griffith in 1891 followed the American Constitution even more closely than the final version, providing for senators to be chosen by the state legislatures, while cabinet ministers were not required to be members of Parliament. By 1898, most delegates favored the direct election of senators and a system of responsible government that required ministers to be elected members of Parliament, but the American Constitution remained exemplary. At Bathurst in 1896 the United States consul general was invited to deliver a speech to the delegates on "'Progressive Liberty'"; and most members of this and other conventions were undoubtedly in agreement with Parkes' 1890 assessment that Americans lived under a Constitution "'...in such comparative happiness and prosperity, and in such comparative glory.'"[97] I think, this admiration for the United States' Constitution must be seen in a wider context, for in the late nineteenth century Australians increasingly saw American society, institutions and technology as providing examples that would allow Australia to become "the future America." The Americans had demonstrated that a public education system and separation of church and state promoted liberty, opportunity, and democracy; that with the application of technology, areas hitherto regarded as uninhabitable could be settled and farmed; that modern mining machinery could extract precious metals quickly and cheaply; and that booming, almost instantly created cities could be efficiently provided with facilities that made life comfortable and convenient. Many Australians believed that the means by which Americans had conquered a continent provided the example for Australia's future. "We in Australia," admitted Melbourne's *Age* in 1908, "have

---

[95] B. Fontana (ed.), *Benjamin Constant, Political Writings*, 309ff., cited in Alastair Davidson, *From Subject to Citizen: Australian Citizenship in the Twentieth Century* (Cambridge: Cambridge University Press, 1997), 20–21.

[96] Hirst, *Sentimental Nation*, 255.

[97] Constitutional Conference (1890), 45.

more constantly turned our eyes to America for light and guidance than we have to the mother country."[98]

The entrenchment of ideas of liberty and the establishment of institutions of responsible and democratic government involved complex processes of cultural transmission, resulting in the intermingling of imported ideas and institutions from pre-industrial and modern Britain, other European countries, and the United States. Perhaps it was the recognition that these were imported (even if they were reworked in the antipodean context into a unique set of institutions and political cultures) that subsequently led Australians to downplay the political achievements involved in establishing representative and democratic institutions. In an age in which poets and politicians stressed that nations were born and manhood tested on the battlefield, Australians were also less likely to believe that the proclamation of the Australian Constitution on January 1, 1901 marked a heroic moment and signaled the arrival of nationhood. In the context of the times, the story of the Anzac landing at Gallipoli on April 25, 1915 was quickly seized upon as a more appropriate foundation myth, an event that proved the mettle of the country and the bravery of its soldiers. Unlike America's Founding Fathers, the architects of the Australian Constitution were soon forgotten and Australians took for granted that the establishment of representative and democratic institutions was secured without much struggle.

In 1794 a Church of England clergyman wrote back to a fellow minister in England contradicting the mostly negative accounts of NSW that were regularly reported home. "The soil is capital, the climate delicious. I will take it upon me," he added, " to say that it will soon be the region of plenty, and want only virtue and liberty to be another America.... ."[99] A hundred years later many Australians believed that they were on the verge of fulfilling this prediction, although the facts that the nation's foreign policy was still conducted from Westminster and the British government still insisted on the right of appeal from Australian courts to the Privy Council were evidence that full independence and nationhood did not come with federation. The fact that Parliament did not believe it was necessary to legislate for an Australian flag and an Australian anthem reflected a continuing commitment to an Anglo-Australian identity. In the 1930s the nation assumed the right to conduct its own external relations, and several decades later (1986) the federal Parliament legislated to eliminate appeals to the Privy Council. The adoption of *Advance Australia Fair* as the national anthem in 1984 was a sign that most Australians now accepted that they possessed a culture and identity of their own. Complete national freedom, however, may only come when the British monarch ceases to be the Australian Head of State and, as in the 1890s, Australia again follows the American constitutional path, this time to republicanism.

---

[98] Quoted in Noel McLachlan " 'The Future America'; Some Bicentennial Reflections," *Historical Studies*, vol. 17, April, 1977, 382–3.

[99] HRNSW, vol. II, 870, Reverend Thomas Fyshe Palmer to Reverend Jeremiah Joyce, 15 December 1794, 870.

9

How Much Did Institutions Matter?

Cloning Britain in New Zealand

James Belich

New Zealand is a long thin country in the South Pacific. It has no neighbors –
Australia is 1,200 miles away. New Zealand is small relative to Australia, but it is
larger than Britain and stretches for 1,200 miles through a variety of environments, ranging from subtropical to sub-Antarctic. In human terms it is perhaps
the youngest country in the world; the first settlement, by Polynesians, appears to
date back less than 1,000 years and European settlement less than 200. In these
blinks of history's eye New Zealand has created two new peoples, the Polynesian
Maori and the European "Pakeha." These characteristics of small size, isolation,
and youth make New Zealand historically translucent, a natural laboratory for
the study of settler societies in general and British-derived ones in particular.

According to its mid-twentieth-century historical mythology, New Zealand
developed along three steady and inexorable trajectories after it was acquired
by Britain in 1840. The indigenous Maori were transformed from independent
warriors to peaceful subjects; New Zealand nature was transformed from
unproductive wilderness to very productive and surprisingly highly urbanized
civilization; and white settlers were transformed from Britons into New
Zealanders. All these changes did eventually take place; the mythical element
lies in the notions of steadiness and inexorability. Early settler mass acquisitions
of land, to the 1860s, were restricted mainly to the South Island. Most Maori
lived in the North Island, and here they remained largely independent until
about 1880. Their last sanctuary was conquered only in 1916, after a gun battle
in which ten people were killed and wounded.[1] "Steady" is just about the last
adjective one should apply to the conversion of New Zealand's landscape from
forest to pasture, or to the general growth of the New Zealand economy. On the
contrary, growth took place in two great bursts, from about 1850 to 1866 and
from 1872 to 1886. New Zealand's settler population increased eightfold in the
first period and more than doubled in the second. In all, the white population

---

[1] James Belich, *The New Zealand Wars and the Victorian Interpretation of Racial Conflict*,
Penguin, Auckland, 1988 (original 1986), 309.

rocketed from about 1,000 in 1840 to half a million in forty-six years, a rate of growth dwarfing that of all subsequent periods. As for the steady transformation of Britons into New Zealanders, there were in fact ups and downs. In some ways, New Zealand's identification with Britain actually strengthened between the 1880s and the 1950s. New Zealand was in some respects *more* independent of Britain in 1880 than in 1920.

New Zealand's great booms (1850s–1880s) are usually attributed by historians to the export of wool and gold. In fact, the first boom began before significant exports of either and always extended to regions that had neither. Wool and gold helped at some times in some places, but the economy's main game was growth itself: the encouragement, organization, support, and supply of immigration; the building of towns, farms, and a transport infrastructure; the stocking of new farms; the provision of food and feed, wood, shipping, and work animals; and the public and private borrowing of £71 million pounds from Britain to finance all this. When a socio-economy was doubling in a decade, you did not need export markets. It was these booms, at least as much as hard-fought and narrow military defeat in war, that swamped and marginalized Maori, first in the South Island, by the 1860s, and then in the North Island by the 1880s. Maori were a match for normal European colonization, cooperating and conflicting with it on the basis of rough parity in the 1840s. It was *explosive* colonization that proved too much for them.

Too late to help the Maori, the settler booms ended in busts, relatively mild in 1867–70 but devastating in the 1880s. Even the 1880s bust was not necessarily a technical depression, in which wages fall further than prices and the economy actually shrinks. But it was a huge, sudden, and permanent downward shift in the rate of growth, a change in history's speed. From this nadir, the settler socio-economy was rescued by new kinds of exports it could not and did not predict: the mass shipment of refrigerated sheep-meat, cheese, and butter to Britain. By the 1930s, it was providing half of Britain's imports of these products, carried in 127 great refrigerated ships, each running the 12,000 miles between Britain and New Zealand several times a year – a ferry service so massive, cheap, and regular that it amounted to a virtual bridge. This re-integration of Britain and New Zealand was cultural as well as economic, and I have somewhat controversially described it as "re-colonization."[2] "Export rescue" is a more neutral alternative. Re-colonization was essentially a counterintuitive re-integration of colony and metropolis. It was based on the mass export of staples but had a crucial cultural dimension, whereby "re-colonized" New Zealanders saw themselves as Britons as late as the 1960s. It is important to note that there was little that was supine or cringing about white New Zealand's identification with Britain. New Zealanders saw themselves as co-owners of the British empire, not subjects of it, and denizens of part of a fragmented metropolis rather than a periphery. New Zealanders were

---

[2] For a critique of the concept see J. G. A. Pocock, *The Discovery of Islands. Essays in British History*, Cambridge University Press, New York, 2005, 194.

Britons, but better Britons; New Zealand was Britain without the mistakes. New Zealand's relationship with London was more like that of Nebraska and New York than that of Nigeria and London.

In short, the New Zealand pattern was a period of slow, incremental settlement (normal colonization), followed by great booms that swamped hitherto resilient indigenes (explosive colonization), followed by disastrous busts, followed in turn by re-colonization or export rescue. It would be a coup for New Zealand exceptionalism, and no doubt a relief to non-New Zealanders, if this pattern was unique. It was not. On the contrary, it was stock standard throughout the Anglophone settler societies of the nineteenth century, western American as well as British, and it represented a sharp upward shift from the pace of settlement in the eighteenth century. From Adam Smith, Benjamin Franklin, and Thomas Malthus to many distinguished historians in the present, commentators have noted with astonishment the rapid growth of Anglophone settler populations and economies in North America in the eighteenth century. They did grow much faster than in old Europe, doubling in twenty-five years. Yet they grew much more slowly than in the nineteenth century. During booms, nineteenth-century settler socio-economies typically at least doubled in a single decade, very often from a substantial base. All Australian colonies, most British North American ones – and most western American states – experienced this remarkable decennial doubling at least once. Demographic growth is not necessarily economic growth, and extensive economic growth is not necessarily intensive development, where economies become more complex, specialized, and urbanized. But it was all three in these exploding Anglophone settler societies. Busts were frequent, like those of 1842, 1867, and 1891 in Australia and those of 1819, 1837, 1857, 1873, and 1893 in the United States. Export rescue usually followed, tightening the links between the settler society and its metropolis, whether New York or London. Busts joined booms in building settler economies. Farms and businesses went broke in droves and were picked up for a song by surviving neighbors. In this respect, collective futures were built on layers of individual fiscal corpses, more like coral insects than rational *homo economicus*.

This chapter sets out to assess the contribution of political and legal institutions to the rollicking growth of nineteenth-century Anglophone settler societies in general, and New Zealand in particular. Let me make it plain from the outset that I am wary of institutional determinism – defining determinism as the promotion of one of several major historical forces to a master variable. In extreme forms it can stretch beyond the evidence and achieve liftoff from history to mystery. Yet I am also wary of over-reacting by reflexively downplaying the role of institutions. Some English institutional practices, such as secure and transferable property rights, can be shown to be growth-enhancing, even boom-triggering, in settler contexts. Secure property rights enabled settlers to borrow on their security, and transferability fueled speculative markets. Borrowing and speculation were core features of settlement booms. It is plausible that, by the seventeenth century, the English had developed a suite of institutions that happened to be peculiarly growth-prone in a context of globalizing capitalism, and that these were successfully transferred to their settler colonies. Something must explain the fact that the Anglophones leapfrogged their rivals, Spanish, Portuguese, and Russian, as a reproducer of peoples. Between 1790 and 1930 the number of Spanish-speakers grew about threefold and the number of English-speakers tenfold, and the economic discrepancy was even greater. In terms of the growth of settler societies, there *was* an Anglophone divergence, and it may be that peculiar institutions were at the bottom of it.

I focus on two trios of institutions, one British and one "neo-British" – my term for British-derived settler societies. One key British institution was representative government, which extended consent and allowed for the cooption of newly powerful groups even when it was far from democratic. This form of government tended to be transferred to nineteenth- century neo-Britains in three steps. The first was unelected representation, in which a few appointed members of a settler elite joined officials on a governor's council. Nominated upper houses of colonial parliaments descended from this, and were thought to match the House of Lords. The second stage was representative government, in which an elected assembly controlling local taxation sparred with an appointed executive. The third was responsible government or full self-government, in which the executive was either elected, as in American states, or drawn from the assembly and responsible to it, as in British colonies from 1848. Our second British institution was the common law, which derived not only from statutes, as with continental European civil law, but also from custom and precedent, and which featured trial by a jury of peers. Sourcing one's law horizontally as well as vertically may not have delivered better justice, but it may have made the law more adaptable, more beneficial to social cohesion, and more supportive of a freeholder's sense of full citizenship. The average English jury verdict might be no fairer than that of French or Chinese magistrates, but it did come from one's peers as well as one's rulers. The third British institution was the "public sphere," a public space outside the state in which the state could be criticized and reform advocated. An active free press can be taken as our indicator of this.

Neo-Britains also featured another trio of institutions, or consistent political habits embodied in law. The British derivation of these institutions is not obvious, and they did not flower in old Britain until the late nineteenth century at the earliest, so they are better described as "neo-British" than British. One was a broad franchise, tending to near universal suffrage of adult white males. This derived partly from the English tradition of enfranchising freeholders, dating from about 1430, but also from the greater availability of freeholds in new lands and from the belief that a wide franchise was more attractive to potential immigrants. The second neo-British institution was the interventionist state. In the nineteenth century, British colonial governments tended to be far more economically interventionist than the London model. This was arguably also true of the United States, especially when the interventions of state and municipal governments are added to federal. For example, in the British settlement colonies and the United States, canals and railways were typically built with state help in some form, which was not the case in old Britain. The third neo-British institution was "cloning": the tendency to expand settlement by the creation of small new polities rather than the extension of old large ones, as was the Spanish practice. Around 1775, Spain ruled its 10 million or so American subjects through two or three giant vice-regalities, while Britain ruled its 3 million or so subjects through no less than thirty separate colonies. Again, cloning was not an old British practice – there, the trajectory was toward greater centralization, with the incorporation of Wales, Scotland, and Ireland between 1536 and 1800. Not all of these six institutions can reasonably be called "liberties" – the interventionist state is the most obvious exception – and only half were "English." But, as a package, these institutions were important in the rapid growth of Anglophone settler societies, especially in the nineteenth century.

Cloning was among the most marked yet least studied of neo-British institutional peculiarities, and it warrants a little pre-history. Initially, the formation of small separate settlements was standard practice for the great European settling societies – Iberian, British, and Russian. Governments short of cash licensed private individuals or groups to plant settlements, as with the contract conquistadores Cortes and Pizzaro, the Donatory Captains of Brazil, the Stroganov merchant clan in Siberia, and the Virginia Company. Iberian and Russian monarchs then re-asserted control to a greater extent than did British monarchs. The resulting proliferation of British colonies was a contingent development, not a transfer of long-standing British tradition. Cloning could produce political units too small for viability, but in some respects it was intrinsically growth-friendly in settler contexts. Old settlements were reluctant to use their revenues or borrowings to develop new frontiers. If the frontiers split off, they could tax and borrow for their own development. Migrants and money were attracted by the "boosting" or promotion of potential destinations, through publications, publicity, and letters back home, and cloning gave new frontiers a separate brand to boost.

Representative government and the common law may also have stimulated growth. Other settler societies had elements of representative self-government before 1800, but it does seem fair to say that the Anglophones had more of it. Colonial assemblies date from 1619, and were pretty much standard practice for settler colonies by 1689 – a period during which the power of the English Parliament also increased massively. Assemblies represented mainly elites, but they did broaden consent, support local interests, and allow for the cooption of newly powerful groups through extensions of the franchise. One expert has recently argued that most Old Britons did not believe that English common law was automatically or totally transferred to settler colonies, but by the eighteenth century settlers themselves believed that it was, and by the nineteenth century the imperial authorities accepted this.[3] The law, of course, protected property rights, which could then be used as security for debt, and encouraged

---

[3] Daniel J. Hulsebosch, "The ancient constitution and the expanding empire: Sir Edward Coke's British jurisprudence," *Law and History Review*, 21, no. 3, Fall 2003. Also see P. G. McHugh, "The common-law status of colonies and Aboriginal 'rights'; how lawyers and historians treat the past," *Saskatchewan Law Review*, 61, no. 2, 1998, 393–429.

the repayment of debts, which made for willing lenders. Whether English common law was uniquely good at protecting property rights is another matter – European civil law and Chinese law were good at this, too. But the English common law probably was different in another respect – it was thought to derive from the community as well as the authorities, as symbolized by its use of juries. As Jack Greene has argued, this augmented settler community, consent and cohesion, or social and cultural capital.[4] Furthermore, familiar law encouraged metropolitan investment in, and migration to, colonies. French law would have done just as well in this respect if the money and migrants had been French, but they were not.

One problem with institutional explanations for the Anglo divergence in settler growth was that the divergence was primarily a nineteenth-century phenomenon. The opposite assumption is still common: "Clearly, then," writes Anthony McFarlane, "the colonies of English North America showed far greater vitality in the 17th and 18th centuries than did those of the other European nations."[5] But it is increasingly contested. Recently, two eminent American economic historians, Kenneth Sokoloff and Stanley Engerman, have attempted a comparison of gross domestic product per capita in Anglo America and Latin America in 1700 and 1800. Given the sparse and uneven nature of the statistics, this is a heroically speculative enterprise, but it may be better than mere inherited assumption. It suggests that, in 1800, the United States was well ahead of Brazil, Chile, and Mexico, but that Cuba and Argentina were a little ahead of it. Packaging institutions under the term "national heritage," Sokoloff and Engerman conclude that:

The relationship between national heritage and economic performance is weaker than popularly thought. During the colonial period, the economies with the highest per capita incomes were those in the Caribbean, and it made little difference whether they were of Spanish, British, or French origin .... It was not until industrialization got under way in North America over the nineteenth century that the major divergence between the United States and Canada and the rest of the hemisphere opened up.[6]

The number of Spanish settlers and English settlers, excluding subject peoples, appears to have been roughly equal in 1780, at around 2.5 million, with Spanish America well ahead in such things as the size of cities and the number of universities. In size, at least, the cities of Spanish America dwarfed those of Anglo America before 1800. In 1790, the three biggest cities in *North* America were Havana in Cuba, Puebla in Mexico, and Mexico City. At

---

[4] Jack P. Greene, "Social and cultural capital in colonial British America: A case study," *Journal of Interdisciplinary History*, 29, no. 3, 1999, 491–509.

[5] Anthony McFarlane, *The British in the Americas, 1480–1815*, Longman, New York, 1994, 154.

[6] Kenneth L. Sokoloff and Stanley L. Engerman, "History lessons: Institutions, factor endowments, and paths of development in the New World," *Journal of Economic Perspectives*, 14, 2000, 217–232.

105,000 people, half of them European, Mexico City was three times the size of New York.[7] In 1701, Spanish America had nineteen universities, compared to British America's three.[8] We could debate this, and might conceivably conclude that the Anglos did have an edge in dynamism, but until 1780 it was quite modest. If Anglophone institutions were intrinsically growth prone, why did they take so long to have much effect?

One possible and partial explanation is that the peculiar Anglophone institutions experienced a Second Coming, or second evolution, after American independence in 1783. Of the thirteen American colonies, seven had claims to potentially rich lands in the west. Extension west of, say, a "Greater Virginia," rather than the creation of new and politically equal states, was a real possibility. "There was potential for an empire of Virginia."[9] But the Northwest Ordinance of 1787 famously ensured that the template of American expansion was to be cloning rather than extension.[10] Some Founding Fathers were motivated by convictions that new settlements should be constitutionally equal to the old, to avoid fresh rebellions, and that republics should be small. The resentment of those states without western lands, and the desire to use the sales of western lands to defray the costs of the war of independence, were also factors. The ordinance ordained that new settlements would achieve self-government in three stages: initial territorial status involving separation and direct rule by federal appointees; full territorial status with an elected assembly sharing power with appointees; and full elected self-government in the form of statehood. This template was in fact very similar to that which developed in Britain's remaining settler colonies after 1783. Canada and Nova Scotia were split into five provinces by 1791; Greater New South Wales had become seven colonies by 1859. Most of these neo-Britains went through stages of direct rule, mixed appointed and elected government, and full elected self-government. Philip Buckner has shown that substantive self-government in British North America did not have to wait for Lord Durham and his report of 1839.[11]

The structural homology between American and British "wests" is unlikely to have been coincidence, and was partly the fruit of an Anglo-American rivalry for settlers. To attract and keep Loyalists, late Loyalists, other Americans, and

[7] H. S. Keline, "The demographic structure of Mexico City in 1811," *Journal of Urban History*, 23, no. 1, 1996. Also see J. C. Sola-Corbacho, "Urban economies in the Spanish World: The cases of Madrid and Mexico City at the end of the eighteenth century," *Journal of Urban History*, 27, no. 5, 2001, 604–32.

[8] J. H. Elliott, *Empires of the Atlantic World, Britain and Spain in America, 1492–1830*, Yale University Press, New Haven, CT, 2006, 245.

[9] John C. Weavers, *The Great Land Rush and the Making of the Modern World, 1650–1900*, McGill-Queens University Press, London, 2003, 96.

[10] Peter S. Onuf, *Statehood and Union. A History of the Northwest Ordinance*, Indiana University Press, Bloomington, 1987.

[11] Phillip A. Buckner, *The Transition to Responsible Government: British Policy in British North America, 1815–1850*, Greenwood Press, Westport, CT, 1985.

new migrants to Canada against the competing attractions of the United States, Britain had to offer comparable freedoms. "Governor Haldimand was shocked when the Associated Loyalists insisted upon 'a form of government as nearly similar as possible to that which they Enjoyed in the Province of New York.'"[12] But he and other British officials soon overcame their surprise. In 1796, one official remarked that "good policy . . . requires that we should leave as little for them [the Canadian settlers] to gain by separation [independence] as possible."[13] "This theme," writes a Canadian historian, "with almost innumerable variations, would sound through the history of Upper Canada until it received its fullest orchestration at the hands of Lord Durham."[14] After American independence, writes another, "successive [imperial] governments accepted that Imperial rule must bear lightly on the colonials" and conceded "a very considerable amount of self-government."[15]

British competition with America was not just a matter of shared borders, but of the well-known tendency of British and Irish emigrants to prefer the United States as a destination, at least until the 1880s. This was much-lamented by many Britons, and quick cloning, liberal constitutions, and wide franchises were seen as ways of limiting the losses. Elected self-government remained problematic in the Australian penal colonies until the 1840s but was explicitly anticipated for free colonies. A British act of Parliament in 1834 – five years before the Durham Report – envisaged early self-government for South Australia.[16] The bidding war for settlers between the American West and the British colonies, I suggest, was a major stimulus to the proliferation of cloning and its institutional allies. By 1840, most imperial politicians and officials – though not necessarily colonial governors – were predisposed toward the transfer of cloning and parliamentary self-government at least to nonconvict settler societies, and this was the situation that New Zealand inherited.

New Zealand came under British rule in 1840. Historians differ on whether the key event was a proclamation by the governor of New South Wales extending his jurisdiction to New Zealand (January 14, 1840) or an agreement with some Maori chiefs on February 6, 1840, known as the Treaty of Waitangi. One ramshackle European settlement, Kororareka, already existed in northern New Zealand, and it was joined in the north in 1841 by Auckland, founded by the first governor, William Hobson, as his capital. In central New Zealand, three settlements (Wellington, Nelson, and New Plymouth) were established

[12] Norman Knowles, *Inventing the Loyalists: The Ontario Loyalist Tradition and the Creation of Usable Pasts*, University of Toronto Press, Buffalo, 1997, 18.

[13] Quoted in Helen I. Cowan, *British Emigration to British North America: The First Hundred Years*, rev. ed., University of Toronto Press, Toronto, 1961, 11.

[14] Gerald M. Craig, *Upper Canada: The Formative Years, 1784–1841*, Oxford University Press, London, 1963, 12.

[15] Phillip A. Buckner, *The Transition to Responsible Government: British Policy in British North America, 1815–1850*, Greenwood Press, Westport, CT, 1985, 8.

[16] W. R. Prest et al., eds., *The Wakefield Companion to South Australian History*, Wakefield Press, Kent Town, South Australia, 2001, 503.

between 1840 and 1842 by the Wakefieldian New Zealand Company. Two further settlements, Otago and Canterbury, were founded in the south, in 1848 and 1850, respectively, by affiliates of the company. Until 1853, New Zealand was governed as a Crown colony by an imperial governor assisted by small appointive executive and legislative councils. Several newspapers were established in the early 1840s, but many were short-lived and their freedom was initially contested by the local governors. By 1844, however, the governors accepted the freedom of the press and it was soon performing its public sphere role as "the major public arena in which ... conflict between authorities and settlers was staged."[17] The first purely European law in New Zealand pre-dated British rule and was somewhat informal. In the pre-annexation settlement of Kororareka an association of settlers acted as police, judge, and jury, and subjected one man to the well-known common-law punishment of tarring and feathering – for the crime of debt collecting. Despite this, and despite an early dalliance with the laws of convict New South Wales, it was soon clear that free settler New Zealand was to be an abode of the common law. A raft of ordinances of 1840–1842 made this explicit. Jury service, for example, became a formal right and duty for every white male freeholder between the ages of twenty-one and sixty in 1841, and the first Supreme Court opened for business in January 1842. Only nine people were executed between 1840 and 1853, but 100 were transported to Van Diemen's Land for terms ranging from seven years to life.[18]

The imposition of British law on the Maori was a more complicated matter. There were some intriguing attempts at syncretic legal systems, beginning even before New Zealand became British. In 1835, a mixed Maori and European jury found a missionary guilty of sexual intercourse with "two native females, one of whom was baptized." His punishment, if any, is not recorded, but another jury in 1838 found two Maori guilty of murdering a European and asked local chiefs to execute them both. They obligingly killed one but spared the other on account of his youth.[19] After 1840, the government initially recognized that English law was not yet appropriate for Maori districts, and a "Native Exemption Ordinance" remained in place until 1846. But governors and settlers alike were eager to apply the law to Maori – an indication of their conviction that this would hasten economic progress and help part the Maori from their land.

From 1846, resident magistrates in Maori districts were "assisted" by salaried Maori "assessors," usually local chiefs. The number eventually reached 200, but these were concentrated among tribes friendly toward the government and usually allowed Maori customary law to take precedence over English law

[17] Patrick Day, *The Making of the New Zealand Press: A Study of the Organizational and Political Concerns of New Zealand Newspaper Controllers, 1840–1880*, Victoria University Press, Wellington, 1990, 34 and passim.
[18] John Pratt, *Punishment in a Perfect Society: The New Zealand Penal System 1840–1939*, Victoria University Press, Wellington, 1992, Ch. 3.
[19] Richard Hill, *The History of New Zealand Policing*, Volume One: *Policing the Colonial Frontier*, Government Printer, Wellington, 1986, Part One, 73, 84.

anyway. Under one scheme, from 1858, some Maori tribal assemblies or *run-anga* were acknowledged to have some local governmental and legal authority in their districts, theoretically under the supervision of a European civil commissioner, to whom European resident magistrates were also subordinate.[20] Also in 1858, the government published a pamphlet in the Maori language explaining English law. "Whether the Law Be Human or Divine, It Ought to Have the Same Fountain, that is GOD."[21] Among the most interesting developments in Maori-European jurisprudence was a thirty-three–article code of laws promulgated in 1864 by the great Maori nationalist organization, the King Movement, which emerged in the central North Island in the 1850s and became the backbone of Maori military resistance in the 1860s.

It forbade murder, feuding, and some other customary practices, just as British law would have liked. But it was rather un-British in that almost half its articles dealt with sexual conduct and licensed sex between unmarried women and men, and it decried but specified no punishment for sex between unmarried men. "If an unmarried man sins with another unmarried man they must cling to the faith and the provision of the Law."[22]

But, broadly speaking, the common law did not apply to most Maori until the 1880s, and alien regulations such as taxes were honored mainly in the breach until the 1890s. In 1858, the Maori rate per capita of assault and drunkenness convictions in European courts ran at 4.2 percent and 2.7 percent, respectively, of the settler rate.[23] "English law has always prevailed in the English settlements," wrote Governor Thomas Gore Browne in 1860, "but remains a dead letter beyond them."[24] As late as 1869, an Auckland journal waxed sarcastic about Maori immunity to the law:

> I would I were a Maori
> To be above the law;
> To row, and fight, and yell, and shout,
> and give the policeman jaw! ...
> Then I would I were a Maori
> To do whate'er I choose
> Without the dread of magistrates
> Or those detested "blues."[25]

Maori engagement with English law intensified from 1865, when a Native Land Court of European judges began work. Its purpose was to individualize and document Maori land title to facilitate purchase by Europeans. While

---

[20] Ibid, Part Two, Ch 10. Also see Alan Ward, *A Show of Justice: Racial "Amalgamation" in Nineteenth Century New Zealand*, Auckland University Press, Auckland, 1973.

[21] Alex Frame, *Salmond. Southern Jurist*, Victoria University Press, Wellington, 1995, 64.

[22] James Belich, *Making Peoples. A History of the New Zealanders from Polynesian Settlement to the End of the 19th Century*, Allen Lane, London, 225.

[23] Calculated from statistics kindly provided by Miles Fairburn.

[24] Quoted in Belich, *The New Zealand Wars*, 78.

[25] Quoted in Belich, *Making Peoples*, 224.

notorious as a subtle instrument of nonviolent colonization, it was mainly effective in areas in which Maori had already been militarily conquered or demographically swamped. The notion that Maori were conquered by courts, shared by legal determinists and some Maori radicals, is largely false.

There were at least three important qualifications to the picture of a tragic but not untypical European colonization of indigenes. First, the New Zealand version was relatively slow. Maori political, legal, and economic independence was ground down largely by 1890 and entirely by 1916 – half to three-quarters of a century after the events of 1840 made Maori nominal British subjects. The slow pace of subjugation permitted some survival of social and cultural autonomy, which was important to the late twentieth-century Maori revival. Second, partly because New Zealand happened to be acquired at Imperial Britain's most humanitarian moment, there was at least a "show of justice."[26] Maori consent was initially sought, and Maori land was generally purchased by the Crown, though often at derisory prices and from the wrong people, not simply annexed by fiat as "waste land" or "terra nullius." Third, especially after the withdrawal of imperial troops from active operations in 1866, Maori allies, known as *kupapa*, were crucial to the eventual colonist victory and initially shared the spoils. These included four Maori seats in the lower house of Parliament, allocated in 1867 and surviving to this day.

Across the Tasman in Van Diemen's Land, the 1820s had witnessed cloning (separation from New South Wales in 1825), a modest element of unelected representation, and the application of the common law to free settlers, as well as a flurry of newspaper founding. This demonstrated that the colony was not solely penal, stimulated an upturn in free immigration and investment, and so helped trigger the southern hemisphere's first settlement boom, which began in Van Diemen's Land in about 1828, extended to New South Wales in about 1830, and lasted until 1842.[27] But the same set of institutional developments in New Zealand in the 1840s, including separation from New South Wales in 1841, failed dismally to trigger a boom, and the eastern shore of the Tasman world languished in recession until 1848 – the settler population was static in 1842–4 and actually declined in 1845–6.[28] From that year, however, a fresh surge of institutional transfer did correspond with the beginning of a boom.

Agitation for self-government began in New Zealand as early as 1840, and was soon prominent in the press. It was a fundamental part of the New Zealand Company's plans. The governors resisted it, partly because it threatened their own power but also because it seemed premature in an embryo colony and risked clashes between settlers and Maori. But even the governors sought to

[26] Ward, *A Show of Justice*.
[27] R. M. Hartwell, *The Economic Development of Van Diemen's Land 1820–1850*, Melbourne University Press, 1954; Lloyd Robson, *A History of Tasmania. Volume I: Van Diemen's Land from the Earliest Times to 1855*, Oxford University Press, Melbourne, 1983; W. A. Townsley, *Tasmania. From Colony to Statehood, 1803–1945*, St. David's Park, Hobart, 1991.
[28] M. F. Lloyd Prichard, *An Economic History of New Zealand to 1939*, Collins, Auckland, 1970, 36.

postpone, not prevent, self-government, and as far as London was concerned the settlers were pushing an open door. The permanent head of the Colonial Office, "Mr. Over-Secretary" James Stephen, was from the outset "anything but hostile to the pleas from New Zealand for some measure of self-government."[29] In 1846, Earl Grey and William Gladstone passed legislation establishing self-government in the six-year-old colony – surely a remarkably precocious autonomy. But they were persuaded by New Zealand Governor George Grey to suspend implementation for five years. The settlers resented this delay and were not placated by Governor Grey's offers of unelected representation on his councils, or his interim cloning of the colony into two provinces, New Ulster and New Munster, in 1848. In 1852, new London legislation gave New Zealand its constitution, and self-government began being implemented the following year.

"A parliament based on the British model was taken for granted,"[30] so much so that the system did not actually have to be very Britain-like. Governor Grey claimed to have designed the new constitution himself, inspired by the United States Constitution and "by talking to the hills and trees."[31] Not only was it "quasi-federal,"[32] dividing the colony into six provinces with their own elected superintendents and councils, which had no British precedent, but state interventionism was always much stronger and the franchise was always much broader. In the words of leading historian J. C. Beaglehole, "New Zealand has never been, in the strict sense, an individualistic society. From the very beginning of colonization the individual and the state ... worked together, and from the very beginning the state was called on actively to aid the individual over an increasingly large area of his life."[33] There was a very modest property qualification for the vote – £50 worth of freehold land, or rented property worth £10 in town or £5 in the country. This immediately allowed about 60 percent of adult white males to vote if they chose, about four times the old British percentage of the day.[34] The colonial press also flourished after 1853. Between 1840 and that year, some 20 newspapers had been founded. Between 1854 and 1879, the number was about 200.[35] The central government, or general government, as it was known, consisted of an elected lower house and an appointed upper house or legislative council. Both met first in 1854 and for the next two years struggled to share power with the governor – a

---

[29] A. H. McLintock, *Crown Colony Government in New Zealand,* Government Printer, Wellington, 1958, 261.

[30] Raewyn Dalziel, "The politics of settlement," in G. Rice [and W. H. Oliver], eds., *The Oxford History of New Zealand,* 2nd edn., Oxford University Press, Auckland, 1992, 92–3.

[31] Quoted in James Milne, *The Romance of a Pro-Consul: Being the Personal Life and Memoirs of the Right Hon. Sir George Grey,* 2nd edn., Chatto & Windus, London, 1899, 160.

[32] W. J. Gardner, "A colonial economy," in Rice and Oliver, eds., *The Oxford History of New Zealand,* 64.

[33] Quoted in Frame, *Salmond,* 53. Also see Michael Bassett, *The State in New Zealand 1840–1984,* Auckland University Press, Auckland, 1998.

[34] Belich, *Making Peoples,* 409.

[35] Day, *The Making of the New Zealand Press.*

very brief intermediate phase of representative but not responsible government. From 1856, after a slap on the knuckles from London, the governors accepted that most executive power rested with a ministry drawn from, and responsible to, the lower house. However, through their control of imperial resources such as troops, the governors retained considerable power until 1867.

In 1856, then, a settler population of fewer than 50,000 had seven elected governments, besides the governor and several dozen independent Maori tribes – "more like the Holy Roman empire with its 300 states than the solid British pink of the old school atlas."[36] With an average of roughly 2,000 voters per government, New Zealand was the cloning capital of the world. The six provinces were based on the original settlements, minus Kororareka. A further four provinces were added by 1872. In accordance with North American precedent, the stimulus behind the formation of new provinces was the conviction of frontiersmen that the old settlements were not doing enough for frontiers in terms of boosting and borrowing. Separate foundations, somewhat different characters, and difficult interprovincial communications were factors in New Zealand's extreme case of cloning. So too was the fact that Britain-sized New Zealand seemed much larger to the early Victorians than it does to us.

Because the provinces were set up in 1853, before the general government, they may have had somewhat more power than was originally intended. They received all revenues from the sale of Crown land within their boundaries, plus a share of customs revenues. They needed central government permission to borrow, but this was given readily during the first New Zealand boom, to 1866, which was largely led by the provincial governments. "The provinces accepted responsibility for colonization and development."[37] The main modus operandi was energetic boosting, in which the free press joined with great enthusiasm, and the equally energetic borrowing of British money to assist immigration and for public works. Initially, the plurality of New Zealand brands helped the colonizing crusade in other respects, too. Otago and Canterbury were able to distance themselves from Auckland and New Plymouth, where Maori resistance was rife in the 1860s. "The New Zealand model had different makes, catering for all preferences, with teething problems such as the massacre of customers restricted to a few only."[38] Competitive development, such as the use of different railway gauges and the building of neighboring ports in two different provinces, was inefficient, but it doubled the action in terms of growth through growth. But the boom ended in 1867, at least partly because "government borrowing by both general and provincial governments had exhausted the colony's credit on the London money market."[39]

---

[36] James Belich, "The governors and the Maori" in Keith Sinclair, ed., *The Oxford Illustrated History of New Zealand*, Oxford University Press, Auckland, 1990, 76.
[37] Dalziel "The politics of settlement," 99.
[38] Belich, *Making Peoples*, 285.
[39] Gardner, "A colonial economy," 70.

Borrowing, mass immigration, and rapid growth recommenced about 1872, now under the aegis of the central government and its master-booster, Julius Vogel. Sometimes treated as an exceptional risk-taker and visionary, Vogel was in fact merely the flagship of a fleet. Colonization was the main business of all politicians, none of whom wanted the process to be slow. As Vogel put it:

We have set ourselves the task of making New Zealand the home of millions of human beings sooner than, in the natural course, that result would have been arrived at. There must be no suspension of the policy of progress .... The statesmen of New Zealand should remember that their work is the heroic one of colonization.[40]

Vogel's political rivals were more cautious about borrowing for rapid progress than he was, but not by much. One, Edward Stafford, the longest-serving colonial premier of the nineteenth century, was convinced that New Zealand was "intended by nature and God to carry twenty-five millions of people," and tried to play his full part in this manifest destiny.[41] The distinction was not between bold borrowers and cautious borrowers, as is sometimes suggested, but between bold borrowers and very bold borrowers. If politicians chanced to forget this, they were swiftly reminded by their constituents. "Get us the Million," wrote one settler to his local member, "We'll forgive anything but want of success."[42] This ideology of "progress," of explosive colonization, of making a great future happen fast, was common to press and politicians, public and private sectors, provinces and central governments.

The law was sometimes a useful ally of the colonizing crusade. Pastoralism, the extensive farming of sheep on cheaply leased Crown land using animals and methods imported from Australia, was an important early activity. One problem was that sheep farmers did not own their land and therefore could not borrow on the security of it. In 1858, a "Wool and Oil Securities Act" was therefore passed, based on New South Wales precedent.[43] This converted the wool on sheep, which might or might not be shorn, and the blubber on whales, which might or might not be caught, into a tangible property right on which money could be borrowed. The first documented action for defamation, in 1842, was against the allegation that the defamed was a bad credit risk – the worst possible allegation in a booming settler society.[44] British legislation limiting the liability of joint-stock companies was quickly adopted in 1860.

[40] Raewyn Dalziel, *Julius Vogel, Business Politician*, Auckland University Press, Auckland, 1986, 172, 234.
[41] Edmund Bohun, *Edward Stafford. New Zealand's First Statesman*, Hazard Press, Christchurch, 1994, 296.
[42] Dalziel, "The politics of settlement," 103.
[43] G. R. Hawke, *Law and Economic Development: The Case of New Zealand*, Victoria University of Wellington Economics Department, Wellington, 1983.
[44] Rosemary Tobin, "The Defamation Action in mid 19th century New Zealand," *Australia and New Zealand Law and History E-Journal*, 2005, 49–59 [http://www.anzlhsejournal.auckland.ac.nz/].

However, where British precedent or the sanctity of property rights appeared to clash with the progress imperative, the latter prevailed. Among the first acts of the New Zealand Parliament in 1854 was the repeal of a British usury law restricting interest to 5 percent.[45] Land transfer regulations, culminating in the Torrens system, facilitated sales more than did those of old Britain, as was also the case in other colonies.[46] A strong strand of legislation, stretching from 1844 to 1895, such as the abolition of imprisonment for debt in 1871, eased the consequences of bankruptcy – surely a blow *against* the property rights of lenders and investors.[47] In 1894, New Zealand enacted and implemented legislation enabling the compulsory purchase and subdivision of large landed estates. The perceived need to place small farmers on the land was one incentive for this, but so was the desire to restart progress, which had stalled in the 1880s, by expanding the new refrigerated dairy exports best produced by family farms. Property rights were sacred, but progress was even more sacred. All in all, it is hard to dissent from the view of New Zealand's leading economic historian, Gary Hawke: "There is little independent role for law in the process of economic development. It is easy to trace the influence of economic development on the law.... It is more difficult to trace the reverse influence."[48]

What was true in law was also true in cloning and Parliament. Under Vogel, the central government took the lead in stimulating explosive colonization but continued to find the provinces a hindrance. So, in 1876, it abolished them, lock, stock, and barrel. "The passing of provincial institutions was unregretted in most of the Provinces."[49] Canadian unifications in 1842 and 1867, and Australian federation in 1900, may also have been influenced by a need to prime the pump of explosive colonization, particularly through the extra borrowing power of a united cluster of colonies. In New Zealand in 1893, the legislative council, or upper house, blocked progressive measures such as the compulsory land purchase of large estates and was therefore castrated by regulations allowing the government of the day to appoint fresh members to ensure a majority. The upper house became a cipher and was finally administered euthanasia in 1950. In the final analysis, the sanctity of progress outranked that of cloning, property, and even Parliament.

The Britishness of New Zealand law, like the Britishness of New Zealand in general, appears to have increased under re-colonization in the twentieth century. Appeals to the Privy Council were much more common after 1890 than before, even in proportion to population. There were thirteen New Zealand appeals between 1840 and 1890 and seventy-nine between 1890 and 1930. In

---

[45] Jeremy Finn, "Development of the law in New Zealand," in Peter Spiller et al., *New Zealand Legal History*, 2nd edn., Brooker's, Wellington, 2001, 76.

[46] Jeremy Finn, "The English Heritage" in Spiller et al., *New Zealand Legal History*, 40.

[47] Jeremy Finn, "Development of the law in New Zealand," in Spiller et al., *New Zealand Legal History*.

[48] Hawke, *Law and Economic Development*, 69.

[49] W. P. Morrell, *The Provincial System in New Zealand 1852–1876*, 2nd edn., Whitcomb and Tombs, Christchurch, 1964 (orig. 1932), 264.

the period 1914–60, writes one leading legal historian, "Parliament and the legal profession appear to have possessed ... an Anglocentric focus on the world that to some extent reversed the 19th century trend towards a distinctively New Zealand character and legal identity."[50] "In 1956," states another scholar, "the [New Zealand] Court of Appeal considered itself bound by the House of Lords."[51] As late as 1966, a third could write:

In New Zealand the policy of the Courts has been to preserve uniformity with the common law in England. This is partly for reasons of convenience and partly because of the assumption prevailing in New Zealand that there is a single common law, the law of England, and that there are not separate, though similar, common laws in different countries.[52]

John Salmond, "New Zealand's most influential and renowned jurist," in the 1920s "publicly disclaimed any New Zealand international personality separate from the British Empire."[53]

Re-colonization may have worked both ways. Salmond's textbooks, one of which ran to twenty-seven editions by 1992, were influential throughout the common-law world. Despite some divergences, Salmond on the whole supported legal theorists such as John Austin, whose views tended to empower the almighty state. An interventionist state eventually emerged in old Britain, from about the 1890s, and from the 1920s there was also a new tendency toward decentralization or devolution, which might be compared to cloning. The trend of old Britain following, not leading, is even clearer with suffrage. In New Zealand, never less than 50 percent of adult white males had the right to vote. The percentage rose to 84 percent in 1881, and women received the vote in 1893.[54] Between 1832 and 1867, about 20 percent of the men of England and 14 percent of the men of the United Kingdom as a whole had the vote. "As late as 1911, only sixty-three per cent of all adult males [and no women] were on the electoral lists."[55] Australian, Canadian, and western American levels of suffrage varied, but they were much more similar to those of New Zealand than those of Britain. What we may have here is a re-colonial ricochet, whereby old Britain derived institutions from the neo-Britains rather than the other way around. Other old British developments, such as Irish land legislation in the 1890s, general welfare legislation from that time, and housing policy between the wars, also smack of colonial precedents. British emigration increased to a torrent in the period 1900–1914, increasingly aimed at the Dominions, and

[50] Finn, "Development of the law in New Zealand," 78.
[51] Hawke, *Law and Economic Development*, 23.
[52] "Legal system," in A. H. McLintock, ed., *An Encyclopaedia of New Zealand*, 3 vols., Government Printer, Wellington, 1966, vol. ii, 295.
[53] Frame, *Salmond. Southern Jurist*, and "Salmond, John William," in *The Dictionary of New Zealand Biography*, Volume Three, Auckland University Press/Department of Internal Affairs, Wellington, 1996.
[54] Belich, *Making Peoples*, 409.
[55] D. G. Wright, *Democracy and Reform, 1815–1885*, Longman, London, 1970, 195.

possibly the British ruling class was being forced to match dominion institutions to keep someone to rule.

It seems clear that British and neo-British institutions did form a growth-enhancing package in Anglophone settler societies in the long nineteenth century. As Australian historian Geoffrey Blainey has shrewdly noted, "to possess a parliament house and a civil service was to possess the hormones of growth."[56] But institutions were only one of several steroids in the nineteenth-century settler races and need to be seen in the contexts of the others. These included the rise of mass transfer, the "settler transition," and the "boom mentality." These three key shifts all took off from about 1815; none was exclusively Anglophone but all were Anglo-*prone*, and each had both general and particular manifestations.

The nineteenth century witnessed a huge surge in the capacity of European metropoli, including the northeastern United States, to shift all sorts of things across mountains and oceans. An obvious element was the effect of industrialization on transport technology: steamboats, which made rivers two-way highways, and railroads, which put rivers where you wanted them. But industrialization was far from the whole story. Several early Anglo booms, including Australia's first (1828–42) and New Zealand's first (1850–66), occurred without steam transport playing a significant role. A flowering of *non*industrial technology preceded and merged with the effects of industrialization on mass transfer. The ancient technology of sailing ships improved enormously; changes in banking practices eased the flow of money; and the rise of literacy and postal services eased the flow of information. Settlement booms normally featured the sudden mushrooming of banks, newspapers, and postal services. Especially on settler frontiers, with their vast resource endowments, the constituents of pre-industrial technology were abundant – wind, water, wood, and work animals. Booms usually correlated with a surge in horse numbers even greater than the increase in people. Ten-ton wagons hauled by twenty span, 12 acre lumber rafts on rivers, long canals, and seven-masted sailing ships were as much the icons of explosive colonization as were the steam ship and the locomotive. The overlap of two full suites of technology doubled the action. Even without steamships or railroads, things, thoughts, people, and money ceased to trickle across oceans and mountains, and began to flow. Many peoples participated in this trend, but for various reasons the Anglophones benefited the most. Throughout the nineteenth century, if you hailed a ship in mid-ocean, the chances were that it would answer in English.

Before the mass advent of rail in mid-century, water transport was the most effective for settlement as well as everything else. The Mississippi River system, the Great Lakes, and the St. Lawrence probably outranked the covered wagon as settler transport even in North America. In Australasia, the Tasman Sea was more a bridge than a barrier. Whaling and the transport of convicts established sea links with Britain, and shippers were eager to add migrants to their

---

[56] Geoffrey Blainey, *A Land Half Won*, Macmillan, Melbourne, 1980, 206.

business. After 1815, land grants attracted a new type of migrant to New South Wales and Tasmania – free, moneyed, and well-connected in London. These forerunner settlers made it their business to try to trigger booms, sometimes in alliance with colonization companies of various kinds. They succeeded in Tasmania from 1828 and New South Wales from about 1830, but initially failed in South Australia and New Zealand. From about 1848 – *before* the discovery of gold in Victoria in 1851 – a fresh set of Australasian booms began, this time extending to New Zealand with the help of cloning, state-led borrowing, and state-assisted immigration.

The "settler transition" was a sharp upward shift in the status or standing of migration. Before 1800, Britons saw emigration as social excretion, the last resort of the desperate and disreputable. Americans naturally contested this and may have been successful on their side of the Atlantic, but not on the other. "Emigration," stated Lord Sheffield in the 1780s, "is the natural recourse of the culprit, and those who have made themselves the objects of contempt and neglect."[57] In the early nineteenth century, the British still "looked upon a life in the colonies as socially degrading, and having much in common with penal transportation."[58] This attitude was later famously summarized by Charles Buller. Emigration was "little more than shoveling out your paupers to where they might die, without shocking their betters with the sigh or sound of their last agony."[59] Yet at some point in the first half of the nineteenth century, there was clearly a somersault in British attitudes to emigration. In the long eighteenth century, about half a million British and Irish emigrated. In the long nineteenth century, about 20 million did so.

The shift in emigration and attitudes to it are sometimes associated with Edward Gibbon Wakefield and his fellow "colonial reformers," and dated to around 1830. But it appears to date to 1815. In 1815–20, there was a surge in British emigration and overseas investment corresponding with the first Anglo-booms in Canada and the American West.[60] Unlike eighteenth-century emigration, the great bulk was voluntary. There was a corresponding surge of emigration literature. These early nineteenth-century emigration books noted a

[57] Quoted in Doron S. Ben-Atar, *Trade Secrets: Intellectual Piracy and the Origins of the American Industrial Power*, Yale University Press, New Haven, CT, 2004, 112.

[58] S. C. Johnson, *A History of Emigration from the United Kingdom to North America, 1763–1912*, Routledge, London, 1913, 21.

[59] Quoted in Peter Gray, "'Shovelling out your paupers': The British state and Irish famine migration 1846–1860," *Patterns of Prejudice*, 33, 1999, 47–65.

[60] P. D. McClelland and R. J. Zeckhauser, *Demographic Dimensions of the New Republic: American Interregional Migration, Vital Statistics, and Manumissions, 1800–1860*, Cambridge University Press, New York, 2004 (original 1982), 96–112. They estimate an inflow of 108,000 people into the United States between 1815 and 1820, most of whom were British and Irish. Deduct about 15,000 for other immigrant groups (Hans-Jurgen Grabbe, "European immigration to the United States in the early national period, 1783–1820," *Proceedings of the American Philosophical Society*, 133, 1989, 190–214). Add an inflow of 70,000 into Canada and add 10,000 emigrants to Australia between 1815 and 1819 (Wray Vamplew, ed., *Australian Historical Statistics*, Fairfax, Syme, and Weldon, Broadway, New South Wales, 1987, 105).

shift in the quality as well as the quantity of emigration after 1815.[61] "Emigration assumed a totally new character; it was no longer merely the poor, the idle, the profligate, or the wildly speculative, who were proposing to quit their native country." "The mania for emigration is not now, as formerly, confined to the poorer class and such as could not gain a living at home."[62] The upward shift in the standing of emigration is symbolized by a sudden rise in the use of the word "settler." In Britain, *settler* was used in its current meaning at least as far back as the seventeenth century, but it was used infrequently. By the early nineteenth century it had connotations of a higher status than "emigrant," taking the stigma out of emigration and implying that migrants now retained a metropolitan, first-world status. The rise of the settler over time can be traced through fully searchable databases of newspapers and journals. In the 1790s, the *Times* used "settlers" in 7 articles and "emigrants" in 870; in the 1800s the numbers were 22 and 149. In the 1810s, the use of "settlers" suddenly shot up to 110, compared to 192 for emigrants, and "settlers" actually exceeded "emigrants" in the 1820s, 280 to 272. Emigration, re-branded as "settlement," was losing its stigma.

Respectable settlement replaced disreputable emigration, but most potential destinations had to achieve their own particular "settler transition" as well. At best, this involved overcoming the ignorance of potential settlers and investors about New Zealand or Oregon. At worst, it involved transforming a pre-existing negative image into a positive one. Through the efforts of its gallant boosters, Wakefield to Vogel, New Zealand ceased to be the Cannibal Isles and became the Better Britain of the South.

The settler transition combined with a boom mentality to form the ideology of explosive colonization, noted above in its New Zealand manifestation. The boom mentality involved an intense flurry of speculation, risk-taking, and optimistic projects and prognoses. Both contemporaries and historians leave no doubt of the boom mentality's prominence and pervasiveness, but tended to define it as "frenzy" or "mania" at best, or mass fraud at worst; in either case it was a culpable aberration. Yet it happened numerous times. It was most obvious during "land rushes," particularly urban ones, when the same piece of land could sell several times at multiples of the original price in single year. But a "gambling spirit" was pervasive in other circumstances, too. Visiting the

---

[61] E.g., Anon., *The American Traveller and Emigrant's Guide ...* C. Hilbert, Shrewsbury, 1817; *British Traveller, The Colonial Policy of Great Britain considered ...*, Baldwin, Craddock and Joy, London, 1816; Anon., *The Emigrant's Guide to the British Settlements in Upper Canada and the USA*, T. Keys, London, 1820; E. Dana, *Geographical Sketch of the Western Country, Designed for Emigrants and Settlers*, Looker, Reynolds and Co., Cincinnati, 1819; Francis Hall, *Travels in Canada and the United States in 1816 and 1817*, 2nd edn., Longman, London, 1819; Anon., *The Emigrants Guide, or, A Picture of America; also, A Sketch of the British Provinces Delineating Their Superior Attractions, by an Old Scene Painter*, W. Simpkin and R. Marshall, London, 1816.

[62] Henry Bradshaw Fearon, *Sketches of America ...*, 3rd edn., Longman, London, 1819, xi; A. J. Christie, *The Emigrants' Assistant*, Nahum Mower, Montreal, 1821, 21–2.

American Old Northwest in the 1830s, Alexis De Tocqueville was told that "almost all our tradesmen play for double or quits."[63] Charles Dilke, author of the original *Greater Britain*, found exactly the same phenomenon in booming New Zealand in the 1860s.[64] We should be cautious about dismissing the boom mentality as a spasm of collective hysteria egged on by crooked speculators. There was a crusading fervor about even the wildest boosters and speculators, who usually risked their own lives, money, and children as well as those of others. There was an assumption that, at least on frontiers, both nature and the human capacity to transform it were inexhaustible. Like buffalo hunters on the Great Plains in the 1880s, New Zealand whalers and sealers spent a season being mystified at the nonarrival of the prey they had just locally exterminated. Forests were burned off for pastures on hillsides too steep even for sheep. There was a sense in which old bets were off; previous assumptions about the spread of opportunity and the speed of history no longer applied. Busts were attributed to scapegoats, or simply forgotten. There was a kind of bounded rationality – people did make fortunes, cities did sprout, and new lands did rocket in population and wealth. The illusion was that this would go on indefinitely.

These "steroids," technological and ideological, sometimes converged with institutions and sometimes diverged. In the later case, ideology tended to take precedence over institutions, at least during booms and efforts to start or restart them. The important but essentially secondary role of institutions can be demonstrated in another way – a quick trip to Siberia. The settler explosion of the nineteenth century, in which socio-economies doubled in size in a single decade, was mainly but by no means entirely Anglophone. From the 1870s, it was emulated in places such as Argentina and Siberia. Between the 1880s and 1914, Russian settlement in Siberia experienced the same pattern of boom, bust, and export rescue. No one has yet accused late Tsarist Russia of a sudden injection of common law, wide suffrage, a free press, representative government, or regional autonomy, let alone all five. English institutions may have helped to better convert booms and export rescue into long-term stability and prosperity. But they cannot explain explosive colonization itself. What Siberia did have was an interventionist state, plus mass transfer, a settler transition, and a boom mentality.[65]

---

[63] Quoted in Howard Bodenhorn, *A History of Banking in Antebellum America*, Cambridge University Press, New York, 2000, 111.

[64] Charles Dilke, *Greater Britain: A Record of Travel in English-Speaking Countries during 1866 and 1867*, 2 vols., Macmillan, London, 1868, vol. I, 331–2.

[65] Mark Bassin, "Inventing Siberia: Visions of the Russian East in the early nineteenth century," *American Historical Review*, 96, 1991, 763–94; Willard Sunderland, "Peasant pioneering; Russian peasant settlers describe colonization and the eastern frontier, 1880s–1910s," *Journal of Social History*, 34, 2001, 895–922. Also see Sunderland, "Peasants on the move; State peasant resettlement in Imperial Russia, 1805–1830s," *Russian Review*, 52, 1993, 472–485, 478 and footnote 27, and "An empire of peasants..." in Jane Burbank and David L Ransel, eds., *Imperial Russia: New Histories for the Empire*, Indiana University Press, 1998; David Moon, "Peasant migration and the settlement of Russia's frontiers, 1550–1897," *Historical Journal*, 40, 1997, 859–893.

The long nineteenth century witnessed a European settler explosion that comprehensively transformed and re-peopled half the world – central and western North America, Australasia, Siberia, and parts of South America and South Africa. This extraordinary explosion was not exclusively Anglophone, but it was Anglo-prone. Anglo settler societies "exploded" earlier, more universally, and on a larger scale than non-Anglo. Thus, in mass settlement at least, in the nineteenth century at least, there was an Anglophone divergence from even European norms, and this requires historical explanation. A suite of political and legal institutions and structures were indeed part of the explanation. They included the cloning of many polities rather than the extension of a few, parliamentary government, wide franchises, a predilection for state intervention in the economy, an active free press, and the pragmatic use of the common law. Some of these institutions and tendencies can be traced back to English precedents, but some cannot – cloning, the wide franchise, the interventionist state. These were products of a space between fragment and frontier, and were reinforced in the nineteenth century by a bidding war for immigrants between, and within, the United States and the British empire.

The New Zealand case suggests that these institutions were helpful to settlement booms but were outranked by technological and cultural factors. Apart from land wrested from indigenes, you also had to have mass transfer, a settler transition, and a boom mentality. One indirect but important effect of institutions thought to be metropolitan-like was in buttressing the settler transition, enhancing the sense that, unlike other migrants, nineteenth-century Anglophone settlers retained their metropolitan-ness, their full citizenship, their first-world standing. The willingness of Britons and Americans to migrate to each other's settlement colonies suggests that this "virtual metropolitan-ness" outranked nationalism. "Progress," or "the heroic work of [explosive] colonization," took precedence over attachment to institutions as such. When regional autonomy, the sanctity of property rights and debt collection, and an effective upper house seemed to clash with progress in New Zealand, they were unceremoniously ditched. This, together with the Siberian example, puts institutions in their place as an important but not necessarily crucial or dominant contributor to the settler explosion. Institutions did matter, but they mattered most when they converged with shifts in other dimensions of history, which sometimes mattered more. "English liberties," adapted, amplified, and sometimes even invented overseas, did enhance the development of settler societies, and historically anthropologizing them is an important scholarly enterprise. But they were not the master key to the massive Anglophone demographic and economic growth of the long nineteenth century. We need to look to ideologies and technologies, as well as liberties, to explain this growth.

10

The Expansion of British Liberties

The South African Case

Christopher Saunders

It is a natural or at any rate an expectable thing that colonists who have emigrated from a mother-country to settle in new lands, but remain attached to their mother-country after their emigration, should carry with them a stock of political ideas, and should preserve and even expand that stock – partly because it is in their blood; partly because it is kept intact by continuing association with the mother-country; and partly because the new conditions of colonial life demand new responses which are found most naturally in new applications of old ideas. The colonists will vindicate the rights and liberties of the mother-country as *their* rights and liberties; they will even, in the free and bracing air of colonial conditions and colonial enterprise ... attempt to carry these rights and liberties to a farther point and a higher reach than they have attained in the mother-country.[1]

The transmission of British ideas about liberty, consensual governance, and the rule of law to South Africa is a neglected topic.[2] This is at first sight surprising, given the importance of those ideas in South Africa today, but both British rule and liberalism have taken hard knocks in recent South African historiography, which has tended to be critical of the British role in southern Africa as highly illiberal. This is not because such historiography accepts the view, expressed by a leading Afrikaner in a propaganda tract on the eve of the Anglo-Boer war of 1899–1902, that the preceding century had been a "Century of Wrong" done by the British to the Boers, though some writers still subscribe

---

[1] E. Barker, *Ideas and Ideals of the British Empire* (Cambridge: Cambridge University Press, 1942), p. 50.

[2] I have found no work that directly discusses this topic. It is touched on in T. R. H. Davenport, "The Consolidation of a New Society: the Cape Colony," in M. Wilson and L.Thompson, eds., The *Oxford History of South Africa*, volume I (Oxford: Oxford University Press, 1969); A. Bank, "Liberals and Their Enemies," unpublished Ph.D thesis, Cambridge University, 1995; and T.Keegan, *Colonial South Africa and the Origins of the Racial Order* (Leicester: Leicester University Press, 1996).

to less extreme variants of that proposition.[3] Radically minded scholars have argued, rather, that it was the use of British power and the extension of British rule in the nineteenth century that ended the independence of most African polities, and that people of British origin, rather than Afrikaners, were mainly responsible for the creation, in the late nineteenth and early twentieth centuries, of the system of racial segregation and exploitation for which South Africa became known, in the late twentieth century, as "the polecat of the world."[4] Such an interpretation has tended to downplay the vast contributions that the British made to the development of South Africa, whether in economic, cultural, or other spheres of life.[5] For while the British took class prejudices and concepts of racial classification to South Africa,[6] they also introduced their ideas of liberty.

Liberalism has often attracted a bad press in South Africa, and liberals have been accused of hypocrisy, arising from their privileged position in society, in which they had the luxury to be concerned with individual rights rather than collective survival. Liberalism has been seen as a cloak for imperialist designs, often linked to the extension of capitalism.[7] The negative view of Britain's role has been linked to the view that liberalism has meant above all the freedom to exploit,[8] while Marxists have scorned liberalism's gradual, noncoercive means to achieve its goals. But, while it is true that historically the reach of liberalism in South Africa was limited, with many excluded from its purview, liberal ideas took root there. The roots may have remained relatively shallow, but liberal ideas prevailed in the democracy born after the collapse of apartheid.

---

[3] J. Smuts, *A Century of Wrong* (London: Review of Reviews, 1899). The author, ironically, had been educated at Cambridge, and was to become a member of the Imperial War Cabinet and vice-chancellor of Cambridge University. For more recent interpretations see especially H. Giliomee, *The Afrikaners. Biography of a People* (Tafelberg: Cape Town, 2004).

[4] See in general P. Maylam, *South Africa's Racial Past* (Ashgate: Aylesbury, 2004). The key article to advance such an interpretation was A. Atmore and S. Marks, "The Imperial Factor in South Africa in the Nineteenth Century: Towards a Reassessment," *Journal of Imperial and Commonwealth History*, 3 (1974).

[5] One who does not minimize the British contribution is A. Sparks, who, in *The Mind of South Africa* (Durham: Duke University Press, 1989), says "The British created modern South Africa" (p. 46).

[6] For racial ideas from Britain see, e.g., S. Dubow, *Scientific Racism in Modern South Africa* (Cambridge: Cambridge University Press, 1995); Maylam, *South Africa's Racial Past*.

[7] E.g., D. Taylor, *The Role of the Missionaries in Conquest* (n.p., 1952). In the 1970s, leaders of the Black Consciousness Movement accused white liberals of being de facto defenders of apartheid. On South African liberalism in general see R. Vigne, *Liberals Against Apartheid. A History of the Liberal Party of South Africa* (London: Routledge, 1997).

[8] E.g., S. Newton-King, "The Labour Market of the Cape Colony, 1807–28," and S. Trapido, "'Friends of the Natives': Merchants, Peasants and the Political and Ideological Structure of Liberalism at the Cape, 1854–1910," both in S. Marks and A. Atmore, eds., *Economy and Society in Pre-Industrial South Africa* (London: Longman, 1980).

I here follow those who see the core liberal ideas as fundamentally political, relating to individual freedom, the rule of law, and accountable government.[9] No one should be incarcerated without charge or trial or tortured to produce a confession. One should only be charged for contravening an existing law, and one had a right to trial by a jury before being sentenced to imprisonment. Accompanying such ideas were others that had developed by the end of the eighteenth century relating to government: that it should rest, at least to some extent, on the consent of the governed, so that there should be no taxation without representation, and that it should be limited by law, even if that law was not embodied in a written constitution. There developed in Britain, too, the concept that all people were capable of assimilation to British culture through education and Christianity. In ways too complex to explore here, the idea of freedom became deeply intertwined with concepts of equality and justice, many of which emerged in the course of the French and American revolutions.

This chapter is concerned with how and by whom liberal ideas were transmitted from the island in the North Atlantic where they largely originated to the southern part of the African continent, and how in the process these ideas underwent reformulation and contestation in a new environment. Such reformulation was inevitable, given that these ideas were transmitted to, and were then embedded in, a very different society, a colonial one in which the majority of the people were from the start, and remained – unlike the other major white settler societies colonized by the British – not settlers from Britain but either slaves brought in from Africa or Asia or indigenes of one kind or another.

When the British arrived at the Cape they found, as they did not in Australia and New Zealand, an existing colonial society. That society had, like that of French Canada, been in existence for almost a century and a half. When the British took over the Cape there were more slaves than settlers of European descent and a large indigenous population, initially mainly Khoi (who were known by the derogatory term Hottentot).[10] As British rule expanded into other parts of the region in the course of the nineteenth century, the ratio of settlers, whether of old stock or more recent immigrants from Britain, to indigenous black people progressively widened, for the indigenous people did not, as some whites predicted they would, die out, but ever-increasing numbers were brought under white rule. The question then became whether ideas of individual rights that had been developed for "free-born Englishmen" would be applied universally in South Africa as British rule spread into the interior. In the event, as we shall see, one of the main ideas of freedom that came from Britain – that people should have the right to rule themselves – helped promote illiberalism in the particular circumstances of South Africa, for it meant that power was transferred

---

[9] E.g., J. P. Parry in P. Mandler, ed., *Liberty and Authority in Victorian Britain* (Oxford: Oxford University Press, 2006), pp. 71–72.

[10] In 1798 there were more than 25,000 slaves and fewer than 22,000 "free," plus an unknown number of Khoi: M. Boucher and N. Penn, *Britain at the Cape* (Johannesburg: Brenthurst Press, 1992), p. 179.

to minority regimes that did not promote liberal values and did not promote the extension of those values to the majority, who were not regarded as citizens.

In general works of South African history it is sometimes suggested that when the British took the Cape by force of arms from the Dutch in 1795 they suppressed ideas of liberty that had entered the colony from Europe in the late eighteenth century, that the initial decades of British rule were highly authoritarian and illiberal, that British ideas of liberty only began to take root in the 1820s, and that they did so as a consequence of the arrival from Britain of new settlers who successfully challenged the authoritarianism of the British officials then ruling the colony.[11] Such an interpretation is not supported by recent research. Only a very small minority of the settlers in the colony established by the Dutch East India Company (DEIC) in the 1650s ever sought to challenge the authoritarian ways in which they were ruled by DEIC officials. Such a challenge came most notably in 1779, when those who called themselves Cape Patriots, influenced by events in Europe, petitioned for a range of what they saw as freedoms, including the right to flog their slaves without restraint. The Patriots achieved nothing significant, however, and their movement soon collapsed. In 1795, before the British arrived, settlers in the frontier area in the eastern part of the colony, where DEIC rule was especially tenuous, declared their independence from Cape Town, but this rebellion was, as the historian C. W. de Kiewiet wrote many decades ago, "the result of what the burghers considered an unwarranted intrusion [by the DEIC] upon their freedom to deal with their Kafir neighbours as they saw fit."[12] Not many months after they threw off the company's yoke, the newly arrived British – acting to keep the colony together and impose order on an unruly frontier – put down the revolt, ending the short-lived republic of Graaff-Reinet.

The new rulers were not certain that their rule would endure when the wars then taking place in Europe came to an end, but whether it would or not, they saw themselves as modernizers, bringing enlightened ideas to the Cape, including that of relaxing restrictions on trade. General Craig, the first military ruler, acting on instructions from London, wrote of "the liberal arrangements which will soon be carried into effect," and he selected six of the most prominent Dutch citizens – key members of the collaborating class with which the British chose to work – to serve on a Burgher Senate to help rule the colony.[13] It was Craig who suggested to his superiors that the use of torture to extract confessions and to accompany capital punishment, especially where slaves were concerned, be stopped. Slaves, he said, no longer needed to be sent such a brutal message, given the strength of British rule at the Cape. His suggestion led to instructions being given in London to the first civilian governor, Earl

---

[11] E.g., E. A. Walker, *A.History of Southern Africa* (3rd ed., London: Longman, 1957).
[12] C. W. de Kiewiet, *History of South Africa Social and Economic* (London: Oxford University Press, 1941), p. 31.
[13] A. P. Newton and E. A. Benians, eds., *The Cambridge History of the British Empire*, volume 8 (Cambridge: Cambridge University Press, 1936), p. 179.

Macartney, to abolish all forms of torture in criminal proceedings, in line with prevailing ideas in Britain itself.[14]

Macartney's order of 1797 was as momentous a turning point as the ending of capital punishment almost two centuries later by South African President F. W. de Klerk. It would be over a century and a half after Macartney's order before torture would again become routine in South Africa, and then not openly, as in the eighteenth century, but in the offices of the Security Police, where Steve Biko and other political prisoners were tortured, sometimes to death, on the go-ahead of men who had in some cases been Nazi sympathizers in the Second World War. On coming into office in late 1989, de Klerk did not admit that there had been official sanction for such actions, but he gave the orders to the security forces that brought South Africa back to where Macartney had taken it in 1797.[15]

Horrific public executions continued to take place at the Cape in the early years of British rule, but, as in England, they declined in number. Bodies were now less frequently left to rot on the gallows on the outskirts of Cape Town. It took more than seven decades from the arrival of the British for public executions to cease altogether, following the example of Britain itself, but from the time the British arrived the trend was toward more humane punishments.[16] When Macartney saw a slave who had been flayed, he sent the master a message saying that if it happened again "he would take from him every slave he held and render him incapable of ever becoming the proprietor of another slave."[17] And in 1800 the leading Cape diarist of the time wrote that the colonial secretary could not "without legal powers and proofs" arrest "a man of a fair character." That man had himself, on his voyage out to the Cape from Britain, referred in his diary to "the liberty of an Englishman" while criticising the French for spreading, "under the specious Mask of Liberty and Equality ... their pernicious doctrines to the ruin and destruction of all who listen to their infernal creed."[18]

---

[14] See, e.g., Newton and Benians, eds., *Cambridge History of the British Empire*, 8, p. 178. The Irish-born Macartney had served much of his life outside Britain, as governor in the West Indies and Madras and envoy to Russia and China. So, too, had James Henry Craig, a Scot born in Gibraltar who had been wounded at Bunker Hill. See their entries in the *Oxford Dictionary of National Biography*, eds. H. Matthew and B. Harrison (Oxford: Oxford University Press, 60 vols., 2004) and Boucher and Penn, *Britain at the Cape*. On torture cf. J. H. Langbein, *Torture and the Law of Proof* (new ed., Chicago: University of Chicago Press, 2006).

[15] In both cases, some individual examples of torture occurred afterward, but without official sanction.

[16] The last public execution was in Grahamstown in 1868. I thank Mr. Justice Ian Farlam for providing information on this legal history.

[17] National Archives, Cape Town, Samuel Hudson Papers: "Essay on Slavery". Elsewhere in the essay, Hudson writes of the "mercy seat where black and white should have equal justice." My thanks to Edward Hudson of Stoney Stratford for these references.

[18] B. A. le Cordeur and M. Lenta, eds., *The Cape Diaries of Lady Anne Barnard* (2 vols., Cape Town: Van Riebeeck Society, 1999), 2, pp. 255–56; National Archives, Cape Town, Samuel Hudson Papers: Journal, 10 December and 25 November 1796. My thanks to Edward Hudson for these quotations.

After British rule was confirmed at the end of the Napoleonic wars, parties of settlers were sent out to the Cape from Britain, but the idea that the largest party, that of 1820, brought with them liberal ideas and so began a tradition of liberalism in South Africa is a myth. The 4,000 "emigrants" of 1820 were, though selected from a large pool of applicants to represent a range of occupations and different religious denominations, mainly unsophisticated people, not schooled in ideas of liberty. Placed on a hostile frontier, they, not surprisingly, soon exhibited illiberal and racist behaviors. Like many others who came from Britain in later years, they were soon extremely critical of British policies to their adopted country. What was appropriate for Britain, the settlers would often say, were not applicable in the particular circumstances of southern Africa. Though in making such arguments the 1820 settlers sometimes appealed to British liberties as applying to them, only the most remarkable of them has a claim to be called one of the founders of liberalism in South Africa. This was Thomas Pringle, who had edited literary magazines in Edinburgh and been influenced by the Scottish moral philosophers Dugald Stewart and Adam Ferguson before he left for the Cape. Before he moved from the eastern Cape to Cape Town, the capital, Pringle persuaded John Fairbairn, with whom he had read classics at Edinburgh University, to join him in South Africa. To his invitation Fairbairn responded enthusiastically that they might become "the [Benjamin] Franklins of the Kaap."[19]

Before we consider how Pringle and Fairbairn took a stand for liberal values in Cape Town in the mid-1820s, it is necessary to notice other ways in which liberal ideas were transmitted from Britain, and how liberties were extended at the Cape for Khoi and slaves. In the first two decades of the nineteenth century, those who worked for the London Missionary Society (LMS) in the colony were among the chief bearers of liberal ideas. These missionaries came from a variety of European countries, but they were all, albeit to different degrees, influenced by ideas from the country in which their society was based, whether in previous life they had been a medical doctor in the Netherlands or a carpenter in Essex.[20] Like others with backgrounds in the Enlightenment and the Evangelical Revival, these men took with them to the Cape ideas of racial equality not found among Europeans at the Cape previously. The LMS missionaries soon put these ideas into practice by taking Khoi wives and partners and adopting the way of life of those among whom they worked, whether Khoi or San or slave. They sought to pass on their ideas to their converts through their teaching and example, and to the "native agents" they trained.[21]

---

[19] S. Dubow, A *Commonwealth of Knowledge: Science, Sensibility and white South Africa, 1820–2000* (Oxford: Oxford University Press, 2006), p. 32. On influences on Pringle, see ibid, p. 29. See also the entries on the two men in the *Oxford Dictionary of National Biography*.

[20] These were the backgrounds of the two leading LMS missionaries in the first decade of the nineteenth century, Johannes van der Kemp and James Read.

[21] The fullest recent study is E. Elbourne, *Blood Ground: Colonialism, Missions, and the Contest for Christianity in the Cape Colony and Britain* (Montreal: McGill University Press, 2003). Van der Kemp married a freed slave, forty-five years his junior, in 1806 and had four children with her.

Perhaps even more than the LMS missionaries, however, the British government was, in the early nineteenth century, a major transmitter of liberal ideas to the Cape. These ideas traveled from London to its officials there, but not always in a direct and unambiguous way. Perhaps the main example of a liberal measure passed by the British Parliament that had significant consequences when implemented at the Cape was the act of 1807 that ended the slave trade. From 1808 a British naval squadron, stationed at the Cape, was active in intercepting foreign ships in the waters off the colony and along the east African coast, to prevent anyone from continuing the trade. Those released by the squadron from intercepted slave ships – called at the time Prize Negroes or Prize Slaves, and later Liberated Africans – were not taken back to where they had come from, but remained at the Cape as a new labor force, for they were "apprenticed" for fourteen years in conditions little different from those pertaining to the slaves. What was often presented as a humanitarian mission meant a new form of forced labor at the Cape, where well over 4,000 Prize Negroes were landed. They had been saved from the Atlantic passage and, had they survived that passage, from life as a slave in the Americas, but their freedom at the Cape was very limited, at least until their period of "apprenticeship" came to an end, and often after it ended as well.[22]

The British wanted order in their new colony, and their idea of order included the expulsion from the eastern districts of thousands of Xhosa-speaking Africans in 1812, who were seen as intruders, without rights in the colony. The Khoi, by contrast, were conquered people, and while many European settlers continued to view them as inferior people without rights, the British accepted that they were within the colony to stay, and therefore that they should be subjected to colonial laws. Concerned to make their rule of the Cape more efficient, British officials first tightened up the conditions in which the Khoi lived, insisting that they must have a fixed place of abode. Though the missionaries condemned Governor Caledon's so-called Hottentot Code of 1809 as restrictive, it brought the Khoi within the law, an essential preliminary for extending them rights as citizens, and it regulated relations between settlers and their Khoi servants, with the aim of protecting the Khoi from abuses of settler power. The Khoi were now informed that they could take complaints to local authorities.

Though local officials were told by Cradock, Caledon's successor as governor, that he was following "instructions I myself have received from His Majesty's Government ... to extend to all classes of persons 'equal justice' and 'equal protection,'" he did not merely pass on instructions from London. His circular to local officials added that "in the dispensation of Justice, no dispensation is to be admitted – whether the Complaint arise with the Man of wealth,

[22] C. Saunders, "Liberated Africans at the Cape of Good Hope," *International Journal of African Historical Studies*, 18 (2) 1985. Money collected from the distribution of Prize Slaves went to build the South African College School: see W. Ritchie, *The History of the South African College, 1829–1918* (Cape Town: T. M. Miller, 1918).

or the poor Man, the Master or the slave, the Christian or the Hottentot: the same patient and equal attention is to be paid to the representation, and the most careful inquiry is to ensure that unbiased justice follow. ..." He added that special vigilance should be given to "the lesser description of offences, which, from their obscurity and supposed insignificance, escape observation and punishment." He concluded by expressing his concern over "the uncontrolled severity of the Powerful over the Weak," because "such persecutions evade the direct Interposition of the Law, and are alone to be remedied by the energy of an active and enlightened Magistrate, intent to advance the progress of true religion and Christianity."[23] Cradock's instructions were not only passed on to lesser local government officials; leading members of the Dutch collaborating elite with whom the British worked took them over as well and helped propagate them.[24] Thus, when J. A. Truter opened the new premises for the Court of Justice in 1815, he called for the administration of laws to "be effected with unbiased judgment, and without respect of persons."[25]

Caledon's Code meant that Khoi could now bring cases against colonists before the courts, and in the so-called Black Circuit of 1812 they did just that, alleging ill-treatment by white farmers. All this was a far cry from the DEIC days, when there were laws but no equality before the law – a man of European origin who murdered a slave in 1793 was given no more than a reprimand[26] – and when the Khoi were not within the ambit of the law at all.[27] By the 1820s, when a white farmer murdered a Khoi or slave, he was sentenced to death.[28]

---

[23] Circular to Landdrosts, 1812, quoted in N. Penn, "The Onder Bokkeveld Ear Atrocity," *Kronos*, 31 (November 2005), p. 84. Cf. W. Dooling, *Slavery, Emancipation and Colonial Rule in South Africa* (Pietermaritzburg: University of KwaZulu Natal Press, 2007), p. 70. John Francis Cradock, son of the archbishop of Dublin and governor at the Cape from 1811 to 1814, like other British officials at the Cape, spent much of his active career abroad, not in England itself. How he and other British officials at the Cape were influenced by prior careers in India (Cradock had served in Madras) remains to be researched. Cf. the relevant entries in *Oxford Dictionary of National Biography*.

[24] The British ruled their new possession through the old ruling class, which was allowed to remain in place; it acquiesced to British rule in return.

[25] Dooling, *Slavery*, p. 75, citing A. Du Toit and H. Giliomee, *Afrikaner Political Thought* (Cape Town: David Philip, 1983), p. 101.

[26] Dooling, *Slavery*, p. 16.

[27] In "The Rule of Law at the Cape of Good Hope in the Eighteenth Century," *Journal of Imperial and Commonwealth History*, 1980, Robert Ross criticized Rodney Davenport's statement in *The Oxford History of South Africa*, vol. I, that there was no rule of law then, but Ross did not understand the concept as Davenport was using it. As Ben Beinart pointed out in "The Rule of Law," *Acta Juridica*, 1962, A. V. Dicey (*Introduction to the Study of the Law of the Constitution* [10th ed., London: Macmillan, 1959]) contrasted the rule of law "with every system of government based on the exercise by persons in authority of wide, arbitrary, or discretionary powers of constraint" (p. 101). After associating the rule of law with individual rights, Beinart concluded that "the basic and indispensable element in the maintenance of the Rule of Law must remain an independent and impartial judiciary administering justice according to law where the government and officials as well as citizens can be brought to book" (p. 138).

[28] Dooling, *Slavery*, pp. 78–79. Cradock had referred a case of 1812 to London, when a farmer who had killed a slave was given a mere three-month sentence.

The British did not think it politic to overturn the existing body of Roman-Dutch law when they arrived at the Cape, and that it remained in place did not facilitate the extension of liberties, but it was slowly amalgamated with the principles of English common law.[29] In that process, one of the main developments was the new Charter of Justice of 1828, which provided for trial by jury in both civil and criminal cases, that having been one of the recommendations of visiting commissioners sent out by London to see how the Cape could more closely be brought within the practice of other parts of the empire.[30] Though the law relating to juries contained no color bar, juries were dominated by whites, which led a British writer to observe that trial by jury in South Africa was sometimes "an arrangement whereby a white man who had forgotten himself in dealing with a black man could be relieved from the consequences."[31]

John Philip, LMS superintendent in South Africa from 1819, took up the Khoi cause more vigorously and effectively than anyone else. A preacher from Aberdeen who had briefly studied in London, where he had gotten to know Thomas Buxton and the missionary John Campbell,[32] Philip gave Adam Smith his authority for his demand that the Khoi should be allowed freely to participate in a free labor market.[33] He identified the pass system as the cornerstone of their oppression, and his lobbying was responsible for the passage first of Cape Ordinance 50 of 1828, which removed restrictions on them and "free persons of colour," and then of the British Order in Council of 1829, which put Ordinance 50 beyond the power of the local government to amend, except with the consent of the British government. The significance of the Order in Council was shown in 1834, when a Cape draft vagrancy law that would have re-introduced some of the restrictions done away with by Ordinance 50 was disallowed by the British government.

As with other freedoms, those granted by Ordinance 50 were heavily circumscribed in practice: Though Khoi and the "other free persons of colour" mentioned in the ordinance were in theory free to take their labor to the employer of

---

[29] For this complex process see, inter alia, R. Zimmermann and D. Visser, *Southern Cross: Civil Law and Common Law in South Africa* (Oxford: Clarendon Press, 1996).

[30] Cf. Davenport, "Consolidation", p. 302, and A.Sachs, *Justice in South Africa*. (Brighton: Sussex University Press, 1973), ch. 2. The commissioners had recommended that trial by jury not apply in cases involving people of different races, in the interest of protecting non-Europeans, but were overruled. There were continuing links between liberalism and legalism, and even at the height of apartheid a commitment to law did something to temper the authoritarianism of those in power, which is why a judge such as Richard Goldstone could be as effective as he was. Cf. R. J. Goldstone, *Do Judges Speak Out?* (Cape Town, University of Cape Town graduation address, 1993) and *For Humanity* (Johannesburg: Witwatersrand University Press, 2000).

[31] Sachs, *Justice*, p. 60.

[32] On Philip see the classic works by W. M. Macmillan, *The Cape Colour Question* (London: Faber and Gwyer, 1927) and *Bantu Boer and Briton* (1929; 2nd ed., Oxford: Oxford University Press, 1963), and A. Ross, *John Philip: Missions, Race and Politics in South Africa* (Aberdeen: Aberdeen University Press, 1986). Other missionaries (the Wesleyan Methodists from 1816 and the Presbyterians from 1821) were less active politically.

[33] J. Philip, *Researches in South Africa* (London: James Duncan, 1928), vol. I, pp. 367–70.

their choice, their societies had been destroyed and many were dependent on the white farmers who employed them. They could now own land, but, besides plots in the Kat River Settlement on the volatile eastern frontier, none was given them. Some Kat River people said that they appreciated that Ordinance 50 had given them "a first taste of freedom," but others asked in vain for more land to be restored to them.[34] Yet it is wrong to downplay the significance of Ordinance 50. The idea that rights belonged to all who lived in the colony, not only people of European or British descent, was one that was to grow, not only among those who came from Britain but also among those with no British roots. The most striking example of this is Andries Stockenström, the Cape Town–born son of a Swedish-born Cape official. He became a liberal administrator, thanks in part to the discussions he had with Philip and Pringle in the eastern Cape.[35] Other administrators of the 1830s and 1840s in the frontier region were also receptive to the mediation of British ideas and were consequently relatively liberal in their attitudes to Khoi and did not display the deep hostility of most settlers to the Xhosa and Thembu across the colonial border.[36] An important strand of liberal thought at the Cape in the early nineteenth century was criticism of British frontier policy as too harsh and pro-settler. These critics called for the people beyond the frontier to be seen as equals, with whom treaties could be signed, and not as enemies to be conquered. Philip and others accepted that British rule should be extended, but only if it protected Africans in their lands. This tradition of liberal imperialism would fall into disrepute as the century wore on.[37]

On his arrival at the Cape, Philip denounced slavery as "injurious to morals, to industry, to wealth and comfort"[38] but he chose not to campaign on that issue, and instead threw himself into the campaign to improve the condition of the Khoi. The issues of ameliorating the condition of slaves, and then ending slavery itself, were taken up in Britain itself and transmitted via official channels to the Cape. A series of British laws, made applicable at the Cape, required

[34] E. Elbourne, "Freedom at Issue: Vagrancy Legislation and the Meaning of Freedom in Britain and the Cape colony, 1799 to 1842," *Slavery and Abolition*, 15 (2) August 1994, p. 145.

[35] On Stockenstrom's liberalism see especially Du Toit and Giliomee, *Afrikaner Political Thought*, pp. 78–126, and A. Du Toit's recent article on Stockenstrom and Gandhi in *Journal of Southern African Studies*, 2007, which sees him as a champion of human rights. It is not surprising to find that he is buried in Kensal Green churchyard in London.

[36] E.g., Charles Stretch, for whom see B. A. le Cordeur, ed., *The Journal of Charles Lennox Stretch* (Cape Town: Maskew Miller Longman, 1988).

[37] Cf. especially C. W. de Kiewiet, *The Imperial Factor in South Africa* (Cambridge: Cambridge University Press, 1937). In calling on the British government to institute an enquiry when a leading Xhosa chief was killed in 1835, Philip wanted "even the men of our Colonies to call things by their proper names," so as to "prevent the British name from being [handed] down to posterity like that of the Spanish loaded with the execrations of all Nations": A. Lester, *Imperial Networks. Creating Identities in Nineteenth-Century South Africa and Britain* (London: Routledge, 2001), p. 126.

[38] Macmillan, *Cape Colour Question*, pp. 76–78.

improvements in the conditions of life of the slaves.[39] The idea, again coming from Britain itself, was "to confer upon them [the slaves] one civil privilege after another, as they shall be found capable of bearing it, till at length they shall rise insensibly to the rank of free peasantry."[40] Only a few Cape slaves came to believe that they should take up arms to fight for their freedom, an idea that Galant and the rebels of 1825 found to their cost did not work, for they did not win their freedom but were executed. Other slaves were, from 1830, able to take their masters to court, which they often did successfully.

The slave owners reluctantly went along with the new rules, being concerned above all with their slaves as property, for, if emancipation came, would they be compensated adequately for the loss of their property in slaves? The only local attempt to end slavery came in the form of the Cape of Good Hope Philanthropic Society for Aiding Deserving Slaves to Purchase their Freedom, established in 1828, and all that society achieved was the manumission of 126 slaves.[41] Fairbairn was one of those who in the 1820s distanced themselves from those who advocated "liberty" for the slaves on "moral and religious grounds." He argued instead for a "statecraft" determined by the "principles of Political Science," which meant that slaves should only be freed if adequate compensation was paid. Others might follow the Ten Commandments, he wrote; he was "content with the Multiplication Table."[42] In the early 1830s, however, he came to accept, on utilitarian grounds, that abolition should come as soon as possible. When the British Act of 1833 brought an end to slavery, the slave owners continued to be most concerned with the level of compensation they would receive, especially as the slaves had to serve four more years as "apprentices" before being able, in theory, to move freely about the colony.[43]

While the idea of a free press came from England – though in the 1820s a greater degree of press freedom was to be found in the United States than in the British Isles – it had to be fought for at the Cape. A fierce struggle was waged, first against the British governor and then against "procrastination and vacillation in London."[44] In 1823 Pringle and Fairbairn, who became Philip's son-in-law, decided to begin a *South African Journal*, of which two issues were

---

[39] For example, in 1812, Cradock abolished the statute forbidding the sale of Christian slaves, for slave-owners had been discouraged from educating their slaves in Christianity; in 1813, the governor limited the number of lashes a slave could receive. Further improvements came in 1826, 1830, and 1831, even by Lord Charles Somerset.

[40] Quoted in J. Walvin, *England, Slaves, and Freedom* (Basingstoke: Macmillan, 1986), p. 151.

[41] R. Watson, *The Slave Question. Liberty and Property in South Africa* (Johannesburg: Wits University Press, 1991), ch. 4 and p. 85.

[42] South African Commercial Advertiser (SACA), 2 March 1831.

[43] On all this see Watson, *Slave Question*, and J. Mason, *Social Death and Resurrection: Slavery and Emancipation in South Africa* (Charlottesville: University of Virginia Press, 2003).

[44] B. le Cordeur, "The British Contribution to the Newspaper Press in South Africa," *Bulletin of the South African Cultural History Museum*, 10 (1989), pp. 28–39.

published in early 1824.[45] In their introduction to the first of these, they praised
Britain above all countries: "[W]ith a self-protecting Constitution, and ... a
noble spirit of love for the whole human family suffused through the mass of
her population ... Britain stands at the head of the history, – and of the reality, –
almost of the hopes of Man."[46] When an article by Pringle appeared that was
critical of the way the settlers were being treated, the autocratic High Tory
Governor, Lord Charles Somerset, "who lived in hourly terror of Jacobin-
ism,"[47] insisted on pre-publication censorship for both the *Journal* and the first
nongovernmental newspaper, the *South African Commercial Advertiser*, which
George Greig, another settler not part of the 1820 group, started in the same
year. Pringle, Fairbairn, and Greig refused to submit to such censorship, the
Journal was closed (though a variant continued in Dutch), and the issue of the
freedom of the press was taken to Britain. In 1828 Fairbairn won the right to
publish without pre-censorship, at a time when the press in Britain itself was
still "circumscribed by a variety of legal and fiscal restrictions."[48]

The principle of a free press then won – and it was given legal force by Cape
Ordinance 60 of 1829 – survived and, though often infringed by the state
during the apartheid era, especially in the state of emergency imposed in the
mid-1980s,[49] remains to this day, now as a bulwark of South African democracy. As Basil le Cordeur has pointed out, until about the Second World War,
most of the senior staff on English-language newspapers in South Africa were
British born and British trained. They looked to Fleet Street as their model and
relied on contacts there for much of their news.[50] And after the indigenization
of the press, links with Britain were important in sustaining press freedoms in
South Africa.[51]

Pringle and Fairbairn also took with them to the Cape from Britain the idea
that voluntary societies, independent of the state, were important parts of what
we would today call civil society. Until he left for the Cape, Fairbairn had been a
member of the Literary and Philosophical Society of Newcastle,[52] and within
months of arriving he and Pringle had founded both an independent school and

---

[45] On Fairbairn see H. C. Botha, *John Fairbairn in South Africa* (Cape Town: Historical Publica-
    tion Society, 1984); J. L. Meltzer, "The Growth of Cape Town Commerce and the Role of John
    Fairbairn's *Advertiser* (1835–1859)", MA thesis, University of Cape Town, 1989; B. A. Le
    Cordeur, *The Politics of Eastern Cape Separatism, 1820–1854* (Cape Town: Oxford University
    Press, 1981).

[46] *South African Journal*, I (Jan.–Feb., 1824), p. 7 (reprinted Cape Town, 1963).

[47] Le Cordeur, "The British Contribution," p. 28.

[48] B. le Cordeur, "International Aspects of the Struggle for the Freedom of the Press at the Cape:
    New Perspectives," *Acta Academica*, 23 (3), August 1991, p. 140; W. Wickwar, *The Struggle for
    the Freedom of the Press, 1819–1832* (London: George Allen and Unwin, 1928).

[49] Cf. C. Merrett, *A Culture of Censorship* (Cape Town: David Philip, 1994).

[50] Le Cordeur, "British Contribution," p. 33.

[51] The title of the most important newspaper of the past two decades, the *Mail and Guardian*,
    indicates its continuing ties with *The Guardian*.

[52] S. Dubow, *A Commonwealth of Knowledge* (Oxford: Oxford University Press, 2006), p. 33 and
    n. 60.

a literary society. The Classical and Commercial Academy they founded in Cape Town in December 1823 had enrolled fifty pupils within a month of its launch. Though Truter and other local luminaries joined the South African Literary Society that Fairbairn and Pringle began, it was soon prevented from continuing by the autocratic governor, who refused to consent to "the establishment of an association which might have a tendency to produce political discussion."[53] Fairbairn revived the society after Somerset left the Cape. Through such societies, the many newspapers that were founded after the *South African Commercial Advertiser*, some in the smaller country towns, yet which carried news of what was happening in far-away corners of the empire, and through publications such as the *Cape Monthly Magazine*, which first appeared in 1857 and ran into the 1870s, ideas from Britain were transmitted to the broader literate community at the Cape in the Victorian age and beyond.[54] And the secondary schools that began to open – the South African College in 1829, the Diocesan College in 1844, and a host of others as the century wore on – drew their staff overwhelmingly from Britain, retained close ties with "the mother country," and formed vital transmitters of ideas from there to South Africa. On their playing fields, boys in particular learned the concept of "fair play." Of the schoolteachers recruited from England, James Rose Innes, who became the Cape's first superintendent of education in 1839, gained a reputation for promoting liberal ideas, and his son became the leading liberal at the Cape in the late nineteenth century.[55] From the South African College would develop in the early twentieth century the University of Cape Town, which, along with other English-speaking universities, would, through their ethos and teaching, pass on liberal ideas to generations of students.[56]

From Britain came too the idea that as a colony of settlement – though one that had been conquered – the Cape should become self-governing. At the Cape the emerging middle classes strongly supported this as a way to check the arbitrary power of government, as shown in the actions of a series of autocratic governors. Fairbairn and Philip were ambivalent on the self-government issue, for while they favored representative institutions in principle, they feared that the introduction of such institutions would mean a transfer of power from the colonial government to settlers, whether of Dutch or English origin – and Fairbairn viewed all who made Africa their home, whether from "England or Holland," as "all Africans"[57] – who would rule illiberally. The existence of slavery did delay the grant of any kind of representative institutions,[58] and it was not

---

[53] *Papers of the South African Literary Society* (Cape Town, 1825), p. 23.

[54] Cf. Dubow, *Commonwealth*, esp. ch. 2, on the *Cape Monthly Magazine*.

[55] H. M. Wright, ed., *Sir James Rose Innes: Selected Correspondence* (Cape Town: Van Riebeeck Society, 1972).

[56] For the late twentieth century this may best be traced in S. Saunders, *Vice-Chancellor on a Tightrope* (Cape Town: David Philip, 2000), and M. Shear, *Wits: A University in the Apartheid Era* (Johannesburg: Wits University Press, 1996).

[57] *South African Commercial Advertiser (SACA)*, 17 March 1824.

[58] Watson, *Slave Question*, pp. 71, 191.

until 1834, almost forty years after the British first arrived, that an entirely nominated legislative council was instituted, with some unofficial members. A further two decades were to pass before the Cape Parliament was born.

That the Cape should be given representative government was agreed in principle in London in 1846, but a mass settler protest helped bring it about. When in 1849 the colonial secretary in London sent convicts to the Cape, breaking a promise that they would not be landed there, Fairbairn and others created an Anti-Convict Association to put pressure on London to concede self-government. Fairbairn reminded readers of the *South African Commercial Advertiser* of the social contract made by "Englishmen" in the Glorious Revolution of 1688 and of the need to "resist despotism," the "dry rot of the constitution."[59] The colonists argued that were convicts to be allowed to land, colonial society would be degraded; their protest was "framed in terms of middle-class respectability."[60] In the face of the protest, London agreed that the convicts should be sent on to Australia, and an elected assembly was now agreed to. By then it was accepted, by British officials working on the instructions of, and with the support of, governments in Britain, that all legislation at the Cape should be nonracial and applicable to all. Though humanitarianism was on the wane in the late 1840s, this principle had become entrenched a decade and more earlier, when concern for the rights of indigenous people in the empire was at its height.[61] In introducing the Cape Masters and Servants Ordinance of 1841, which did not mention race, the governor said that "a law applying only to Coloureds would perpetuate their status as an inferior people."[62] Similarly, the British proclamation annexing Natal in 1843 ruled out discrimination on grounds of race.

What property and/or educational qualification should be required for the Cape franchise? After the Reform Act of 1832 a high qualification was perhaps unlikely, but that the Cape ended up with one lower than Britain would get until 1867 was thanks in large measure to Fairbairn and the Cape's attorney-general, William Porter. An Ulster Protestant of dissenting liberal Presbyterian views, Porter respected England as "the home of freedom" and was progressive enough to advocate the abolition of capital punishment.[63] He and Fairbairn wanted the franchise to be low enough to include both Afrikaners and those of indigenous or mixed descent, in the belief that a low franchise would foster common loyalties and interests. Porter famously said that he would rather

[59] *SACA*, 23 May 1849.
[60] K. McKenzie, *Scandal in the Colonies* (Melbourne: Melbourne University Press, 2004), p. 176.
[61] See especially A. Bank, "Liberals and Their Enemies."
[62] H. J. and R. Simons, *Class and Colour in South Africa* (Harmondsworth: Penguin, 1968), p. 20; J. S. Marais, *The Cape Coloured People* (London: Longman, 1939), p. 200.
[63] J. McCracken, *New Light at the Cape of Good Hope: William Porter. Father of Cape Liberalism* (Belfast: Ulster Historical Association, 1993), p. 95. There is no entry for Porter in *Oxford Dictionary of National Biography*.

"meet the Hottentot at the hustings voting for his representative than ... in the wilds with a gun in his hand."[64]

The representative government granted in 1853 did mean, as Philip and Fairbairn had feared, that white settlers in what was effectively a "parliament of masters" could pass legislation that, though nominally nonracial, was not in the interests of the black majority. A revised Masters and Servants Act of 1856, approved in Whitehall, bound black servants to their white employers.[65] British liberalism and the grant of representative government, then, was no challenge to white supremacy, but reinforced it, for whites still had virtually exclusive access to power and wealth.[66] Despite this, it was but another step from representative government – which at the Cape, as elsewhere, was unstable, because the legislature did not control the executive – to the grant of full self-government. That further step was again assumed in Britain to be natural, given what had happened elsewhere in the empire; full self-government "belonged of right to settler colonies."[67] As Niall Ferguson has recently written, responsible government was a way of "reconciling the practice of empire with the principle of liberty"; there was no question of refusing it and having to fight another battle of Lexington in the streets of Cape Town.[68] Those who fought for responsible government at the Cape were led by the farmer John Charles Molteno, who was born in England and knew of the Durham Report of 1839 and what had happened in Canada.[69] The Colonial Office in London was so frustrated by colonial opposition to representative government that the colonial secretary wrote to the Cape governor in 1869: "If the colonists will not allow themselves to be governed, it follows that they must adopt the responsibility of governing."[70]

With responsible government inaugurated at the Cape in 1872, the colony was freed from any effective intervention from London.[71] The low qualification of occupying property worth £25 was maintained, and the Cape liberal tradition was held up as a model for other parts of the not yet united South Africa,

---

[64] Quoted in S.Trapido, "The Origins of the Cape Franchise Qualifications of 1853," *Journal of African History*, 5 (1) (1964), p. 48. In a famous memorandum prepared for the governor in 1848 Porter wrote: "I deem it to be just and expedient to place the suffrage within the reach of the more intelligent and industrious of the men of colour ... because by showing to all classes ... that no man's station is, in this free country, determined by the accident of his colour, all ranks of men are stimulated to improve or maintain their relative positions": J. McCracken, *New Light*, p. 105.

[65] J. S. Marais, *The Cape Coloured People* (London: Longman, 1939), p. 205.

[66] R. Elphick and H. Giliomee, eds., *The Shaping of South African Society* (3rd ed., Cape Town: Maskew Miller Longman, 1989), p. 561.

[67] A. B. Keith, *The Sovereignty of the British Dominions* (London: Macmillan, 1929), p. 5.

[68] N. Ferguson, *Empire. How Britain Made the Modern World* (London: Penguin, 2004), p. 112.

[69] Cf. J. McCracken, *The Cape Parliament* (Oxford: Clarendon Press, 1967), p. 8; P. A. Molteno, *The Life and Times of Sir John Charles Molteno*, 2 vols. (London: Smith, Elder, 1900); P. Lewsen, *John X. Merriman* (New Haven, CT: Yale University Press, 1982); C. Saunders, "The Annexation of the Transkeian Territories," *Archives Year Book for South African History*, 39 (1976) [Pretoria, 1978].

[70] Granville to Wodehouse, 11 December 1869, quoted in Davenport, "Consolidation", p. 330.

[71] In theory, London could refuse assent to any Cape legislation in a two-year period, but in practice this was not exercised.

where the contrary principle of "no equality in church or state" prevailed, and where the majority of the large number of new arrivals from Britain, those attracted by the changed economic fortunes of the region after the discovery of first diamonds and then gold, were to settle. In the late nineteenth century, the Cape tradition did come under attack in the colony itself, when large African territories east of the Kei River were annexed, in the new era of industrial capitalism, with the almost insatiable demand for labor for the mines. The qualifications for the vote were tightened in 1887 and again in 1892, when an educational requirement was added. Though there was no bar to it, no black person ever became a member of the Cape Parliament. The Cape tradition survived into the twentieth century, and continued to have meaning and strong supporters, but its limits were clear.[72]

Once the Cape had become fully self-governing, the smaller colony of Natal could hardly be denied that status, even though it had no effective color blind franchise.[73] Nor could the republics conquered in the Anglo-Boer war, which had then become British colonies. Nor could the Union of South Africa in 1910, which resulted from two campaigns with different origins that converged in 1909, the one driven by imperial officials and the other by South African politicians, Jan Smuts prime among them. At the National Convention held to discuss the making of a union of South Africa, John X. Merriman, Walter Stanford, and F. S. Malan from the Cape all tried to extend the Cape franchise to the rest of what would become South Africa, but they found that the best they could do was keep it for what would become the new Cape Province in the new Union of South Africa. So the united South Africa began life with a color bar in its constitution, for it was laid down that no black person could become a member of the new Union Parliament. Some liberals suggested that South Africa should follow Canada and Australia and become a federation rather than a union, and a federation might have provided more protection for the Cape liberal tradition, but it was not to be. When the British settlers in Southern Rhodesia, most of whom had come from the Cape, decided not to join the Union in 1922, they did so because they did not want to come under Afrikaner rule and wanted the freedom to rule as they wished; the biography of the leading settler in the movement to win self-government in that colony refers to "the liberation of Southern Rhodesia."[74]

---

[72] Cf. P. Lewsen, "The Cape Liberal Tradition: Myth or Reality?," *Race*, 13 (1971), and Lewsen's chapter in J. Butler, R. Elphick and D. Welsh, eds., *Democratic Liberalism in South Africa* (Middletown, CT: Wesleyan University Press, 1988).

[73] In Natal, wrote A. B. Keith, "the natives were denied the franchise save on almost impossible conditions, and their overwhelming numbers presented exceptional difficulties.... It was indeed obvious that the colony was not ripe for self-government, but, after hesitation ... responsibility was conceded in 1893, with the reservation of a vague sphere of authority to the Governor as supreme chief. In this capacity he was not to be bound to act on ministerial advice, and certain funds were rendered available to him beyond Parliamentary control": *Dominions*, pp. 69–70.

[74] J. P. R. Wallis, *One Man's hand: The Story of Sir Charles Coghlan and the Liberation of Rhodesia* (London: Longmans, Green and Co, 1950). I thank Donald Lowry for pointing out this highly ironic phrase, given the nature of settler rule in that colony.

Liberals in Britain played a leading role in selling out the black majority in South Africa. The liberal government hailed the new Union as a triumph of reconciliation between Briton and Boer. A strong Union, it was said, would be able to act justly toward that majority. But all that was done effectively to restrain the power of the whites to whom power was now transferred was to keep the three small High Commission territories outside the new Union, out of concern for their African populations. The conditions laid down in 1909 for any future incorporation in the Union to take place would ensure that the three territories would remain outside the Union, though this was not what was initially expected to be the case. Union meant that the white minority could do what it liked internally – it was of little significance that appeals could still be taken from the Appellate Division of the Supreme Court to the Privy Council – and in 1936, by which time even the right of appeal to the Privy Council had gone and South Africa had acquired full freedom by the Statute of Westminster, the battle to retain the Cape as a nonracial franchise for black Africans was lost, when at last the necessary two-thirds vote of both Houses of Parliament to remove it was obtained. As the most enlightened both at the Cape and in London had feared, the liberal grant of the power of self-government opened the door for racist rule, which from 1948 took the form of apartheid, the most advanced form of white supremacy.[75]

Because this topic has been so neglected, much about the process of transmission of liberal ideas from Britain to South Africa remains unclear and demands further research. South African historians lack the detailed biographies and studies of intellectual thought that have so enriched American and British historiographies. No one has trawled through the relevant publications to track, for example, the use in South Africa of the idea of "free-born Englishman" and the different meanings given to that term over time. No one has done a systematic study of the spread of print media in the nineteenth-century Cape and the way it helped in the dissemination of liberal ideas. We lack the kind of detailed analysis of the metropole– colonial relationship to be found in Catherine Hall's book on England and Jamaica in the early Victorian era, and no one has demonstrated the role of sport, say, in the transmission of values from Britain to southern Africa.[76] But certain things are clear. One is that the ideas that came from British, whether via British officials or missionaries, did not remain confined to British settlers in South Africa, but filtered through to such

---

[75] For all this see especially G. Fredrickson, *White Supremacy. A Comparative Study in American and South African History* (New York: Oxford University Press, 1981).

[76] C. Hall, *Civilising Subjects. Colony and Metropole in the English Imagination, 1830–1867* (Chicago: University of Chicago Press, 2002). On sport cf. A. Odendaal, *The Story of An African Game* (Claremont, South Africa: David Philip, 2003), which is about "Black cricketers and the unmasking of one of cricket's greatest myths, South Africa, 1850–2003" (back jacket), the myth that blacks did not play cricket.

Anglicized Afrikaners as Henry de Villiers, later Lord de Villiers,[77] and to others, including, for example, Saul Solomon, born of Jewish parents from England, educated at the new South African College in Cape Town, member of the Cape Parliament, strong advocate of responsible government, and opponent of state aid to churches.[78] And these ideas were also taken up by black South Africans, most notably from the 1880s, when through the influence of teachers from Britain such as the influential James Stewart of the Presbyterian Lovedale College, men such as John Tengo Jabavu became firm adherents of British values and ideals, even though they continued to suffer social discrimination. The mission schools that provided such education were closely linked to mother churches in Britain itself, themselves often linked to the London-based Aborigines Protection and Anti-Slavery societies. Imperial propaganda was strong, especially on occasions such as the Diamond Jubilee of 1897, at which it was stressed that Britain stood for justice, fairness, and equality before the law.[79]

Jabavu was able, as editor of his own newspaper in King William's Town, to help spread such ideas among the African community of the eastern Cape. Though he would become disillusioned with Britain in the Anglo-Boer war, when his newspaper was closed down by the government because of his criticism of the British "war-party," he and other black people nevertheless remained hopeful that Britain would act to restrain whites from carrying illiberal policies further. In the Anglo-Boer war, Abraham Esau hoped that Britain would intervene to help black people and led "coloured" resistance in the Cape on the side of Britain.[80] Even after the war, and the grave disillusionment of the Treaty of Vereeniging, which did not extend the Cape franchise to the conquered republics, most black leaders continued to place hope in the idea of appealing to Britain on the basis of the values that they associated with that country, only to find Britain refusing to interfere in what it now said were internal South African issues, such as the infamous Native Land Act of 1913. Yet faith in British ideals remained strong among many black people well beyond the 1920s. The leading black intellectual of the early twentieth century, Solomon Plaatje, did much to propagate British ideas; he spent most of the First World War in Britain and was the first person to translate Shakespeare into an indigenous black African language.[81]

---

[77] De Villiers was of Huguenot descent, born in Paarl, Cape. As an Anglicised Afrikaner, he worked for responsible government and was eventually to head the National Convention that agreed the terms of Union in 1909: see E. A. Walker, *Lord de Villiers and His Times: South Africa, 1842–1914* (London: Constable, 1925).

[78] W. E. G. Solomon, *Saul Solomon* (Cape Town: Oxford University Press, 1948).

[79] C. Saunders, "African Attitudes to Britain and the Empire before and after the South African War," in D. Lowry, ed., *The South African War Reappraised* (Manchester: Manchester University Press, 2000).

[80] B. Nasson, *Abraham Esau's War. A Black South African War in the Cape* (Cambridge: Cambridge University Press, 1991).

[81] C. Saunders, "African Attitudes"; B. Willan, *Sol. Plaatje, South African Nationalist, 1876–1932* (London: Heinemann, 1984).

As Ernest Barker pointed out, when Britain was facing its greatest challenge, in the early years of the Second World War, "the liberty of British settlers is not the only liberty. There is also the liberty of native populations."[82] Ideas of individual freedom, transmitted through imperial officials, missionaries, and settlers from Britain, could clash when applied. Settlers appealed to ideas of liberty to justify ruling themselves, but settler rule was often intolerant. In the early nineteenth century, in the heyday of humanitarian liberalism, British officials brought from London the idea that all people in the colony should be treated the same, and that laws should not discriminate on the grounds of race, but where masters were white and servants were black or brown, the effect of a nonracial Masters and Servants Ordinance was to consolidate, not weaken, racial domination. As Albie Sachs has written, the effect of such measures "was not to constitute a revolution, but to remove certain barriers to emancipation; not to eradicate racial domination, but to sanction its class rather than its colour or cultural aspects; and not to destroy privilege, but to regularise its operation and restrain its arbitrary exercise."[83] So British ideals of freedom were transmitted in complex and contradictory ways. They spread from the British to the Dutch/Afrikaner collaborating elite and, largely through teachers at the missionary schools, to blacks. They entered a society in which slavery and a racial hierarchy were firmly in place and became intertwined with racial ideas that suggested that not all people were equally entitled to liberty. The question became where one drew the line. Local white settlers tended to confine ideas of liberty to their own kind, and from the mid-1840s British officials were less inclined to promote equality, as humanitarian liberalism declined.[84]

Yet, for all their contradictions, all the limitations on them in practice, liberal ideas had long-term significance. As we have seen, by the mid-1840s they had been taken over by those residents at the Cape who accepted as a matter of principle that no racial line should be drawn. By the late 1840s such individuals were defending what they saw as colonial liberties against the oppressive British state. For Philip, Pringle, Porter, and others in their tradition – and in South Africa of the 1960s that would include, say, Alan Paton, leader of the Liberal Party – liberalism meant working to end the oppression of the majority and extending to that majority "equality in church and state." In the Boer republics, established by those who had moved away from British rule precisely because they did not like the measure of equality the British had introduced at the Cape, black people were denied such equality, and after the Cape became part of the larger Union of South Africa in 1910, and those of British descent found themselves without effective political power, it seemed that liberal ideas might be

---

[82] Barker, *Ideas and Ideals*, p. 79.

[83] Sachs, *Justice in South Africa*, p. 40.

[84] Cf. A. Bank "Losing Faith in the Civilizing Mission – the Premature Decline of Humanitarian Liberalism at the Cape, 1840–1860," in M. Darnton and R. Halpern, eds., *Empire and Others* (London: UCL Press, 1999).

eliminated altogether in South Africa. But though post-Union governments were more and more segregationist and oppressive, liberal ideas were nevertheless kept alive, transmitted to the larger whole and embodied institutionally in organizations ranging from the Joint Councils of the 1920s to the Liberal Party of South Africa, which was founded a century after the grant of representative government to the Cape. Though it long seemed that such ideas, propagated by only a relatively few individuals, were of little or no account in a society that seemed intent on moving in the opposite direction, they survived. When apartheid collapsed, they were there to be tapped by those who now sought a negotiated transition to a new order. Liberal ideas were at the heart of the constitution forged for the new South Africa.[85] How deeply they have sunk into South African soil in the twenty-first century, however, remains to be seen.

---

[85] Some play down the influence of liberal ideas from Britain and look instead to other traditions: e.g., K. Asmal with D. Chidester and C. Lubisi, *Legacy of Freedom: The ANC's Human Rights Tradition* (Jeppestown: Jonathan Ball, 2005), and H. Ebrahim, *Soul of a Nation* (Cape Town: Oxford University Press, 2003).

Index

Aborigines, Australian, 240–42
  denied right to vote by Commonwealth
    Franchise Act (1902), 241
Acadians, 47, 117, 164
Act of Settlement (1701), 3, 84, 91, 114
  elements not extended to Ireland, 91
Adams, Amos, 125
Adams, John, 122, 133
  correspondence with Thomas Jefferson,
    139
  on American ignorance of rights,
    113
Adams, John Quincy, 158
Addison, Joseph, 68
Address to the Committee of
  Correspondence in Barbados, 67
  Barbadian response to, 67–68
Administration of the Colonies, 121
Alcaçovas, Treaty of (1479), 29
Alleyne, John Gay, 68
American colonies. *See also*
  individual colonies
  ambiguity of English liberty in, 32, 35,
    39, 43–44
  and 1688 Revolution, 42, 43
  and legislative authority of Parliament,
    115
  as virtually independent after 1688, 121
  assemblies, 52–53, 140
  assemblies, as models of English
    governance, 54
  autonomy enjoyed by, 116–17
  charters of proprietary colonies, 40

  denial of Parliament's role in military
    affairs, 124
  emulation of House of Commons, 7
  fears of Catholics in, 42
  locus of real authority, 116
  non-English settlers, 46
  political situation compared to Ireland,
    96
  protection of English rights, 55
  role of assemblies as affirmation of
    English liberty, 33
  seventeenth-century struggles over
    English liberty, 36
American Revolution,
  anti-metropolitan nature, 150
  as British war over meanings of liberty,
    28
  as moment of historical awareness, 114
  as movement for corporate privileges,
    152
  British ban on incorporation, 148
  class-consciousness in, 137
  distinctiveness, 136
  imperial vision of patriots, 135
  invoked in New South Wales, 235
  Loyalists. *See* Loyalists
  seen as incomplete, 138
  slavery used to clarify concepts of
    liberty, 27
Anti-Convict Association, 282
Antifederalists, 143–44, 147
Antigua, 39
  adoption of elected assembly in, 52

289

Archbishop of Canterbury. *See* Church of England, Archbishop of Canterbury
Argument on behalf of the Catholics of Ireland, 105
Armitage, David, on global expansion of concepts of liberty, 212
Asiatic Society, 209
asiento, 44
Associated Loyalists, 255
Australasian Chronicle, 231
Australia. *See also* New South Wales
 aboriginal population, political rights of, 226
 Aborigines denied right to vote by Commonwealth Franchise Act (1902), 241
 Aborigines, considered British subjects, 241
 Aborigines, constitutional rights of, 20, 240–42
 anti-transportation movement, 238
 Bathurst Convention, 243
 changes to franchise qualifications, 236
 Chartism, 236
 Chartist unrest, 231
 committee petitions for right of trial by jury (1819), 227
 Commonwealth Franchise Act (1902), 241
 constitution, adopted (1901), 247
 constitution, drafting of, 244–45
 constitution, importance of U.S. constitution to, 246
 constitution, influenced by, 246
 constitution, limits on right of Aborigines and others in, 245
 constitutional reform in, 223
 constitutions adopted in, 231
 convict population of colonies as emergent polity, 19
 convict uprisings, 225
 convicts, end of transportation, 230
 discovery of gold, 239
 early elections, 234
 Election Act (1842), 233
 emancipists, 226–28
 expansion of advisory council, 19
 Federal Conference (1890), 242
 government of, 230, 234
 government of New South Wales, 221
 imperial development compared with South Africa and New Zealand, 220
 influence of Durham Report on, 230
 motivation for federation, 242
 New South Wales Corp. *See* New South Wales Corp.
 nineteenth-century identity, 242
 people's conventions, 243
 popular sovereignty in, 244
 population in, 242
 racism in, 241
 review of New South Wales Corp. by colonial office, 226
 right to trial by jury in, 222
 Rum Rebellion, 223
 transported convicts, importance of language of liberty to, 225
 women's suffrage, 241, 243
Australian, 228
Australian Government Act (1850), 233
Australian Government Colonies Act (1850), 238
Australian Natives' Association, 242
Ayscue, Sir George, 39

Bacon, Nathaniel, 1
Bailyn, Bernard, 163
Baldwin, Robert, 180
Bancroft, Edward, 128
Bank of the United States, 145
Bannister, Jerry, on importance of customs in Newfoundland, 168
Barbadoes Packett, 61
Barbados, 214
 adoption of elected assembly in, 52
 assembly, defense of colonial authority, 55–56
 assembly, denial of parliament's right to legislate, 55
 establishment of bicameral legislature in, 53
 government as royal colony, 56
 population of, 60
 reaction to Stamp Act in, 67–69
 relationship of slavery to Englishness in, 60
 submission negotiated with Commonwealth government, 39

Barbados Gazette, 60
Barker, Ernest, 287
Barnard, Samuel, 54
Bathurst Convention, 243
Bayly, C. A., 215
Beaglehole, J. C., 259
Beckford, William, 120
Bell, Philip, 53
Bengal, 18, 195
  government of compared with
    Philadelphia, 202
Bent, Ellis, 222
Bentham, Jeremy, 217, 223
  on government of New South Wales,
    222
Bermuda,
  adoption of elected assembly in, 52
  assembly, 33
  transition to civilian government, 33
Bigge, J. T., 226
Biko, Steve, 273
Bill of Rights (1689), 43
Blackstone, Sir William, 2, 3, 4, 74, 114,
    115, 118, 119, 130, 170, 199
Blainey, Geoffrey, 264
Blayney, Andrew Thomas Blayney, Baron,
    107
Blenman, Jonathan, 57
Bligh, William, 223
Board of Trade. *See* Lords Commissioners
  for Trade and Plantations
Bolts, William, 202
Bonaparte, Napoleon, 146
Bourke, Nicholas, as author of *The
  Privileges of the Island of
  Jamaica Vindicated*, 61–63
Bourke, Richard, 229
Breaches of Contract Act (1877), 174
Brett, Jasper, 94
British Columbia, 17, 165, 166
British Empire
  alternate history of, by American
    writers, 125
  ambiguity of status of slaves in, 154
  as federal government, 134
  as political community, 132
  colonial administration, 43, 116
  concept of liberty distinguished from
    other empires, 27

development of liberty as an
    abstraction, 28
  diffusion of liberty in, 22
  diversity of population in, 198
  identity exaggerated by provincials, 133
  importance of liberty of commerce and
    navigation to, 44
  liberty as central to identity in, 26, 61
  limits of self-government in, 24
  nature of constitution in, 116
  obligation to protect liberty of subjects,
    48
  reevaluation of as consequence of
    American Revolution, 17
British North America Act (1867),
    17, 184, 189
Brockholls, Anthony, 40
Brodrick, Alan, 92
Brownists, 34
Buckingham, James (Silk), 213, 214
Buckner, Philip, 254
Buller, Charles, 265
Burke, Edmund, 10, 117, 123, 131, 195,
    196, 205
  conflict with Warren Hastings, 205
  on importance of maintaining British
    freedoms in India, 206
  opposition to India acts, 206
  views on relationship of English law to
    Indian society, 195
Burt, William, 72

Cabell, Joseph C., 156
Calcutta, 192
  as British settlement, 192
  as center for radicalism in British India,
    211
  as center of constitutional conflict, 203
  government of, 192
  petition of 1779, 192–94
  relationship with East India Company,
    195
Calcutta Journal, 213
Calcutta Telegraph, 211
Caledon, Du Pre Alexander, Earl of, 275
Caledon's Code, 276
Callender, James Thomson, 15
Calvert, Cecil, second Baron Baltimore,
    36

Campbell vs. Hall (1774), 71
Campbell, Alexander, suit against export duty, 71
Campbell, John, *Political Survey of Britain*, 10
Canada. *See also* individual colonies
  blacks in, 183
  Breaches of Contract Act (1877), 174
  British North America Act (1867), 184, 189
  central theme of historiography, 160–161
  Confederation of 1867, 165, 184–85
  Constitution of 1791, 170
  deportation of Acadian population, 164
  establishment of Supreme Court, 182
  government in, 177
  government of, 165, 171, 186–87
  importance of newspapers in, 179
  importance of property rights in, 188
  lack of founding moment, 167–68
  Loyalists in, 164, 165
  movement for responsible government in, 17
  Native peoples in, 175–76, 185, 190
  Official Languages Act (1969), 189
  political reform in, 177–78
  population of, 166
  provincial assemblies in, 169
  Quiet Revolution, 161
  rebellions of 1837, 180
  religion in, 173, 176
  representation on right to trial by jury in, 173, 180
  seigneurial tenure in, 173
  Statute of Westminster (1931), 165
  Tory touch in, 161
  trial of Joseph Howe for libel, 179
Canada Act (1791), 131
Canadian Bill of Rights (1960), 188
Canadian Charter of Rights and Freedoms (1982), 185, 188
Canadian colonies, concessions to as consequence of American Revolution, 17
Candid Observations on Two Pamphlets lately published, 68
Cape Breton, 45, 125, 164, 165, 169, 171

Cape Colony. *See* South Africa
Cape Monthly Magazine, 281
Cape of Good Hope Philanthropic Society for Aiding Deserving Slaves to Purchase their Freedom, 279
Cape Patriots, 272
Cape Town, 274
Care, Henry, 2
Carleton, Thomas, 171
Cary, Mary Ann Shadd, 183
Cateau-Cambrésis, Treaty of (1559), 30
Catholicism,
  and anti-Protestant ideology, 79
  association with French colonization, 30
Catholics. *See also* Ireland, Catholics
  access to English liberties in seventeenth century, 80
  Argument on behalf of the Catholics of Ireland, 105
  expulsion from Canada, 47
  fears of, in American colonies, 42
  in Canada, 173, 176
  in Caribbean, 46
  in Maryland, 8
  Ireland, political rights in, 87
  limits of liberties in British America, 47
  Popery Laws in Ireland, 77
  population in Acadia, 164, 176
Cavendish-Bentinck, Lord William Henry, 215
Ceded Islands. *See also* Dominica; Grenada; St. Vincent; Tobago; West Indies, British
Chambers, Robert, 204
Charles I,
  proclamation on liberty of settlement, 37
  view of Virginia as royal colony, 32
Charles II,
  and liberty of conscience, 40
  colonial expansion, approach to, 39
  mercantilist policies of, 39
  review of colonial charters, 41
Chartism, 236
  impact on New South Wales, 236
Church of England, 232
  Archbishop of Canterbury, 34, 36
  attempts to establish in Maryland, 42
Church of Ireland, 79, 84, 85, 87, 101

Church of Scotland, 114
Clare, John Fitzgibbon, Earl of, 105–06
Clay, Henry, 145
Clive, Robert, Baron Clive of Plassey, 201
Cloning, as analytic concept, 251–52
Clonmell, John Scott, Earl of, 106
Coghill, Marmaduke, 92
Coke, Sir Edward, 1–3
Colden, Cadwallader, 115
Colebrooke, Sir George, 200
Colonial Leviathan, 161
colonies, inclusionary and exclusionary
    nature of polities, 8. *See also* American
    colonies; Ireland
Commentaries on the Laws of England
    114, 170
common law, 2
Common Sense, 136
Connecticut,
    as aristocratic, 139
    assembly, 37
    Fundamental Orders, 37
    inclusion in Dominion of New
      England, 41
    merged with New Haven colony, 38
Conolly, William, 92
consensual government. *See*
    representative government
convicts. *See* Australia, convicts.
Cordeur, Basil le, 280
Cornwallis, Charles, Marquess
    Cornwallis, 206, 207
Cortés, Hernan, 30
Country Whiggery, in Ireland, 95
Court Whiggery, philosophy of liberty,
    170
Courtis, Edward, 39
Cowper, Charles, 240
Cradock, John Francis, Baron Howden,
    275
Creasy, James, 193
Creighton, Donald, 162
Cromwell, Oliver, policy regarding
    Ireland, 80
Cunningham, James, 72
Cunningham, Philip, 225

Dalling, John, 72
Daniehy, Daniel, 232

Dargo, George, on English liberty and
    colonial settlement, 51
Darling, Sir Charles Henry, 229
Davies, Sir John, 79
Davis, Sir John, 1
De Laudibus Legum Angliae, 1
Deakin, Alfred, 242
Declaration of Independence (1776), 26,
    28, 129, 141, 155
    as act of union, 135
Declaratory Act (1720), 14, 91, 92, 94,
    113
    repeal, 100
Declaratory Act (1766), 14, 73
Declaratory Act (1778), 16, 130
DEIC. *See* Dutch East India Company
democracy, 137, 156, 158
    negative connotations of, 136
Democracy in America, 135, 136
Democratic-Republicans, 138, 144, 151
Dempster, George, 10
Dickinson, John, 67, 68, 122, 126–28
    as author of *An Address to the*
      Committee of Correspondence in
      Barbados, 67
Dilke, Charles, 267
Dominica, assembly established, 70
Dominion of Canada, 165
Dominion of New England, creation, 41
Domville, Sir William, 82, 89
Dow, Alexander, 202
Drennan, William, 103
Ducharme, Michael, 160
due process of law, 2, 26, 47, 52, 59
    limits in American colonies, 47
Dulany, Daniel, 125, 126
Dunmore, John Murray, Earl of,
    proclamation of 1775, 155
Dunn, John, 137
Durham, John George Lambton, Earl of,
    19, 180
Durham's Report. *See* Report of Lord
    Durham on the Affairs of British
    North America (1839)
Dutch East India Company, 272, 276
Dutch Republic,
    beneficiary of seventeenth-century
      European turmoil, 38
    commercial ascendancy of, 38–39

Eagar, Edward, 227
East India Company, 15, 17, 33, 45, 115,
    129, 147, 149, 191–97, 200, 202,
    203
  and Calcutta Supreme Court, 195
  and Cornwallis regulations, 207
  attempted takeover by Charles James
    Fox, 206
  authority compared with other British
    colonists' polities, 200
  disappointment with Regulating Act,
    203
  global expansion of liberty as threat to
    authority of, 213
  government organization of, 201
  government structure in India, 201
  Regulating Act (1773), 193
  restrictions on liberty of the press, 214
  restrictions placed on officers of, 203
  review of charter by parliament,
    214
Edwards, Bryan, as author of the *History,
    Civil and Commercial, of the British
    Colonies in the West Indies*, 72–74
EIC. *See* East India Company
Elizabeth I, 30, 79
Emancipation Act (1832), and the end of
    slavery in the Cape Colony, 21
emancipists. *See* Australia, emancipists
Engerman, Stanley, 253
England. *See also* Great Britain; British
    Empire
  attempts to regain colonial authority,
    39
  Bill of Rights (1689), 43
  civil wars, 38
  civil wars, impact on constitutional
    development of colonies, 54
  colonization, role of joint-stock
    companies in, 32
  Commonwealth, free trade as
    concession to colonies, 39
  Commonwealth, negotiation with
    Barbados, 39
  concepts of liberty, 28
  culture of liberty compared with
    France, 31
  early colonial settlements, 25
  ideologies of expansion, 25

Massachusetts Government Act (1774),
    44
merchants in overseas expansion, role
    of, 31
metropolitan views of liberty, compared
    with colonial, 27
Navigation Acts, 31
parliament, legislation to reduce
    royalist colonies (1650), 39
Petition of Right (1628), 40
Revolution (1688), 41
traditional aspects of liberty, 28
English Separatists. *See also* Pilgrims
Englishness, importance in West Indies,
    57
*Essay Concerning Slavery, and the Danger
    Jamaica Is expos'd to from the Too
    great Number of Slaves*, 63–65
Estwick, Samuel, 65
Eyre, Edward, 76

Fairbairn, John, 274, 279–83
Federal Conference (1890), 242
federal government, 134, 143
federalism, 12, 134, 138, 147, 148,
    151–58, 186, 188, 190, 242, 246
  and British Empire, 149
  rejection of, in South Africa, 22
Federalists, 134, 143, 144
  in New England, 158
Ferguson, Adam, 274
Ferguson, Niall, 283
Field, Barron, 226
fisheries, North Atlantic, 33
Flood, Henry, ix, 96–97, 100
  compares Ireland's political situation to
    American colonies, 96
Fortescue, Sir John, 1
Fox, Charles James, India Bills (1783),
    206
France
  and toleration of Protestants, 31
  assertion of liberty of passage and
    commerce, 30
  strategy of colonization, 30
Francis I, 30
Francis, Philip, 205
Franklin, Benjamin, 123, 132, 250
French Revolution, 136, 138

impact on American political history, 138

tree of liberty as symbol of hope in Ireland, 103

Gladstone, William, 259
Gordon, Thomas, 3
Great Britain. *See also* Union Anglo-Scottish (1707); England
as parliamentary monarchy, 114
expansion of suffrage in 1867, 24
overseas trade dependent on African slavery, 48
Great Fundamentals, 35
Greene, Jack P., 133, 168, 253
Greig, George, 280
Grenada, assembly established, 70
Grey, Charles Grey, Earl, 238
Grey, George, 259
Griffith, Sir Samuel, 246
Grotius, Hugo, 30, 59
Guilford, Frederick North, Earl of, 99, 193, 202
Gunpowder Plot, 83

Habeas Corpus, 3, 169, 212
Haldimand, Sir Frederick, 255
Hale, Sir Matthew, 26
Hall, Catherine, 24, 285
Hall, Edward, 229
Hamilton, Alexander, 143
Hamilton, Archibald, 57
Hardwicke, Philip Yorke, Earl of, 66
Hartford Convention (1814), 146
Hartz, Louis, view of Canadian society, 161
Hastings, Warren, 204, 205, 208
notion of ancient constitution in India, 204
Hawksley, Edward, 237
Hay, Douglas, on English juries, 173
HBC. *See* Hudson's Bay Company
Henry, Patrick, 142
History of New England, 38
History, Civil and Commercial, of the British Colonies in the West Indies, 72–74
Hobson, William, 255
Hooker, Thomas, 49

Hopkins, Stephen, 124
Howe, Joseph, libel trial of, 179
Howick, Henry, 229
Hudson's Bay Company, 33, 45, 164, 165, 174, 175
Huguenots, 30, 46, 47
expulsion from France, 31
Louis XIII's attempts to break influence of in overseas trade, 30
Hume, David, 126, 229
Hume, Joseph, 218
Hurwitz, Samuel J. and Edith, views on strength of representative government in colonies, 75

imperium in imperio, 148, 151
Impey, Elijah, 193, 204
India Act (1784), 206
India, British. *See also* East India Company; Calcotta; Bengal
abolition of sati, 215
ancient constitution in, 205
arguments for extension of royal authority in Bengal, 202
"Black Act" (1836), 216
Calcutta, government of, 192
Charter Act (1833), 216
conflict between British and Mughal concepts of law, 209
conflicts between British law and Indian society in, 194
controversy over liberty of the press in, 213
Cornwallis code of administrative regulations in 1793, 207
emergence of new public men in, 215
English law in, 191
historiography of, 197
impact of French Revolution in, 211
impact of the American Revolution on governance of, 17–18
importance of Calcutta petition in, 195
India Bills (1783), 206
judiciary reform in, 204
presidency towns as grounds for radicalism in, 211
pressures for reform in, 215
Regulating Act (1773), 193, 202
representative government in, 18

India, British (*cont.*)
  utilitarian turn, 217
  Vellore Mutiny (1807), 213
indigenous peoples, concepts of self-
    empowerment, 5
Innes, James Rose, 281
Ireland,
  abolition of Parliament, 109
  Act of Settlement (1701) not extended
    to, 91
  Act of Union (1801), 109
  American Revolution, impact of, 99
  ancient constitution, 89
  arguments for rights as equivalent to
    English rights, 89–90
  aristocracy, creation of, 80
  basis of Protestant Ascendancy, 14
  Catholic rights, limits on, 80
  Catholicism argued as incompatible
    with liberty, 106
  Catholics, accommodation toward, 100
  Catholics, impact of Revolution of
    1688 on, 86
  Catholics, political rights of, 87
  censorship, 88
  Church of Ireland, establishment of, 79
  compared with American colonies in
    imperial context, 8–10
  constitutional concessions made by
    Westminster, 100
  Cromwellian actions in, 83
  Declaratory Act of 1720, 14
  Dublin Corporation, attempt to reform,
    95
  early eighteenth-century shift in
    political discourse, 94
  English and Scottish colonization
    compared with American provinces,
    7–8
  English settlement, 78
  establishment of conservative clubs to
    support George III, 104
  failure of political reform, 101
  fears of attack on constitution by
    George III's ministers, 98
  French Revolution, impact of, 102–03
  heads of bills, 84, 87, 93
  Insurrection Act, 107
  Irish Council, 84

  Jacobite parliament, 85
  kingdom, creation of Tudor, 79
  legislative authority of Parliament
    eclipses Privy Council, 93
  Money Bill dispute of 1753–56, 95
  Navigation Acts suspended, 14
  Orange Society, 107
  Parliament of, 86
    diminished by Westminster, 91
  parliamentary independence, 88, 100
  parliamentary legislation denied by
    England's Privy Council, 91
  parliamentary rights of, 82
  Penal Laws, 87
  perception of as a colony, 92
  political situation compared to
    American colonies, 96
  political system under James VI and I,
    81
  Popery Laws, 77
  Protestant Ascendancy, fundations of,
    81–83
  Protestants assume practical control, 92
  Rebellion of 1641, 83
  Rebellion of 1798, 107–08
  relationship of Irish protestants with
    William III, 85–86
  relationship with English and Scottish
    invaders, 5
  repeal of Declaratory Act of 1720, 100
  repeal of Poynings' Law, 14
  Revolution of 1688, impact of, 84–85
  settlement, landownership as incentive
    to English and Scottish, 80
  undertakers, 92, 95, 98
  United Irishmen, 102, 103, 105, 106,
    107
  Volunteers, 99, 100
  Whig Club, 101, 102
  Wood's halfpence, 94
  Wood's halfpence dispute, 92

Jabavu, John Tengo, 286
Jackson, Andrew, 145
Jacobite Parliament, 85
Jamaica,
  adoption of elected assembly in, 52
  applicability of Poyning's Law to, 9
  as slave society, 59

assembly, abolition of, 16, 76
assembly, as mediator between Britain and American colonies, 69–70
assembly, constitutional crisis over, 61–63
assembly, defense of colonial authority, 56–57
government of, 54, 56
government, constitutional impact of anti-slavery measures on, 75
Morant Bay uprising (1865), 16
petition of 1682 to restore constitution, 58
population of, 60
slave revolt in 1776, 71
slavery in, 63–65
James VI and I, 29, 34, 36, 81
James VII and II, 11, 37, 41, 42, 84, 89
as New York proprietor, 40
Jamison, Sir John, 227
Jefferson, Thomas, 49, 73, 128, 133, 135, 139–41, 144–49, 151, 155–59. *See also* Declaration of Independence
and French Revolution, 138
and balance of constitutional power, 146
and metropolis as specter, 155
correspondence with John Adams, 139
on ancient constitution, 128
Statute of Virginia for religious freedom, 139
views on aristocracy, 139–40
Jeffersonian Republicans, 138
Jews, in Canada, 173, 177
Johnson, Edward, 38
Johnson, Samuel, 154
Johnson, William, 144
Johnston, George, 223, 224
Johnstone, George, 201
Jones, William, 207, 209
Joseph Howe, libel trial of, 179
juries, 2, 11, 21, 26, 28, 52, 74, 107, 147, 169, 193, 194, 196, 202, 206, 212, 215, 216, 221, 222, 226–28, 277

Kammen, Michael, on assertiveness of colonial assemblies, 53
Keith, Sir William, 115

Kenyon, Cecilia, view of Antifederalists, 143
Kercheval, Samuel, 156
Khoi, 21
pass system, 277
practical limits to freedom, 277–78
Kiewiet, C. W. de, 272
King, William, on Irish legislative independence, 88
Knox, William, 123

landholding, in British American colonies, 9
Lang, John Dunmore, 237
Laurier, Sir Wilfrid, 187
Lawrence, Charles, 44
Lefroy, A. H. L., 187
Leiden, English Separatists in, 34–35. *See also* English Separatists; Pilgrims
Leisler, Jacob, 42
Letter from a Merchant at Jamaica to a Member of Parliament in London, Touching the African Trade, 59–60
Letters from a Pennsylvania Farmer, 122
Levant Company, 33, 45, 46
Lewthwaite, Susan, 171
Liberal Party of South Africa, 288
Liberalism, 145
liberty. *See also* American colonies, Australia, British Empire, Canada, England, Great Britain, India, Ireland, New Zealand, South Africa, United States, West Indies
ambiguity of, in English colonization, 32, 35, 39, 43–44
and English identity, 3–4
and tension with equality in American context, 135
as English inheritance, 22–23
as European legacy, 27–28
as iconic in American context, 28
as social property, 38, 49
as strengthened by slavery in American mind, 154
conceptual development in American colonies, 5
contradictions of, in British context, 48
creation of, as consequence of British expansion, 49

liberty (*cont.*)
  development of within British Empire,
    23
  English concepts of, 28
  extension in India, 17–18
  protected by provincial assemblies, 54
  seventeenth-century English concepts
    of, 2–3
  tension between individual and
    corporate liberties in early United
    States, 136–41
  traditional English aspects, 28
  unrelated to property ownership in
    United States, 153
  views of Virginians compared with
    Plymouth settlers, 36
liberty of commerce and navigation, 29,
  45
  centrality to British Empire, 44
  threatened by Spanish, 45
liberty of conscience, 26, 27, 30, 34, 36,
  38, 40–43, 46, 47, 49
liberty of movement, 25, 29, 34, 37, 38, 49
  and slavery, 29
liberty of person and property. *See* due
  process of law; juries
liberty of self-government. *See*
  representative government
Lincoln, Abraham, 159
Littleton, Edward, 60
Locke, John, 89, 91, 102, 103, 235, 237
London Chronicle, 113
London Missionary Society, 274
London, Treaty of (1604), 29, 30
Long, Edward, 65
Lords Commissioners for Trade and
  Plantations, 43, 44, 115
  established, 43
Louis XIII, 30
Louis XIV, 46, 118
Louisbourg, 125
  surrender of, 45, 164
Lowe, Robert, 234
Lower Canada, 16, 129, 165, 166, 169,
  172–77, 180, 181
  abolition of seigneurial system, 181
Lowther, Robert, 57
Loyalists, 16, 137, 144
  in Canada, 161, 165, 255

Lucas, Charles, 95, 96
Lyttelon, William Henry, 61

Macarthur, James, 229, 232
Macarthur, John, 223, 224
Macartney, George Macartney, Earl,
  273
Macaulay, Thomas, 217
Mackenzie, Holt, 217
Mackenzie, William, 180
Maclean, Charles, 211
Macquarie, Lachlan, 224
Magna Charta, 2, 3, 26, 40, 55, 65, 66,
  193, 228, 237
Maier, Pauline, 147
Maine, inclusion in Dominion of New
  England, 41
Maitland, F. W., 112, 113, 130
  view on limits of parliamentary
    sovereignty, 112
Malan, F. S., 284
Malthus, Thomas, 250
Man, Yunlong, on political development,
  53
Mancke, Elizabeth, 167
Mansfield, William Murray, Earl of, 65,
  66, 71, 116, 154, 155
Maori, 248
  and British law, 256
  as impacted by colonization, 258
  colonial relations with, 256–57
  colonial situation, 256
  compared with Australian Aborigines,
    20
  independence eroded, 258
  political rights, 20
Mare Liberum, 30
Marshall, John, 144
Marshall, P. J., on consequences of slavery
  on British perceptions of India, 207
Mary of Modena, and birth of Prince of
  Wales, 41
Maryland,
  attempts to establish Church of
    England, 42
  charter, 36
  establishment of bicameral legislature,
    53
  veto of claim to assembly as right, 43

Mason, John, 40
Mason, Matthew, 158
Massachusetts Bay, 36
  as aristocratic, 139
  attempt by crown to revoke charter,
    36
  charter, 37
  establishment of bicameral legislature,
    53
  inclusion in Dominion of New England,
    41
  interprets assembly as right, 43
  Massachusetts Government Act (1774),
    44
  Pequot War, 37
  protests against parliamentary
    oversight, 39
  Recharter of 1691, religious toleration
    in, 40, 42
  religious intolerance, 36
  splintering of Puritans in, 37
Massachusetts Bay Company, 36
Massachusetts Government Act (1774),
    43, 44
Masters and Servants Act (1856),
    283
Mather, Increase, 41, 42
Maxwell, Henry, 87
McCully, Jonathan, 183
McFarlane, Anthony, 253
McKay, Ian, 162
merchant shipping, shipboard
    governance, 33
Merivale, Herman, 239
Merriman, John X., 284
Mexico City, 254
Mill, James, 217
Mill, John Stuart, 196
Missouri, ban on slavery, 156
Moira, Francis Rawdon Hastings, Earl of,
    107
Molteno, John Charles, 283
Molyneux, William, 89
  adaptation of Locke, 89
  argument for Irish equivalency of
    English rights, 89–90
  hostility of Westminster Parliament
    toward pamphlet of, 90
monarchy, concepts of, 1–2

Montesquieu, Charles de Secondat, Baron
    de la Brede et de, 10
Montreal Gazette, 129
Montserrat, adoption of elected assembly
    in, 52
Morris, Valentine, 71
Morton, W. L., 168
Munro, Thomas, 213, 218
Murdoch, Beamish, 169, 170

Nantes, Edict of, 31, 46, 47
Narragansett Bay, 36, 37. *See also* Rhode
    Island
Natal (colony), 22
Native Americans, 47, 175–76, 185, 190
Navigation Acts, 39, 113, 121
  importance of, 54
  renewal of at Restoration of Charles II,
    117
  suspended in Ireland in 1780, 14
Nevis, adoption of elected assembly in,
    52
New Brunswick, 16, 17, 117, 164, 165,
    169, 171, 173, 175, 189
New England, Council of, 35
New England, Dominion of, 35
New Hampshire,
  as royal colony, 40
  assembly, 40
  inclusion in Dominion of New England,
    41
New Haven (colony), 38
New Jersey, inclusion in Dominion of
    New England, 41
New South Wales, 254
  colonial government of, 19
  constitution drafted in 1853, 239
  debates over constitution, 232
  gerrymandering in, 239
  government of, 228
  harmed by absence of English liberties,
    221
  immigration to, 231
  impact of Chartism on, 236
  separated from Victoria, 233
  settlers challenge authority of governor,
    224
  threats to citizens compared with
    American Revolution, 235

New South Wales Corp., 222
  review of regulations, 226
New York
  as proprietary colony, 40
  assembly first called, 37
  charter of 1683, 41
  inclusion in Dominion of New England, 41
  incorporation of businesses in 1811, 150
  Leisler Uprising, 42
  Long Island settlements, 37
  veto of claim to assembly as right, 43
New York City, 254
New Zealand. *See also* Maori
  appeals to Privy Council, 262
  boom mentality, 266
  characteristics, 248
  colonial government, 20
  colonial status, 255
  economy, 249–50, 261–62, 264
  emigration to, 266
  extension of English law to, 256
  government of, 256
  growth of representative government, 21
  historiography, 248
  identity, 263
  maritime trade, 264
  pastoralism in, 261
  population, 249
  relationship with Maori, 256–57
  reliance on imperial economy, 260
  self-government, 258
  settlement, 260
  suffrage, 260, 263
  Treaty of Waitangi (1841), 255
  Wool and Oil Securities Act (1858), 261
New Zealand Company, 256, 258
Newcastle, Henry Pelham Fiennes Pelham-Clinton, Duke of, 238
Newenham, Edward, 98, 99
Newfoundland, 174
  settlement, 164, 173
Nicholson, Sir Francis, 42
Nootka Sound Agreement (1790), 45
Normanton, Charles Agar, Archbishop of Dublin, Earl of, 99
North America, British. *See* Canada

Northwest Ordinance (1787), 254
Nova Scotia, 8, 16, 17, 44, 47, 117, 164–66, 169, 171–75, 182, 254. *See also* Acadians
  first assembly called, 44

O'Connor, Roger, 103
Ontario, abolition of civil juries, 182
Orr, William, execution, 103
Otis, James, views on parliamentary sovereignty, 122

Paine, Thomas, 136, 236. *See also Common Sense*
Pakington, Sir John, 231, 238
Palmer, Robert R., 137, 140
  views on distinctiveness of American Revolution, 136
panchayats, 215
Papineau, Louis, 180
Parke, Daniel, 57
Parkes, Henry, 236, 242
Parliament. *See also* England, Great Britain, American colonies
  abolition of feudal tenures, 119
  and legislative authority over American colonies, 115
  and restoration of Charles II, 128
  as democratic model for Americans, 137
  attempts to legislate for American colonies, 44
  conceptual relationship with colonial assemblies, 6–7
  extent of authority in Britain, 115
  views of sovereignty within British empire, 117
Parry, David, 72
Paton, Alan, 287
Patriotes, 180
Pennsylvania, 117
  government of Philadelphia compared with Bengal, 202
People's Advocate, 235, 237
Pequot War, 37
Petition of Right, 40
Philadelphia, government of compared with Bengal, 202
Philip, John, 277

Philipps, Richard, 47
Phillip, Arthur, 221
Pilgrims, 49. *See also* English Separatists
  Code of 1685, 35
  disaffection, 36
  expectation of, in transatlantic
    settlement, 35
  Great Fundamentals, 35
Pitt, William, the younger, 169, 207
  and East India Company, 206
Pitts, Jennifer, 217
Plaatje, Solomon, 286
Plea for the Constitution, 222
Plymouth colony, 35
  government of, 35
  inclusion in Dominion of New England,
    41
Pocock, J. G. A., 163
Political Survey of Britain, 10
Popery Laws, 77
popular sovereignty, 150
  as fiction in United States, 153
Porter, William, 282
Portugal, demand on prohibition of
  English trade with Africa, 30
Pownall, Thomas, 10, 121, 126, 200. *See
  also Administration of the Colonies*
  views on constitutional situation of
    American colonies, 121–22
Poynings, Edward, 79
Poynings' Law, 14, 56, 79, 81, 84, 88, 93,
  96, 97, 100. *See also* Privy Council
Price, Richard, 11
Prince Edward Island, 9, 16, 17, 164, 166,
  169, 171, 173, 174, 181
  as exception to other American colonies
    in terms of landholding, 9
Pringle, Thomas, 274, 278–81, 287
*Privileges of the Island of Jamaica
  Vindicated*, 63
Privy Council, review of colonial laws, 9
Proclamation of 1763, 48
property rights, 142, 153, 158
  and slavery, 155
Provincial Freeman, 183
Puritans,
  and liberty of settlement, 37
  view of liberties expressed in *History of
    New England*, 38

Quebec, 6, 15, 16, 17, 21, 22, 44, 48, 76,
  161, 165–69, 171–74, 176, 182, 187,
  189
  Civil Code (1866), 182
Quebec Act (1774), 168

RAC. *See* Royal African Company
Reeves, John, 104
Reform Act (1832), 282
Report of Lord Durham on the Affairs of
  British North America (1839), 20,
  129, 180, 230, 255, 283
representative government, 3, 5, 147
  actual compared to virtual
    representation, 152
  established at Jamestown in 1619,
    32
  parliamentary sovereignty, 115
  unevenness of applicability across
    British empire, 17
republicanism, 149, 151
responsible government, 17, 22
  in Canada, 17
Revolution of 1688
  impact on Ireland, 84–85
  legacy for concepts of liberty,
    43
Rhode Island, 37
  inclusion in Dominion of New England,
    41
  religious toleration in, 37
  reputation for independence, 38
Richelieu, Armand Jean du Plessis de,
  Cardinal, 30
Riddell, William Renwick, 188
Risk, R. C. B., 185
Roman law, invoked by France and
  England versus Spain, 31
Romney, Paul, 180
Roy, Raja Rammohan, 215
Roy, Ram Mohun, 218
Royal African Company, 33, 45
Rozbicki, Michal, on nature of liberties in
  medieval world, 49
Rule of law, 142
  unevenness of applicability across
    British empire, 17
Rum Rebellion, 223
Russell, John Russell, Earl, 230

Sachs, Albie, 287
Salmond, John, 263
Sandys, Sir Edwin, 32, 34
Sati, abolition of, 215
Scotland. *See also* Union,
    Anglo-Scottish (1707)
  commercial competition with English
    merchants, 46
Scottish enlightenment, 199
Seeley, J. R., 130
Sempronius, 60
Seven Years' War, 22, 48, 97, 117, 125
Shadd, Abraham, 183
Shannon, Henry Boyle, Earl of, 95,
    96
Shore, John, 208, 209
slave trade,
  abolition of, by Britain, 75
  asiento, 45
  in British Empire, 48
slavery,
  and British concepts of liberty, 27
  and liberty of passage and commerce, 29
  British overseas trade dependent on, 48
  in Cape Town, 275
  in Virginia, manumission, 154
  in West Indies, 50–52
    impact of anti-slavery movement on,
      74–76
    relationship with British identity,
      69–70
    resistance to ameloriation in, 75
  reinforced by American concepts of
    liberty, 154
Smith, Adam, 11, 13, 46, 133, 145, 250,
    277. *See also Wealth of Nations*
Smith, H. W., 182
social contract theory, 141
social Darwinism, 241
Society for the Abolition of the Slave
    Trade, 75
Sokoloff, Kenneth, 253
Solomon, Saul, 286
Somers Island Company, 33. *See also*
    Bermuda
Somerset Case, 64–66, 69, 116, 154, 155
  and Britishness in West Indies, 64–67
Somerset, James, 64
Somerset, Lord Charles Henry, 280

South Africa. *See also* Cape Town
  Aborigines Protection and Anti-Slavery
    societies, 286
  Anti-Convict Association, 282
  as variant in colonial relationships to
    British ideas of liberty, 21
  assembly, as protector of settler
    privilege, 22
  Black Circuit, 276
  Caledon's Code, 276
  Cape Ordinance 50 (1828), 277
  Cape Patriots, 272
  Charter of Justice, 277
  colonial situation of Khoi, 275
  colonization, 271
  elected assembly introduced, 282
  erosion of blacks' rights, 285
  executions in, 273
  extension of equal protection to Khoi
    and others, 276
  first settlers from Britain, 274
  government in, 282–84
  government of, 282
  Hottentot Code (1809), 275
  ideas of self-government, 281
  impact of abolition of slavery on, 279
  Liberal Party, 288
  liberty of press in, 279
  pass system, 277
  population, 271
  racial discrimination in the law, 282
  slaves in, 279
  transmitters of liberal ideas to, 274–75
  Union of, 284, 287
South African Commercial Advertiser,
    280–82
South African Journal, 279
South African Literary Society, 281
Spain, colonization, theories of, 31
Speech on American Taxation, 131
St. Christopher, 39
  adoption of elected assembly in, 52
St. Vincent, assembly established, 70
stadial theory, 23, 217
Stafford, Edward, 261
Stamp Act (1765), 119
  British views of, 113
  reaction to in Barbados, 67–69
  repeal of, 120

Stamp Act Congress, 122, 124
Stanford, Walter, 284
state formation theory, 12, 161
Statistical, Historical and Political Description of the Colony of New South Wales and its Dependent Settlements in Van Diemen's Land, 221
statute law, distinguished from common law, 2
Statute of Westminster (1931), 165
Stephen, James, 259
Stephen, Sir Alfred, 233
Steuart, Sir James, 199
Stewart, Dugald, 274
Stewart, James, 286
Stockenström, Andries, 278
Strafford, Thomas Wentworth, Earl of, 81
Stuart, James Francis Edward (son of James VII and II), 41
sugar
  and slavery, 50
  British trade in, 50
Sugar Act (1733), 113
Swift, Jonathan, 91, 94
Sydney Gazette, 227
Sydney Morning Herald, 230
Sydney, Algernon, 4

Tabatabai, Ghulam Husain Khan, 209
  critique of British government, 210
Tasmania, 226
  colonial government of, 19, 228
Taylor, John, 148
Taylor, Miles, 214
Thirty Years War, 38
Thomson, Edward Deas, 232
Thynne, Andrew, 243
Tobago, assembly established, 70
Tocqueville, Alexis de, 135, 267. *See also Democracy in America*
Toleration Act (1701), 114, 116, 176
Tone, Wolfe, 105
Townshend, George, Marquess Townshend, 97, 98, 99
Tracy, Destutt de, 145, 146, 148
Treaty of Aix-la-Chapelle (1748), 125

Treaty of Alcaçovas (1479), 29
Treaty of Cateau-Cambresis (1559), 30
Treaty of London (1604), 29–30
Treaty of Paris (1783), 13, 164
Treaty of Tordesillas, 29, 45
Treaty of Utrecht (1713), 164
Treaty of Waitangi (1841), 255
Treaty of Zaragoza (1529), 29
Trenchard, John, 2
trial by jury. *See* juries
Truter, J. A., 276
Turner, Frederick Jackson, frontier thesis, 49

Union, Anglo-Irish (1801), 109
Union, Anglo-Scottish (1707), 46, 114
Union of South Africa, 287
United States. *See also* federalism
  American system, 145
  and absence of metropolis in, 136
  and aristocratic threat, 145
  and corporations, 150
  and social contract theory, 141
  Antifederalists. *See* Antifederalists
  as slaveholders' union, 156
  Bank of the United States, 145
  compatibility of liberty and slavery in, 156
  constitution, ban on foreign slave trade, 157
  constitution, Bill of Rights, 134
  constitution, influence on Australian constitution, 246
  constitution, model for state constitutions, 143
  constitution, opposition to, 143–44
  constitution, ratification, 134
  corporations, 147–48
  federal government as synthesis of individual and corporate privileges, 136
  Hartford Convention (1814), 146
  impact of French Revolution on, 138, 139
  imperium in imperio, 148
  lack of class-consciousness in, 137
  language of aristocracy in, 144
  legacy of British views of liberty in, 135
  liberty as iconic, 28

United States (*cont.*)
  Missouri crisis, 157
  political mobilization in, 141
  popular sovereignty as fiction in, 153
  popular sovereignty in, 142
  property ownership in, 152
  rejection of Jeffersonian democracy,
    159
  republicanism in. *See* republicanism
  rise of democracy, 147
  shaped by principles of federalism,
    134
  slavery and westward expansion,
    157
  state constitutions, 133, 142
  states as corporate entities, 151
  views of aristocracy and democracy in,
    140
  virtual representation in, 152
  War of 1812, 158
University of Sydney, 232
Upper Canada, 16, 167, 171, 173–75,
    177, 178, 180, 182, 255
  perspective of rural people in, 171
  population, 165
  proposed creation of aristocracy in,
    169
utilitarianism. *See* Bentham, Jeremy; Mill,
    James

Van Cleve, George W., 154
Van Diemen's Land. *See* Tasmania
Vansittart, George, 209
Veridicus, 60
Vernon, Edward, as British hero, 45
Villiers, Henry de, 286
Vipond, R. C., 185
Virgin Islands, assembly established, 70
Virginia
  applicability of Poyning's Law to, 9
  assembly, importance of for settlers, 33
  assembly, meanings of, 34
  establishment of bicameral legislature,
    53
  manumission, 154
  negotiation with Commonwealth
    government, 39
  shift to royal control, 32
  transition to civilian government, 33

Virginia Company of London, 32–34
  dissolution, 32
  invitation to English Separatists, 34
Vogel, Julius, 261

Wakefield, Edward Gibbon, 265, 266
Walpole, Sir Robert, 45, 96
War of 1812, 158
War of Jenkins' Ear, 45
War of the Austrian Succession, 45
War of the English Succession, 42
War of the Spanish Succession, 44
Wealth of Nations, 11, 46, 133. *See also*
    Smith, Adam
Wellesley, Richard, 211
Wentworth, William Charles, 221, 227,
    232, 239
  proposes colonial aristocracy, 232
Werden, Sir John, 40
West Indies, British
  abolition of slave trade in, 16
  and Englishness, 57
  assemblies in, 52
  assemblies, American Revolution and
    older colonial, 72
  assemblies, impact of American
    Revolution on, 70
  assemblies, impact of anti-slavery
    movement on, 74–76
  assemblies, resistance to metropolitan
    intrusions, 54–55
  defense of British identity in, 61
  economy of, 50
  government, constitutional revolution
    in, 76
  impact of American Revolution on,
    15–16
  impact of American Revolution
    on imperial relationships of, 14
  legal status of servants and servitude in,
    51–52
  relationship of slavery to Englishness in, 60
  settler identity, 51
  slave unrest in, 71
  slavery, opposition to attempts to end, 75
  slaves, vulnerable to insurrection of,
    60–61
  Somerset Case used to affirm Britishness
    in, 64–67

West, Francis, 33
Westmeath, Thomas Nugent, Earl of, 104
Whately, Thomas, 120
Whig Club, 101, 102
Wilkes, John, 98
William III, 86
  conflict with parliament over colonial
    oversight, 43
  role in the Revolution of 1688, 41
  vetoes colonial legislation defining
    assemblies as right, 43
William of Orange. *See* William III
William the Conqueror, 26
Williams, Roger, 36
Wilson, James, 134
Winthrop, John, 36, 37

Wise, S. F., 162
Wolfe, Arthur, Viscount Kilwarden, 108
Women's Christian Temperance Union,
  243
Wood, Gordon, 163
Wood, William, 60
Wood's halfpence. *See* Ireland, Wood's
  halfpence
Worsley, Henry, 57
Wyatt, Sir Francis, 32

Yeardley, Sir George, 32
Young, Arthur, 1, 10

Zaller, Robert, 4
Zaragoza, Treaty of (1529), 29